WHAT'S GOOD?
A MEMOIR IN FOURTEEN INGREDIENTS

PETER HOFFMAN

WITH A FOREWORD BY
ADAM GOPNIK

ABRAMS PRESS, NEW YORK

To Susan, my wise partner and devoted champion.

To Olivia and Theo, who learned alongside me much of what's described here and carry it forward as avid cooks and global citizens.

CONTENTS

RECIPES

First-rate raw materials are the very foundation of good cooking. Give the greatest cook in the world second rate materials and the best he can produce from them is second rate food.

—Paul Bocuse

Eating with the fullest pleasure—pleasure, that is, that does not depend on ignorance—is perhaps the profoundest enactment of our connection with the world. In this pleasure we experience and celebrate our dependence and gratitude, for we are living from the mystery, from creatures we did not make and powers we cannot comprehend.

—Wendell Berry

A FOREWORD

ADAM GOPNIK

Some friendships start, like the universe itself, in high heat and gradually cool down; others are more like the movement of the tectonic plates, proceeding in long, slow passage through the years until they bump into one another for good and merge to form a continent. My friendship with the author of this book is of the second kind. We began as client and chef, became collaborators and colleagues, and have ended, I think, as the best of friends—so much so that I take partial, guilty responsibility for the inspired title he has given this book, as one among many in the annoying chorus of greedy people who, visiting the New York City greenmarket at Union Square with him, or merely bumping into him there, demand urgently: "Peter! What's good?"

As we ask, we're confident that, whether talking ramps or beans or shrimp or pea pods, spring strawberries or summer peaches or winter potatoes, Peter Hoffman knows what's good and will quietly point you to the one right stand to get it. (Or even actually accompany you there, where his friendship with the farmer selling the good goods makes for a ten-minute catch-up before the normal business of buying and selling commences.) Peter's intimate relation to the greenmarket and its farmers is, ironically, one of the purest forms of urbanism I know: it is the place where "weak ties," the "bumping-into" relationships that broaden the spectrum of intimacy in cities, still lives, even at the height of a pandemic.

But this book, in addition to being as good a market guide as one could hope to find, with wisdom applicable to farmers' markets far outside New York, is something more: the story of an artist who is also an artisan. I keenly recall seeing Peter for the first time in the early 1990s, in his magical SoHo restaurant Savoy. What made Savoy unique among the first-rate restaurants of New York was its presciently handmade quality, and its insistence on practicing the craft of cooking within the happy, normal range of experience. It was not a place to go for ten courses and a long lecture with each one—it was just where you went, planned or, sometimes, on impulse, for a perfect dinner.

Perfect is a scary word to use, but Savoy's perfection was achieved in part by imperfection, by the place not trying too hard. Perfectly lit by a copper mesh light above, perfectly served by an attentive but not servile staff, with his wise wife, Susan Rosenfeld, often in attendance—and early on working there as still the best pie-maker of my experience—my wife and I watched as the host and owner and chef moved among tables, a guy my age whose care and attention were divided among the entire house.

But I sensed too what I did not yet know—that the appealing young man was also an artist in the grip of a peculiar passion that, like all artists' passions, proposed previously impossible reconciliations: to make a new kind of eclectic, Mediterranean–inspired, yet wholly American cooking; to scrub away the last encumbering barnacles of the old slavishness to French cooking without neglecting the glory of France (I knew from our first table-side conversations that he, like me, was an admirer of the arch Francophile writer Richard Olney); above all, to make a place for a weekday dinner that was also a place where minds could meet and make values, to cook from an American palette without being tiresomely "local." I was engaged at the same time, in my own writing about food and the philosophy of eating, in what I imagined to be a similar obsession, wanting to bring the brio and tone of the *New Yorker* writers on appetite I loved, A.J. Liebling above all, safely into the end of the century. We were sharing a new time, when we drank less, cared for our children more, cooked home as much as we ate out, and, generally, with significant exceptions, ate less for spectacle and show and more for company and conversation.

I left for five years in Paris with that ambition in mind and had our farewell meal there . . . I still have pictures taken that night. Coming home in 2000, Peter and I discovered, in the way of generations, that our paths had coincided even more: we came home from Paris with a baby girl named Olivia—a name we had thought uniquely original and "Shakespearean"—and found Peter and Susan with . . . a baby girl named Olivia. (Everyone had a baby girl named Olivia in the late nineties.)

Peter and I grew closer as I entered ever more deeply into the world of food, and we began to collaborate on "talking" dinners, some of them unforgettable, not least celebrations of the great French trilogy of bouillabaisse, cassoulet, and choucroute. They remain highlights of my own life as a speaker—seminars in gastronomic history that were underlit by actual gastronomy—talking about food while eating it.

Yet one need never have eaten at Savoy, or even seen it in passing, to relish this narrative. What Peter offers the world in this memoir is, really, the history of the passion that was incarnated in that restaurant. Even if that restaurant, like too many good New York things, became the victim of real estate madness and neighborhoods altered, the passion still lives, and even rages. In this beautiful, bittersweet, confessional, yet still appetite-fueled reminiscence he has written about many objects—that memoir of the rise and fall of a neighborhood and a restaurant, a testament to a particular vision of food, and a useful guide to what is good in any greenmarket and how we might go about discovering that for ourselves; his real subject is the life of a chef, or cook, as an artist. For cooks, he reminds us, are as much artists as any other kind, yet work with material and circumstances more resistant than any other kind of artist knows.

Here is the whole history of an artist as committed as any composer or novelist to his own form of lyrical expression, with all the familiar steps: first, the inspiration from a remote hero (Paul Bocuse in this case); then, the slow awkward formation by mentors, kind and cruel; next, the joyful discovery of yourself as part of a generation of like-minded makers; finally, the opening of a restaurant—the cook's equivalent of publishing that first novel; and then the inevitable struggle with idiot reviewers, who give you three stars out of annoyance at someone else having given you four, and all of standards while raising a disputatious family.

I tried to dramatize the complexities of this life in a musical I wrote with the composer David Shire, *Our Table*—about, exactly, a chef, his front-of-the-house wife, and their two children—in which the moral is that on every menu there are prices on the right side and choices on the left, and that restaurant people make their lives between them. In the end, we all do. The difference, of course, is that where writers or painters or even musicians depend on a network and have to live ultimately in the real world of supply and demand, chefs are on the cutting edge of commerce every night, even as they dream of the outer edge of innovation every morning.

Opening a restaurant is like publishing that first novel, with the difference of having to publish it again the next night. Writers struggle with their sentences no more or less than cooks struggle with their plats, but writers don't have to pay a staff of comma cleaners or depend for the success of our last paragraphs on the mood of an inebriated last-paragraph chef, as chefs must do on pastry chefs—last-paragraph chefs who would be, so to speak, hired on a flyer from another writer who forgot to mention that she's no good after 10 P.M. and a second bottle of Sauternes.

All of that artistry—and all of the resistance it meets—is recorded here. The story of an artist with a chain of keys at his waist and an intimate relationship with a refrigerator repairman essential to his vision—that's what gives this book its comic grace, and its ultimate meaning. What's really good? You will learn more about the outer life of a restaurant, and the inner life of a chef, from this book than from just about any other I know. The moral one takes away from it is somehow both simple and precariously complicated—that what's true about the history of ingredients he tells us is true about the life of a cook who truly cares: "what's good" is . . . all that's hybrid, historically complex, constantly in dialogue between honest terroir and exotic temptation, sizing up the place you come from and the pleasure you serve.

A single walk with Peter Hoffman across the Union Square Greenmarket supplies enough ethical tests—this one or that one? Too soon or too late? Sustainable or bad for the soil?—to harden anyone's moral fiber. This book makes those walks with Peter Hoffman available to anyone who opens it and gives permanence to his passion.

PROLOGUE

ON THE CORNER

I peer across the intersection of Prince and Crosby Streets at the corner building in SoHo where I ran a restaurant for twenty-six years. I feel pride, a touch of sadness, and relief. Several months earlier I had sold off the contents to a dizzying stream of devoted customers, tourist shoppers, and bottom-feeders. One last time, I removed from my pants pocket the custodian-sized ring of keys to every door, closet, back entry, and cash drawer in the place, the ones always on me, inexorably abrading my pocket lining and my spirit. I set them down. The lease had been assigned; I'd gotten paid and gotten out.

The two floors I occupied during most of my tenancy are now wrapped in a large plywood construction shed, wheat-pasted with posters boldly announcing the impending arrival of a fast casual food concept: a modernized cafeteria that keeps office workers calorie-fueled and close to their desks. Conceptually, it's not wholly different from the restaurant that came before me, the Rodriguez, a rice and beans luncheonette that served food dished out of a steam table or quickly griddled but for a different set of daytime workers. Back then, sweatshop and factory employees inhabited this dwindling manufacturing district by day, all but deserting it on weekends.

Standing on the corner and reflecting on all this history, I'm struck by the realization that my restaurant, Savoy, a beloved place where people came to break bread with old friends, celebrate marriages and birthdays, clinch business deals, and mark inevitable life losses while enjoying the pleasures of the table, occupied a unique moment in time. Savoy was bookended by two food businesses offering streamlined cafeteria-style food service, neither one a dining experience. This moment marks the end of an era for me but presages what has been happening to many restaurants in the middle—those neither fast casual or fast food nor high-end luxury houses. Operating in NYC had become problematic, maybe untenable.

When I first discovered this corner in 1989, gazing from the same spot I'm now on, I saw a neglected shop, its brick filthy with graffiti and bent scissor gates pulled forebodingly over the windows. It sat on the backside of Broadway, a grand allée of high buildings that were fast becoming home to design and creative professionals. Just across Broadway lay the heart of SoHo, epicenter of the modern art world. The Rodriguez was closed on Saturdays when the curious art crowd crawled the neighborhood to view the latest works of an entire generation of contemporary artists; it probably wouldn't have appealed to most of them anyway. I saw a sad spot with good bones and huge potential, in need of love, attention, and a vision. Together with Susan, my wife and partner, we brought all of that to the corner in a huge infusion of energy that created a hive of community.

Our modest place (originally forty seats with no bar) hummed with cooks excited to explore the worlds of flavor, to uncover the stories of how and where our ingredients were sourced, and to deepen their culinary skills. Front-of-house folks passed along that excitement and those stories to diners while also introducing them to beverages that prompted awe at the extent people go to produce something delicious. As we figured out how to make it all work in this spot and defined our cuisine, we also learned who our diners were and what their interests were. To say that we built a clientele of regulars misses the point and reduces many rich and varied relationships down to narrow transactional exchanges. The people who ate our food, paid our bills, and partook in our culinary journey became integrated into the very fabric of the place; they were part of the vibe. A room devoid of customers is but a ghost of a restaurant. It's obvious that a place lacking customers can't remain open but our customers, in supporting and funding our ongoing work in progress, solidified a food community. As the restaurant dug deeper into direct sourcing, the community extended far beyond the walls of the little Federal-style building at the edge of SoHo, beyond the borders of the city, out onto the land into the farming communities of our region and beyond. Orchestrating this community and making its story apparent to all who entered our shop was my job and my passion for over twenty-five years. It fed me in all the ways I dreamed that running my own restaurant might and fed my family and the families of many people who worked here during that period as well.

Running a restaurant is performance art, a nightly show that requires myriad parts to align in order to execute a service that sings for everyone involved. When the place was humming, the cooks in tune with each other, turning out beautiful food smoothly and seemingly effortlessly, and the servers were helping diners navigate the menu and wine list while facilitating a good time in the room, I absorbed that energy and heart and mirrored it back to everyone in the house. Those nights more than made up for all the uphill pushing I had expended to keep breathing life into the place over many years. Cooks could feel the optimism emanating from me as I walked into the kitchen to share a story from the dining room and felt pride.

The window of opportunity for this fine dining establishment opened up as manufacturers deserted SoHo and were replaced by the pioneers, artists, gallery dealers, and idiosyncratic shop owners, all of whom supported our creative endeavor. The window closed when the neighborhood, a product of its own success, became so heavy with retail shoppers that it attracted national and international firms willing to pay astronomical sums for brand exposure. And we didn't fit the brand.

This was never clearer to me than in our final sale days when an endless stream of shoppers flowed through looking for something, anything, to buy, their thirst for acquisitions all too apparent. The moment played to our advantage since we were depleting our entire inventory and cashing out, but it was also melancholy. In all this stunning traffic, few had any knowledge of or interest in what had transpired here over the last twenty-six years. I shared something in common with the Rodriguez. Over time we both became incapable of sustaining our rents. I had participated in the gentrification of the neighborhood and gentrified myself right out of a job.

Between the bookends of those cafeteria-style food operations is our Savoy story, but it is also the larger story of our changing relationship to food as a nation. Along with many compatriots around the country, we changed the culinary landscape in ways we never could have imagined. At Savoy's start, we were in search of something simple: good ingredients to cook with and a room in which to serve them unpretentiously to people who shared our values. It was a modest undertaking, but its underpinnings were profound:

conceptual, aesthetic, and political. We didn't realize at the time that our endeavor would be part of a drive for a broader social and ethical inquiry, instigating a national conversation about food and social priorities and the kind of world we want to live in, a conversation that continues to this day.

What's Good? is the story of what happened between those bookends and a deep dive to answer the question I ask all the time, whether shopping at the Union Square Greenmarket or thinking about life choices. Chapters alternate between ones pulling back the curtain on the mechanics and business of starting and operating a restaurant, and others that revel in the stellar ingredients available in the market. The ingredients chapters are profiles in taste, inquiries into how the plants and animals we cherish eating can deepen our appreciation for the marvel of creation. The thrills of building community and offering friends and strangers a place to *restaur* themselves (hence the term "restaurant"), the struggle to balance family and work, my discouragement as the landscape changed—it's all here. The two timelines are interwoven: a year of the growing season—from the moment sap begins running in maple trees, a spring awakening we cannot see, up to the hard frost in November when most plants have either been harvested or died back—alongside the four-plus decades of my professional development as composer and conductor of that human orchestra of appetite.

LEEKS AND POTATOES

I like to start my day with a tour of the universe. Living as I do in an urban environment of stone and glass, I need a portal into the green, growing world, into the benign and the miraculous. I get that by riding my bike to the Union Square Greenmarket and doing a shop at the farmers' market. It used to be my first stop after dropping my kids off at school, three days a week at 8:30 A.M. before heading to the restaurant. Now that they are grown and I am restaurant-free, my timing is less prescribed, but I know that if I want what's good, the earlier I arrive, the better.

What is laid out on the farmstand tables reflects what's happening outside the city, in the soil, on the land, a result of the season maker, the planet's tilted rotation. My visits let me experience the slow revelation of spring, new crops unfurling each week. It's a kind of time-lapse photography, only I get to eat the subject. The summer is an inundation, too many ingredients to choose from, each ripe, fecund, and rich. My fall market runs can jolt me. I may think I am about to make one more great tomato-basil salad when an unexpected cold snap moves in and shocks all the basil brown. Done, over. Buy rosemary, instead. Think about a quick-cooked tomato bean soup to take the edge off the chilly evening air.

Once I've completed the market run, I have location and trajectory. I know what the weather really is and a notion of what to cook for dinner. I like to do the buying. You might even say I *need* to do the buying. Without it I feel untethered, unstuck in time. I pedal home, ready to take on the day.

* * *

It's January. How did that happen? Summer's abundance quickly slipped into autumn's parade of send-off dishes, the last corn, beans, and peppers. Plummeting temperatures and low horizon sunlight brought ingredient diversity to a nadir. A few weeks back, Christmas markets were celebratory, bright with princess pine roping sold by the yard and fir wreaths trimmed with plaid scarlet ribbon. Specialty items that farmers held in reserve to prompt holiday spending have all been offered up: a last pass on dried Sorana beans; the final cuttings of the chicories; braided garlic to adorn a wall; and the reserve bottling of best-of-the-season maple syrup. Once this final transfer from farm cellars to apartment cupboards is complete, many growers pack up for the season. Those who remain have less to offer; there is a dreary predictability to what is available.

If a media consultant were to analyze the farmers' market messaging they would be all over their client for projecting the cardinal sin of mixed signals. At the height of the growing season, farmers' markets are selling the allure of food in the moment: today's superb ingredients will never be more delicious than they are right now. Nowhere else can better be bought; airfreight and a global economy be damned. These ingredients are highly perishable and not designed to survive the pummeling and extended shelf life required by mainstream food handlers distributing on a national scale. Chefs and home cooks alike cherish this market moment and scramble in the early morning to procure wild Mexican cherry tomatoes, Tristar strawberries, and butter lettuces, rushing them back to their kitchens before the day heats up. The beauty of the shortest possible supply chain between the farm and the kitchen is apparent; everything in the market seems to shout, "Eat this glory now."

But come the hard frost, it's transformative: on the landscape, to availability, and for the seasonal cook. The market messaging flips, now suddenly selling shelf life and longevity—promoting the hardy plants that hold energy stores for later use. As a cook, it's a hard transition to go from merely pointing ethereal raspberries or luscious tomatoes in the direction of a plate to create a great dish to then literally bottom out, becoming reliant on root crops that need effort, heat, and cooking time to coax out their flavors and release their nutrients. In it for the long haul (or at least until next spring), these plants assist us humans in getting to the other side of winter.

I get that it's a challenge to find excitement in the January market. During this period of damp and cold, low-light days, it can be daunting to go out and troll for inspiration and come back with potatoes. When I suffer from post-December party depression, the pull to hibernate is strong. By the time I finally spill out on the street, the sun is often beginning to sink and I wonder if it's worth bundling up and heading to the market. Maybe it's better to order dinner on my phone and let the immigrant deliverymen on bikes brave the weather instead. Or head to Florida or Mexico. Or walk into the chain supermarket where, in a kind of reverse migration, they've brought Florida and Mexico to us and with it a profusion of sunlight and chlorophyll.

Urban life can fool us into thinking we are masters of the universe with access to whatever we want, whenever we want; all it takes is money. I can go to the supermarket and shop in a world with no time or place (and also no community) but instead I give myself over to this market, cooking, eating, and sustaining myself from its offerings, which this morning are meager.

I buy an array of heirloom apples—pears are long gone—some super-sweet nugget carrots, a knob of rutabaga. I come upon some yellow chard that has been grown under plastic, hardy leaves that have become tougher and sweeter with the rises and falls in temperature over these last few months. I move on to the stand of a South Jersey farmer with a mountain of wintered over leeks and scallions, their root hairs vibrant with new life, beards on gnarly vegetables mustering through the snow and sleet.

There's a truth to the January market: the weather is in alignment with the offerings—unlike the market in late April, when warm, sunny downstate days shout for spring food even though snow may still be on the ground upstate. January shoppers show a clarity of purpose: we are here for foods of sustenance, necessary in order to stay put. Confronting the seasonal weather changes, animals must choose whether to leave or stay put—migrate or hibernate. Migration was a proven hedge against the winter long before snowbird retirees began establishing themselves part-time in Boca or Palm Beach. Ducks and geese fly south, bluefish and stripers do the same in our coastal waters, and many indigenous peoples were nomadic, tracking the migrating fish and game in order to maintain a continuous food source.

Plants lack the Boca option. Unable to move under their own power, they developed an array of survival strategies that can be categorized by life cycle: annual, perennial, and biennial. Annuals sprout each spring from seed, then mature, flower, produce seed in quantity for next year, and finally die back. Lettuces, peas, squashes, and corn are all annuals. It's a quick in and out approach. They live fast and die young. Perennials adapt to their climactic conditions, go dormant during the cold months, and then begin growing again

3

once temperatures rise and days lengthen. In devoting significant energy to building biomass and staying put, they will produce seeds each year under good weather and growing conditions. All trees (fruit and nuts), shrubs (blueberries), canes (raspberries), vines (grapes), and plants with underground root crowns (asparagus and rhubarb) are perennial. It's a great long-term approach—creating abundant offspring over a broad stretch of time.

Biennials split the difference, spreading their growth cycle out over two years. In the first, they concentrate on establishing themselves by building infrastructure (aka biomass), taking the year to establish that the site is suitable before reproducing the second. This strategy is particularly useful in places where there is intense competition between species, as in a meadow with abundant light and fertile soil. Carrots, beets, turnips, fennel, radishes, and onions are all biennial.

In preparation for continuing life into their second year, biennials hoard surplus sugars below ground in tubers before going dormant for the winter, a reserve to ensure having enough energy for reproduction. Growers snag these plants at their energy zenith in the fall or, as with parsnips, leave them in the frozen earth overwinter and dig them in early spring before they bolt and go to seed. Nothing beats a bowl of beet borscht drizzled with sour cream or a handful of carrots tucked around slow-cooking short ribs as a delicious means of transferring stored energy from plant to human. Biennial bulking up gives us hibernator types the option of hunkering down, of not playing the Boca card, myself included. I stick around town and troll the market for caches of stored energy.

Craving the vigor and sweetness of nutrient-dense plants, I'm ever on the hunt for whatever dwindling bits of live chlorophyll I can find. Why eat wan arugula from a plastic bubble box that isn't really satisfying, shipped a few thousand miles by burning nonrenewable fossil fuels? I prefer to search the market, reacquainting myself with vegetables that at other times of the year I pass up: the rutabagas, daikons, and celery roots. There is a recent trend of growers harvesting tender spinach leaves from unheated, high tunnels as the days lengthen. This method while delicious comes at a price point that I can only justify as the occasional garnish to a wintry braise.

For my leafy green needs I turn to the biennials that don't produce tubers and bulbous roots: the brassicas—the kale, mustard, cabbage family—aboveground biennials, they're fall hardy but rarely make it all the way through winter. Open, flat-leaved varieties (kale and mustard) have more exposure and so succumb earlier in autumn. Collards, possibly the toughest of the flat leaved, do qualify as winter hardy; their leathery leaves can withstand punishing weather—great for survival but with a cost to us cooks: they demand a slow and low approach in the pot.

The winter hardy brassicas tend to tightly fold their leaves up into heads (cabbage and Brussels sprouts) utilizing a Russian doll-like method of protection—enclosing leaf upon leaf, as insulation, until the innermost kernel is immune from freezing. Market farmers successively peel away rotten outer leaves that froze, until pale yellow ones are all that remain. Even though any vestige of summer's bright green is all but gone, stored cabbages, when shredded into slaw, offer a crisp and refreshing counterbalance to a rich, wintry braise. Seek out cabbages that were stored in a root cellar instead of a mechanically refrigerated walk-in. The difference in water content and freshness is startling.

By January, with the brassicas gone, leeks have become my saving grace for local greenery, the last plant standing and standing tall at that. Uniquely adapted to temperate life, leeks are a series of leaves folded and wrapped around each other in a circular pattern; the outer leaves protect the inner ones just as in a cabbage, but unlike cabbage, each leek leaf end is exposed to the sun, ready to photosynthesize whenever there is light and temperatures are ten to fifteen degrees above freezing. Stiff outer leaves help the plant stand tall, able to compete for sunlight, and their high cellulose/low water content help them withstand repetitive freezes and thaws. That's why cooks toss the tough outer leaves and woody, deep green tops in the stockpot or in the trash. The remaining cylindrical leaf layers, fading from forest to lime green, finally becoming white where they bunkered in the soil, are tender and ready to sweeten up any stewed chicken or pot of potato soup.

Two conventional farmers I worked with extensively over the years, both now retired, figured out how to extend their season of market viability and keep leeks coming to market deep into the winter. It's costly to drive a truck into the city, pay for market space and people to work the stand all day. Without diversity on the table, the trip doesn't pencil out. Exploiting leeks' cold hardiness, Alex and John would harvest them late in the fall, lay them outdoors on crates, well aerated to prevent rot but covered to protect them from snow. Gathering them for market days was a simple task and kept leeks coming into the market well into February.

Alex and John both farmed the black dirt mucklands of Orange County, New York, remnants of ancient lakebeds from the Pleistocene era, North America's last period of glaciation. Driving on a narrow highway thick with forest but thin on sightlines, the road dramatically descends and the view opens up to what appears to be a lakebed with a shoreline of forest and houses on the far side. Instead of blue water, the surface is black, a flat expanse of yards-deep organic matter accumulated from thousands of years of algae and fish settling on the lake bottom. Considered to contain the highest percentage of organic material anywhere in the nation outside of the Everglades, the soil is by-grace-of-glacier Miracle-gro. Nearly impossible to farm until Polish immigrants in the late nineteenth century trenched runoff canals to drain the lands as if cutting curd to separate the whey, only on a geologic scale, the drained flats support farm machinery, but little else. Only seventy miles from New York City, the black dirt acreage is not under threat of development; it's unsuitability for building is nature's conservation easement.

The surrounding town names—Pine Island, Big Island, Merritts Island, Black Walnut Island—aptly describe the high, stony ground, where homes can be sited without sinking into the muck. Without a pebble or a stone to divert a biennial root's downward trajectory, every carrot and burdock root grows straight and full, every onion round and rich in flavor. In addition to its high nutrient content, the black soil absorbs the sun's heat, keeping the plants warm on cool nights, giving a boost to early season growth and extending it in the fall. The flip side comes in July, when annuals like herbs and lettuces get heat stressed and shut down or bolt. Black dirt farmers are well represented in the greenmarket; their tables display the soil's magnificent output—mountains of carrots, beets, radishes, and leeks—a panoply of biennials.

* * *

I work leeks hard in my winter cooking. Their luxurious, melting texture is alluring, especially in contrast to the fibrous brassica leaves that never develop a silken mouthfeel, even with long cooking. I could use them up in a hurry but given that they are the very last green things to come into the market and will not make it to the Promised Land of spring, I hoard them, carefully doling them out to myself. I confess; I am an ingredient hoarder. Farmers may use root cellars and outdoor racks to extend the season but I have a few urban tricks of my own. Copying what I noticed in Japanese grocery stores, I wrap each leek individually and push them to the rear of the fridge. Rather than viewing my hoarding as aberrant behavior, I channel being a biennial. The moment presents me with the opportunity to live within my limits. Me and the biennials; we are both conserving, holding back, banking on getting to the warmer, brighter days of spring. Restraint as a time-tested survival strategy has served us both well.

Biennials keep my fall cooking interesting, but they can't fuel me through the winter. I need more calories, many of which I get from carbohydrates, particularly from annual grasses or grains—wheat, barley, rye. But the grains are culturally and agriculturally problematic. On the positive side of the ledger, growing annual grasses produces quick results—heavy seed output in a single harvest—and being self-pollinating, they easily maintain genetic consistency over multiple generations. The first farmers domesticated a wide variety of annuals in the Near East around 9000 BCE: lentils, peas, wheat, and barley. Once a farmer found a variety they liked that grew well in their region, they could save seed, replant the following year, and get the same crop. Annuals made the experiments in cultivation easy for these new agriculturists; the rewards could be swift and the yields high, sometimes even miraculous. The negative side was that with quick and easy also comes higher risk of loss. Crops could fail, completely. Droughts, floods, locusts, you know the Old Testament drill with the Ten Plagues, exposed a deep and real vulnerability of early civilizations. Theirs was a precarious boom and bust eco-economy reliant on annual plants.

Neither annual nor biennial crops were able to reliably supply the caloric demands of Europe's population from the Middle Ages well into the Industrial Age. Even though grains—wheat, rye, and barley—were grown extensively and could be stored from one season to the next, widespread famines consistently caused upheaval and instability. It wasn't until the sixteenth-century arrival of a perennial from South America that the feast-and-famine cycle was broken and allowed the population of a few European nations to grow rapidly and then assert dominion over the entire globe. The perennial was the potato.

Taking a long-range reproductive approach, perennials extend their organism across time and geography; their success is not dependent on a single harvest. Cross-pollinating with other potato plants nearby offers countless opportunities for adaptation to a range of conditions. In the Andes, where they originated, unraveling the genetic lines of potatoes is next to impossible. It's a spud mosh pit of related entities more than an orderly set of identifiable species. With over five thousand varieties still grown today, there is little agreement among plant scientists about how to categorize all the various species, subspecies, and landraces. And unlike grains, which require the consolidation of wide areas of acreage under singular control or ownership, the potato is well suited for small plot production and its caloric yield per acre is far higher than any of the annual grains. Subsistence farmers could produce a hefty crop for their personal use, especially through the winter.

In order to maintain consistency in potatoes, propagation is done clonally, by planting pieces of last year's tubers as this year's crop. The result is that this year's potato is genetically exactly the same plant as last year's. In the Andean version of the Wall Street axiom, "spread the risk," most small-scale Bolivian farmers grow on average twenty different types of potatoes. It's no surprise then that when a narrow gene pool is geographically isolated and then repeatedly propagated clonally that it would become prone to disease. This is what happened when a single variety of potato, adapted for life in the cold, dry, and high-altitude Andes was brought to Europe and grown exclusively in the hot and humid lowlands of Ireland. The perfect potato storm—the proliferation of late blight, a fungus that spread through the countryside in a matter of days devastating the entire Irish crop in the 1840s, the widespread monoculture of a single variety, and a huge number of poor people heavily dependent on the potato for survival—caused the potato famines and the deaths of over one million people.

***

I didn't grow up being exposed to anything close to five thousand varieties of potatoes; I think we ate two: the thick-skinned, elliptical Russet Burbank for baking; and the spherical thin-skinned Red Bliss or Norland, the ones my mother called "new potatoes" (even though most times they weren't new) for potato salad. Eating true new potatoes, also known as creamers, is a wonderful thing. Harvested from young living plants as the tubers are just beginning to form, the immature potatoes haven't developed the complex starch cells that both allow the potato to withstand storage and handling and contribute to the mealy texture. With higher sugar levels, they are both sweet and have a smooth mouthfeel. Look for creamers in June and if the stars align, these newbies cooked with early peas are an unsurpassable treat.

As good as potatoes can taste they are superlative carriers of flavors in the form of fats, herbs, and acids. Twice-fried French fries, duck fat potatoes or potato salad bathed in mayonnaise are crowd-pleasers and moneymakers. Guaranteed to provoke choruses of gushing from happy customers, scores of restaurant reputations have been built on their potato preparations. As a carrier of fat flavors, the potato probably reached its apotheosis with three-star Parisian chef Joël Robuchon's "pommes puree," a meticulous recipe for mashers enriched with half their weight in butter. His adoring customers thought they were eating potatoes when in fact he had hoodwinked them, cloaking a stick of butter in a few spoonfuls of spud. Robuchon was serious about his potatoes. He heralded fingerlings, the thin-skinned, digit-shaped, European varieties, which only became a thing in the United States in the nineties, when chefs and diners strived to replicate his magic trick. Known in French as *le ratte* or rat potatoes due to their rodentate resemblance, fingerlings are not mealy but dense, waxy, and wonderful for boiling or sautéing.

In the United States, we "prefer" the Russet Burbank. Claiming 40 percent of the entire U.S. potato market, the Burbank has a long storage life, high yields, and is resistant to late blight, the killer fungus of Irish potato fame. Taste and texture are not two of its best features although we have become accustomed to it. I have split open more than my share of aluminum-wrapped bakers and doused them with butter or sour cream and chives. Bolivians consider the Burbank to be a joke, a flavorless facsimile bred for white Europeans who are content eating industrialized food. They swear that the ultimate French fry can only be made with the papa amarilla, the yellow potato from the altiplano, the high plains of the Andes.

For many years, at Franca Tantillo's Berried Treasures stand, I would occasionally stumble on a bin of potatoes labeled Papa Amarilla. When asked about its origins, Franca's answers were vague. I could tell that it wasn't because she didn't know; she was being cagey. Just as I had learned not to ask certain employees how they obtained a social security card, I knew not to ask farmers how they got certain items onto their farm or into the country. Some extra-legal activities are beneficial to society (and delicious). Many a passionate winemaker has circumvented the quarantine requirement (that imported grape vines live for five to seven years at UC Davis) by sewing a few cuttings into their sports coat sleeve lining or tucking them inside the dirty laundry section of a suitcase. Franca's papa amarilla probably had a clandestine journey similar to those contraband vines.

They are nothing like a Yukon Gold. Purple-skinned, small as a golf ball, almost pine cone-shaped and with prodigious, deep-set eyes, a nightmare for any prep guy working for a chef who doesn't want to see a speck of skin, the interior flesh is an intense bright yellow. Cooked, their color holds and they have a nutty flavor some compare to chestnuts. I could never get enough of them mostly because Franca could never grow enough; they were disease-riddled, not adapted for life in the warm, low altitude Catskills and she was always holding back most of the crop, hoping for a better planting next year. I haven't seen them in the market for years. A former partner of Franca's is rumored to be growing them out west in Idaho or Montana, a climate better suited for a potato whose home is at ten thousand feet in dry soil. Maybe the only way I'll get to taste them again will be to head to the Andes and order up some local French fries.

* * *

Reliance on the winter market can indeed be monotonous. It's far more exciting to walk into a supermarket and experience growing seasons from other regions. As a cook I live to experience the peaks of sparklingly vibrant ingredients. I love cooking to wow people, but I don't want to cook a lie, the lie that we can eat this way all the time or live this way all the time. There are peaks and valleys in food availability and in life. Acting as impresarios, chefs and owners are expected to put on a dazzling show, night after night. Trying to maintain those heights is exhausting and inevitably leads to collapse, burn out, or self-destructive habits to stay jacked up, either personally (cocaine) or culturally (fossil fuels).

If, instead of basing our economy and life goals on the boom and bust cycle of annual grains, we based it on the more balanced approach of the perennial potato, we might sit more comfortably with the idea that some days are about hard work and completing the tasks, for which there may not be a shower of brilliance upon completion. Instead there is the security of survival in the present and the possibility of propelling into the next moment, into spring when brilliance might re-emerge again. Consuming carbs is the best way to get the hard work done.

One of the beauties of the potato is that after harvest, no further work or equipment is required. No backbreaking grinding corn on a metate, no trips to the licentious miller to obtain flour. A pot with some water or a pan with some cooking fat is all that's needed. My favorite dead-of-winter potato dish is Jansson's Temptation. There are no flashy ingredients, only three larder staples: potatoes, onions (or leeks), and anchovies married together with a splash of cream. It is a breeze to prepare. After eating this gratin on a chilly night you are bound to feel invincible against any winds blowing in from the Arctic, ready to take on the world with energy and verve. Watching Theo, one of my cross-pollinated offspring, reach across the table and shovel a large second helping of Jansson's onto his plate, it's clear that this potato dish too, even in the depths of January's winter market, is shouting, "Eat this glory, now."

JANSSON'S TEMPTATION

This is a rich, deeply satisfying, and fortifying potato dish with anchovies, leeks, and cream to round out the flavors. It's origins are Scandinavian and it is a much loved Christmas dish there but will soon be a winter regular in your family any day of the month. I use garlic and leeks in my version, and although the Swedish recipe calls for sprats, most Americans preparing the dish use cured anchovies in oil. Some people prefer to use heavy cream, which is a bit rich for my tastes. During the baking the dairy reduces and gets richer, so I find that the half-and-half is plenty rich.

1 large leek, sliced
2 cloves garlic, sliced
1 pound (455 g) fingerling potatoes, thinly sliced
6 anchovies, roughly chopped
Freshly ground black pepper
1 cup (240 ml) half-and-half, plus more as needed

1. Preheat the oven to 375°F (190°C).
2. In a small bowl, combine the leek and garlic. In a medium baking dish, layer the potatoes and leek–garlic mixture, sprinkling in the anchovies and black pepper as you go. Drizzle in the half-and-half. Bake for 1 hour, checking after 30 minutes to see how cooked the potatoes are by inserting a paring knife into them. Some areas will feel resistant to the knife, others softer and more cooked. Look also at how the cream is reducing. If it has cooked away, leaving too many exposed potatoes, turn down the temperature to 350°F (175°C) and perhaps add a splash of half-and-half to slow down the cooking. The dish is done when a knife passes easily through the potatoes and there are golden brown patches on top.

CITY BOY, COUNTRY BOY

I grew up in Tenafly, New Jersey, a bedroom community of New York City, just over the George Washington Bridge, in the sixties and early seventies. For some, the suburbs were a stifling place full of rigidity, pressures to conform to the norms of appearance, achievement, and success. For me, it was a bridge between the worlds of trees and skyscrapers. A stone's throw from the city, I enjoyed regular museum forays with my parents to the forest floor dioramas at the American Museum of Natural History, a Dalí show of melting clocks at the Huntington Hartford on Columbus Circle, and the Tinguely moving sculptures at MOMA's *Man and Machine* show. Sometimes my mom would use the FAO Schwarz toy store as drop-in day care, leaving me to wander the floors alone while she shopped at Bergdorf's across the street. She'd pick me up in the model train department and we'd go for lunch at Chock full o'Nuts, where I enjoyed the spinning counter stools and eating date-nut bread sandwiches. We also explored food in immigrant enclaves scattered around the city: at Mrs. Herbst's, a Hungarian bakery on the Upper East Side, I used a licked finger to collect every last flake of their marvelous strudel; in a Bronx Armenian bakery we bought lavash full of burnt dough bubbles, scooping up their cucumber yogurt dip with it; and Sahadi's, their apricot leather challenged me to exercise enough control to make it last beyond the date of purchase—I rarely succeeded. From these surprise food excursions, I began to sense that the city was full of foods that told stories of people who had traveled here from other lands, often escaping from their homelands.

We lived nearby an Armenian church and my dad attended their annual festivals, partaking in their delicious cuisine. In his eyes, too much eggplant was not enough. He bought a copy of their spiral-bound church community cookbook and began a decades-long practice of perfecting *beyli baghli*, a dish that became one of his classics: baked eggplant slippers topped with ground lamb, more eggplant, tomatoes, and pine nuts. My sisters and I would watch the process and sometimes he allowed one of us to help. He would cut the eggplant into precise axial wedges, salt them, and after sweating them for an hour, scrape off the bitter droplets with his knife, brush them with olive oil (my job), and top them with the lamb sauce and pine nuts. In the midst of the prep, he relayed the story of the Armenian genocide, their suffering under the Turks during the run up to World War I. He'd get fired up into a fury about how the Turks had brutally starved and slaughtered a million Armenians and to this day were still denying that it had ever happened. My father always served the completed dish on a bright orange, baked-enamel platter commanding everyone's attention with its theatrical scale and the drama of the all-day preparation. I was grateful for the leftovers: cold eggplant and a chilling history lesson.

My mom grew up in Nuremburg, Germany, for the first ten years of her life until 1934, when the Nazis took over her father's industrial ceramics factory and put him under temporary "protective custody." Upon release, my grandfather was sure the political unrest would blow over, but my grandmother insisted that they leave. After a brief stop in New York City, my mom, her sister, and their parents settled in Teaneck, New Jersey. No sooner had they unpacked their boxes and enrolled the children in school than they began sponsoring countless Germans for entry into the United States: relatives, distant relatives, friends, relatives of friends, anybody and everybody that they possibly could. Today some call it chain immigration. Back then they just knew they were saving lives and livelihoods.

Their house, known by its house number, 601, was the social hub for our relations and a community center for the displaced, the itinerant, and the just passing through. At Sunday summer parties in the backyard I'd overhear the older people speaking German, the frequent outbursts of laughter and exclamations of "*Wunderbar!*" followed by hearty nods of agreement. Even though *wunderbar* and *raus* (my grandfather's loving way of telling us to get out of the car) was nearly the extent of my German, I could sense that at these summer gatherings everyone felt at home in their words and in their skins, a comfort we never experienced in the more stilted and formal English they spoke with us. With surnames like Teutsch, Lutz, Zeiller, and Holzinger, each had tales of their escape and struggle to start a new life. *Bündnerfleisch*, air-dried beef, graced every summer hors d'oeuvres table and most gatherings concluded with my grandmother's *muerbeteig*, a buttery pastry using whatever fruit was in season and ripest: plums, peaches, apricots. In winter, there was spaetzle, sauerbraten, and *lebkuchen*, the clove-spiced cakes that were sent every December from Germany in decorative metal tins. We watched in fascinated horror at the gross stuff my grandfather loved: head cheese, tongue, and pickled pig's feet. He would have loved the nose-to-tail cooking we did at Savoy decades after his death.

Europe was never far away at 601; as soon as I entered the house, we'd hang our coats in the "*schranke*," a huge Biedermeier armoire. My grandfather would be at his wood inlay desk seated in a stiffly upright medieval-looking chair with carved wooden arms and brocade fabric. I'd run to visit the "museum," a highboy vitrine that displayed objects from our ancestors, and gaze at the Meissen porcelain musicians, a gold pocket watch, an embossed silver ciga- rette case, and miniature portraits of unidentified ancestors. The house was Tudor-style with dark exposed beams and plaster stucco walls, appointed with hand-embroidered tablecloths, cut-glass wine goblets, and blue Delft china on the table evocative of a refined, ordered, and distant world. It even smelled European—the bathroom always had a bottle of 4711 (like 601, the address of the original cologne from Cologne had become a brand) at the sink.

Regardless of the season, my grandmother set a small flower arrangement on the dining room table: in summer, a selection of roses from her garden; in winter, a tiny spruce bough and a few twigs of winged euonymus clipped from the yard, sitting in a low bowl, almost Japanese in its sparseness. A silver bell sat on a doily off to her side to ring for the cook when the next course was needed. I fought with my sisters and cousins about who would get to ring the bell, both oblivious and tantalized by the power dynamics its use implied.

My mom didn't grow up learning how to cook by hanging around in the kitchen. Their live-in cook didn't encourage others to enter her domain and her cooking wasn't worth emulating anyway. When my mom married my father, her mother-in-law, looking out for the interests and well-being of her darling son, handed her a copy of Irma Rombauer's *The Joy of Cook- ing*. It became the rock of her kitchen, where every crucial recipe could be found: roast chicken, pot roast, pineapple upside-down cake, and candied grapefruit peel along with Irma's down-to-earth bits of advice and calm voice of reason, perfect for someone who was starting out clueless in the kitchen. My mom didn't have a vast library of cookbooks. Coffee table food porn volumes barely existed yet. Not even the groundbreaking Time-Life Foods of the World series, marketed as a mail-order series, made it into our house, although I'd longingly flip through these volumes at a friend's house. I had a vague sense that my friends' moms were preparing elaborate French dinners, assiduously following Julia Child's steps for boeuf bourguignon or blanquette de veau with the dads matching their wives' endeavors with a supply of first-growth Bordeaux wines (or as close an approximation as they could afford). I longed to be from the household hosting those affairs but that wasn't my mom's way. Her connection to Europe wasn't from a book; it was still live, the memories quite present, some still painful. During the sixties, my mom was receiving reparation payments from the German government for the disruptions to her education and life that she had endured. As a cook, she was all about good ingredients and straightforward cooking and she put it on the table every night for decades.

My dad was all about flash and gusto, in his dress, his opinions, and in his cooking. If my mother reluctantly added garlic to a dish, his version led with it full frontal. If my mother felt somewhat bound to Mittel-European traditions, my dad, also Jewish but a born and bred New Jersey boy, felt freer to wander the map, especially into the lands of eggplant, peppers, and shellfish. Nothing made him happier than purchasing corn at a farmstand, returning immediately to the house to drop it into boiling water that he had put on the stove before he departed on the corn run. He was triumphant at the idea of measuring in minutes the time elapsed between when the ear was pulled from the corn stalk to when he dropped it into his pot. Invariably he would exclaim that tonight's corn was the best ever, completely believing it each time and was incredulous if someone didn't share his passions. Ignoring my resistance to eating fresh tomatoes, each August when they really kicked in, he would gush enthusiastically and say, "You've got to taste these, no really, how can you not like them?"

***

It's true. I was "a locavore before the word existed." I shopped at farmers' markets and sought out local suppliers long before I realized what I was doing or why it mattered. It was just what I did. Only later did I begin to think about the implications of what I was doing and build on it. That is also how I cook. A recipe only exists when I've finished. In hindsight, there is a breadcrumb trail of obvious decisions I made along the way—ingredients that can now be quantified and steps articulated. In the mix of the moment, there was only action and process, hunches followed intuitively, whether fistfuls of herbs making a sudden cameo or a sprinkling of acid to brighten the dish in a last-minute addition.

It's equally plausible that I could have become a biologist or a therapist but my path to becoming a cook began with a sliced egg sandwich when I was four. I was fixated on the lunch my mom packed me for summer day camp: sliced hard-boiled eggs on Pepperidge Farm white bread with Hellman's mayonnaise, a touch of mustard, and iceberg lettuce. Not only could I eat it every day, but I did, not because I was a finicky eater but because as summer lunch food it was so right and so good. Unable to contain my anticipation I usually consumed the sandwich on the car ride to camp. I'd had breakfast so it's not like I needed the calories. But I was ravenous for that perfect flavor combo.

The best part was how the power of the taste motivated my desire to acquire fundamental culinary techniques. Sense memory resides in our fingers in ways that tongs or spatulas can never know. Long before I learned how to make crepes from *The Joy of Cooking* or bought a chef's knife in anticipation of my first prep job in Stowe, Vermont, I was eager to master culinary tasks and free myself of parental dependence. I wanted to graduate from being handed pre-peeled foods to ones where I had agency—peeling oranges and shelling hard-boiled eggs were the firsts. I strived to produce masterfully smooth, unblemished eggs or intact oranges, facsimiles of the world as whole and perfect. I learned to use my fingernail for the first part, breaking through the skin and then slipping my thumb in for the second, tracing the circumference to remove the peel, sometimes in one piece. I discovered that I could peel an egg without tearing up its planetary surface by matching up the convex curvature of the spherical egg with the concave curve of my thumb running between the knuckle and the first joint. It was far superior to chipping away at it with fingertips. To call it a revelation might be a bit grand, but it was a technique that I incorporated into my body, into my body of knowledge, forever.

And then there were tools, implements of civilization: the wire-guitar egg cutter. Pulling it down through an egg, I was Superman at the cutting board, transforming an orb into slices with a single swipe. In a house absent of toy guns or play swords, my executioner's swath with the egg cutter was a good substitute. We've all got to start somewhere. I guess I started by brown bagging it in the back of a car.

For a friend's tenth birthday, we were taken to Luchow's for dinner, the German restaurant on East Fourteenth Street that dated back to the late nineteenth century, a time when the East Village was filled with German immigrants. The place was a wonderland filled with murals from Bavaria, trophy racks of deer, and elk and a man carrying a chalkboard sign edged with bells around the frame shaking it as he paraded through the rooms to let people know if they had a phone call. Bemused by my curiosity, my friend's mom encouraged me to order the pricey wild game dish of venison with chestnuts, neither of which I had ever tasted before. I was stepping out in my tastes and beginning to dip my toes into cooking as well.

As a middle schooler, in the late afternoon when I had either finished my homework or was avoiding it, my mom would set me up with simple prep jobs on a stool at the end of our narrow galley kitchen: a pile of English peas to shuck or a mess of string beans to snip. We'd hang out and talk, the shared menial tasks a kind of meditation. With peas, the beauty of the repetitive action, the rhythm and sounds of success were enchanting: pop, zipper open, slide the peas into a bowl, toss the pods. Repeat. Pop, zipper, slide, toss. It was a repetitive dance with the occasional variation: pop, zipper, slide, eat. Focused on the project at hand, I would begin sharing my thoughts and worries with her; she'd listen, offering an occasional comment, the mountain of peas in the bowl growing larger as our discussion topics went deeper.

Mesmerized by how the ladies at La Crepe effortlessly rotated their little wooden rakes to spread the crepe batter around the griddle, my mom guided me to a recipe from her still sturdy but now tattered copy of *The Joy of Cooking*. The instructions said to make a well with the dry ingredients and then pour in the wet ones and incorporate. Without the recipe's accompanying sketch, I would have had no idea what a well was. Using the well to work in the wet ingredients felt groundbreaking. Choosing to add the optional lemon rind was thrilling and edgy. Recipes, I discovered, had a structure to adhere to, a series of discrete operations to follow, but they also allowed room for improvisation and variation. This was big. My parents honored my new interest and bought me a black steel pan. Saturday mornings began with well making and rind zesting, far more satisfying than trying to succeed in Little League.

At fifteen, I became a de facto only child; both my older sisters had left the house for college and beyond. My parents began to include me in more city adventures: recitals by great musicians and refined dining experiences. They took me to Casa Brazil, for feijoada, the black bean dish of Brazil, jam-packed with porky bits and sausages. Its myriad accompaniments were exotic, the rich complexity of smoked pork, dark sausages, and beans incredibly delicious. To this day it remains on my short list of great celebration dishes. Seduced by the tropical decor and understated elegance I imagined that I had magically left New York.

But it was at Zabar's on Broadway and Eightieth Street late on Saturday nights, the place completely abuzz with boisterous post-theater, food-obsessed people stocking up for a Sunday appetizing spread of babka, bagels, and smoked fish, where I became convinced that the city's round-the-clock vibrancy was totally cool and a necessity of life. The intense verve was an intoxicant and I couldn't wait until I would be of age to partake; I was going to live here.

* * *

Suburbia during the sixties was filled with people trying to escape their pasts, to assimilate and become mainstream. Diversity hadn't been identified as valuable yet. Strivers were conformers, their origin stories and culinary traditions were often hidden from view. In a way, the blandness of Tenafly and the pressure to blend in became the very thing many of us rebelled against. The city was one antidote; the color and vibrancy of the woods right outside my door was another.

We lived on a piece of forested land with barely a small grassy patch. It neither qualified as lawn nor faced the street, clearly suburban no-nos. We groomed it with a push mower. Why couldn't my dad buy one of those gas-powered two-stroke polluters that everyone else had? We were completely surrounded by split-level houses built in the late fifties. Our land was a steep lot that the developer thought was either too difficult to build on or wouldn't appeal to his target audience, so they sold it off cheaply. My parents crafted a unique modernist glass home surrounded by a sea of conformity. At the time, the town still had quite a few large tracts of undeveloped land. The forest floor was still moist with runoff, the water not yet hydro-engineered away into culverts and storm drains. Our property was carpeted in spring with Canadian mayflowers, spring beauties, and trout lilies, even the occasional lady's slipper. I was fascinated by the beautifully grotesque plants: jack in the pulpit, skunk cabbage, false hellebore, as well as the wintergreen fragrance of black birch twigs. This was my playground; with guys I constructed forts and tree houses, feeling all-powerful from our commanding overlooks. With girls, I scouted for spots where we could withdraw from the world and hide. I was probably never more than fifty feet from the house, within easy vocal range of a parent, but I felt like I was deep in a forest, beyond civilization.

I went away to a summer camp where instead of playing baseball or tennis I learned canoeing, tree identification, and orienteering by compass. We never tired of singing "Power and Glory" by Phil Ochs, the Woody Guthrie of the Vietnam period. It being 1968, the song was both patriotic and a protest song, passionate but cynical about the glaring hypocrisies of our land and our democracy.

In the summer of 1969, I later went to a hippie camp in Vermont. I learned to throw the I Ching, make ceramic coil pots, danced like Martha Graham in a black leotard to Carmina Burana, and drank Ripple, my first bottle of cheap wine while listening to Buffalo Springfield. Everyone gathered in the camp dining hall to watch the lunar landing on a small rented black-and-white TV. Being proper counterculturists, there was live sitar accompaniment to Cronkite's commentary as we gazed at the full moon overhead.

Movement in and out of camp was very loose. One group drove off to a rock festival in a town called Woodstock. I was invited to go but at age thirteen, I wasn't ready to "trip" much less smoke a joint. I opted instead to go road-tripping with two counselors and a small group of campers. We drove all day by VW bug over the mountainous spine of New Hampshire down to the Maine coast, where I had my first lobster pound experience: you select your lobster live, pay for it, it gets tagged with your name on it, then when your name is called you pick up the lobster cooked, ready for cracking. We sat out on a pier, watching the sunset. I would have more cachet today if I had gone to Woodstock but my prized takeaway was a culinary one: the time from ocean to plate when measured in minutes makes a world of difference.

My explorations expanded from the backyard to the backwoods. What had begun as a place of wonder and curiosity had grown into a retreat from all the things I was against. I was anti-war, anti-industry, and anti-materialist, and like so many of my contemporaries, I wanted nothing to do with "the establishment." Critical of our culture's arrogant belief in man's dominion over nature with no regard for the air and water pollution created, I wanted to live with nature and to experience the wonder of creation instead of the folly of what money could buy. Given all my against-ness, the outdoors was the only thing I was for.

My answer was to be in charge of the roof over my head (a tent), to need only what I could carry (my backpack), and to get off the grid (a candle lantern for illumination); everything else I deemed indulgences that contributed to planetary misery. I happily sustained myself cooking over an open fire or with a small Svea stove and sleeping under the stars. Colin Fletcher, the author of the backpacking how-to book, *The Complete Walker*, became my guru for stripping back to the bare essentials. He preached "Leave No Trace" before the slogan was coined and created ultra-light gear by trimming extraneous parts off his equipment. I emulated everything he preached including the ultimate strip down—hiking nude as he did solo in the Grand Canyon. I chose the more populated Olympia National Park in 1970. Not surprisingly, this didn't go over too well with the hikers we encountered.

My backwoods explorations helped me develop a spiritual connection. I was raised an atheist. It's not that my parents didn't believe in God; I never knew what they really believed. My father vehemently rejected all organized religions and their orthodoxies. He'd blurt out venomous words before even entertaining a spiritual consideration. He was irrational about his rationality. I never asked my mother her views, because my father was so loud that I didn't realize she might have a different view or wisdom on the topic. Only much later was I able to see that my dad's commanding bravado was actually brittleness that overlay his fears. In her solo years after my dad's death, my mother openly embraced spiritual examination and even began practicing some Jewish rituals from her childhood.

As a teen though, I had to figure the religious stuff out for myself. Backpacking trips became spiritual opportunities as much as they were tests of self-sufficiency. In my reverence for "the creation" I studied wildflower identification books and read the rocks, intent on unraveling the story of planetary life. I found answers to my questions high on a mesa, looking into canyons carved over millions of years, and in tidal pools watching invertebrate dramas play out, life incrementally slow, infinitely small but connected to the larger forces of galactic movement and time.

Eating well in the woods gave me joy. I wanted no part of the corporatized freeze-dried fake food that I had been introduced to by the Boy Scouts. I cooked real food. After a National Outdoor Leadership School course in Wyoming, I began packing in a holster of used Kodak film canisters filled with spice blends to flavor lentils or bulgur. I'd shovel coals atop a covered skillet to make peach cobbler from rehydrated dried peaches mixed with Bisquick. Eating this slow-baked dessert beside a crystal-clear mountain lake, far from any electric light or stove, was a triumph of everything I stood for. Spiritual, yes; ascetic, no.

Euell Gibbons, the wild foods forager and author of *Stalking the Wild Asparagus*, became my first crossover hero from the outdoors into the world of food. Following his lead, I subjected my parents to many renditions of Japanese knotweed pie, pickled poke stems, and a batch of birch beer that fermented improperly and produced rank odors from our utility room. I tapped a row of sugar maple trees on our suburban town's main road and in the boiling off process nearly destroyed our kitchen ceiling with all the evaporating moisture. We discovered that the 40:1 ratio of sap to syrup is real; thirty-nine on the ceiling, one on the French toast. An even more powerful culinary figure was about to enter my life, a figure who became a beacon to steer by for many years.

BUTTER UNBOUND

Growing up, our butter dish was stocked with margarine. Its smooth texture and lightly salted flavor was familiar but it was of little use in preparing my two earliest dishes—cinnamon toast and scrambled eggs. If margarine came in tubs in those days, my parents didn't buy it that way; they purchased it in stick form to masquerade on the butter dish. I wasn't fooled. I'm not certain where their habit or preference came from. They had lived through World War II, when butter, sugar, and gasoline were rationed and a black market thrived on these most desirable goods. Open season returned when rationing ended in late 1945, but my parents soldiered on with the margarine. Is it what they had become accustomed to? Was it a Jewish thing, since it was always kosher, neither meat nor dairy? My mom recalls that during those years, margarine was sold colorless, accompanied with a small capsule of colorant to hand-mix in. This was the result of Wisconsin butter producers successfully lobbying the federal government to prohibit ersatz manufacturers from a passing off margarine as butter (not unlike the present-day dairy lobby assault on nut "milks" or the suits against use of the word "burger" for plant-based meat replacers). Believing that margarine's unsaturated fats and lower cholesterol levels were healthier than butter, whole wheat toast with a schmear of margarine remained my parents' breakfast staple until the nineties when the dangers of trans-fatty acids were revealed. My opinion was that margarine was good for moistening dry toast, but not much else.

Hortense Goodrich, our housekeeper from just before I was born until I was a teenager, had a different view on things. She liberally cooked with butter and lard. I quickly came to prefer things her way. Hortense came to the house on a weekly basis to clean, iron, and cook, always a high point in my week. She knew a slew of dishes, was keyed into flavor, and I was always happy to taste her compositions: creamed spinach, chicken with giblet gravy, baked custard with nutmeg shavings, and apple brown betty. I would sit on a stool nearby and she would instruct me while she made gravy: start with a butter and flour roux; cook out the flour's raw taste; deglaze the roasting pan to get all the tasty bits into the sauce; and slowly and gradually add milk to avoid any lumps, season it with salt and pepper, cook it until it thickened.

Family battles were fought over Hortense's apple brown betty. She would patiently sauté cubes of Pepperidge Farm white bread in plenty of butter, toasting them to a golden brown, then sprinkle the crisp cubes on top of apples tossed in brown sugar, spices, and probably more butter, and then bake it. It was delicious the night of but even better the next morning for breakfast, cold—the crusty bread now impregnated with solidified butter, resting atop the pectin-firm baked fruit. Breakfast allotments were negotiated the night before since my oldest sister went off to school earlier than my other sister and me and we needed assurance that we wouldn't get shortchanged. With property lines staked out along baking dish quadrants, everyone went to bed peacefully.

Hortense was the first person of color I ever had contact with. I remember looking at her hands and asking her why they weren't the same color as the rest of her skin—I must have been three years old. She told me it had rubbed off from working hard. Originally from the Carolinas, she was a single mom raising her daughter in Englewood, the neighboring town and commercial center for the area. It's where my dad practiced dentistry and was home for many Black people working service-class jobs. Barely three miles from our home but an ocean away in terms of opportunity.

Hortense came to work one day each week and would put on a uniform—a white zippered dress—before beginning her tasks: making beds; washing laundry; ironing our cotton sheets and my dad's shirts; and of course cooking. I viewed her uniform as a sign of professionalism and her respect for the work at hand, not a sign of subservience—not dissimilar from the white jacket my dentist dad donned each day before he began his work.

I am not sure if Hortense openly communicated her disdain for margarine to me, directly undermining my parents, but she wasn't shy about sharing her belief that butter was the secret to the fabulousness of her apple betty and her gravy, and that lard was the crucial ingredient in her flaky piecrust. My absolute faith in her good sense about fats marked the beginning of my inevitable separation from my all-knowing parents. When she'd leave for the day, any unused butter would remain in a dish next to the margarine in the refrigerator. Once I began opting for butter on my toast, my cinnamon toast game vastly improved and I insisted that two dishes run concurrently.

Hortense's recipes and techniques for making giblet gravy and béchamel sauce with roux represented a long passage that began in France; crossed the Channel to England before traversing the Atlantic to the Carolinas onto plantations or into households where enslaved men and women cooked for white families; passed down by Black cooks to future generations; and then in the great twentieth-century migration of Black people from the South, traveled northward to places like Englewood, New Jersey; until finally landing at my house and on my plate. Being a good cook offered Hortense a pathway out of poverty, as it has been for so many immigrant groups in our culture, towards upward mobility, if not for herself then for the next generation. Hortense's daughter had a white-collar job at Best Foods, makers of consumer products like Hellman's and Skippy peanut butter, and rose to become a key advisor to corporate executives—a groundbreaking position for a young, Black woman during the sixties. If Hortense's recipes were about butter bound with flour, her recipes were also bound up with hardship and exploitation.

* * *

The sauces I later learned to prepare in French restaurants were about butter unbound, freed of flour, freed of the oppressive constraints of rule-laden, French haute cuisine. Those recipes had traveled direct, from Paris to New York in the late seventies when nouvelle cuisine was the culinary "it girl" of the moment. Beurre blanc was its star sauce, the prefect expression of a new generation's desire for lighter and more spontaneous cooking. Translated as "white butter," the sauce is an emulsion of reduced white wine vinegar and chopped shallots with whole butter gently incorporated over low heat. The butter's milk solids and fats are held in suspension. Delicate in flavor, silken in texture, and lighter than the classic flour-bound sauces, beurre blancs were also finicky. Lacking flour's stabilizing power, they needed to be made daily.

Improvisations on the classic shallot and white wine vinegar combo were legion. Some restaurants built entire menus around the beurre blanc, offering a choice of up to sixteen different ones to mix and match with an array of fish and meat entrées—grilled Norwegian salmon with Jack Daniels beurre blanc was one possible combo, though probably not recommended. The signature dish at the midtown English wine bar where I worked in 1979 was sautéed monkfish with a raspberry vinegar–pink peppercorn beurre blanc. Making the sauce was always the last thing we did each night just before opening for dinner service. On any given night I would make several pounds, hold it in a bain-marie, a warm water bath, and regularly dunk in pieces of baguette, my dinner on the fly.

Another element of nouvelle cuisine was spontaneity and à la minute cooking. Pan sauces, made to order, replaced complex master sauces bound with roux like espagnole or Mornay that traditionally could be prepared for the week and then held on steam tables ready to ladle out during dinner services. Instead we deglazed pan drippings with wine or brandy, hit it with a ladle or two of stock, tossed in some herbs and reduced it to concentrate the flavors. The last element of this à la minute cooking was to toss in a pat or two, or three of butter and mount it, a term for slowly incorporating it to give body and heft to the reduction. Many a novice line cook thought they had graduated to saucier just by learning how to swirl and shake some butter in a pan. We wanted to mount anything that was in a sauté pan—vegetables previously blanched in water, mushroom sautés, pasta dishes, steamed clams, or mussels. The base stocks or deglazing spirits might change but every stovetop recipe ended with a hunk of butter tossed in. Its addition tasted rich and extravagant; it was also monotonous and heavy, fatiguing the diner as well as the cook. Butter had become a flavor shortcut, a way of avoiding the slower, more labor-intensive layering of taste from careful deliberate cooking.

Nouvelle cuisine was the fashionable food of the moment when I entered the world of high-end restaurant kitchens but I never felt at home in those kitchens. I was cooking rich food for rich people in restaurants that flaunted their high prices. The general assumption among cooks was that luxe cooking was at every chef's pinnacle and the expected trajectory was to work one's way up in the hierarchy of exclusive dining palaces until eventually running or owning one. I could see that serving the wealthy opened doors and provided opportunities. Hortense understood that too; but wealth is relative. She cooked for our middle-class family and now I was cooking for people far wealthier than me. My white chef's coat with checked pants and an apron were still viewed by many as the uniform of the service staff and with it they expected a certain level of invisibility and subservience. I also knew that as a white man of some privilege and education I had options beyond being kettled in the back of house. The chef coat and apron hadn't yet become fashion statements, but I wore them with pride. This was also the moment when the perception of chefs began to shift, joining athletes and rock musicians as power-culture figures.

When Sue and I began to dream and define what kind of place we would one day open, we were clear that it would be moderately priced, not catering to the one percent. We wanted to create structural relationships in the workplace that didn't replicate the class and racial stratifications we had experienced in most of the restaurants where we had worked. Savoy was not employee-owned, but cooperation and reciprocity were built into the compensation structure. In the front of the house everyone equally shared the work and the single tip pool. There were no busboys (the word itself an oppressive anachronism), the bartender was an equal member of the pool, and servers were expected to help out in all sections. Servers rotated as the kitchen runner/espresso maker—a position that in many fine-dining houses is often relegated to young people of color, a gateway position to a better share of the pool.

In the back of the house, I refused to create a tiered structure of prep cooks and line cooks. Everyone was responsible for their own mise en place. There was no daytime person peeling garlic, cleaning kale, and butchering chickens for the dinner crew. It was a kitchen full of college-educated (read: white) cooks who had turned their backs on white-collar careers, choosing instead to develop a craft requiring tactile skills and join the working class. I corrected new employees not to address me as "chef" but rather as Peter. We were peers, except I signed the checks.

Along with casting off the French hierarchical structure in the Savoy kitchen, butter and the beurre blanc got pushed aside as well. The advent of the Mediterranean diet—the hypothesis that people from cultures more reliant on olive oil than on animal fats in their cooking lived healthier and longer lives—opened up a new world of flavor possibilities. Olive oil was lighter and healthier and, more important, it tasted of the place where the olives were grown, expressing specificity of flavor and place akin to wine. As the foundational fat in cuisines of the Mediterranean—Italian; Spanish; Moroccan; Tunisian; and Palestinian—our interest in olive oil's use marks the beginning of the decolonization of our collective culinary outlook, of looking beyond France for extraordinary cuisines and beyond the Christofle-and-linen luxe dining rooms for unforgettable dining experiences. Olive oil opened the door for not only the Mediterranean cuisines to rise in popularity but by extension a vast range of non-Eurocentric cuisines including Mexican, South American, and Korean.

I turned my back on butter and relegated it to Sue in the pastry department—for her fruit tarts and crisps—except for the occasional appearance of sliced compound butter to garnish grilled meat or fish. I was not an oven butter baster, the technique of repeatedly spooning butter over every roasting protein as so many American chefs descended from haute French houses did, and I dispensed with making stock reduction–butter finished sauces. Instead, the counterpoint to rich proteins were either bright and acidic compotes or condiments containing raw elements, like gremolata for example—the lively Italian combination of parsley, garlic, and lemon rind. Two other house favorites that we utilized in endless combinations and applications were romesco sauce—a Spanish blend of almonds, garlic, chiles, and tomatoes—and zhoug, the Yemenite green sauce composed of cilantro, serrano peppers, garlic, caraway, and cardamom seeds. I had broken free of the tyranny of the butter sauce.

Hortense's sauces were bound—physically and culturally—to be consistent and integrated, predictably draping the entrée protein. This demonstration of order and command reflected a colonialist worldview that attempted mastery over people and ingredients. Nouvelle cuisine heralded lighter emulsified sauces of fats, magically held in harmonic suspension, independent of binding, the appearance of freedom from bondage while maintaining the illusion of continuity and control. Following that, the introduction of unemulsified sauces and broken vinaigrettes represented yet another worldview—an acceptance that some things are irresolvable, unable to be fully unified into one, different parts allowed to speak for themselves. Salsa verde and its ilk existed long before Jean-Georges Vongerichten was born, but my first encounter with a fine dining chef abandoning the goal of integration was at his restaurant, Jojo, in 1991. Looking down at a few golden green circles of oil floating atop a carrot jus on the plate was exciting and unnerving; the lexicon of how to construct flavor profiles was suddenly up for grabs. Infused oils replaced the beurre blanc, and soon every appetizer from edgy kitchens was squirted with globules of green chive or red chili oil intermixed with a briny shellfish broth or chicken pan jus. Breaking up the monotony of the mounted sauce, fats and jus coexisted on the plate, interspersed but unresolved, like chords that leaves us hanging with uncertainty, even a bit of tension. Maybe we no longer needed uniformity and control mirrored back at us by our creations. We were more comfortable embracing a respect for the random, the unpredictable, the differences in history and legacy. It suggested a shift in control—food was not a servant for the cook to demonstrate their ego or power on the plate. Cooks were now servants of the ingredients, less creators than conduits of flavor.

Much of farm-to-table cooking seeks to overturn the expectation of homogeneity in flavor and ubiquitous availability, the uniformities we have grown accustomed to in an industrialized food system. It's a celebration of specificity and individuality. Composing seasonal menus using the available fruits and vegetables from a farmers' market is a demonstration of this idea. Olive oil is both fruit and fat and easily shows seasonality and site specificity. Tuscan versus Provençal oil, comparisons of taggiasca to picual olive oils and the flavor of the new September harvest all became conversations among aficionados. Butter wasn't eliminated from the table. With the farm-to-table movement it moved from the entrée plate, playing a supporting role to the star protein, and onto the side plate, in its own breakout role served alongside some whole grain, slowly fermented bread, and sold as a menu starter, no longer a gratis accompaniment.

* * *

In addition to being the first person of color I got to know, Hortense's relationship with my mom was also my first experience of class distinctions and the power differential between worker and boss. I sensed that my mom's feelings for Hortense weren't always as positive as mine. Family lore had it that when I was a toddler my parents left me with her for the afternoon only to return and find me tied up, like a dog, to a tree in the front yard.

When I first heard the story, I found it amusing and couldn't comprehend why it upset my mother. It contradicted everything I ever experienced from Hortense. Years later, she told me her version of the story—that my parents expected her to keep track of me in addition to accomplishing a host of household chores. Ever on the move, racing on all fours towards a busy street, I needed some restraint if the beds were ever going to get made, the dishes washed, and her employer pleased. A boy on a leash tied to a tree seemed like a simple solution.

From the story, I began to consider the possibility that as an employer maybe my mom had a narrow view and unreasonable expectations of her employee. It gave me a small window into my mom's sense of entitlement or at least her obliviousness to the work challenges Hortense faced. Years later, well after Hortense had stopped working for us, she filed a claim that my mom had failed to pay Social Security benefits on her wages. My mom's explanation was "this was how it was done." The thinking was that everyone benefitted. By not taking deductions out of someone's pay and not contributing the additional employer's share to the IRS, employees had a higher take-home pay and the employer had a lower outlay. My mom paid the penalties and past due contributions but harbored resentment about it for many years. Sadly, Hortense's good work faded from her memory.

* * *

I was not able to sustain the nonhierarchical kitchen. One chef de cuisine, who came from a well-run quality restaurant, convinced me that our efficiency and my profitability would increase if we created a prep position. With this division of labor came not only stratification but a racial and language divide as well. The people in New York City most qualified and most willing to peel garlic and butcher chickens for ten hours a day tend to be Spanish speaking, from Puebla, the state in northern Mexico, many of them undocumented. I went down this road and efficiency increased; some of these cooks were technically more proficient than any culinary school grad who'd come in looking to be hired as sous chefs. I demonstrated how to bone a chicken to our best and last prep cook, Mariano. In a very short period of time, he far surpassed his teacher. With repetition and focus, he mastered how to move through a case of chickens with speed and precision. Mariano had become critical to the operation, if not indispensable.

Prior to Mariano's arrival, one of my chefs, after being hired, brought in "his" butcher, contending that line cooks were interchangeable and easy to come by but that his quiet, highly skilled technician, working nonstop in a corner of the basement, was the linchpin to keeping the operation consistent and cranking. When that chef left a few years later (without giving full notice) and took the butcher with him, I learned how right he was. Mariano, my undocumented butcher, in the basement was paid sous chef wages, more than any line cook. He had a certain invisibility but was a cornerstone to our humming operation.

In the early years of Savoy, cooks were only interested in negotiating a weekly take-home pay number: "What's the net?" I didn't know that by law, cooks needed to be paid an hourly wage. I had never been paid that way. In trying to be competitive with some of the bigger, flashier houses with deeper pockets, I paid every cook one hundred dollars in cash each week in addition to their check. Like my mom, I was trying to reduce my costs and keep a little more in everyone's pocket. We were complicit in playing the system for our mutual benefit. Like my mom, I would have been angry if the guys receiving the Ben Franklin in their pay envelopes exposed me to the Social Security Administration.

With the passage of the Affordable Care Act, I wondered if I was ever going to be able to offer my employees a benefit that I believed should be a right. Given the incredible pressure I was under to keep the restaurant viable, it seemed completely out of reach. Walking through the kitchen one day I exchanged greetings with a documented Pueblano line cook who had taken on a leadership role, nurturing and training inexperienced cooks. The sadness in his eyes, reflecting years of struggle and hard work, met my own sadness and discouragement, knowing that even with this moderately busy restaurant I couldn't provide what he deserved and what we as a society had a responsibility to offer employees. Farm to table might be great for raising people's awareness about farm and agriculture issues but it wasn't shining a light on the inequity of restaurant economies.

* * *

I recently went back to Paula Wolfert's cookbook *Mediterranean Cooking*, a font of de-colonialized flavor combinations during Savoy's early days, and prepared "her" Moroccan chicken and chickpea stew, redolent with ginger, saffron, and cinnamon, the complex perfume of spices we pursue when we imagine Moroccan food. Surprisingly the recipe called for a pad of butter at the end. I tasted the broth that I had been developing over several hours. It had depth but the liquid quickly departed from my tongue. Contrary to habit, I added the prescribed butter and the broth took on a silkiness that elevated it from thin to round, from elusive to persistent. It wasn't sauce but the broth now had body, the flavors lingered on the tongue. It was a revelation—to come home again, to the glory of (some) butter.

Hortense's gift to me as a boy had finally found a balanced place in my cooking. Her struggle to be seen, paid fairly, and appreciated for her hard work and delicious food can be seen as one that continues, especially in today's restaurants as operators endeavor to strike a balance between paying people fairly, the price that diners are willing to spend for dinner, and remaining financially solvent. "Value" in restaurant pricing has largely been predicated on buying cheaply produced food and keeping wages depressed. The system was and remains broken.

How do we create an economic structure that incorporates the true cost of the ingredients and the people making our food into the price of going out for dinner? How do we change what people expect to pay for dinner out? Hortense's gravy was bound in the love of good flavor, the desire to be seen, and the long sadness of deliberate oppression. Her recipes and their journey to my plate hold a place in my cooking. Hortense's gravy, enrobing my roasted chicken, is rich and deeply pleasurable even with its history of domination over people and ingredients. My salsa verde, drizzled over roasted fish, an unbound sauce of herbs and olive oil floating freely in suspension, contrasts the richness of the fish. Each sauce is delicious, broken, and both are forever part of my repertoire.

INSPIRATION PLEASE

I was struggling in high school. Not with academics, that was fairly easy for me. It was the big stuff. How was I going to figure out a career and how was I ever going to get a girlfriend? These were not sophomoric questions; at sixteen they felt truly foundational. Said another way, what path did I want to take and with whom could I share that path? I wasn't withdrawn in high school but that didn't mean I wasn't lonely. I hadn't found my people yet or figured out how to find them.

I decided to pursue a friendship with the son of family friends. He was a wrestler so I chose to make dinner on a Saturday night after his match. Wrestlers are always playing a feast-and-famine weight game, starving themselves all week long in order weigh in at the top of their weight class to dominate their opponents with bulk as well as skill. Following the morning matches he could eat with abandon on Saturday evenings before beginning the whole weight-loss regimen again the following week. I prepared a huge casserole of lasagna. We demolished the lasagna and built a friendship that continues to this day. My big takeaway was I learned that cooking for other people was a gift that opened their hearts; people are thrilled, seduced even, to be seen and honored.

***

People would ask me, "What are you into?" "Nature," I'd reply. But I didn't have a clue where to go with that, how to turn that into a career. The obvious paths like forestry, environmental science, and wildlife biology all lacked some sparkle that I yearned for. When I told my rationalist intellectual German grandfather that I might go into forestry, the conversation fell flat and abruptly ended. I desperately wanted to avoid the professional tracks that kids around me were following. Cooking as a path was still proto-lingual.

Then one Sunday morning midway through high school in 1972, I eagerly pulled the *New York Times* in from the doormat where it had been sitting since dawn. My goal was to get the front page of the Arts and Leisure section before my sister did so I could be the first one to search for the Ninas hidden in Al Hirschfeld's weekly caricatures; Hirschfeld would draw his daughter's name Nina hidden in folds of clothing or wisps of hair, and just knowing about the game meant that you were a New York insider. In order to get to Arts and Leisure I'd quickly flip past other sections including the magazine. On this particular morning, I stopped short to take in the striking glossy photo of a handsome chef. He was standing in an outdoor farmers' market proudly surveying an abundance of fruits and vegetables. Who was this guy and what was he doing? Pre-breakfast and still in pajamas, I read the article. The Ninas could wait.

The cover photo was of Paul Bocuse, aged forty-six, chef of his family's Michelin three-star restaurant outside of Lyon, France, and a leading spokesperson for a new generation of chefs who were modernizing fine dining in France. He was standing in an outdoor market surveying a farmstand table abundant with pristine fruits and vegetables. From that single cover photo I saw a path. Here was an occupation that married culture and nature, the city and the country. There was enormous room for artistry and intellectual stimulation and the work, rooted in physical labor and tangible productivity, maintained a connection to the beauty of the natural world. I wasn't alone in having this realization. Bocuse represented the possibility of an honorable alternative career path for countless American kids. We didn't have to go into law, medicine, or finance. He legitimized the career and brought prestige to work that had previously been viewed in this country as merely service work. Along with sports heroes and rock musicians, chefs were elevated into the cultural elite. Bocuse was the first to be lauded in this way. Many consider him the original celebrity chef.

Interestingly, Bocuse represented far more than a career possibility for college-bound kids. He represented an entire generation of French chefs who were breaking away from the classic Escoffier-modeled kitchen with its mechanistic approach to cooking and menu development. Escoffier had codified French cooking into a series of sauces, stocks, and garnishes that allowed it to be exported internationally and produced en masse in restaurants, hotels, and banquet halls. It was a rigid approach to cooking, leaving little room for creativity, which might have satisfied the hotel owner but not necessarily the chef. This was a stultified cuisine still mired in the baronial opulence of the pre–World War I era. Of the mid-twentieth-century three-star Parisian restaurants—La Tour d'Argent, Maxim's, Laperouse, and Lasserre—their chefs were barely known; their names aren't even listed in the Michelin Guides of the time. The food had to be good but chefs, like the garnishes, were interchangeable. A house's reputation was built not on who was in the kitchen but on who greeted you at the door. There was little room for personal expression in cooking much less the modern notion of seasonal spontaneity.

Bocuse and his generation of chefs pushed against this old guard. France was slowly rebounding from World War II, which had devastated the people, the landscape, and the country's infrastructure. Food scarcity and privation was real and lasted for many years after liberation in 1945; it wasn't until 1950 that Michelin awarded three stars again to any restaurant, having ceased publication of the guide from 1940 until 1946 and deemed awarding three stars inappropriate until the nation had rebounded. The post-war-generation chefs that began to emerge were adventurous, wanted a fresher, lighter, and a more modern approach to cooking and dining. They refused to be relegated to the stoves. They came out into the dining room, proud to be the face of the restaurant, and the power center of the restaurant returned to the kitchen, its source of creativity and innovation. Paul Bocuse was the face of that change.

Concurrent with this change in France was the growth of the middle class in the United States. With more disposable income and the increased ease of air travel, they began traveling to France, enjoying not only the cafés and bistros of Paris but the haute cuisine spots throughout the countryside as well. These American visitors weren't penniless, struggling artists or passionate lefties as the "lost generation" of the teens and twenties and partisans of the thirties had been. Instead they were food and fine-dining obsessed gourmands. A.J. Liebling and M.F.K. Fisher wrote inspirational prose about their Parisian dining exploits; Julia Child and James Beard deconstructed traditional French fare making it accessible to the American home cook. While all of these writers shared their love of French cooking and culture, they were neither professionals nor French. The nation and the cuisine needed an ambassador chef of its own. Paul Bocuse became that chef. Landing on the cover of the *New York Times Magazine* signified that change for France and the world.

With the image now burned into my head, the text resonated as well. The author, Waverly Root, asked Bocuse why he didn't "delegate the irksome chore" of shopping at the market when he could just as easily have sent an employee. He replied, "Because first-rate raw materials are the very foundation of good cooking. Give the greatest cook in the world second rate materials and the best he can produce from them is second rate food." Obvious, but revolutionary. Bocuse went even further to say that scale of production has a direct impact on the quality: ". . . all the mass wholesaler, who pours all his produce into the same hopper, is able to sell is the average." The first quote underscored seasonal sourcing as a fundamental chef credo and the second raised questions about scale and quality in our food and agriculture. It would take a few more decades before I fully understood that comment and still grapple with it to this day. As critical to the quality of his cooking as market shopping might be, Root muses that Bocuse shops in the market because "I suspect . . . that Bocuse *likes* to do the buying." I follow in his footsteps.

MAPLE SYRUP

Although you would never know it from a quick glance at the landscape, it's spring. The forest is a gray scale study: silvery trunks, branches in shadow nearly black, and granular corn snow an apology for white; there's the occasional brown of exposed leaf litter but the only color in this wintry palette is the occasional patch of sky blue. I'm wearing a heavy wool sweater, a cap, and gloves; without activity even that's not going to be enough to maintain comfort outdoors for any duration.

Spring stirs deep inside the trees, in ways we cannot see, and by the time our eyes do actually spy swollen tree buds poised to unfurl as leaves, the moment has long passed. With longer days and the sun higher in the sky, winter's back has been broken. In early April, with the arrival of ramps and wintered-over rabe in the farmers' market still weeks away, Sue and I went off in search of the real spring awakening. Instead of heading southward as so many travelers do to jumpstart its arrival, everyone eager to shed clothing and gaze at magnolias and cherry blossoms, our contrarian compass was oriented northward towards the Northeast Kingdom of Vermont.

On the surface, it looked as if we were heading right back into winter. The highway medians throughout Westchester County and Connecticut were dappled with patches of green but the visual field was still mostly brown and tan. Some tree buds had color—swamp maple red, weeping willow yellow. By the time we hit the Massachusetts Pioneer Valley even those small bits of color were gone. When we turned off the I-91 lowlands hugging the Connecticut River and climbed onto the Green Mountain spine running through the middle of the state, plenty of snow covered all but the most exposed southerly facing slopes.

We were heading north to see maple syrup get made by Howie Cantor of Deep Mountain Maple who, along with his wife, Stephan, has been sugaring in West Glover for thirty-five years. Howie left New York City for Vermont, fell in with the Bread and Puppet Theater, the agitprop theater group that

37

creates art and theater pieces around the state, around the world, and at their theater barn just a stone's throw away from the Deep Mountain sugarbush. The theater group also runs a sugaring operation on their property, which is where Howie caught the bug during the 1983 season. Taking his pay in syrup, he headed to New York City, rented a temporary stand at the Union Square Greenmarket, and saw that not only was this work he liked and a good source of income, but it could help him resist the oft-tempting offers to go on the road again with Bread and Puppet.

Spring for a maple tree begins when its winter dormancy is over and sap, the tree's lifeblood, begins running from its roots, up through the trunk and branches, out to the leaf buds. Think of the roots sending sugars back up into the tree as a way to kick-start the season, offering a boost from last fall's bumper crop of photosynthetic activity until the buds unfurl into leaves and can begin again doing what leaves do, acting as little green solar panels, photosynthesizing sunlight into energy. Photosynthesis, though well studied, remains a magical, almost sleight of hand process: take six molecules of carbon dioxide, add six molecules of water, reshuffle them inside a leaf cell with the addition of sunlight, and they will yield one molecule of sugar for tree growth and six molecules of oxygen to offset our CO_2 production: $6CO_2 + 6H_2O = C_6H_{12}O_6 + 6O_2$. Nature's card trick that is good for the tree and good for the planet. All deciduous trees go through this process but sugar maples have a high percentage of sugar in their sap and unlike oaks and ash they lack any off flavor tannins. Good news for my bowl of yogurt.

A stand of maple trees used for sugaring is known as a sugarbush. To the untrained eye these forests might appear to be wild, their growth checked only by weather and the forces of natural selection. But a maintained and well-groomed sugarbush advances both the human's and the tree's needs. Clearing out intrusive brush, culling closely spaced trees, dropping dead or dying ones, and removing some but not all of the non-maple species facilitates the reproductive success of the maples, allows for easy movement in the sugarbush and, as a kicker, provides the very fuel needed to boil down the diverted sap into a bottle of maple syrup. It's a neatly closed circle of a renewable resource.

In February, Howie snowshoes around his 5,200 tree sugarbush, drills a single hole into each mature sugar maple, inserts a spile or tap into each one, and connects all of them via a zigzagging web of neon-blue-colored plastic tubing. Once the sap starts flowing, usually sometime in March, the tubing directs the sap downhill into large repurposed stock tanks, for giving water to cattle in the field, until it can be transferred to the sugarhouse where it will be boiled down into syrup. For most of the nineteenth and twentieth centuries, sap collection consisted of crews either snowshoeing or using a horse-drawn sleigh through the sugar bush, emptying the lidded buckets into larger containers and then hauling it back to the sugarhouse, a tedious process to be sure. Tubing usage became widespread in the eighties and represented a huge savings in time and labor. Howie, more of a back-to-the-lander than an early adopter type, didn't switch over from buckets and horses until 1990.

Even though Howie and Steph sell at the farmers' market, you wouldn't exactly call sugaring farming. Ethnobotanists put sugaring into a category of food production activities called proto-farming—stewarding and facilitating the success of a wild population that as a side benefit produces food for human consumption. Beekeeping, oyster aquaculture, gathering wild rice, and arguably today's lobster industry—which uses the lobster pots as feeding troughs to feed the lobsters until they reach regulation size—are all examples of proto-farming. Since Neolithic times, farming grain has necessitated monocropping large areas of acreage to the exclusion of all other plants, using any means necessary to discourage intruders, whether it was a plow or herbicides and pesticides. As an occupation, sugaring is more about facilitating or curating the landscape than controlling or manipulating it.

As Howie tells it, when he arrived in Vermont, the prevailing farming model was to run a small and diversified operation: divide time between tending a small, fifty to one hundred head dairy herd year-round, logging during the winter for fuel and cash, haying and growing feed corn in the summer, and sugaring from Vermont's Town Meeting Day (the first Tuesday in March) until the fields were dry enough to plow. As thrifty dairymen, they spread the herd's manure over the pastures, building nutrient material, and harvested the pasture hay for feeding the herd during the colder months, a closed circle utilizing renewable resources.

Sugaring then was just one activity of a diverse farm, almost a sideline gig of dairymen. "The old saw was that sugaring paid your taxes." Most sugaring operations were small scale and site specific. Like wine from small vineyards, they expressed the taste of a very specific place. Old-timers have always maintained that the best syrup comes from sugar maples on high rocky land. They identified both the sugar maple, only one of many maple species that have sweet sap, and the rocky high ground as the topography best suited for making syrup of the highest quality. They snubbed the syrup obtained from faster-growing red swamp maples not only because their sugars are lower, requiring more fuel and boiling time, but because the flavors are considered less complex, lacking the minerally and buttery flavors of the high-ground "rock" maples.

***

We are holed up in a hotel room in a nearby ski resort. Over at Deep Mountain everything is locked up. For the past three days temperatures have held steady in the high twenties—too cold for sap to run. There is a complete maple standstill from tree to barrel: sap isn't running, the neon-blue plastic tubing supposed to direct the sap downhill from the trees is frozen and all of the collection tank valves are frozen up as well. Howie discourages us from arriving too early in the day although he expects the sap to start running later in the afternoon. Slithering our way through their mud soup of a driveway, we bottom out the rental car more than once, park, and then, carefully planting our feet in someone else's snow tracks, we descend the fall line to the sugarhouse. Lying on his back next to a 250-gallon collection tank, Howie is switching out a tiny one-half horsepower electric pump that burnt out after hours of unsuccessfully trying to push frozen sap through a line. It's overcast. I feel the chill, and no sooner than I wonder how long it is going to take to thaw out the forest and all the gear, Howie engages us in a deicing project. We take a propane torch to a metal valve and heat it until the sap in the frozen line defrosts. There is a wonderful whooshing sound as sap, now released, flushes through the lines and flows from an upper collection tank down to a tank near the sugarhouse. "We are almost there," Howie says, moving on to the next locked-up pipe connection.

Maple sap does not come out of trees pancake ready. Unlike pine tree sap, which is persistently tacky when I've gotten it on my hands while climbing a tree or collecting branches for firewood, maple sap resembles water with just the slightest but unmistakable maple tinge of sweetness on the tongue. Sap circulates in the tree through the xylem, one of the tissues on the circumference of the tree just inside the outer bark. We know why sap flows in the spring: to jumpstart the new growth before photosynthesis can begin. How sap flows is less understood. Sugarmakers have always known that a good sap season is dependent on the regular and prolonged fluctuations of temperatures above and below freezing, preferably alternating between day and night, that occur as spring tentatively edges out winter.

Contrary to common wisdom, flowing sap is not akin to turning on your faucet allowing it to run up the tree. In fact, runs occur when the sap is moving back down into the roots, away from the tree's extremities. When temperatures fall below 32°F, sap in the tree freezes, starting from the most exposed small twigs and limbs, working its way back to thicker sections of the tree. The frozen sap physically expands, just as ice does, and pushes into nearby air-filled cell chambers, called rays. This action of removal from the xylem creates suction or negative pressure and pulls more sap up into the tree from the roots. The longer the freeze, especially if it is a gradual freeze, the more sap that gets pulled into the rays. Sugarmakers have long observed that some of the longest and sweetest runs occur after a sustained freeze. When temperatures rise during the day as the sun warms the tree, the frozen sap thaws and pushes back into the xylem, creating pressure that pushes the sap down the tree (or out of the tree if somebody has come by and drilled a small tap hole).

Traditionally, sugarmakers have also observed that bad weather systems play a positive role in contributing to a good run. If barometric pressures fall as a storm system moves in, there is a greater differential between the pressure inside the tree and the outside air, producing a stronger run. Bad hair days are good sugaring days. In the nineties, people figured out how to make this an everyday affair. They attached a vacuum pump to the plastic tubing lines and created a constant negative pressure at the tap. Contrary to what many might think, the vacuum line doesn't suck the sap out but maintains a micro-atmosphere of low pressure around the tap, aiding a strong and steady flow. For a long time, Howie resisted vacuum pumping, feeling like it wasn't a natural process. He is now in favor of its use having found that it allows him to drill a smaller hole in the tree, which causes less damage and stress on the tree while still extracting a higher yield. Now regardless of size, his trees only get a single tap.

We move to another tank, this one on the uphill side of the sugarhouse. This reservoir when opened flows directly into the sugarhouse pans for boiling off sap into syrup. There is sap here that didn't get boiled off at the end of the previous run when the temperatures began to plummet. It's iced over, two inches of pure H_2O, nature's cold method of concentrating sap. Howie charges me with removing the ice. I perch on a ladder leaning out over the tank wearing thin rubber kitchen gloves and lift sheets of ice, drain them of their sap, and toss them into the snow. Meanwhile, Howie futzes with another frozen valve, this one a toilet float mechanism used to prevent an overflow of sap into the tank. The propane torch trick works again and fresh sap gushes into the tank. My hands are numb from handling ice with only rubber gloves. I recall Howie's comment from hours earlier about being "nearly there" and wonder when we're ever going to light a fire. In order to keep working I need the benefit of some radiant heat.

Howie capitalizes on the three-day freeze and my expert ice removal to boost the sap's sugars. It's not a reliable method, but a modern technique for concentrating sap called reverse osmosis (RO) is. RO inverts the concept of a water purification system by passing sap through a filter. In water filtration systems, the larger "impure" particles are discarded leaving pure potable water. In maple syrup operations, the water is tossed and the blocked sugar molecules are concentrated and reserved.

On an average day, maple tree sap is around 2 percent sugar. Some people push their RO and get it up to 22 percent sugar, cutting their boiling-off time and fuel bill by a factor of ten. Howie and many others believe that flavor is lost in sap that has undergone extreme RO. Depth of color is lost and some of the ineluctable flavors that come along with the slower caramelization process in the evaporator pan may be lost as well. Howie does use some RO in his operation but reluctantly. He only pushes his sap to 6 percent and then blends non-RO sap back into the mix to produce 4 percent sugar, a level that he justifies as possible from a tree under optimal conditions. It's a bit of a moral calculus that keeps the process honest for Howie, allowing him to benefit from the decreased time and fuel cost while still remaining committed to the craft of creating deep, complex flavors.

While we are propane torching the valves, the sun is doing the same thing to the trees; sap is now flowing freely. It's late afternoon, the typical time of day for the sap to run. Highly susceptible to fermentation, sap must be boiled off immediately after collection to preserve it. Not unlike making jams from summer fruit, raising sugar levels—i.e., removing the water—acts as a preservative. Afternoon runs turn into nighttime boil-offs, making sugaring work largely a late-night activity.

"It's time to start a fire in the arch," Howie says using the archaic term for the firebox (it used to be a brick-built arch) that supports the evaporator pan, a wide expanse of a vessel allowing the greatest possible amount of the surface area for water evaporation. Howie's stainless steel pan, six feet across and sixteen feet long, sits on top of the arch, and is partitioned into six interconnected troughs with a spout on either side of the pan for drawing off finished syrup. As night is beginning to fall, Howie sends Sue and me to the woodpile to assist Dante, one of his crew, to move wood closer to the arch. There are two fuel types—small diameter branches that will burn fast and furious and thicker logs, more of a slow burn. We clamber up onto the behemoth woodpile, and shift logs from the far and high end forward closer to the arch, restocking the depleted end to give Howie easy access and ample fuel to feed the fire.

These days, not everyone burns wood. Some syrup producers burn oil to boil off the sap after running it through multiple RO passes, yet another trade-off of labor for capital. Using limited and costly fossil fuels to boil off when the sugarbush itself offers up the renewable fuel right at hand reminds me of Wendell Berry's comment on the paradox of modern farming. "They can take a solution and neatly divide it into two problems." He was referring to a farmer's dependence on synthetic fertilizers to add nutrients back into the soil for crops while at the same time factory dairy and cattle operations need to dispose of massive quantities of manure. Burning oil strikes me as a foolish use of fossil fuels.

Transforming maple sap into maple syrup requires boiling off. In culinary parlance, we call that reducing stock into a sauce. Common kitchen ratios are 4:1 or even maybe 8:1; one or two gallons of stock will produce one quart of sauce. Out in the sugarhouse, the reduction ratio is rarely less than 40:1—a huge amount of water to separate from the dissolved sugar in order to produce syrup, as I learned first-hand in my parents' kitchen.

Howie lights the arch and dons his sugaring garb, a red cotton pullover, Carhartt overalls, and depending on the temperature either a woolen New England Patriots pom-pom hat or a Boston Red Sox cap. The uniform is sugar encrusted from an accumulation of wet hand wipes and ladle splatters. I doubt he launders the gear until the season is over; with at least two more weeks of sugaring to go, I reckon there will be at least a half pound of maple sugar on his shirt alone. Howie now feeds the fire every few minutes. With each addition, he gracefully unlatches the arch doors with a wrought iron poker, stokes the fire, and then swings the doors shut again in a choreographed move he's practiced for nearly forty years. I admire the expertise of his motions remembering how completely comfortable I was in front of my own arch—the stove on Savoy's cooking line. Even as an older, slower cook I could still keep up with the younger cooks because, from practice, I had eliminated extraneous motion. It's the same with Howie's motions. When he switches off to take a break, his helper, with only six years under his belt, is less fluid.

Sugaring is hard work and during the six-week season there is often little time to rest or get a full night's sleep. Steph is down in New York selling syrup at the market, leaving Howie and his two-man crew to fend for themselves. Last night's dinner plates are still at their place settings on the table, clothing and outdoor gear is strewn about on random surfaces. But this hard work is nothing compared to producing sugar from sugar cane.

In the late eighteenth- and nineteenth-century maple production was heralded as a way to obtain sugar without participating in the slave trade. Abolitionists looked to the sugarbush as a means of opting out of a system that was exploitive of people, destructive of the land on which it was grown, and damaging to comity among all people. The *Farmer's Almanac* of 1803 exhorts its readers in March to "prepare for making maple sugar, which is more pleasant and patriotic than that ground by the hand of slavery, and boiled down by the heat of misery." To this day, the height of maple syrup production in the United States, even with the recent explosion in maple operations, was in 1860, surpassing today's output by more than 150 percent.

In possibly the first instance of food boycotts (tea parties aside) and a "vote with your fork" philosophy, citizens opposed to slavery refused to purchase one of the most visible products of the slave economy and purchased their sugar from stands of maple throughout the Northeast and Midwest. Not only does maple sugaring represent a gentle approach to living with the ecosystem, it also represents a source of sweetness in our diets that is not exploitive of people.

The viability of the small diverse Vermont farm largely collapsed with a crash in the dairy business. Beginning in the 1950s, dairymen saw that grain in a cow's diet boosted milk production and increasingly corn became a larger portion of the farm's crop rotation. The trend intensified as dairies found that by replacing hay production and pasturing outdoors with a heavy grain diet, they could maintain larger herds on far smaller plots of land, confine them to sheds, and even relocate dairies to places with little or no pasture. By shipping in the grain from the Midwest, even states like Arizona and Texas could become major dairy producers. This approach produced large volumes of milk at prices far below the cost of production on the green meadows of New York and New England and resulted in the collapse of the dairy industry throughout the Northeast.

Without dairy at the center of the Vermont farm economy, many have looked to turn sugaring from the sideline gig into an efficient, technologically driven business that could be scaled up. Prior to tubing systems, a farmer could maintain about five hundred trees. With tubing, Deep Mountain taps ten times that, just under five thousand trees. There are operations that now routinely tap thirty thousand trees and way up north in Island Pond there is a sugaring operation financed by a Greenwich Connecticut hedge fund that is tapping over two hundred thousand trees. Between 2004 and 2018, Vermont maple syrup production quadrupled. Much of it goes into developing new markets globally and into value-added products like maple-sweetened beverages.

With the scaling up of the industry has also come a loss in specificity of taste. Not unlike blended négociant wines that are less expressive of the place and the maker, maple has gone in the same direction. Howie points out how ironic this is given that at a time when artisanal food production is ascendant, with some of the best farmstead cheeses and craft beers in the country being produced in Vermont, sugaring in the state is moving in the opposite direction, towards larger scale production, with less individuality and specificity of place expressed.

I am standing over the evaporator pan getting a maple steam facial, peering into froth and bubbles. The bubbles can become so voluminous that they overflow the pan, akin to how we used to enthusiastically blow bubbles into a milkshake at a diner until the froth cascaded over the rim. Sugarmakers periodically add de-foaming agents, usually some form of fat, during the boiling off to avoid this. The addition of any fat breaks up the surface tension of bubbles. Old Vermonters used to hang a slab of bacon over the pan, producing a double whammy of maple-cured pork and a placid surface from the occasional fat drip during the boil off. Howie's fat of choice is an occasional squirt of half-and-half into the back pan. As the sap reduces, the bubbles get smaller, their surfaces thicker. Howie sidles up to me and points to the thermometer on the side of the pan. It is marked off in black hatch marks measuring only from 0 to 10, with a "7" as the only number written. "Syrup is made at 7 degrees above boiling or 219°F. That's what we are watching for." The needle is on what would be 5. Howie begins another of his well-practiced dances; he holds a square-shaped ladle and, in a repetitive sweeping arm motion, he moves sap from less-reduced pan sections into the final bay, slowing down the reduction and building up the quantity of what will be the final batch to draw down. Knowing that 5 will soon become 7, he is also simultaneously testing the syrup by watching the drips of syrup falling off the ladle. "I'm looking for sheeting, the moment when drips merge into a continuous ribbon. Not yet." Howie's arm sweeps again back into the pools of froth, ladling, feeling, watching. "It's time," he exclaims and hops off our perch and begins to draw off close to ten gallons into nearby stainless steel pails.

Howie begins testing the thickness of the draw with a hydrometer, a calibrated floating bobber that measures the specific gravity of a liquid; the thicker the liquid, the higher the bobber floats. As human hydrometers, we are more buoyant in saltwater than we are in a freshwater pond. There is more material around us to support our flotation. Howie knew that we had gone past 7 and the hydrometer attests to that; the bobber is higher than the red mark he has drawn at the state-mandated 66.9 Brix mark or

66.9 percent sugar to be called pure maple syrup. He funnels in some reduced but unfinished sap from the pans, measures again and adjusts until it has the right specific gravity. Walking around to the other side of the sugarhouse, he hands off the syrup to Larry, a transplanted New York City accountant, for its final cosmetic treatment—the removal of all the particles of ash, bark, and other unknown bits, collectively known as "nighter," to produce a beautifully clear and lustrous syrup.

Larry runs the syrup through a superfine filter of diatomaceous earth, the ground-up fossilized remains of diatoms, marine phytoplankton. When I asked Howie about this setup, he tells me that he used to hand pour each batch through filter paper set in a galvanized bucket like drip coffee, only on a grander scale. It was inefficient and slow, as you know if you have ever waited interminably for a pour-over coffee at a hipster coffee bar. "We used to change the filter for every draw down. When I realized that I didn't know what the paper was made of and how it had been chemically treated, I decided that I preferred using twelve-million-year-old plankton." Larry switches on the pump and we insert its steel output hose into a stainless steel barrel, the size of an oil drum, the receptacle for tonight's boil off. A thick stream of syrup begins to flow. I divert the hose for a moment into a coffee mug. Sue and I drink it warm, straight, no chaser. "It'll never taste this good again," Howie says. We know he is right.

Once the air temperatures swings have evened out, the pressures inside the maples are only marginally positive, and the massive sap flows cease. Bud break also occurs, changing the flavor of the sap to more bitter and bubble gummish, that Vermonters call "buddy," and it is no longer suitable for sugaring. Sugarmakers call the final run the frog run, a recognition of spring's debut on the forest floor. Spring peepers, little forest floor frogs, emerge from their hibernation and call out incessantly in the night, searching for mates and telling the sugarmakers to go home and find theirs.

THE BACK FORTY

MAKES 1 COCKTAIL

This was the house cocktail at Back Forty and a huge favorite, so much so that some people would order Back One-Twenties. A turn on a classic whiskey sour using maple for the sweetener and Tennessee whiskey for the spirit, it is a simple drink to assemble. Always in season.

2 ounces (60 ml) Tennessee whiskey (we chose George Dickel #12)
¾ ounce fresh lemon juice
¾ ounce Maple Simple Syrup (recipe follows)
2 dashes orange bitters (preferably Fee Brothers)

Pour the whiskey, lemon juice, maple simple syrup, and bitters into a shaker. Add ice, shake, and strain into a rocks glass. Add fresh ice and serve.

MAPLE SIMPLE SYRUP

Combine 1 cup (240 ml) maple syrup and ½ cup (120 ml) hot water. Stir to incorporate the maple syrup, then allow to cool. Store in a Mason jar in the refrigerator for future drinks. Keeps indefinitely.

MY SPRING AWAKENING

With Bocuse as a beacon to steer towards, I devised a plan of escape from the tyrannical narrowness of high school. I'd test the culinary waters by taking a year off—now called a gap year—and get a cooking job. My parents were supportive, some of their friends mortified. I remember fighting back tears of fury at my dad's best friend's insistence that I'd never go to college if they let me take a year off, a slippery slope into hell, implying that my parents' permissiveness was a grave mistake. I persisted with my plan, doubling up on core requirements, taking English literature in summer school, and graduated a year early. I moved to Vermont, worked construction on a hotel renovation, and parlayed that into my first kitchen job in the hotel's kitchen as a dishwasher and prep guy, at a place called Topnotch, where the food was anything but. Very little fresh produce made it our way in the middle of winter. In those days, northern Vermont got the warehouse floor sweepings of the big city produce wholesalers. The once-a-week fish delivery from Boston invariably became a shellfish velouté, that hotel-ready creamed fish sauce cooked for hours to extract ultimate flavor. It was either dolloped into "patty" shells or glopped atop pieces of baked cod. With a shake of paprika and a boutonniere-sized garnish of curly parsley we produced the finest in European resort cooking.

I loved the pace of restaurant life; it's slow build each night into the 8 P.M. climax with everyone playing their practiced roles. I loved the repetition of running the big Hobart dishwasher, the jangling sound of plates and glasses as I organized them into the racks, sliding the tray into position and lowering the door in an action akin to using an old paper cutter, an affirmative *fazhunk* that set the nozzles spraying against the steel doors, like brushes on a drummer's high hat. Most of all I loved the community experience. It was theater and we were a troupe: the often bad-tempered mustachioed Austrian chef in clogs, his devoted sidekick sous chef of Irish extraction always ready to party, the assortment of ski bum dudes like circus high-wire actors there to wash dishes by night, bomb the slopes by day, and provide entertainment for all the servers, the circus acrobats who had come to ski and party. And then me, the overly earnest guy who'd moved to Stowe to learn how to cook and ski cross-country alone in the forest. Regardless of its flaws and deficiencies, I was proud to be a member of this troupe and they were proud of me in spite of and because of my earnestness. I was underage and keeping my nose particularly clean since I had been arrested as a minor, back in New Jersey for cultivating marijuana. While the other dish guys were bombing National and Star, the famed double black diamond trails, on dump days, coming into their shifts with their thighs wrecked and carousing at night after their work shift, I was leading a nearly ascetic life: learning to clean mussels, organize a store room, and use a chef's knife, by day; living in a renovated milking parlor under a former dairy barn, reading Orwell's *Down and Out in Paris and London*, and pining for the unattainable daughter of the Jewish weekenders from Montreal, by night. When the snows melted, I returned home to my native Bergen County and signed on as a fisherman on the Hudson River, knowing that in the fall I'd be heading to college at UC Santa Cruz.

* * *

In joining the crew of the last stake-net shad fishermen on the Hudson River, I tapped into my deep passion for all the living species in the natural world, particularly the edible ones. My job, as the least experienced man in the crew, was to pick shad from our nets as we pulled our way across the pole-staked row. There I was, in the bilges of a twenty-four-foot square-ended scow, wearing calf-high rubber boots and Helly Hansen "skins," aslosh in fish slime, iridescent scales, bloodied river water. As the pick progressed, I was increasingly enveloped by hundreds and hundreds of dead and dying shad, and happier by the minute. It was like being buried in sand at the beach except this gentle compression was wet and fluid and fabulously gross. I had never imagined anything more energizing and life affirming than witnessing shad's cyclical return to the Hudson estuary, with the Manhattan skyline as my backdrop.

As air and water temperatures change with the seasons, animals respond more rapidly than plants. We animals can head south, crawl into dens, grow or don extra coats instead of literally dying on the vine. That's one of the perks of being warm-blooded and ambulatory. Animals keep their engines running all winter, albeit slower, while plants die or die back after the hard frost. Come spring, annual plants require a lot more energy and work to get going, but once up and running they power through their life cycle in a matter of weeks giving us fruit in two to three months. Animals and perennial plants require more time, measured in years or even decades. Hey, I didn't bear fruit until well into my fourth decade.

Migratory fish are the first responders to the seasonal shift. The slightest changes in water temperature and longer days promote phytoplankton blooms that migratory fish feed on, and the fish begin to move northward. Meanwhile, terrestrial surface temperatures continue large diurnal fluctuations. The risk of an overnight killing frost persists until the end of May in the Hudson Valley when soil temperatures finally reach the mid-fifties. Elevated soil temperatures really promote growth. Without it, nothing in the market really screams spring, certainly not in any abundance.

Shad, the largest member of the herring family, are anadromous, meaning that, like salmon, they live their adult lives in the ocean before returning to spawn in the freshwater place of their birth. As the Atlantic coastal waters slowly warm each March well in advance of the terrestrial snowmelt, spring shad and herring "runs" head into the East Coast estuaries from Florida all the way to Maine. These runs kept many indigenous North Americans and early colonists from the brink of starvation in a way that rhubarb and asparagus never could, an abundant and immediate protein on the dinner tables of many New England and Mid-Atlantic homes. Extending its shelf life especially prior to refrigeration gave rise to all the salted, smoked, and pickled herring recipes. The spring runs signaled the end of the harsh lean winter season and became the impetus for many local festivals celebrating their return.

In the early twentieth century, as many as four thousand rows of nets extended into the Hudson, each a staked claim on this "limitless" protein source. Most of these fishermen were drift netters working the slack tides of the mid-Hudson; in Ossining, Tarrytown, Piermont, Newburgh, Stony Point, Verplanck, and Beacon. They persisted longer than downriver stake netters because the method was simpler, requiring less infrastructure, only a boat and a net. In 2010 barely a dozen guys were still pulling shad nets and those few were all above the Bear Mountain Bridge in Poughkeepsie, Hudson, and Kingston. The decline was a result of many forces—overfishing and habitat destruction but also changing culinary tastes, shifting skill sets in the labor pool, and new sources of "cheap" protein, notably farmed fish.

In 1974 I crewed for Ron Ingold and Charlie Smith in Edgewater, New Jersey, and bunked on a barge that Charlie bought for a dollar from Penn Central Railroad, back when the nation cast off its land-based infrastructure in favor of "more efficient" air travel. Charlie's row was opposite 137th Street, the elevated section of Riverside Drive, where Columbia's new campus is now. Ronnie's was just north of the George Washington Bridge off Ross Dock in Englewood opposite 190th Street and Inspiration Point.

In the lower section of the river, the tides are too strong for drift netting. Instead, we drove a row of poles into the mud stretching from a hundred yards or so offshore into the middle of the river. Poles were cut from hickory and white oaks, trees selected for their even-tapered straight runs, never shorter than sixty feet. They could have been ship masts. We set the poles in early April using a floating derrick, driving them deep into twenty or thirty feet of Hudson muck. At the end of each season, the crew reversed the derrick action to pull them and deposit the poles onto the tidal mudflats to await next year's season. Benefiting from the preservative qualities of the Hudson's silty, salty brine, they didn't seem to rot. New poles were expensive so Ronnie and Charlie bought out retiring shadders' inventory, accumulating a library of old poles, some cut seventy-five years earlier.

With a row of poles driven in place, we'd set nets on the downstream side of the poles at the end of low tide, as the last of the slack waters left the estuary, emptying into the ocean. When the tide turned and the water flowed back upstream, the net would gently sink, and begin collecting shad as they caught a ride on the flood tide, trying to head home to the place of their birth. We would lift at high tide, always a tricky proposition to time, since the tide turns sooner along inshore eddies, later mid-river, and other factors affected the timing as well: onshore winds, the lunar cycle, and changes in freshwater runoff following heavy rains.

Two men lifted the net; one pulled up the weighted bottom "ring" line, the other took the "top" line, helping to keep the pockets of gathered fish intact. Along with shad, each lift pulled in scads of other estuary denizens: striped bass, herring, fluke, Atlantic sturgeon, short nosed sturgeon, window-pane, white perch, catfish, spiny dogfish, seahorses, weakfish, blackfish, spear-ing, monk, winter flounder, sea robins, scup, bluefish, the occasional eel, and hundreds of silvery anchovies. Today this would all be called bycatch—jargon for unintended victims of a catch—a critical factor in evaluating the sustain-ability of a fishery because most of the hauled fish are dead when they hit the deck and cannot be thrown back. The bycatch for wild Gulf shrimp can be 10:1, ten pounds of discarded bycatch for every pound of shrimp caught. For me, the bycatch was a wondrous display of the vitality and diversity of what thrived below the placid river surface, beneath civilization's triumphant span, the George Washington Bridge.

Charlie and his oft-drunk German first-mate Hugo would lift the net and drop it into the boat for me and my buddy Chris to pick. The shad, on the swim upstream, would ram themselves into the net, get gilled and suffocate. Our job was to quickly unlatch them from the net and push them behind us, making room for more net, more fish. I loved the repetitive action. How quickly and efficiently could I unlatch a big roe (female) from the net? How smoothly could I move, over and over again, pulling the net back, keep up with the speed of Charlie's sweep down the row? A roe could weigh eight to ten pounds and since I picked up a fish by reaching over the gill plate with just my thumb and index finger to gain purchase, I developed huge muscles between my thumb and forefinger. It was a dance, not unlike the thrum in a busy restaurant kitchen. There were big hits of fish, when the moon was full or new, the tides stronger and the evening warm, reminiscent of the first balmy spring nights in the city when couples wander the streets in search of a meal, connection, and love.

We worked around the clock, the schedule progressing an hour forward each day with the tides. Two sets at low tide, two lifts at high. During daylight hours between tides, we weighed, sexed, separated, and boxed the fish, and dried, cleaned, mended, and re-boxed the nets. Sunny days meant net work; rainy days might allow for a welcome nap. As the season hit its stride, we'd barely get two hours of sleep between nighttime pulls and the next set. The saving grace was the escapement period—shad's Shabbat, mandated by New York State—from Friday afternoon to midday Sunday when no nets could be set, a thirty-six-hour period allowing the fish to pass on upriver. Unfortunately for the shad, there were usually other fishermen upstream awaiting them when the escapement period ended.

Roes fetch more money because they contain the prized ovaries or roe sacs. There was a time when the daily special in every fish house in New York and Philadelphia—Sweet's, Sloppy Louie's, Gloucester House, the Oyster Bar, Bookbinder's, and Snockey's—was a pair of roe with two thick rashers of bacon laid cross-wise over them. Connoisseurs knew that bucks (males), especially downriver ones, taste better than roes, preserving a market for the guys. Females invest more physiological energy into reproduction while males retain muscular strength for faster travel, yielding sweeter, richer flesh.

For easy eating, shad required the services of John at Smitty's Fillet House at Fulton Fish Market or some other highly skilled cutter who can bone them. The myriad tiny bones can only be removed with multiple deft triangular cuts. Up and down the flesh, John would caress the fillets with a pencil-thin blade. On the downstroke he removed wedges of bony tissue and on the upstroke he cleared the cutting board of water and slime. Mesmerized I'd watch, trying to decipher and internalize the moves awaiting my future attempts. After Smitty's, I'd grab fried egg sandwiches and a 6 A.M. beer at the Paris Hotel, just up Front Street and across from Fulton's main arcade.

As spring progressed, the fish came in waves or runs. Old-timers had named the runs after blossoming spring flowers and not just shadbush. The first run was the forsythia, followed by magnolia, climaxing with dogwood, and ending with the lilac, a run laden with huge roe fish, multiple spawners, rotund mamas who survived after laying eggs upstream their first year to return in successive years. At this point in the season I was bleary eyed, practicing by rote my learned motions, and looked with anticipation to Friday when I could go to my parents' house for a shower and a night of uninterrupted sleep.

When we caught the first backrunner—a buck shad swimming back to the ocean after having made his reproductive deposit—we knew the season was winding down. These fish were spent, exhausted from the stress of not eating during their five-hundred-mile journey from the continental shelf off Barnegat Light to Troy and back. The lifts began to lighten and the daytime workload eased. With the lilacs fading, June approached, and the season ended. I swam in the Hudson one warm day as we pulled up the shad poles and reburied them in the marsh mud, preserving them until next year.

I loved the work and the physical exhaustion that came with it. It was the first of many repetitive actions, both skilled and mundane, that I was to practice, movements that offered a connection to the past, to humble workers using their hands to make a living and to staying in touch with the seasons through food.

GREEN FOOD

April in the Northeast can be so tough. In some years, floods, snow, and cold snaps can span the entire month, even reaching into May. The days might be longer, we're on daylight savings time, and the Yankees are playing ball but plenty of signs still point back to winter. One day I'm in short sleeves and the next I'm searching for the hat and gloves I foolishly tucked away in the winter drawer. It's part of what makes April so tortuously cruel. It's a month when as a chef/owner I can't please anyone: cooks, customers, even myself.

This April is worse than usual. I've lost my chef. He took a high-paying midtown job and gave three weeks' notice, inconveniently overlapping with the sous chef's previously scheduled two-and-a-half-week honeymoon. A former cook is lending a hand. She is waiting for Back Forty to open, where she's going to be the chef, her first go at writing the menu and leading a team. It's nearly May. Menu changes need to be made; the winter dishes are tired and we are tired of them. Customers want a changeup and, on the days when the weather completely delivers, we don't have the food to match it.

The new chef and I are meeting to discuss possibilities. Following that, a health inspection drill is planned. Not five minutes into our discussion, a manager flies up the stairs and shouts, "Health department!" The meeting is over. Donning hats and gloves, everyone scampers to various hot spots making sure things are hygienic. Only an hour before, the general manager informed me that the hot water for the entire building was out. The repair call is in. But how far was that going to fly with the health inspector? Not very. No hot water for the hand sink, no hot water for patrons in the bathroom, no high temp on the dishwasher? I foresee an immediate failure, possibly an argument to avoid an immediate closure.

The inspection commences at the hand sink, the inspector washing his own hands. I cringe, breathe deeply and tell it to him straight. There won't be any hot water during this inspection unless a miracle occurs and the technician arrives in far less time than his habitual five hours. Things don't go badly, although half my violations points result from the lack of hot water. Once he's gone, I conduct a server wine meeting because I recently fired the wine director. He texted in sick on Easter, after unsuccessfully trying to manipulate the servers into surreptitiously opening the restaurant so that he could spend the holiday with his wife.

It's over two hours later before I can get back to the culinary conversation, but my brain is still too rattled from the health inspection for any deep creative thinking and besides it's too close to dinner service, with the chef on the line tonight. I listen to her menu ideas—asparagus salad with a farm poached egg, grilled sardines with a romaine Caesar salad, and roasted striped bass in saffron broth with clams and snap peas. I grimace. Asparagus isn't in the market yet, farm-grown lettuces are still weeks away, and worst of all, snap peas won't be in until early June. I tweak her ideas but avoid addressing the seasonal issue head-on. It can wait for another day. Better to make sure the food tastes good and that all the cooks are in a positive frame of mind.

The toughest part is not about cooking; it's about figuring out how to balance cooking seasonally while also remaining relevant, keeping up with the chef Joneses, staying part of the scene, and holding people's attention. It's easy to find April menus from "market-driven" chefs that abound in English peas, favas, string beans, sugar snaps even though none of these vegetables could possibly be growing in our region yet. Should I give in, jump-start the season, and serve the flashier "spring" foods or should I hold my ground and continue cooking from the market at the risk of being perceived as tired or stale?

I put in a few hours at my desk attending to the ever-growing stack of papers and items needing my attention. I send an email to a chef candidate asking him to draft a sample seasonal menu, hunt down the architect for Back Forty to finalize the façade design, submit a menu idea for the Citymeals on Wheels fundraiser, and sign the first-quarter payroll returns. I call it a day. All things considered, it is a positive one at that. The new chef will be terrific in time. She has a lot of growing to do but she is eager to glean culinary, management, and life lessons.

The proposed menu nags at me, though. I am not comfortable that our local and seasonal cuisine isn't really local and seasonal. The worst of it are the snap peas. They are fruit after all, a plant's life cycle climax, the creation of offspring to ensure a future. There are no plants producing fruit yet in the region. I can justify asparagus and romaine. They are leaves, the first plant parts we harvest, and it really is only a matter of days before they'll be available at Union Square. A little stretch of the region is OK in certain instances; one might be in April, a truly challenging moment. But that doesn't mean all standards go out the window. It's not like we can then apply the "it's five o'clock somewhere" cocktail axiom to our purchasing. The peas are still wrong. We have barely expressed the spring moment of leaves and sprouts and already there is drift to order up some pea pods; tomatoes are not far behind. It's easy to do. Just pick up the phone and it will be here in the morning.

Admittedly, it's an arbitrary and formal construct. I happily use lemons trucked from Florida and olive oil shipped from Spain. Green garlic, fava beans, sides of snap peas litter the menus in popular dining rooms all over town and I'm still struggling with the moral dilemma about peas? I need to move on but I remain unsettled. If the "it's five o'clock somewhere" quip is to justify someone's drinking issues, then the same logic applied to seasonal cooking is a justification for a commodified food system. As individuals, the result is we end up untethered in time and space.

I compose dishes with what's available in the market to paint a landscape of the seasonal moment, of where we are in time right here in New York City, not New York City with an assist from Florida and California. It's an art statement as much as a political statement. I consider myself a Hudson River School landscape painter, only my canvases are ten-inch round plates.

Later in the week, I go to the market and find the first asparagus and some wonderfully delicate romaine lettuces. I buy. Not really enough for the restaurant's needs but enough to honestly say we are in season, cooking of a place and from a place. I sprint back to Savoy in time for lunch service. Breathless, not from the bike ride but from the journey across the meager winter months, I hand off the asparagus to the sous chef, a baton in the last leg of a relay. I almost didn't make the final lap. I almost gave in to the international distribution system that brings Mexico and California and Florida to our doorstep anytime, anywhere. I prefer the truths of my inconveniences.

* * *

Asparagus spears are stems of a perennial, shooting up from their buried and mulch-protected root crown. Even if some supermarkets try to use international shipping to convert it from hyper-seasonal into a ubiquitous product, they are the ultimate harbinger of spring. The etymology of "harbinger" derives from the fifteenth-century usage of an advance military scout sent to search for safe lodgings (as in "auberge" and "harbor"). Asparagus define the term—the advanced guard of seasonality but also the safe harbor of food in the new growing season.

Singular in our gardens, asparagus is possibly the only cultivated perennial whose fruit we don't eat, harvesting instead for its dense, full-flavored stalks. The spears can be cut once, maybe twice, and then the plant needs to be left to grow out into its feathery and delicate maturity. The fruit are small, inedible, peppercorn-sized red berries. Maybe because of its perennial nature, asparagus has a vigor and robustness that other spring greens lack. They show off the power of having grown and extended for many years deep into the nutrient-rich soil. We can taste that it's not their first rodeo. I used to prefer pencil asparagus, possibly a holdover from the baby vegetable food trend during the eighties but these days I tend to like the bigger, fleshier ones. They are vegetable meat just as artichokes—another perennial—have a density making them a meal in themselves. I love laying into a pile of fatties, hot, oven roasted, and sprinkled with capers and dill or napped with hollandaise (call me old-school), a sauce that still seems like a perfect application even though its cultural trappings are obsolete. People think that having asparagus on the menu proves that they are in season. It can be a false proclamation. Locally though, there isn't asparagus in most years until the third week of April and that's from South Jersey; it's mid-May before the Hudson Valley comes on hard.

Until then the fields are wet and muddy; no tractor work can take place for fear of getting stuck in the field, and the wet soil mostly rots newly sown seeds instead of germinating them. This is especially true for organic farmers who use seed that hasn't been sprayed with fungicides to reduce rot under damp conditions. Test if I'm right. Do conventional farmers in your market come to market with vegetables earlier than organic farmers even if they are from the same region? Is our haste to get the season going and get the farm in production worth making choices that bring more poison onto the land and into our food?

What is in the market are greens: leaves, shoots, and stems. It's not exactly new growth, plants from seeds germinated this season. Rather these are the regenerative leaves of winter annuals both cultivated—broccoli rabe, spinach, leeks, and scallions—and wild—chickweed, miner's lettuce, and ramps. These are plants that were either intentionally planted or went to seed in the fall, got a head start on life by developing a strong root system, and then hung on through the winter in suspended animation until longer days and warmer soil got them growing again. What might grow in two weeks' time with the warmth and long days of May can take two months of incremental progress in February and March even if grown under hoop houses. None of these greens have the heft of asparagus but in this moment they scream of new life, of vitality, of chlorophyll.

I liken it to the current craze of drinking matcha, the green tea drink originally from Japan, made from the first spring flush leaves and buds on tea plants. The small lime green leaves produce a tea that is brilliant, almost neon green, both bitter and sweet. It tastes supercharged, not just with caffeine but with life. When we drink matcha, we are drinking the cells of new life and all its vibrancy, dried, ground, and then whisked into a beverage. If red Burgundy sipped out of a balloon glass expresses the ripe, ample lushness of maturation then matcha, whether from a paper cup or a ceremonial tea bowl, expresses youth, and vibrating awakeness. No wonder it's become a thing.

My thirst for spring greens in the market is similar to the matcha fixation. You might say I am a choloholic or a chlorophyllaphile. No matter how well hydrated the California kale at Whole Foods is, it doesn't have the life energy found in the local, new growth leaves of April. The bundled greens that come closest to having the full flavors of asparagus are Kenny Migliorelli's wintered-over rabe from Tivoli, New York. Market wisdom is that fall greens after the frost are the sweetest because the plant's starches, complex carbohydrates, are broken down into simple carbohydrates, sugar. I tend to cook a lot of kale, mustard, and rabe in October and November, skipping the summer crop, a doldrum time for brassicas. But wintered-over greens are the vernal equivalent of the autumn story. The new growth is all sweetness, with a delightful tinge of bitterness. The stems are tender, only just able to support themselves; none of the stringy cellulose needed for structural support has developed and no sugars have converted to starches for longer-term energy storage. It's all new construction. Down here in the city we certainly understand the allure of new construction.

Microgreens are examples of this desire for new life in our diet also and explain why so many chefs adorn their dishes with them. Sadly though, they are little more than eye candy. Coming from greenhouses, often hydroponically grown, they lack the true taste of life from out of doors soil. But Kenny's rabe stems are the stars on the plate, sweet and tender. I make an entire meal out of a bunch of rabe sautéed in flavorful olive oil with a lot of garlic and a liberal sprinkling of chile pepper flakes. Add to the mix a sheaf of spaghetti with some grated Parmesan and Sue's in heaven too.

Alliums (onions, leeks, scallions, chives, and ramps) are the other group of plants in addition to the brassicas (kale, rabe, mustard, cabbage, Brussels sprouts) that are Northeast winter hardy, particularly the wild ones: chives and ramps. The brief window of ramp availability reveals a marvelous adaptation of the plant to arboreal life. To access the rich humus produced by all the rotting leaves falling from a mature forest canopy, a place with few competitors due to the low light conditions for most of the year in the understory, ramps developed a warp-speed life cycle, sending out wide leaves—uncharacteristic for alliums—that act like solar panels, quickly collecting as much sunlight as they can prior to the trees leafing out and the canopy filling in. In more open areas with longer windows of sunlight, ramps would face far more competition: perennial grasses, innumerable annuals, and plants with highly evolved structures for reaching up towards the light. But in the few spring weeks prior to leaf out, ramps have their day in the sun. Afterwards, the leaves die back and for much of the summer are almost dormant, difficult to locate except for a brief time when they send up a flower spike.

In the saucepan, ramps retain their call of the wild with a pleasant pungency and bite, far different from the roundness of garlic, even the green garlic of June. Chefs love grilling ramps whole or sautéing the bulbs and tossing the leaves in off the heat as a verdant finale. Cranky food journalists have remarked that ramps are hyped and overrated, claiming not to understand what the fuss is about. If they don't cook or eat seasonally and spring ingredients have been around for months, shipped in from wherever, then there is nothing to get excited about. It is much ado about nothing, one more trendy ingredient. But cooks who appreciate ramps aren't making a fuss, they're just cooking with them, celebrating the first uncultivated green foods of the season and joining with cooks, foragers, and Appalachian inhabitants who have been harvesting since time wore out memory what's to be foraged in the wild, before the sowed garden crops come in.

I don't and cannot completely forsake tubers and roots in my spring cooking. I need their nourishment and bulk to sustain me, to give me the calories I need to keep my furnace fired up for the brisk days that still regularly blow into town. The challenge is to bring a fresh view to those ingredients and still manage to say spring. In the fall, I roast those root vegetables to concentrate their flavor essences and highlight their earthy elements with dark spices like toasted cumin and chiles or a sprinkling of Moroccan ras el hanout. Now I want to emphasize the refreshing qualities of vegetables. I am thirsty for the racing brook of spring. So I pair the root cellar starches with lots of fresh herbs and raw greens. Steamed parsnip or celery root tossed in an abundance of dill and chives and a touch of fat for a rich mouthfeel, whether it comes from a spoonful of crème fraîche or a drizzle of good olive oil, completely transforms the cellared past into the verdant future.

* * *

The asparagus baton that I handed off in the kitchen that day was a true harbinger—both my advance guard and my harbor. It was the messenger for what lay ahead and it was the harbor itself offering me the security that having held my ground in the face of all the pressures to dilute my mission, I had made it to a safe haven of honesty. The lean and trying times of April are in the past. The soil will warm, the crops will come in, and we can confidently look forward at the fields of what will be, instead of back into the cellar of what was. THIS is spring! Go cook some green food.

RABE WITH GARLIC, CHILES, AND PARMESAN

SERVES 4 AS A SIDE DISH

Wintered-over rabe has the bitterness we love in rabe but all of the sweetness of the new verdant growth found in spring plants. It is available at the green-market early in the spring before any new plantings are harvested because the plants were established in the fall and dormant over the winter. It often only has leaves and a few buds as the California rabe often does but the entire stalks are tender and completely edible. Susan serves this with pasta but it makes a great side dish with roast chicken too.

1 bunch broccoli rabe
¼ cup (60 ml) olive oil
4 cloves garlic, sliced
2 dried red chiles
Salt
Parmesan cheese

1. Wash the rabe. Shake off the water but do not spin-dry if you are using it immediately. Trim off only the dried stem end where the rabe was harvested. Cut across the stems into three or four pieces.
2. Pour the olive oil into a wide pan and toast the garlic over medium heat until golden. Remove the garlic and set aside. Break up the chiles and add to the oil. Allow the pieces to toast a bit and then add the rabe. Sprinkle with salt. Cover for 5 minutes and allow the rabe to steam in the water retained from cleaning it. Check after a few minutes and toss. When all the stems are bright green and wilted, taste for salt. Remove from the pan. Shave Parmesan over the greens and garnish with the garlic chips.

COOK HERE NOW

Two seventies aphorisms tethered my culinary thinking: one a political protest button, the other a book title. The button I bought at the March on Washington in 1969 against the War in Vietnam. It loosely quoted Eldridge Cleaver, minister of information for the Black Panthers: "If you are not part of the solution, you are part of the problem." It was a call to action; neutrality was not an option. The war and other injustices weren't going to end if people didn't work to create the future they envisioned. Cleaver's words implored everyone to engage in finding solutions. I took that to heart but didn't have a clue how to apply that to my career interests. It would be another ten years before I found a culinary grounding for that idea.

The book title, on the other hand, wasn't political, wasn't endorsing collective action, but instead encouraged a personal inward exploration. I never owned a copy, but it was ubiquitous, seemingly infused into every young person's consciousness regardless of whether or not they had actually read it. I would come across it in the back of camping vans as the Grateful Dead played on the radio when I was hitchhiking, on coffee tables along with *The Whole Earth Catalog* for zoning out after smoking a joint, and in laundromats, a community offering to peruse while waiting for the clothes to dry. The title was the message: *Be Here Now*, Baba Ram Dass's primer on Eastern philosophy.

By the time I left UC Santa Cruz I was swirling in a vortex of confusion; even my professor, the renowned anthropologist and social scientist Gregory Bateson, weighed in on my mental state. Commenting on my end of term essay he wrote, "Hoffman creates mental tautologies which paralyze his thinking." Coming from the guru of the cybernetic revolution, these words stung when I read them, but I knew he was right. I stopped attending university after two and a half years. I was, you could say, spaced out—living in a trailer in a redwood forest, with no idea of what to do next. I counted elephant seals and recorded harem behavior for a sociobiology professor by walking a length of beach every day in Año Nuevo State Park near Santa Cruz, California. It gave me insight into how long it took to prove a scientific hypothesis—far longer than I had patience for. Remembering the focus and purpose I had harnessed in the Stowe, Vermont, kitchen, in 1977 I wandered into the Cooper House, a busy tourist trap Santa Cruz restaurant on the pedestrian mall (later destroyed by the 1989 earthquake) and on a whim applied for a cooking position. They hired me on the spot. It was a silly job; I warmed up quiche in a microwave, fried beer-battered fish (the cook next to me made me keep ordering beer "for batter" from the bar so he could drink it) and dished out cioppino, California's mongrel form of a Genovese fish stew.

Line cooking ripped me out of my paralyzing tautologies and set me right down in the present. Line cooking does that; it is all-consuming and consumes many, equally unrelenting in its mental demands as it is punishing to the body. It is a job for the young. Even though the food was far from stellar, every day was an exercise in seeing how much and for how long I could stay focused. I was doing what Ram Dass had written about, staying present.

On the line, decision-making is simultaneously out of our hands and entirely under our control. We give ourselves over to another power: to the printer, the object that spits tickets with no regard for individuals. "I need, I need, I need" it says repeatedly, and our job is to comply. Line cooks relentlessly set and reset priorities with the arrival of each new ticket. I may be about to plate and complete an order, when a new ticket demands the immediate action of placing a pan on a free burner to preheat before returning to complete the task that was at hand. We spin in circles all night long, rotating 180 degrees from the stove to the cutting board and back again to the stove. Little other movement needed, we are belted into a universe contained in nine square feet. Here, now.

Ram Dass also described the importance of developing a practice. I chose cooking the same set of dishes all night long, mindfully (not mindlessly) executing the repetitions in striving for mastery. What does a medium-rare steak feel like? How much more is a piece of fish going to cook after it's out of the oven? The more actions I could make rote, the more brain space I would have for responding to an emergency or even for creative spontaneity. I was fanatic about always having every item on my station located in the same spot: my salt, my pepper mill, the garnishes, my towels. A well set-up line was stocked with the day's prep. Getting all the mise en place (French for "everything in its place"), the prepped components of a dish—sliced mushrooms, picked herbs, diced shallots—organized for easy access is critical to assembling a dish with ease in the heat of the moment. A recipe is not just the list of measured ingredients; it is the muscle memory of movements as well.

There's no room for wandering minds, for wallowing in past sorrows or future concerns. Whatever thick existential fog might envelop the mind dissipates when line work begins. I took energy from the capacity challenge of a board thick with tickets. Listening to the orders called, doing my own cooking, pulling ingredients from the fridge for the next ticket, communicating with my co-workers when to come up on the final plates, asking for clarification on an order from a server, refiring food that comes back undercooked are some of the multilayered tasks occurring simultaneously. Trying to expand my capacity, I would visualize a big redwood tree and imagine that there was no limit to how far I could put my arms around its hugeness, no limit to the tasks I could hold in my brain in a single moment. The mere blink of diversion, a remembrance of psychic wounds past could quickly translate into overly dark fish batter, miscounts on remaining slices of quiche, or a ticket spiked that hadn't actually been completed.

With my métier identified, I decided to get serious about building my career and left Santa Cruz. A friend's mother highly recommended trying to work at an interesting restaurant in Berkeley but I rejected the idea. How could a great restaurant exist in the provinces? Was I being a New York snob or maybe I just needed to head back to my people on the East Coast? I rejected checking out that place, which of course was Chez Panisse. I drove cross-country, stopping in New Orleans to see if that was the right place to set my culinary sights. It struck me as too old-school, too sloppy, with too much partying and not enough focused work. I kept driving. Back home, I exhaled with the deep relief and safety that comes from having a moment of parental protection. It was time for the city.

* * *

I was clueless about how to find a cooking job. I didn't know anyone in the field, my parents couldn't offer much in advice or connections. I answered ads in the *Times*, took recommendations from "gourmet" friends of my folks, and started knocking on a lot of doors. I walked the streets of midtown looking for real French restaurants, asking to see the chef. I didn't land very many jobs but I did get to visit some of the grand old houses: La Caravelle, where chef Roger Fessaguet decided that since I was out of work I must be hungry and made me sit and eat a plate of Dover sole; Regine's, the chic nightclub kitchen run by three-star chef Michel Guérard and helmed by Larry Forgione where they offered me a job preparing crepes for the "club express," little more than an electric stove parked in a dark hallway behind the club; and Café Argenteuil, where the drunk chef chased me out onto the street berating me for coming around during hours of operation. Point taken, I narrowed my visits to only the hours between lunch and dinner. I began to drop in on André Soltner at Lutèce, hoping for a chance spot in his brigade. Always greeted cordially by his sommelier, given a seat in a café chair up in the front of the restaurant, André would eventually appear, toque in place, speak encouragingly but never offer a trail and barely a whisper of hope. "Check back in six months," he would say. Still, I thought midtown was where the action was. Haute, midtown, and French offered the legitimacy, the respectability, that I thought I needed. I had dropped out of university after all, and my parents were professionals; I needed credentials. Finally, at La Côte Basque they sent me over to La Cocotte, a respectable but *deuxième*-level restaurant on East Sixtieth Street that faced the Bloomingdales loading docks.

I was elated. I had broken into the ranks, made it into a real French kitchen. In the traditional French manner, we worked double shifts with a short break between lunch and dinner. Pommes soufflé (blown-up potato chips) accompanied the lunch specials. Sole Grenobloise (lemon and capers) alternated with sole bonne femme (mushrooms and white wine). The most popular dessert was Mont Blanc, prepared by opening a #10 can of *marrons glacé* (chestnuts cooked in sugar) and running it through the meat grinder attachment of a Hobart mixer. The chestnuts would squiggle through, ground beef style and then get topped with sweetened whipped cream. My favorite was riz impératrice, custardy rice pudding inverted from a mold with a crown of gooseberry jam.

The chef would make up the evening specials when he returned from his break at 5 P.M. Consulting his copy of Saulnier's *Repertoire de la Cuisine*, the 1914 crib sheet written for Escoffier's minions around the world and across the century, the chef would "create." Would it be *ris de veau à la financière*, sweetbreads with cockscomb, truffles, and Madeira, or *tournedos à la Marguery*, beef tenderloin with artichokes, kidneys, port, and cream? There are no actual recipes in Saulnier. It's a handbook that classifies dishes, the names shifting as the garnishes get shuffled. Every permutation and preparation had its name, its appellation. Today we are doing bacon, mushrooms, and onions—that must be Grand-mère. Tomorrow it's peppers, onions—and that would be Basquaise. It was a system nearly devoid of creativity, reliant on the lineage of stocks, fonds, veloutés, and reductions, which, when combined with a rotation of garnishes, produce an endless selection of plats du jours. It was a rigid, mechanized systemization applied to cooking, something I was finding out the French were very good at.

Even potato garnishes fit into the system. We would *tournée* potatoes at six o'clock when service started until tickets began to arrive in the kitchen. The chef would lend me his little Sabatier paring knife and instruct. Six sides with a wide face for the base. Each face was equal to the others, a smooth continuous line arcing across the length. These potatoes had orderliness, the culinary equivalent of classical architraves and entablatures. When paired with the codified Saulnier recipes they represented order and control in the world. They staked a claim in the wilderness and raised the flag of French dominion. I strove to get the arc right, to attain faces of equal size. Most times my potato carvings ended up uneven, too short, or pared down to a paltry thinness no longer acceptable on the plate, with more potato in the peelings bucket than remained on the *tournéed* object. I wasn't excelling and knew it. But I kept at it.

I was also responsible for the escargot. During afternoon prep, I was handed a garlicky, green-flecked tub of "escargot butter." I inserted imported, canned Taiwanese snails into shells and then sealed them inside with a generous plug of the butter. During service when an order was called, I would grab a dozen, arrange them on a stainless steel platter with depressions meant to retain the melted butter and keep the snails from rolling about, and place them in a ferociously hot oven cabinet atop of the broiler. To serve, I would take the snails, now swimming in herbs and oil, out of the blasting heat and set them on an underliner. If I couldn't turn potatoes properly then at least in the heat of service maybe I could follow commands and secure my spot.

One evening, chef called for a "pick up" of snails. I grabbed a nearby but damp towel and yanked the platter from the inferno. Reaching high above my shoulder and wincing from the heat, I gripped the snail plate and rotated on the line, platter in hand to set them down. I could feel the heat rapidly conducting through the wet towel. With the chef glaring and no place to rest or time to fake with a quick touchdown and readjustment on the counter I was determined to hold on to the snails and the job. I landed the platter on the underliner in one seamless motion and also delivered a massive burn to my thumb. I hid my feelings and my thumb throughout the rest of the service, overcome with shame and throbbing pain. The sous chef had seen what had happened and pulled me aside and demonstrated a very important lesson—only use dry towels to touch hot trays and handles as water conducts the heat rapidly. "If you are right-handed it's dry in the left for oven work, wet in the right for cleaning up and wiping down. Always and forever." This was a codification worth incorporating into Hoffman's *Répertoire de la Cuisine*.

"Got it. I'll work on it," I said.

They fired me the next day.

* * *

Throughout the eighties I worked in a variety of restaurants honing my cooking and managerial skills and deepening my understanding of the world I had entered. It was exhausting work, rarely less than twelve-hour days. Every service felt like running a marathon, even though line cooks don't always act like athletes. At the end of a busy service we're tired, undernourished, dehydrated, and totally wired. What salve is a better (and faster) cure for all those conditions than a drink? Beer, whiskey, wine; it doesn't matter. With the single tilt of a glass, thirst is quenched, calories shoot into the bloodstream, and the tension of the night becomes a distant memory. Late-night drinking followed by sleeping in, tanking up on coffee and a sugary pastry to get cranked up for another shift with no time for eating during afternoon prep, and the vicious cycle gets repeated again. It's no surprise that alcohol (ab)use is an issue in the restaurant business.

The A-teams in kitchen crews work the heavy weekend services. Their "Friday," the end of a five-day stretch, often falls midweek. Whenever my "Saturday" came around, I was mentally and physically spent. I loved the feeling of floating freely in the world that next day, off when most everyone else was working. Running counter to the flow of humanity suited me. I never had to wonder where to go for Thanksgiving or on New Year's Eve; I went to work. After eating a leisurely breakfast and completing the sole task of the day—dropping off laundry at the wash-and-fold—I'd wander Lower Manhattan, visiting stores that trafficked in tools, ingredients, and cookbooks. In spite of needing to recharge and rest, I would never fully unplug. I preferred to maintain my culinary immersion, good practice, I guess, for the future demands of ownership. I'd fall into shops: Pete's Spice in the East Village, prospecting for novel grains or beans they displayed in open sacks; Casa Moneo on West Fourteenth Street, the only source for dry posole and Mexican chiles; Florence Meat Market on Jones Street to watch the butchers cut steaks and pound veal scaloppine; and some days, drifting uptown to Bridge Kitchenware, the ne plus ultra in imported kitchen equipment.

But Dean & DeLuca on Prince Street in SoHo was the Met museum of consumable treasures with its elaborate Archimboldo-like fruit and vegetable centerpieces at the front door, audacious arrangements of taxidermied birds and boars mounted each Christmas, and their lean modernist aesthetic that everyone emulated from their dinner tables to their spice shelves. D&D set the highest of bars, displaying cheeses, charcuterie, imported jams, mustards, and jaw-droppingly beautiful pastries. It's where I first tasted radicchio, raw milk cheeses, Moroccan cured olives, true balsamico. Dean & DeLuca was ingredient school and I was an eager, if poorly funded student.

My D&D tours invariably ended in the rear corner of the store, home to the city's best-curated cookbook collection—well stocked with the big publishing house releases plus an array of newsletters, chapbooks, and small-press pubs. Without a chef mentor steering me or a strong ancestral cuisine as an anchor, I lacked a clear sense of what to cook or why and looked to cookbook authors for direction and technique. The buyer-librarian in residence was Martha "Matt" Lewis, every New York cook's go-to source prior to Nach Waxman opening Kitchen Arts & Letters. Better than the best Barney's personal shopper, Matt knew how to narrow the vast selection of newly published authors down to must buys: Penelope Casas; Diana Kennedy; Jane Grigson; Paula Wolfert; Marcella Hazan; and Richard Olney's Time-Life Good Cook series, and she clued me in to the latest in culinary esoterica.

I used Matt's recommendations to steer a course in my professional life towards some indeterminate bearing. I started out pursuing traditionally defined excellence: haute French with *Larousse Gastronomique* and Ferdinand Point's *Ma Gastronomie*, only to realize that gilded haute cuisine and its kitchen guild culture held limited appeal. Food of the people, but still confined to the French people brought me Mireille Johnston's *The Cuisine of the Sun: Classic Recipes from Nice and Provence*. Madeleine Kamman's *When French Women Cook* detailed how the taste of a place is an expression of geography, history, culture, and flavor. Richard Olney's *Simple French Food* was filled with improvisations on ingredient themes directing the cook to be in the service of their ingredients, not the other way around. More than any job these books shaped my thinking and influenced my direction.

This brought me to New American cuisine, the fashionable cuisine of the eighties. Here was food of this continent, ingredients grown in our region or in our country, with recipes that grew out of the traditions and varied heritages found here. Evan Jones's *American Food*, Raymond Sokolov's *Fading Feast*, and Edna Lewis's *The Taste of Country Cooking* were inspirational. I was more intrigued by the cultural folkloric stories associated with dishes than the recipes themselves, excited to consider cooking as an extension of anthropology or ethnography.

Connecting food to people's histories and life stories got me closer to answering a question that was still nagging me. Was I part of Cleaver's "problem" or part of a "solution?" I had lingering doubts about whether or not restaurant cooking was indulgent, pandering to the upper class. Was the world a better place as a result of my work? I was a dutiful subscriber to the *Nation* magazine, had gotten arrested for blocking Senator Moynihan's New York office while protesting U.S. involvement in El Salvador, but then I'd go off to work, a member of the servant class cooking for capitalist controllers extracting resources and exploiting labor at home and in the Third World. No one viewed cooking as a route to world change, certainly not anyone in my family, where there was a long tradition of political activism.

"You should read these," Matt said one day handing me what I suspected was yet another small press publication devoted to culinary monomania.

"I can survive without reading an academic paper on when ice cream was first mentioned in the English language," I said, "and I have enough Italian cookbooks printed on cardboard."

"These are different," she said, and put one in my hand and ushered me to the register. It was a quarterly; *The Journal of Gastronomy*, published by the American Institute of Wine and Food (AIWF), had a roster of food and wine writers I recognized, a culturally relevant scope, and even drifted into food politics. The contributors to one of the 1989 issues, "American Food, American Farms" included activist food and agriculture titans: Frances Moore Lappé, Wes Jackson, Anne Mendelson, Gary Nabhan, Alice Waters, Ed Behr, and Wendell Berry.

Berry's essay entitled "The Pleasures of Eating" knocked me over. Its now well-quoted opening premise, "I begin with the proposition that eating is an agricultural act," was a thunderbolt, tangibly connecting me in a single sentence with a broader community and a greater purpose to my work. "Eating ends the annual drama of the food economy that begins with planting and birth." The nagging questions I harbored about my "elitist" and "indulgent" undertaking were settled. I could tell my sister who was saving the world in East New York as a community organizer after that neighborhood had been ravaged by white flight, redlining, and drug wars, that I too was effecting world change. Berry had deputized cooks as stewards of the earth; we were protectors with important work to do in our kitchens and in our dining rooms. With "The Pleasures of Eating" I understood that cooking could be part of Cleaver's "solution." "Sign me up," I thought as I read it. "Of thee I sing!"

Included in Berry's essay is a practical to-do list of things that urban eaters can do to help shift agriculture and the food system in this country—from "prepare your own food" to "deal directly with a local farmer, gardener, or orchardist" and "learn, in self-defense, as much as you can of the economy and technology of industrial food production." With this list, Berry set forth a lifetime of work for me and other active participants dedicated to creating the solution to a problem of our own creation.

The final paragraph though, placed the entire discussion on a different realm:

> Eating with the fullest pleasure—pleasure, that is, that does not depend on ignorance—is perhaps the profoundest enactment of our connection with the world. In this pleasure we experience and celebrate our dependence and gratitude, for we are living from the mystery, from creatures we did not make and powers we cannot comprehend.

Whenever my tautologies would begin to bind me, these words were a clean drink of truth. Berry's words were not about food politics, agricultural economics, or arguments about local versus organic; they were words about our connection with the planet and with others, about our interdependence with every creature that inhabits this earth. They are as close to a religious text as I ever hope to embrace.

I had discovered *how* to work and begun a practice, and now with this essay I had the *why*, the reason to do the work, and the farmers' market to ground my work. Now I needed to find my *where*.

SHRIMP

I cooked shrimp in my kitchen last night for the first time in many years. I sautéed them, head and shell on, in garlic, olive oil, and a bit of Aleppo pepper. I love watching shrimp transform from gray to pink when they're subjected to heat; magic. I flipped them over, then yanked them out of the pan and finished off the job with a swift flourish of lemon squeeze. I proclaim the dish "Shrimp Newburgh."

Decidedly not another version of the 1880s classic lobster dish from Delmonico's: lobster elegantly slathered in multiple applications of brandy, Madeira, eggs, and cream. No, not that Newburgh. I named my dish after my local source, the upriver city on the Hudson. Not a freshwater variety, these saltwater shrimp are the same Pacific white species, *Litopenaeus vannamei*, that most growers cultivate in ponds from Thailand to Belize. These are raised in kiddie pools set up in a basement underneath a motorcycle museum in Newburgh, New York.

They offer up everything we love about shrimp: that mix of brine and sweetness; a snappy firmness; meaty without the sinew of vertebrate flesh; a toasty, smoky, iodide depth that when fried crispy are more addictive than any potato chip. Since way back, shrimp has had us humans begging for another bite, craving another forkful of its explosive flavor. Seafood candy. We can never get enough.

As a kid, I could hardly get any at all. Back then, shrimp was a high-ticket item, most likely wild caught, sometimes sold fresh but probably frozen. In the appetizer section on menus, the description always included the number of shrimp in parentheses, leaving no room for disappointment or discussion. The bright amber-pink tails (6) came hanging over the rim of a cut glass bowl, a ramekin of red cocktail sauce in the center, maybe some leaves of iceberg lettuce to dress it up, and cost twice as much as any other appetizer. I imagine Sophia Loren beginning her evenings with them, martini coupe in one hand, a tiny seafood fork in the other.

In those days going out for dinner was infrequent in our family but when we did Mom clearly laid out the parameters prior. "Order anything you want . . . except for shrimp. It's off the list." Even though it was a treat just to be going out, my sisters and I naturally desired what was rare, out of reach: the shrimp cocktail. On very special occasions, we received parental dispensation and were permitted to taste the forbidden fruit. This was at Gaby's, a red carpeted, red sauce restaurant in Bergen County, New Jersey, serving the finest in Continental Italian cuisine.

Gaby's was where I began, as we all must begin somewhere, to expand my palate beyond home cooking, discovering the larger world of foods and tastes and their terminology. Learning the foreign lexicon was thrilling: cacciatore, scampi, fra diavolo—platters of exotic deliciousness. It was all so much fun to say and even more exciting when I repeated those same foreign syllables in other dining rooms and they were immediately comprehended, bringing me a plate resembling what I'd been served at Gaby's. The words were powerful keys into the world beyond the 'burbs.

In the sixties, our food culture hadn't gotten torqued up yet into an obsessive search for authenticity. Whether it was Italian, French, or Chinese, we were often being served what immigrant chefs and restaurateurs thought we wanted to eat or what they thought we thought their traditional food was (think of the ubiquitous fortune cookie—never made or served in China but what a disappointment if we weren't served a plate of them at a meal's conclusion). Regions melded, aristocratic and peasant dishes appeared on the same menu, co-minglings unheard of in the old country. Spaghetti has never appeared on the same plate as veal scaloppine in Italy, much less on the table at the same time. We didn't know yet about primi and secondi. Marcela Hazan's books and Alberto Viazzi's Florentine trattoria, the first popular northern Italian in Greenwich Village, were still a decade off.

Dinner at Gaby's always ended with tortoni or the tri-colore spu-moni, desserts that even if they had been invented in Italy, had long ago been forsaken in their original home. Like erratics—the geologic term for boulders moved by glaciation and then deposited onto terrain completely strange and distant from their place of origin—these dishes and their makers existed now in their new home, neither related to the surround-ing tract housing nor to the original strata of their homeland. But they established a foothold in the new country, isolated from the home fires, and thrived.

From a biological standpoint, thriving in isolation can either promote change because a special niche can be honed and maximized (think Darwin's finches) or inhibit change because the isolation protects the species from other pressures (think Australian marsupials). Spumoni is an example of the later. Throughout the second half of the twentieth century, the cuisines of Rome, Napoli, and Sicily continued to evolve but Italian restaurateurs in the United States held on to the dish thinking it a signifier of authenticity to American diners. Or maybe customers just came to like it, authentic or not, and so it stayed on the menu, helping to pay the rent. So too it was with shrimp cocktail. There is little inherently Italian about cold poached shrimp and red tomato sauce with horseradish mixed into it. But there it was at Gaby's, my object of desire, and "off the list."

Fast forward ten to fifteen years, a mere blink in cultural time and shrimp went from being rare and dear to ubiquitous and cheap, even featured at national restaurant chains as part of all-you-can-eat specials. The entire nation wanted what I wanted, and this was accomplished through the "miracle" of farm-raised shrimp. Practiced by the Chinese for thousands of years, pond aquaculture was applied on an industrial scale throughout the equatorial regions of the globe, from Ecuador and Belize to Thailand, Vietnam, and Bangladesh, beginning in the seventies. A "pink gold rush" developed in these countries, as hungry for fast currency as the first world was for cheap seafood protein.

On the surface this seemed like a fair exchange. Long coastlines of wild mangrove swamps previously viewed as "non-developable" for human habitation because of high water tables, frequent flooding, or changing tidelines, were cheap to purchase and development was barely regulated. The mangroves were cut down and converted into a progression of ponds with easy access to the ocean for supplying both the input of fresh seawater into the ponds but also the outputs, pumping the shrimp waste and ammoniated water back into the ocean. Intense feeding regimens and the high population density of the shrimp require the heavy use of antibiotics to fight disease, but they are also used sub-therapeutically to boost weight gain and shorten production time.

Sound familiar? All of this is very similar to the challenges and solutions utilized in land-based concentrated animal feeding operations (CAFOs) for cattle, hogs, and poultry. And as with land animal feedlots, these ponds create huge quantities of waste. Once their ponds become nutrient or ammonia saturated, shrimp producers often choose to abandon the ponds and move production down the coastline, repeating the pattern along a seemingly endless stretch of coastal property. To make matters worse, harvesting is often done either by child labor or under slave-like conditions or both. Biodiversity is an issue as well. The "unusable swamps" were in fact home to countless species, protective waters for young fish, turtles, and crabs to develop and protective buffer zones from tsunamis to inland human developments.

Why is it that we always want what is out of reach, what is dear? And why do we take what is dear and in the pursuit of a lower price cheapen it, degrade it, and maybe in the process degrade ourselves or our world? Think of roses, veal, and pearls. Roses used to be a finicky-to-grow domestic flower commanding a premium price at the florist. A dozen long stems signaled commitment and sacrifice on the part of the buyer, hence sent as a conciliatory gesture after a lovers' quarrel. Now grown in South America, heavily doused with pesticides, farmed by pitifully poor people, and flown in daily to JFK, they cost a fraction of what they once did but the signifying meaning remains intact. Another geologic erratic? On Valentine's Day, very few couples would show up in the restaurant without one of them delivering a bouquet to the other.

It's the same with veal, once a seasonal, small-scale, high-priced meat. In order to keep a dairy herd of cows lactating, each milking cow needs to birth a calf once a year. The gals were kept to reinvigorate the herd, and the male offspring were often sacrificed when they were still suckling and hardly walking, which produced tender and pale flesh—veal. Via the wonders of modern agriculture and pharmaceuticals including animal confinement and antibiotics, veal production was transformed to become cheaper, available year-round, and widely accessible.

With shrimp, the unintended consequences were that thousands of miles of tropical coastlines were chopped down, wild mangrove swamps that previously protected the shoreline and human habitation no longer offered shelter from storms and floods. We did indeed accomplish the abundance of all-you-can-eat shrimp but it came at a cost.

I didn't know any of this in the early years of Savoy. As a chef on a mission to create great flavor but also on a budget, I focused on serving the castaway but more flavorful parts of an animal, the trotters and shoulders instead of center-cut loin chops. This applied to shrimp as well. Having discovered frozen head-on shrimp at a nearby Chinese wholesaler on Mulberry Street, I would buy two-kilogram boxes and not only serve the shrimp but make shrimp oil from shrimp heads and peelings, which we turned into a vinaigrette to dress poached skate wing or drizzled over sautéed greens with toasted garlic.

I was employing the French commitment to culinary thrift in my cooking both to stay in the black and because it aligned gastronomically with my sensibility. Never wasting an opportunity to extract or concentrate flavor, the French developed numerous twice-cooked techniques. Their classic shellfish soup is dubbed bisque, once for roasting the shells and twice for boiling the roasted shells into stock. Biscuits or Italian biscotti and German zwieback all refer to twice-cooked: once to bake the dough and the second time to crisp them up. They are great for dunking into milk, coffee, or vin santo and efficient because the method far extends their shelf life. In the case of shrimp, I'd lightly toast the shellfish carcasses and then combine the shells with wine, water, and vegetables to extract a rich stock. These head-based stocks and vinaigrettes became kitchen staples. In addition to being committed to creating great flavor, our mission was also to tread lightly on the earth as we have our fun; to protect the planet as we cooked and ate. After learning about the problems associated with equatorial farm-raised shrimp, these guys went "off the list."

In 2005 we briefly served Louisiana trap-caught shrimp after joining the White Boot Brigade—a loose consortium of folks all along the food distribution chain to help the Gulf Coast shrimpers get a leg up after Hurricane Katrina and the terrible destruction the hurricane brought upon boats, docks, and processing plants. That choice was fraught too. While we wanted to support the fishing communities, their livelihood, traditional culture and cuisines, we also knew that their catch methods often involved habitat destruction or high levels of bycatch. In an ocean of rapidly decreasing species, we were participating in an economy predicated on depletion and decimation. After several months of supporting the Gulf shrimpers during a restoration period, and as delicious as it was, we struggled to find the balance between species depletion and our support of that fishing community and backed away from serving that shrimp. Once again it was "off the list."

Apart from this one-time call to action, for the next ten years only a single species of shrimp appeared on our menus: red Maine shrimp. Known to the Japanese as *amai ebi*, "sweet shrimp," and to scientists as *Pandalus borealis* after Boreas, Greek god of the cold north wind. In the "everything is relative" mind bender, these little guys migrate south from Greenland and Nova Scotia into the warmer coastal waters of the Gulf of Maine to get away from the intense winter cold of the north.

I fell in love with these shrimp, delicious in all our preparations. Tossed in the fryer and then dressed in lime, cilantro, and red onion, they are crunchy and you eat everything. Peeled and then marinated raw in winter citrus juices or quickly sautéed and set atop a swirl of parsley-laden pasta, they provide high payoff: easy, direct, and full of flavor.

There didn't appear to be bycatch problems associated with their harvest and certainly no pond filth or habitat destruction was involved. The season on red shrimp gave Maine fishermen much needed winter cash flow when lobster roll consumption was low and the wind chill of offshore fishing high. They became a seasonal delight that customers and cooks looked forward to when our seasonal cooking mostly amounted to a never-ending supply of gnarly root vegetables. We normally associate seasonal fish with the tuna or bluefish runs of August and September on Long Island or soft-shell crabs of May and June from the Chesapeake but certainly not January as peak season for shrimp from the coast of Maine.

Most years they were cheap, $3 per pound. I always felt like a pro, having the inside track on a great ingredient that hadn't been discovered yet. I was hoping that they wouldn't end up following the destructive cycle of monkfish, whose value soared when chefs "discovered" it, leading to plummeting populations and then the imposition of stringent regulations to protect them and the fishery. Red Maine shrimp seemed to be a species and a fishery in balance: between production and consumption, between desire and availability.

It didn't last, though, but not because of overconsumption. Rising sea temperatures particularly in the Gulf of Maine—where temperatures were reported as increasing at a faster rate than any other area of the global ocean—resulted in plummeting shrimp stocks. Even with limited takes in 2010 through 2012, the stocks continued to drop precipitously. In 2014, for the first time in over thirty years there was no season at all for red Maine shrimp. This continued with only a small quantity caught for research purposes allowed to be sold, at a sticker shocking $14 per pound in 2016. Subsequent seasons have remained closed and in 2019 the Marine Fisheries Commission took the unprecedented step of closing the fishery for three consecutive years. The outlook is not particularly good. Water temperatures continue to rise and the shrimp need colder waters to thrive. This time by governmental decree, shrimp were once again "off the list."

I feel this as a deep loss, a sadness that brings the global climate change predicament right into the kitchen, onto the plate and the food we put in our bodies. What had been a source of joy in its discovery and delight in the cooking and eating was no longer part of our joy in living, in being on the planet. The decline of red Maine shrimp was a direct outcome of our way of life, of our denial and refusal to adjust our patterns of consumption.

In the wake of this seeming final embargo I came upon a stand at the Union Square Greenmarket called ECO Shrimp. Admittedly, I was immediately suspicious. I am preternaturally paranoid about new food technology even if it is local and particularly if it is not produced in its original habitat. I distrust the raspberries and tomatoes available in March from upstate New York grown in fossil fuel heated greenhouses or the beautiful amaryllis from New Jersey in January heated by coal burning generators. I don't believe the future lies in growing microgreens in skyscrapers in Newark, New Jersey, even though all of these products are local. The economics can't really pencil out.

I walked by the ECO Shrimp stand when I first saw it, thinking this was probably one more greenwashing operation, and only took the brochure. How could shrimp be clean, green, and delicious? As it turns out, Jean Claude Frajmund, the ECO Shrimp genius, has been learning to master the complexities of operating a closed and balanced saltwater tank. This requires raising both shrimp and bio-floc, a bacteria that eat the waste of the shrimp and whatever feed pellets (made from trimmings from a Philadelphia fish house) the shrimp don't eat. In an inversion of Wendell Berry's description of modern agriculture dividing one solution into two problems, Frajmund is propagating two solutions to one problem. He is building a community of organisms that live in balance. The bacteria clean the water, keep ammonia levels low, and obviate the need for water replacement in the tanks. No nearby coastline is needed to pump wastewater and the tanks only need to be topped off occasionally due to evaporation. Frajmund is more an invertebrate community organizer than food producer, obsessively balancing pH, oxygen, nitrate, and ammonia levels to maximize the shrimp's need for the bacteria and bacteria's need for the shrimp. The result of all this harmonization in an underground array of kiddie pools is an ingredient I love eating.

ECO Shrimp aren't cheap, but actually few animal proteins should be at this point. They are never going to be part of an all-you-can-eat feast but they are delicious, there's no environmental degradation involved, and the only underpaid worker is the founder himself. Try making a vinaigrette and tossing some celery root and escarole with it and then setting the pan-fried tails on top of it all. Or just sauté them in garlic, olive oil, and a bit of Aleppo pepper. Don't forget a squeeze of lemon.

SHRIMP OIL VINAIGRETTE

MAKES ¾ CUP/180 ML VINAIGRETTE

(ENOUGH TO DRESS A LARGE SALAD FOR 6)

Making this oil is easy to do and it uses the castoffs of the shrimp if you peel them before cooking. I keep the oil in my refrigerator and use it to sauté other shrimp or fish for added flavor or make it into the vinaigrette as described here; it's a great staple to always have on hand. I often collect shrimp shells (and shrimp heads if available) in the freezer until I have enough or want to make shrimp oil. The vinaigrette brightens up any dish, whether drizzled over a piece of fish or over oven-roasted vegetables like celery root, or as dressing for hearty greens like escarole. Garnishing the salad with sautéed shrimp is an added bonus that ties the entire dish together.

For the shrimp oil:
Shrimp shells, reserved from peeling 2 pounds (910g) shrimp
4 cloves garlic
2 teaspoons coriander seeds
1 teaspoon cumin seed
1 teaspoon black peppercorns
3 pieces star anise
1 thin cinnamon stick
2 small red chile peppers
½ cup (120 ml) grapeseed oil or other neutral oil

For the vinaigrette:
Juice of 2 limes, or more as needed
2 tablespoons fish sauce, or more as needed
1 tablespoon sugar, or more as needed
½ cup (120 ml) shrimp oil

1. **MAKE THE SHRIMP OIL:** Combine the shrimp shells and all the spices in a small pot. Add the oil. Cook over low heat, watching as the shells

toast and change color, for 20 minutes until the shells are crispy and fully toasted. The oil should be a deep rose color. Allow to cool.

2. **MAKE THE VINAIGRETTE**: Whisk together all the ingredients and taste for balance, adjusting the fish sauce, lime juice, and sugar as needed. The oil keeps indefinitely in a nonbreakable, reusable plastic container in the refrigerator. The vinaigrette is good for 1 week in the refrigerator.

WOULDA, COULDA, SHOULDA

Every New York story is in some fashion a real estate story. There is the moment of arrival—even for those who grew up here—of beginning the circuitous and aggravating process of finding a place to rest our heads. Regardless of the decade, everyone tries to secure a piece of the bedrock, to stake a prospector's claim to a spot and call it home. Like birth stories still very much alive long after delivery, everyone has a tale to tell of the process. Attached to the triumphal success stories are also the fish that got away; entire loft spaces passed up because we weren't ready to commit only to realize in retrospect what a deal it was, the airy one-bedroom offered to the next applicant on the list due to a missed phone call, or the choice apartment lost in a breakup. Everyone has at least one woulda, coulda, shoulda tale. Here's mine: one that through luck and serendipity I was able to transform into a restaurant.

When I first landed back on the East Coast after my three-year stint in California, I stayed in the small former maid's room tucked behind the kitchen in my sister's Upper West Side classic-six apartment. She shared it with two other women. It was a great location, the company good. There was plenty of room and, in my opinion, I thought I would make a great fourth. I saw no reason to leave. My sister thought otherwise. Through one of her roommates, I found a share in an unrenovated loft down in the Fulton Fish Market area, half of an entire floor, with plywood for a kitchen counter and bare light bulbs for fixtures. Set just outside the central area bustling with fish hawkers, wholesalers, and stevedores in the wee hours of the morning, it was quiet at night but still close enough to offer a strong marine fragrance in the warmer months. I liked it down there and even considered buying an entire building for $40,000—no floorboards, barely a roof—but an entire building, only blocks away from the financial capital of the world. Today that building would sell for eight figures. Woulda coulda shoulda #1.

After a few job misfires, I landed a solid cooking position at La Colombe d'Or, a restaurant focusing on the cuisine of Provence, where I worked for the better part of a year. I learned how to make *soupe des poisson*, tapenade, and Paris-Brest, a dessert named after a bike race. I fell madly in love with an actress enrolled at grad school at NYU and abandoned both the job and the loft in order to follow her to Michigan, to work as a counselor and instructor at a summer arts camp.

When the summer ended, we were still involved but not ready to move in together. I began looking around the East Village for apartments hovering as close as possible to her Seventh Street apartment. In that wonderful way that New York is a small town even with nine million people living here, I ran into a former college roommate from California on the street, hooked him up with construction work on my cousin's Greenwich Village residence, and in the course of the exchange he tipped me off about a real estate agent who leased renovated apartments at fair prices to nice college kids. There was a hitch, though. They weren't actual leases, more like subleases with very scant paperwork and no documentation from the actual landlord. But places were hard to find, none of us knew how long we'd be in New York, and the outfit seemed to have abundant apartment stock. I hastily took a one-bedroom on East Ninth Street, still under a renovation typical in old tenements: moving the bathtub from the middle of the kitchen and joining it with the small toilet stall—a water closet formerly accessed from the hallway—to create a larger and true bathroom. Space was tight and when finished, the area dedicated to the hand wash sink was so narrow that I could not comfortably spread my elbows to splash water on my face. I considered the situation intolerable and after my first morning's ablutions, I marched down to the real estate office to lodge a complaint. They found my outrage laughable and endearing but agreed to solve the problem. An accordion louver door was installed that could be popped out to offer me plenty of arm room when washing or kept flush with the wall when not in use. At the real estate office, I was humorously dubbed "Louver Door Man."

This was my first true New York apartment, a small but real one bedroom with a tiny eat-in kitchen and a small sitting room. My wall demands notwithstanding, I guess I was a good tenant, because in the spring of 1980 I got a phone call from the real estate agent telling me that an even better apartment was available in SoHo. "It won't be available for long. You need to view it immediately and write me a check if you want it." That evening, before celebrating my girlfriend's birthday with her out-of-town sister at Chanterelle, we stopped off to view the apartment. It was more than a huge improvement; it was lovely: third floor, southwest light, corner apartment, nice layout, in an old Italian neighborhood that hadn't been turned into a tourist attraction like Little Italy, a spacious 550 square feet, and all for $425 a month. We went to dinner at Chanterelle, had a sumptuous meal, and continued the party after dinner with more friends at Mama Siltka's on West Broadway, a downtown watering hole for theater types. Giddy and by now fairly drunk, I danced to Stevie Wonder tunes out on the street while smoking a joint. I slipped on the steel diamond-plate sidewalk hatch and landed teeth first, cracking off my two front teeth. I was aghast. As the son of a dentist, broken front teeth were not an acceptable condition for public display and needed immediate attention. Before driving home to New Jersey where I hoped my father would take care of the gaping hole first thing in the morning, I shoved a deposit check under the door of the real estate office, knowing that New York real estate waits for no man, teeth or none.

My dad was furious with me. His first words, upon discovering me in the driveway asleep in my car, were "You stink," and then as I opened my mouth to explain, he saw the damage, and jumped into action. A few days later, after recovering from the trauma of the ordeal, I called the real estate office to follow up on my late-night deposit. They told me to come down to the office. Everyone snickered as they presented Louver Door Man with a completely indecipherable check. Whatever sheepishness I felt rewriting the check was outweighed by the outcome—I had scored a great apartment.

I lived in that SoHo apartment for several years, blissfully paying my $425 every month. One day I ran into a woman I had gone to summer camp with and she told me that she was part of a lawsuit against our same real estate agent because all of his apartments were in fact illegal sublets. Allegedly, he was signing scads of leases as the tenant for rent stabilized apartments and then subletting them instead of offering leases, skimming a nice vig off the top with little regard for the law. In return, he was relieving the landlords of two big headaches: vetting the applicants and maintaining the apartments. With her lawsuit, his sublet empire began to unravel. Not long after, I got a letter from the actual landlord telling me I would now be paying the rent directly to him. The landlord's name was Artie, and Artie was one of the guys who had "friends in the neighborhood," you know, a guy who knew how to take care of things and get things done. Local building lore had it that previous to my tenancy there had been a lady whose air conditioner was always dripping onto the street at the building entry. After numerous requests to take care of it but inaction on her part, there was a knock at the door one day and two men said they were there to fix the air conditioner. She happily let them in to repair her AC. They opened the window, pushed it out onto the street below, said, "Now it's fixed," and left. That's not exactly the kind of landlord you wanted to approach and say that you have been overcharged for three years because of the illegal sublet situation and ask what was he going to do about it, so I kept my mouth shut. Artie passed away soon after. I wrote a letter to his widow and we quickly agreed that it was better to avoid going to court and that a year's free rent more than took care of the problem. She quickly sold the building to a developer who began warehousing empty units in the building in hopes of converting it to a co-op. To entice residents to support his conversion, insiders were offered their apartments for $18,000. Even in 1984 dollars, everyone in the building knew it was incredible price, an offer we couldn't refuse.

I lived there until 1986 when I moved in with Susan and sublet the apartment for additional income. In 1989, the savings and loan crisis was peaking—a crisis similar to the Great Recession of 2008, smaller in scale but no less traumatic for thousands of homeowners. A precursor of the too big to fail moment in 2008, the federal government was forced to take on the huge burden of the failed loans because savings and loan associations were federally insured. In the aftermath, banks tightened up their loan requirements, stipulating that co-ops had to be 75 percent owner occupied in order for unit buyers to qualify for mortgages. As a result, the co-op board for my building passed a resolution limiting the length of time apartments could be rented out. I was feeling the squeeze. The choices were: move back in, leave it unoccupied, or sell.

I was banking on another option entirely. I had hoped to have a tenant in the place and finance the construction of the restaurant by taking a loan with the apartment as collateral. Several shady mortgage brokerage companies—who promised the moon but delivered little while happily fleecing me of multiple $500 initiation fees—later, I was stuck, forced to sell the apartment. If I could have borrowed against the apartment, funded the restaurant, *and* continued to hold on to it for another five years, I would have tripled my money. Woulda, coulda, shoulda #2.

The cash from my SoHo apartment was more than half of the necessary funding to open Savoy. Had toothless "Louver Door Man" not written an indecipherable check I might never have been able to self-finance the Savoy project that provided my income, sustenance, and livelihood for the next twenty-six years. No woulda, coulda, shoulda regrets here.

CONSTRUCTION IS COOKING

When we were building Savoy, we were continually asked the same two questions everyone asks someone starting a restaurant. When are you going to open? And what is the food going to be? Given that no restaurant ever opens on schedule, we didn't attempt to answer the first and, as for the second, it was all kind of vague. We knew but we didn't know. Construction helped us figure it out.

We didn't test recipes in the months leading up to opening. There was no sous chef on payroll busy in a basement kitchen developing dishes and food shots to publish in the fall previews—the stuff that would later become de rigueur for New York openings. No, while we were in the development phase we didn't think about food. Each morning I donned coveralls and went to the jobsite; Sue did research either at the Mid-Manhattan Library or in the sample stacks at the office of our architect, Larry Bogdanow, in pursuit of appropriate fabric, tile, and light fixtures. We were in construction, and more important, we were into construction.

Many people find renovations an exercise in frustration and anxiety management. They feel worn down by the notorious tangle of paperwork, shipping delays, mismeasured site dimensions, botched installations, and finally at the end of the job, the really bad news, the prohibitively expensive black hole of "change orders," the term for additional billing. Even more treacherous is the frequent volley of finger-pointing accusations between architects and builders, or worse, between the contractor and subs (subcontractors) who walk off the job, having taken money for work not completed. None of that deterred us. Sue and I loved the building process. We used it to shape the nature of the dining room and the kitchen that we would work from and also the way we would work with our employees. Our collaborative process with the design team was a precursor to the creative one we would soon develop with cooks in our kitchen. It was operations without customers, management without employees. We were our sole clientele, the only people we needed to satisfy. We were building our workshop.

But what's the food?

I had been to a Kandinsky exhibit and read a wall text explanation about Gesamtkunstwerk, the term Wagner coined for a total work of art. Just reading the term felt like an incredible affirmation of what we were striving for. In a single utterance our desire now had a name (and it was so much fun to say). We might have been working within the small space of 1,100 square feet but right from the start our vision was grand: a total work of art. Kandinsky applied Gesamtkunstwerk to the theater; I was going to apply it to restaurants.

Sue and I were going to be chef operators, concerned with food and wine selections as well as lighting, sound, tabletop, decor, waitstaff demeanor. While I was excitedly arm waving, philosophically rattling on, Susan, recently returned from Vienna, brought a concrete image to the discussion: the Karlsplatz Stadtbahn, Secessionist architect Otto Wagner's Vienna train station. This was a masterful expression of the balance between function and poetry, rationalism and decor—goals we were striving for even if we couldn't articulate it in those terms. We wanted the refined beauty of Le Grenouille's dining room and the easy community spirit of La Taza de Oro's counter, the Hispanic rice and beans joint near our home. The food and decor signifiers of opulence in the eighties—foie gras, truffles, low-voltage lights strung on high-intensity cables, faux-finished walls, and alabaster lamps—weren't going to have a place in our house even if there had been available funds. Sue wanted the graceful simplicity of the Karlsplatz decor along with its total functionality as a working train station. Its small but human scale became the guiding light for our design work. Forty-five seats were sufficient, even in a city with ever-expanding dining rooms. The Karlsplatz Stadtbahn reminded us that small could be uplifting, even enthralling.

OK, but what's the food?

I began hitting the outdoor flea market on Sixth Avenue every Sunday morning picking up items that seemed to fit that aesthetic mix. Known by a variety of names depending on the country: Secessionist (Austria), Art Nouveau (France), Arts and Crafts (United States), and Mission Style (California), it was a design period of pre-modern modernists, when high design had shifted from singly produced wares for the aristocracy to production on a larger, more industrial scale. It retained the artistry and craft associated with handmade work before modernism became spare and solely about line. I bought Stickley furniture, Bakelite flatware, Eastern European Jugendstil vases, mix-and-match plates, anything that seemed to exemplify this pivotal moment when craft scaled up.

I made a defining purchase at the B. Altman liquidation auction—the mid-priced department store on Fifth Avenue and Thirty-Fourth Street that after eighty years had gone belly-up, unable to appeal to a younger, more fashion-conscious clientele. In the employee lunchroom, I stumbled upon thirty-five dark-brown bentwood Thonet chairs. Not the Victorian-style ice cream parlor ones that still proliferate in cafés, but ones from the forties and fifties—when form followed function—utilizing the traditional bending and lamination techniques to create a chair with the comfort of a porch rocker and the clean elegance of industrial modernism. They were institutional chairs—what is now called contract furniture—a category usually devoid of any character or taste, even valued for being devoid of personality. Found in school offices, factory showrooms, hospital waiting rooms, even the United Nations, they had great style and I needed them. They spoke of everything we were trying to be. I biked over to Le Madri, the Italian restaurant where Sue was the pastry chef and, after making a sketch on a piece of menu paper, I got her buy-in and peddled back to Altman's sure that the purchase would represent a major statement in our room. Bidding began at $3. The only other bidder was an East Village antiques dealer with her boyfriend. Lacking all strategic finesse, I eagerly and immediately topped her every bid. Finally her boyfriend, knowing that I would not be deterred, grabbed her by the arm and escorted her out of the room, effectively halting the bidding. Sold. For $17 apiece.

* * *

Our design process was nonhierarchical; ideas were welcome from everyone. Larry Bogdanow, our architect, and Peter Codella, the general contractor, were key players. Larry never issued a complete and final bid set of drawings. Rather than frustrating, this allowed the process to remain fluid. Countless mornings Peter proposed implementing Larry's "cartoon" sketches into an actual work plan in Peter Falk's Colombo mode saying, "You know, I had a thought when I was alone in the space. It's just a thought." Most often his ideas advanced Larry's design.

Our graphic designer, Julie Salestrom, proposed a business card with the image of a spoon, its die-cut handle extending just beyond the rectangular dimensions of a card. Forks and knives, the utensils historically used to represent fine dining, were tools of the aristocracy but a spoon was everyone's utensil—an expression of warmth and comfort—whether it was in a child's hand slurping up a brothy chicken soup or in an adult's, plunging spoon first into a bubbling peach cobbler. The spoon suggested unpretentious nurturing and ease. This moved us closer to a definition of our cooking style.

Artists have been migrating to New York City for decades, probably even centuries: to go to school, find community, set up a studio, hopefully get paid to create one day, but until that day, they need a day job. Chuck Close and Phillip Glass were electricians and plumbers in the seventies before art and music paid their bills. Our construction crew was no different. Peter, whom I'd met at UC Santa Cruz, was a sculptor and with him came a crew of other artists. D.R. Miller, lead carpenter, was a musician and instrument builder with a second-floor studio in the Gansevoort meat market above Dizzy Izzy's bagel factory (now Design Within Reach) and Jeff Mace, metalworker and welder, also lived in a meat market studio, heated with a coal-burning stove, located across the street from my meat supplier, J.T. Jobbagy (now an Apple store). At the end of each day, when work belts and dusty aprons came off, each tradesman went back to their studios to ply their chosen art. Yet each morning with Greek diner coffee cups in hand, their mission was to help build us our studio, our workshop. The crew took us seriously, not because we paid them but because they saw that we were passionate about our dream. Sensing their important role in its actualization, it became more than just a job for them. This crew was working in wood, plaster, and paint; soon to be replaced by one working in garlic, tomatoes, and pork.

All the tradespeople contributed. Our wizard electrician, Jim Meriwether, fashioned flour scoops and funnels we'd rummaged from Bridge Kitchenware into exterior light fixtures. Our masons suggested lifting the hearth off the floor so that we could store firewood beneath it, coincidentally setting it at countertop cooking height. By accident, Larry draped a double layer of the bronze porch screen he had spec'd for the ceiling to hide the acoustical batting. It created a rippling moire pattern that everyone became enchanted with. Confident that this shimmery effect would create a subtle drama in the room, the screen budget immediately doubled. It was by accretion of small discoveries that we defined our look and our style.

And the menu?

Larry understood that we were on a budget—or lacking an actual budget, he understood that we were working with limited funds. The budget was a mantra more than a spreadsheet: "Spend as little as you can but still make it look nice." Blond Masonite as the wall surface and cherry wooden strips to cover the seams created rectilinear wall sections in Arts and Crafts style. End-grain woodblock for flooring, the same material departing SoHo machine shops used because they wouldn't gouge when heavy machinery was moved around, brought the appearance of kitchen butcher block into dining room. Brilliant!

When it came to tabletop, we dispensed with linens. I had grown up eating every night at a walnut Nakashima trestle table so this wasn't a revolutionary step for me. Linens traditionally signify quality, but they also bring formality and added cost to the dining experience, neither of which we wanted. No one in New York's fine dining realm, outside of Japanese restaurants, had presented diners with the direct tactile feel and look of open wood-grain tables. The "budget" didn't allow for solid hardwood tabletops. Instead Larry and Peter proposed Baltic birch, industrial high-grade plywood. Edges exposed, surfaces bleach-white, the tables were both handmade and industrially manufactured. We weren't making apologies for using commonplace materials, not attempting to transform them into something else; we loved them for what they were.

After opening, customers participated in furthering our visual definition, bringing even greater clarity to the place. Max Protetch, the art dealer with a gallery across the street, decided that our Arts and Crafts walls needed a Louis Sullivan–designed baluster from the 1894 Chicago Stock Exchange that he owned. After a week's loan, we acknowledged that it belonged in the space and we negotiated a trade of dinners for art, a tradition we continued over many years with other artists: Chuck Close, Lorie Simmons, Ray Mortenson, Betty and George Woodman, and Susan Hauptman.

I still managed to get within a week of opening before drafting a working menu, but during the months of construction I had clarified what our guiding principles would be: everyday ingredients worked with care and intelligence, on a scale that was neither twee nor cranked for mass production. Comfort and simplicity would prevail over visual gymnastics and mannered plate decoration. We would work collaboratively, not focusing on any one cuisine, but we'd be ingredient proud, keeping the attention on the ingredients, not on the chefs.

Without step-by-step instructions to the build-out, we had found our way, not dissimilar to the relationship between cooking and recipes. Recipes only exist in retrospect, an accounting of a culinary exploration that actually happened at the stove. Our process delivered us a jewel of a restaurant and that's how we were going to cook.

* * *

What about staff? Before there was Craigslist, Culintro, or ZipRecruiter there was the classified section of the *New York Times*, period. There were other local papers, of course. An ad in the *Village Voice* pulled in folks mostly on the fringe: a mix of substance abusers and short-timers all looking for quick money before moving on. Good knife skills and dependability were not top attributes of *Village Voice* respondents. The *New York Post* was where you'd see listings for pantrymen (an antiquated term for working the appetizer cold station in hotel kitchens), hospital dishwashers, and line cook positions in Brooklyn catering halls or Long Island country clubs. Employment agencies were brokers for people in a jam, on either side of the equation; desperate restaurateurs willing to pay a cash premium for a one-off shift dishwasher or laborers desperate in their own way, possibly one paycheck away from becoming homeless or pulling the emergency cord and leaving town. These weren't the outlets where we were going to find folks who wanted to share our dream, to push forward our vision but as yet undefined cuisine.

The only option was the *New York Times*. But the *Times*, being the national paper of record, was an expensive placement. The base fee in 1990 was $200 for a one-time placement in the Sunday classified section. Compare that with $25 for an ad on Craigslist twenty-five years later. But everybody in the business bought the paper on Sunday morning and perused the employment landscape over a cup of coffee. If you really wanted to get a jump on things you could pick up the paper on Saturday night after 10 P.M. at various newsstands known for getting the first drop; the Gem Spa at Second Avenue and St. Marks Place, across from the Waverly Theater on Sixth Avenue, or in Times Square near the loading dock of the *Times*.

Reading the classifieds was also a window into the restaurant news: who was hiring, what places were opening. If you wandered into the nearby real estate section you could see who was looking to sell their business and at the end of that section were the auction liquidation ads where you could read the direst news of all: who had folded up or whose place had been seized by the landlord or the state. Before Eater.com, the classifieds were our community bulletin board and on select Sundays we shelled out $200 to broadcast our news.

The base fee bought four lines, a challenge for real estate agents and employers alike to communicate allure in compressed form, to tantalize while still including the vital stats of wheres and whens. Why else would all those real estate acronyms have developed? 2 bdrm, EIK, wbfp, pqt flr gt lt, dwntn, $1200 WU. Huh? Of course I'd love to rent an apartment with an eat-in kitchen, a wood-burning fireplace, parquet floors, and great light. With all those other attributes the fact that it's a walkup would hardly matter. These once meaningful abbreviations are now obsolete—with Craigslist space is nearly limitless. But in the hot summer of 1990 how could I ever describe in four lines what we were doing? What kind of food were we going to serve? We weren't French or Italian or even "California cuisine"—a category I found completely annoying. The scale of the restaurant pointed towards marketing it as "cozy" even though the last thing we wanted to do was get lumped in with the Village's French boites serving tired bistro food. We were breaking with those old notions of dining and no one even knew where Crosby Street was.

We didn't have a single person lined up to work with us; we were building a team from scratch. Our network was small; no former co-workers were a remote possibility and the pool of cooks from like-minded restaurants to draw from was only slightly larger. The family tree of kitchens—that each begat a new generation of cooks—had barely begun to sprout. At the end of the day, the only phone call to make (and no later than 5 P.M. on Thursday) was to Brenda, in classifieds, at the *Times*. Out of all of this design work and cookbook research I came up with new words to describe our food and our place. Not Gesamtkunstwerk, not chez nous. Taking our best shot I told her:

> COOKS 2 Seasoned Chefs opening 45 seat downtown
> restaurant. Food with guts and beauty. Exp'd line cook &
> entry position available. 219–8992

Food with guts and beauty; *that* was our food.

SKATE

I love skate. It's a wonderfully meaty fish, packed with juice and gelatin. It embraces a multitude of full flavors, effortlessly soaking up sauce, marrying proteins and juices in a way that upper-crust finfish like snapper and bass never can. The flesh pulls apart into striated muscle fibers more like pulled pork, less like the flesh of those classier fishes that sport scales and denser bones. Yet it gets called trash fish by Americans who prefer fish that doesn't taste fishy and above all else, lacks bones. The irony is that skate has neither all the little annoying bones found in the dorsal, pectoral, and caudal fins of finfish nor any of the pin bones that kitchen prep guys in good restaurants extract one at a time with fish pliers. In the Northeast, skate is probably used for lobster bait more often than it is brought home for dinner. I'm not sure why it gets so little respect. Is it because they are "ugly" bottom fish? Maybe it's because they aren't a manly sport fish to catch on a hook and line—instead they are swept up in nets by trawlers? Maybe it's because historically there was so much cod in New England's waters that no one needed to develop an appreciation and a repertoire of recipes for cooking skate? Probably all of the above.

The French have long appreciated skate, calling it *raie*, as in stingray, which it resembles. Its culinary tradition is urban, more renowned in Paris than in its home fishing ports along the Normandy coast. The common French view is that skate improves with travel and a bit of age on it, making it a good choice to ship overland. Classic bistro preparations found all over Paris are *raie aux capres* (capers) or *raie au beurre noisettes* (brown butter). The term "ray" comes from the radiating pattern of its muscle fibers laid atop its cartilage; we call them wings. By delicately undulating their wings, skate almost hovercraft just above the benthic zone in search of an enviable rich man's diet of clams, oysters, and shrimp. No wonder they taste so good. The wings, which radiate out from the central vertebrae and look like an aerial view of a river's alluvial fan, are the only parts that make it into our kitchens. We don't eat the vertebrae or the rest of their body.

I've served skate myriad ways: on a sandwich with aioli, topped with spaghetti squash, and capers, in a broth of red peppers and olives, sautéed with a dusting of porcini powder. I love cooking it on the bone because the horizontal cartilaginous bony plate keeps the flesh moist and juicy. Yet with the tug of a fork, it elegantly separates off the bone. Even the klutziest ichthyophobe can succeed in a formal dining room without embarrassment.

I also love skate because I'm drawn to gastronomic underdogs. I pursue the underappreciated cuts of meat, the neglected vegetables, the ones overshadowed by the premium ingredients high-end chefs and their deep-pocketed spenders can buy with abandon. You'll never find me putting center-cut pork loins, filet mignon, or rack of lamb on the menu. The expression "eating high on the hog" means eating the cuts furthest from the ground, the least active and thus most tender muscles on a pig, and therefore the most expensive. High on the back might yield more easily grilled cuts, but with it too comes less flavorful meat, a result of inactivity and reduced blood flow. Action equates to flavor. The cuts I prefer are ones that did some work, have had blood coursing through their veins and so need a chef's vision and skill to allow them to shine. Good technique and longer cooking times release more flavor and deliver a better bottom line.

Skate are no exception. They are cheap when compared with the price of trophy fish like striped bass or tuna. A chef who can take a low-end-priced fish, properly handle it, and then charge full fare in the right column of the menu ends up the winner.

Skate are challenging, though, because they have a shorter shelf life than bony fish. Why is that? It goes back to how fishes absorb oxygen from the surrounding water. This is one of the challenges for all creatures trying to live in the ocean, made even more challenging by creatures that have a different salinity from the surrounding water. Imagine what your mouth would look and feel like if you had to gargle saltwater constantly in order to breathe. The salt would desiccate your mouth. Invertebrates don't have this problem; they just adopt the ionic concentrations of whatever water they are in. Biologists employ a wonderful term for this, calling them "osmoconformers," which means the animals conform, using osmosis, to whatever ionic conditions they find themselves in. It's kind of like high school biology meets social group dynamics. The term immediately illuminates why oysters taste so differently depending on where they have lived. Or why the taste of a lobster cooked in its Maine seawater is nonpareil. All those oysters filtering and concentrating the waters of the place they inhabit into their bodies yield the true taste of that place. When people talk about terroir (the specific taste of a parcel of land) or merroir (the taste of a specific marine place) what they are talking about is the taste of osmoconformity. Nothing makes me happier than to have a bag of two or three different types of oysters thrown down on a table with a couple of knives in hand, and then delve into studying the intricacies of the osmoconformity of the Maine coast with a glass of steely chardonnay to reset my palate before the next "experiment."

Fish, unlike oysters, are travelers and need to adapt to changes in salinity. Biologists call them osmoregulators, meaning they have the capacity to regulate the salinity of the water they ingest. Bony fish actively lower the ionic concentration of the water as its being filtered through their gills using chlorine compounds that dissolve marine salts and remove them from the water before they ingest it.

Cartilaginous fish evolved a more passive, "If you can't beat 'em, join 'em" approach, but without going so far as becoming osmoconformers. Their technique is to pre-emptively pump high levels of dissolved salts into their circulatory system so that ingested seawater doesn't raise the salt concentrations in their blood. To do this they use salts produced by their own body, urea, a product of their protein metabolism. They are able to maintain high but different ionic levels from the surrounding seawater.

When bony fish die, the flesh remains stable for some time especially when well iced. The cartilaginous fish present a challenge to chefs because when they die, the ionic pump dies too. The urea, with nowhere to go, begins to break down and is released as ammonia. With a few too many days of age on it, skate turns from toothsome and succulent to mushy, bitter, smelling like a Camembert, well beyond *au point* (the French term for the moment when a cheese is perfectly ripe), and with a tacky quality, pieces sticking together, as if glued. Turnover is key, not only in our kitchen but the turnover of the fish supplier and others up the supply chain as well. Skate that came into the restaurant yesterday may or may not be yesterday's skate, depending on how business was for the fishmonger. Every day in the kitchen presents strategic triage decisions that have to be made. Good enough to serve to customers? Good enough to serve for family meal? Only good for the garbage can? Wearing the differing hats of chef and financial comptroller, at times two competing voices say "Serve the fish" and "Toss the fish." Pay the bills, or sate the customer. Sometimes you can do both but there are times when you can't.

In the first year of Savoy, my friend Noel, a man of discerning taste, came in for dinner. I was going into the weekend with some dubious skate. I knew it was borderline but I didn't know how borderline. Vladimir Horowitz, the famed pianist, once said about not practicing, one day he noticed, two days the critics noticed, and three days the public noticed. I served Noel up the skate hoping it was day one on the Horowitz scale. In fact Noel thought it was day three fish and was furious that I used him to determine acceptability in the dining room. He was angry with me for not treating his dining experience as of importance, but more significantly for not showing a higher standard of professionalism because a chef's reputation is at stake with every meal. Ashamed, I deepened my commitment to ask myself the tough question that has to be asked over and over again, every day in the kitchen. Is this food good enough to serve? Is it burnt or is it just a dark spot? Is the overdressed salad gloppy and inedible or just heavily dressed? Rarely was the total value of a tray of ammoniated skate greater than the revenues from one or two skate entrées. But it's hard to bite the bullet and just toss it all in the trash bin. It signifies a defeat, a failure to properly manage inventory.

Recently I went to a restaurant and ordered the skate. Out came a small heap of skate on a mound of vegetables, not on the bone, several thin fillets glued together in a worrisome telltale pile. It was not joyful to eat in any way, bitter without a drop of sweetness or succulence. I pushed it around on the plate, eating small bits to provide some counterpoint to the chickpea stew that came with it, wanting to taste the idea of the dish, but to no avail. I was unhappy. I stopped eating, disappointed, and reflected back on my Horowitz moment from many years before. Who more than me would know and would taste the difference? I was trying to figure out what to say or how to say it, when I saw the chef at the bar speaking with a couple who also seemed to be unhappy. It turned out they had sent back their skate. Confirmation: day three on the Horowitz scale. The CFO had prevailed. All I could taste was disappointment and the breach of trust in my mouth.

I wish I could say that I learned that lesson unequivocally on that day with Noel more than two decades ago, but the tension never disappears. Maintaining financial health in the restaurant business is a constant challenge. Predicting and maintaining proper staffing levels, ordering and prepping the right amount of food without wasting ingredients or shortening their shelf life, never stops being a challenge. Every day, all day, judgment calls need to be made, ones that balance the chef and CFO.

So go buy some skate, one wing is plenty for dinner for two. I recently paid $2.50 for a large and super fresh one at my fishmonger. Have them skin off the top rough and slimy skin. The bottom white one you can just leave on. Being cartilaginous, skate wings are kind of easy to cut through if you want to portion them. Lean on your knife with both hands and it will pass through the cartilage. To cook them season with salt and pepper and then sear the wings in a pan; stick it in the oven to finish cooking. Make a roughly cut moist stew of fennel and tomato, maybe some red or green pepper, spoon a rubble of olives, fennel seed, and parsley on top, drizzle with great olive oil, and you've got something really nice. Or cook it in a broth with some of your favorite osmoconformers—clams or mussels—and swirl in some pesto at the end to tighten the broth into sauce. Whichever way you prepare it, use your fork to pull the muscle fibers off the bone and drag them through the broth and into your mouth. Now that is some good eating.

SKATE ON THE BONE
IN FENNEL-CAPER STEW

SERVES 2 AS A MAIN COURSE

Skate is easy to cook and stays moist whether it is sautéed in butter or stewed in a pot. I prefer to cook it on the bone as it easily pulls away from the bone when you eat it. Look for skate with the rough top-skin already removed, or ask your fishmonger to do it for you. Some skate wings can be quite large so feel free to cut it into the portions you desire. The cartilage is soft—if you cut the top flesh with your knife and then lean hard on the knife it can be easily divided. This stew is but one of many flavorful stews you could create to cook the skate in.

Olive oil, for sautéing
1 medium onion, thinly sliced
2 cloves garlic, thinly sliced
½ cup (90 g) chopped plum tomato
½ cup (120 ml) white wine
1 fennel bulb, trimmed and thinly sliced
1 tablespoon capers
½ teaspoon dried oregano
2 tablespoons chopped parsley
1 pound skate (2 small wings, or 1 large wing cut in half)
Salt and freshly ground black pepper
1 tablespoon unsalted butter

Cover the bottom of a wide sauté pan with olive oil. Over medium heat, sauté the onion and garlic until the onion is soft and translucent. Add the tomato and cook down until most of the liquid has evaporated. Pour in the wine and continue to cook until the liquid is reduced by half. Add the fennel, capers, oregano, and 1 tablespoon of the parsley. Simmer for 5 minutes. Lay the skate wings on top of the stew, cover, and turn the heat down to low. Cook for 8 to 10 minutes, until the flesh is opaque but still pink at the bone. Remove the skate with a spatula and hold. Taste the broth and adjust the seasoning with salt and pepper. Swirl in the butter off the heat. Lay the broth down on a plate and place the skate on top. Sprinkle with the remaining tablespoon of parsley.

PASSOVER

Both my parents were Jewish. I guess that made me Jewish, with an emphasis on the -ish. I didn't feel like it was a religion or community I belonged to. Only in my mid-thirties, celebrating Passover in my restaurant, did I happen into a fascinatingly diverse world of Jewish cultures and then proudly and publicly embrace my heritage.

I was born into a nonpracticing household, dominated by my father's rationalist atheistic views, even if rationality was at times in short ration. My dad, who had been targeted for being Jewish in boarding school and college, had complete disdain for believers in any faith. He didn't deny his heritage but didn't celebrate it either. My dad's insistence on not being a joiner or valuing a sense of belonging translated into distance and isolation for me, from practicing Jews and non-Jews.

Coming home bewildered after the first day of kindergarten, I asked why everyone else could recite the Lord's Prayer. I lost no time in memorizing the jumble of words, but barely a year later, the Supreme Court abolished prayer in public schools. My parents kept us out of school for Rosh Hashanah and Yom Kippur ("because we are Jewish"), yet we didn't go to temple, eat challah, or fast on Yom Kippur like all the other Jewish kids. My paternal grandparents cowered rather than challenge my dad and my observant maternal grandparents didn't approve of this approach and occasionally expressed disappointment about my lack of Jewish education. In contrast, my cousins across town were members of the local synagogue, spent Saturday mornings learning Jewish history and traditions, and enjoyed a social circle connected to that community. Certain friends alerted me that their parents didn't consider me "a real Jew" because I didn't go to temple. We lit Chanukah candles and left juice out for Santa under a small tree. My connection to both the Christian and the Jewish worlds was tenuous. I was on the outside looking in on both, belonging to neither.

Passover was different. Each year, we celebrated the holiday at my grandparents' house, with a traditional recounting of the Exodus story from Egypt. As refugees from Hitler's Germany, the holiday was particularly poignant for them.

To recount the Exodus story, Jews don't read directly from the Old Testament. They use a text called a hagadah, literally meaning "the retelling" and a plate called the Seder plate, "the order" filled with various symbolic foods that offer talking points to structure the ceremony. Passover is a holiday celebrated at home, around the table; synagogue attendance is not required and the story is left open to personal interpretation—key factors that gave my dad license to embrace the holiday.

Hagadahs come in various forms, from ones that were given away free by Maxwell Coffee House beginning before World War II, an early marketing effort in hopes of being the drink of choice at the meal's conclusion, to present-day versions written by leftist organizations with readings about various liberation struggles: the African-American civil rights movement in the sixties; the women's movement; gay rights; and most controversial, the Palestinian struggle for recognition and statehood in Gaza and the West Bank. It is a fluid document lending itself to improvisation with everyone able to contribute important quotes or songs.

Discussion, even argument, is encouraged, with the bulk of it occurring before dinner. Some versions have four different historical rabbis arguing about the meaning of each of the prescribed Four Questions, which meant having to listen to sixteen interpretative answers to some very simple questions. I remember being infinitely bored: hiding under the table; occasionally looking at the woodcut prints in the Maxwell House version; anxious to know how soon we would be getting to the eating part of the evening. The Seder plate has lots of "foods" on it, none of which are meant to satisfy hunger: a roasted lamb bone, a pile of fresh herbs, a bowl of salted water, and a hard-boiled egg. But there is a fruit and nut mixture called haroses, symbolizing the mortar enslaved Jews used to make the Pyramids, a miracle snack that tides over everyone's hunger until dinner. Ashkenazi Jews from Germany, Poland, and Russia make theirs with chopped apples and walnuts, sweet spices, and a splash of wine. Mediterranean or Sephardic Jews use dried fruit to make their haroses, usually dates or figs and almonds. Always eaten on a piece of matzoh, the flat cracker symbolizing the unrisen bread made by the fleeing Jews, haroses is an oasis in a desert of words and prayers and a godsend for anyone with a short attention span. Towards the end, when dinner is finally approaching, there is a lively moment when everyone reads in a call-and-response pattern a summarization of the miracles that the Jews endured in the course of the Exodus. With each miracle named, everyone shouts out "*Dayenu!*" meaning "That would have been enough." "*Dayenu.* It's time to eat."

After leaving home, I realized that I felt untethered if I didn't celebrate the holiday. Once, I knocked relentlessly on the door of the rabbi in Aix-en-Provence, not realizing that this was forbidden during Sabbath, desperate to be matched with a family willing to take in this wandering Jew on a bicycle. Finally paired with an Algerian Jewish chiropractor and his family, I ate my first date haroses and slept on the treatment table before hitting the road in the morning. During my single New York years, I would often celebrate the first night with family and then gather with friends for less traditional Seders on the second. We began gathering readings about fights for freedom over time and around the globe and discussing the idea of Passover less as a religious holiday and more as a holiday celebrating liberation struggles.

When I was trying to summon the courage to dive into the Savoy project and commit to a lease and a concept, I was overwhelmed by fears about how it might (or might not) work out, to the point of near paralysis. I found the needed advice in the Passover story, specifically in the story of Nachshon. As the Jews were fleeing Egypt and came to the Red Sea with the Egyptian army in close pursuit, they felt trapped and were afraid to attempt a crossing. The common story is that divine intervention miraculously parted the sea and showed the Jews a path to escape. But the Old Testament recounts that an elder named Nachshon trusted that irrespective of the outcome, there was no choice but to trust that things would work out and he waded into the water. Only then did the other Jews trust that the waters were shallow enough to cross (or God intervened) and they discovered a path to safety. Not usually included in most hagadahs, I first encountered Nachshon reading Michael Walzer's *Exodus and Revolution*, a left-wing interpretation of the biblical journey (my dad begrudgingly approved).

Nachshon's courage was inspirational for me—diving into unknown waters was imperative if I was going to create the future I envisioned. Maybe if I had attended synagogue, listening to a rabbi sermonize after a Saturday morning Torah reading, I would have internalized this lesson but instead it took until my thirties to find Walzer's book and the courage to make this huge leap of faith.

The first Passover that our fledgling restaurant was open, I was uncomfortable leaving the restaurant to celebrate with family or closing for the night and losing vital revenue. I was also vaguely concerned about revealing my Jewishness to my new and developing customer base. Not that I ever hid my Judaism but closing for a Jewish holiday felt too Jewy; that was for orthodox businesses on the Lower East Side. I wanted to be a nondenominational chef-owner who just happened to be Jewish. Yet, staying open on that first night of Passover hurt my heart.

I shared my conflict with Deb, another Jewish cook in the kitchen, who suggested we quickly pull together the elements of the Seder plate in time for staff meal, that short, inhale-your-food meal period from 5:00 to 5:30 P.M. I sent a server to go buy a box of matzoh; Deb gathered herbs, chopped apples, and nuts into a quick haroses; I roasted a lamb bone, boiled an egg, and grated some horseradish. If matzoh was created because the fleeing Jews didn't have time to let the bread dough rise, then we reenacted that haste explaining Passover and telling the Exodus story in the thirty minutes allotted for family meal with enough time remaining to discuss the evening specials. Most of my employees had never been to a Seder and enjoyed this swift, if novel exposure to the Jewish tradition. Rushing back to my station to get set up for dinner service while happily noshing on haroses matzoh sandwiches, I realized that this was an experience worth sharing with others, maybe even customers. One of the final statements at the Seder is "next year in Jerusalem," as a way of committing to working towards the goal of liberation of all people. For my part, I committed to "next year at Savoy."

For reasons that I no longer completely recall, "next year" actually took three (among other interruptions was the arrival of our first born), but in the spring of 1994 we transformed our staff meal Passover into a dinner open to the public. Committing to a date was easy; figuring out what to cook was not. For a holiday that was supposed to be about breaking free from bondage, my family had stayed pretty tied up by tradition, serving the same fare, year in and year out: gefilte fish, matzoh ball soup, beef brisket, and apple matzoh cake. Even my iconoclastic father enthusiastically toed the traditional line and prepared his braised beef brisket each year. As satisfying and familiar as those dishes were, I needed culinary liberation from that dull and mostly brown palette. I had no interest in cheffing up the recipes by adding foie gras to the matzoh balls or clarifying the broth into consommé. Instead, what occurred to me was that since Savoy was exploring Mediterranean flavors, we should cook the food of the Mediterranean Jews, the Sephardic Jews, those who were cast out from Spain in 1492 during the Inquisition. Once I stumbled on the notion, I realized that this might be a fascinating exploration, broadening my understanding of what Jewish food is and by extension what being Jewish looks like. I was going to get a Jewish education after all.

I found two cookbooks on the subject, *Sephardic Cooking* by Copeland Marks and *Cookbook of the Jews of Greece* by Nicholas Stavroulakis. Claudia Roden's *The Book of Jewish Food* was still several more years away, but it now sports more Post-its than any other cookbook I own, and became an indispensable historical and culinary guide for my Seder menus. From Copeland Marks I gleaned the broad strokes of geography and flavor profiles throughout the Sephardic world (his actual recipes were dreadful) and Stavroulakis forever liberated me from apple and walnut haroses with his recipe using pine nuts, almonds, dried currants, and dates. It quickly became a Savoy classic and each year we printed copies of the recipe for all our customers. That first menu was a pan-Mediterranean tour of Sephardic dishes, from Morocco and Libya to Greece and Syria. It was joyous and exciting to be exploring and cooking Jewish food I had never tasted, much less knew existed. People booked reservations, everyone was seated communally, and we placed the Seder plates as well as the first-course mezze platters family-style, for every eight or ten people. I read from a hagadah that I had cobbled together with heavy reliance on Walzer. One guest, the food historian and writer Raymond Sokolov, stood up and extemporaneously explained to everyone that *huevos haminados*, one of our mezze items, were eggs slowly cooked in the dying fireplace embers in Spanish Jewish homes during Sabbath, when no work was allowed. Often a slow-cooking stew with chickpeas was also placed in the fireplace and then served for dinner on Saturday night at the end of Sabbath. Ironically the very people who expelled the Jews from Spain came to appropriate this chickpea stew as their own, proclaiming it *cocido madrileño*, the classic soup of Madrid. Many Jews who chose to remain in Spain began adding pork to their *cocido* in hopes of demonstrating to the inquisitors that they had converted to Christianity (yet still secretly practicing Judaism). They were known as Marranos, or pork eaters. Inspired by a couple of slow-roasted eggs, everyone had received a poignant history lesson. Who knew?

Listening to this fascinating tale, my sister, Judy, leaned over and whispered to me that I should organize evenings of talking and eating around food history, maybe even asking Ray to be a speaker. This was the genesis of the dinner series, a program I developed and ran for over fifteen years (and will discuss in more detail later). Passover quickly became my favorite restaurant holiday, surpassing the arbitrary but de rigueur New Year's Eve, the cash cow Thanksgiving that requires a week of military precision to properly execute, and the ever-so precious hushed couples' night of Valentine's Day. The holiday was a feast around communal tables abundant with boldly flavored food and important ideas underpinning it as well. Each year I would compose a menu that broke with the stereotypes of what Jewish food is and proclaim, "*This* is Jewish food," "*This* is Jewish food," and "*This too* is Jewish food." After nearly forty years of thinking that the choice was either Ratner's Dairy or the 2nd Avenue Deli, the existence of an alternate universe of flavors was thrilling. Stuffed grape leaves with tomato apricot sauce, artichokes in honey and lemon, fried eggplant with mango pickles—all of this was Jewish food. Which reminds me of an old joke the playwright Arthur Miller would tell. Benjamin Levine, a guy in the schmatta trade, goes to Shanghai on business. Knowing that there are Jews in China he searches out the local synagogue. After finding it and sitting through a service, Benjamin approaches the Chinese rabbi, introduces himself, and tells him he's a Jew. The rabbi gives him the once-over and says, "Funny, you don't look Jewish."

Each spring brought an opportunity for me to explore the cuisine of a different Jewish community. Some Jewish dishes are the foods of the surrounding region, shared in common between Jews and non-Jews. These are foods of a place, not of a religion: Tunisian *mechouia*, grilled red peppers and tomatoes; Iraqi kofte or kefta, seasoned lamb meatballs, and Rome's *carciofi alla Giudia*, fried artichokes in olive oil, are all examples of this. Our food and our traditions derive from where we live. Other dishes though, were different from the surrounding culture, specific to the Jewish community and reflective of their history and otherness, an expression of exclusion or expulsion. We served Greek *boumwelos*, matzoh fritters soaked in honey syrup, a remnant of the very popular Spanish buñelos, transported to Greece by Jews who left Spain during the Inquisition and specific to the Jews of Rhodes and Salonika. I was getting my Jewish education after all, one Passover meal at a time.

The link between our culinary choices and expressions of liberation and freedom struggles didn't find their way onto the menu until Passover 2003, barely a month after President George W. Bush began the Iraqi invasion. I thought that maybe if we cooked and ate the food of the people we were demonizing we might feel some compassion for and tolerance of "our enemy." There is a wonderful moment in the Exodus story after the Egyptian army drowns in the Red Sea when God says, "Are not these my people too." Which I translated as "Is not their food, my food?" That year's Passover menu celebrated Iraqi Jewish food including: *saluna*, sweet-and-sour fish cakes; *kofta mishmisheya*, lamb meatballs in dried lime tomato sauce; and *muhallabeya*, milk pudding with cardamom and rose water. Sadly, our country's interventions in and vilification of other nations didn't stop with Iraq. It seemed as if with each new foreign policy declaration, the U.S. government just kept offering new cuisines and nations for me to cook: Yemen in 2004, Afghanistan in 2005, Iran in 2007, and Syria in 2009.

All we were missing from completing a culinary tour of Bush's Axis of Evil was a Korean Seder menu. In 2010 I considered the tour complete. Researching that year's Uzbeki menu I ate a raw carrot salad at a Jewish Bukharan restaurant in Rego Park, Queens that resembled kimchi, seasoned with raw garlic, hot chile pepper, and vinegar. I learned that in the 1930s, Stalin had deported four hundred thousand naturalized Koreans from Siberian territory and dumped them in Uzbekistan and Kazakhstan to fend for themselves. Tens of thousands died but Uzbeki residents (some of whom were Jewish) incorporated the carrot salad into their cuisine. It lives on in Queens. Serving the salad and telling the story to all our Passover guests gave voice to the story and kept alive other peoples' struggles against injustice.

I developed a Savoy hagadah, offering extemporaneous commentary on the parallels between today's labor and immigration issues and the Jewish experience in Egypt. All the diners had an opportunity to contribute their ideas about what today's ten plagues might be and I made sure that the first glass of the four glasses of wine we drank was dedicated to farmers and farmworkers, the growers and producers of our food, our sustenance, our wealth. Every year the first wine of the evening was a Txacoli, wine from Basque Spain, the ancestral home of the Sephardic Jews prior to that expulsion. I eschewed drinking kosher wines, instead always curating a mix of wines from Spain, Lebanon, and Morocco.

The holiday became so popular that I began booking both the upstairs and the downstairs dining rooms, and read the hagadah in each room separated by forty-five minutes. The Passover menu also ran all week long à la carte, so that people could come in and enjoy the dishes free of all the ceremonial Seder trappings.

I became known for organizing these Sephardic cuisine Seders with a political bent, even appearing on the Food Network and writing about them for *Food & Wine* magazine; they had become core to what the restaurant was and actually who I was. In opening the map up of what and where Jewish food came from, I also opened up the range of possibility for myself to what being Jewish could look like. Gefilte fish and brisket haven't been served at the family table for well over twenty years but cold poached fish with zhoug, spicy Yemenite green sauce, has. I had become a Jew with conviction, finding a practice around the table at Passover celebrating Jewish food and history with friends, family, and strangers. If this is what belonging to a community looked like, then *dayenu*; that was enough.

ZHOUG

I discovered zhoug in Claudia Roden's deeply researched The Book of Jewish
Food. *Like salsa verde or chimichurri on overdrive, it quickly became a Savoy
classic. According to Gil Avital, our longtime Israeli manager at Savoy, Yemenite
Jews emigrated to Israel in the sixties bringing this sauce with them. Usually
fiery hot, adjust the jalapeño dosage to your taste. I love it drizzled in a broth
with poached fish and spring vegetables, but it is delicious over tomatoes or
grilled steak.*

1 teaspoon caraway seeds
6 cardamom pods, hulls removed
6 cloves garlic
6 to 8 green jalapeño chiles (depending on your heat preference),
    halved lengthwise, seeds and white ribs removed, chopped
2 cups (80 g) loosely packed cilantro leaves and stems
½ teaspoon salt
½ teaspoon black pepper
½ cup (120 ml) olive oil

1. Make this with a mortar and pestle or a food processor. If using a mortar and pestle, begin by grinding the caraway and cardamom seeds,
   then add the garlic and mash to incorporate. Add the chiles, cilantro,
   salt, and black pepper. Incorporate, then add in the oil.
2. If using a food processor, first grind the seeds in a spice mill. Put the
   ground spices in a food processor with the garlic and whiz. Then add
   the chiles and whiz until roughly chopped. Add the cilantro and whiz
   to incorporate. Season with the salt and black pepper, add the oil, and
   whiz until the sauce is emulsified.
3. Keeps in the refrigerator for a day or two before the herbs lose
   their vibrancy.

STRAWBERRIES

The most delicious strawberries I have ever eaten don't come in a perforated plastic clamshell trucked in from Watsonville, California, nor are they *fraises des bois* in a fancy wooden box flown over from Europe looking as if they just jumped out of a Flemish still life. These small and deeply fragrant berries have a brief June season—when countless other farmstands from New Jersey and Long Island are flooded with berries, only to disappear after the June flush—and come on even stronger in late August and September. Barely able to make the three-hour journey from the Delaware River watershed to the Union Square Greenmarket in New York City, they get snatched off the table during the course of a few hours and devoured in a matter of days. There is no backup inventory held in refrigerated vaults at the city's Hunts Point wholesale produce market. Their shelf life is short but that's the point; they are that good. Known as Tristars, because the plant produces fruit during three seasons; spring, summer, and fall, the berry is grown almost exclusively in the Catskill Mountains of New York and remains virtually unknown outside the region.

Growing up, apples, oranges, and bananas were the only fruit constants in our home. Strawberries were seasonal—even celebratory—the first fruit of the growing season. No doubt there were berries coming in from Florida in February or California in April, but they probably cost a lot, didn't taste like much, and my thrifty, taste-sensitive mom never bought them. But come June, she would carry home from the grocer quarts of berries in the green paper pulp baskets that still signify "farm grown." We would clamor to eat as many as we could before she slipped the rest into a pot and cooked them down with rhubarb. It always seemed a shame to cook them into that magenta ooze, even though I liked the taste. Another household favorite was vanilla ice cream, topped with sliced berries and a splash of kirsch schnapps for the grown-ups (and qualifying rising grown-ups). Those desserts were fleeting. Strawberries went out of season as fast as they came in and my mom shifted our attention to blueberries and then later to peaches and plums.

The strawberry has held great allure for centuries. Beginning with early Renaissance paintings depicting the Virgin Mary in forests carpeted with white flowers and drooping blood red fruits, strawberries have represented the hard to attain purity and innocence, fragile morsels that only devotion to God can offer. Their fragrance and delicate sweetness tugged at gardeners' hearts and tongues even in the face of being finicky to grow and highly perishable. Unlike apples and pears, which hold for months in cool cellar storage, or grapes, which can be fermented into wine, strawberries were always a fleeting indulgence, never a staple to depend on.

The European woodland berry, known as *fraise des bois* in French, and scientifically as *Fragaria vesca*, resisted improvement by breeding. Even after centuries of sustained efforts by royal gardeners in England and France, the berries remained unsuitable for commercial production because of their small size and low output. It was only after the voyages to the Western Hemisphere, when two different species of strawberries were introduced, did things begin to change. The North American Virginia berry, *Fragaria virginiana*, brought to France in 1624, was hardy, able to sustain heat, drought, and cold winters, which meant that it could be widely grown. But its yields were low and the berries still small. In 1714, a French reconnaissance officer brought back several strawberry plants from the sandy Chilean coastline, *Fragaria chiloensis*, which yielded a large berry but could only be grown in mild coastal regions. In 1764, an accidental marriage of two New World species occurred in an old-world garden, crossing the Virginia plant with the Chilean one to produce *Fragaria ananassa*. All commercial strawberries today derive from that cross.

Breeding a commercially viable berry in North America took an additional hundred years and another sixty years to produce one with good flavor. This may seem like a long time until you consider that other new-world foods brought to old-world gardens had a head start of several millennia by South and Mesoamerican growers: potatoes for 10,000 years, peppers and beans for 5,000 to 6,000, and tomatoes for a piddling 2,500. Strawberries are new new-world plants and still in their breeding infancy.

The first major advance in strawberry breeding that I became aware of was in the early eighties. I was working in the high-end restaurant the Quilted

Giraffe when we started getting in huge, bright red berries in perfect pyramidal shapes. The explosion of food as theater, food as a fashion statement, was in full throttle and the crowning touch at every high society party was a platter of gargantuan, long-stemmed berries individually dipped in chocolate, sometimes alternating white and dark chocolate. We knew them as Driscoll's. We didn't know the meaning of what we were saying; that was our lingo. "Order three flats of Driscoll's." "Do you have enough Driscoll's for service tonight?" I said it breezily like I was asking someone to pass a box of Kleenex. We scoffed if our produce supplier would disappointingly deliver another "inferior" brand either as a bait and switch or because the Driscoll's weren't available that day. Little did we know but Driscoll was a company laying the groundwork to become the most widely recognized berry brand with rows and rows of clamshell boxes in varying berries and colors on supermarket shelves and national annual sales in excess of $2 billion.

The fashion crowd moved on from the long-stemmed berries, landing for a moment on baby vegetables, little pattypan and yellow squashes that looked impressive on the plate but didn't taste like much. My sensibility also shifted but in a different direction. Instead of calling in orders on the telephone, I began visiting the farmers' market. I traded Dover sole from Paris's Rungis market for striped bass from Montauk, Belgian endive for spicy, deep green arugula, and Driscoll's for day-neutrals—the greenmarket buzzword for the petite, incredibly flavorful berries that a couple of guys were selling at one end of another farmer's table. "Day-neutral" became my new strawberry vocabulary, also with no idea what the term meant. "Got any day-neutrals?" had replaced "Got any Driscoll's." I was just parroting sounds.

I finally inquired of Rick Bishop—one of the guys subletting the end of the other farmer's table—what the term "day-neutrals" actually meant. Rick cuts an Olympian stature—ringlets of blond hair, an athlete's body with a dancer's grace, and fingers thick and muscular, cracked and encrusted with soil from years of fieldwork. Thirty years later, Rick is still bringing those berries to market and still has a magician's sparkle in his eyes.

Known to compete with other growers for the highest sugar content by comparing Brix sugar readings on his pocket refractometer, Rick treats farming as an ongoing science experiment as much as an economic enterprise. A graduate of the Cornell pomology department, he keeps data on the yield performance of successive plantings and gives customers a crash course in plant genetics or soil science while weighing a bag of peas. Most of all, he loves singing the praises of his breeders. "Come taste the beauty and music of Frank Morton in these lettuces" (a seed nurseryman in Philomath, Oregon) he said one day. Later, he mourned the recent passing of Calvin Lamborn, the pea breeder who developed the modern sugar snap pea. In 2015, celebrating his thirtieth season of growing the Tristar berry, Rick stamped every craft paper bag for toting away the berries with an image of Eugene Galletta, the Maryland breeder who developed it.

With a white ten-foot-square pop-up tent as his classroom and a table piled high with produce as a lectern, Rick shares botanical tales that conjure up the wonders of agriculture. His infectious storytelling and generously shared wisdom has lured several hardened New Yorkers into becoming farmers. There is an added bounce in his movements and a twinkling side glance meant to snag your attention while he's bagging up berries, making change, grabbing fistfuls of lettuce to put in plastic bags before coming back to finish today's lesson plan. Assisting the professor to help stay on point, I often step behind the stand and perform the same duties along with offering cooking tips on beans and potatoes.

Commercial growers and breeders have long sought to turn the strawberry into a year-round crop, a staple in everyone's refrigerator, joining the shelf-stable pantheon of the apple, banana, and orange. In order to do this, they needed to extend the season for the berries and prolong their shelf life. Extremely sensitive to light and temperature, strawberries don't produce flowers when the days are long or the weather is hot. The berries my mom brought home ripen in June and early July, with a different variety fruiting for about a week or so. Once that fruiting moment is over, the plants put their energy into vegetative growth, producing leaves and runners and stop flowering. Runners are exact replicas of the mother plant, clones to put it another way, and allow the plant to reproduce asexually. At summer's end, the dropping temperature and the shortening day length signals the plants to shift their growth into sexual reproduction—setting flower buds for the following spring. Apples and pears, strawberry's cousins in the rose family, also set their following year's buds in the late summer and early fall. Most strawberry plants only set flowers once, at this time of the year. Day-neutral,

Rick revealed, meant that regardless of the day's length, the plants continue to bud and fruit throughout the late spring and summer. In order to produce a September berry, the plants need to flower just as the days are lengthening in June, the time when most varieties are producing runners.

Before anyone was able to breed a day-neutral berry, breeders tinkered with the plant's clock in other ways. Since June varieties focus their fruit production into about a week's time, breeders looked to stagger the timing of each variety's peak production, developing varieties that would ripen slightly earlier or later than the norm. This broadened a single farm's season to about six weeks of production. This was true for the West Coast growers as well but given the mild Mediterranean climactic coastline, the season could be staggered by growing in a range of locations that ranged from as far north as Washington State all the way down to Baja, Mexico. The bulk of production has always been in Central Coast California, around Watsonville.

Growers also realized that they could temporarily stop the plant's clock by keeping the plants "conditioned," essentially refrigerated, extending their winter dormancy before being transplanted into the field. This was a way of delaying the growing cycle and pushing the window of productivity further into the season before it got too hot and the days too long. But none of these ploys were enough to really establish the fresh strawberry as a year-round staple in people's homes. Day sensitivity needed to be overcome in order to accomplish that.

The key to cracking the problem was not found in a breeding lab but rather high in the Wasatch Mountains of Utah. While on summer vacation hiking in Big Cottonwood Canyon of Utah's Wasatch Mountains, UC Davis's brilliant breeder Royce Bringhurst found a single flowering plant under a ski lift. In spite of growing at high altitude and with a short growing season—bracketed by late snow melt and early winter onset—this individual plant had evolved to continue flowering throughout the long midsummer days. This was just the trait breeders needed. Bringhurst had long suspected that the day-neutral trait would be found in wild strawberry plants, particularly in a species found only in the Rocky Mountains. Thought to be its own distinct species, *Fragaria ovalis*, the Rocky Mountain species later turned out to be genetically identical to the Virginia berry, *F. virginiana*, and has since been reclassified as a subspecies. Having been geographically isolated for so long, it had evolved independently of the rest of the North American *F. virginiana* population.

For both coastal California and continental growers this discovery offered a treasure trove of diverse genetic material to weave into the narrow Chilean-Virginia blend that everyone had been working with for the last two hundred years. Bringhurst began breeding trials at Davis for the California climate but shared the crucial plant material with his colleague Eugene Galletta at the USDA facility in Beltsville, Maryland, who focused on selecting for conditions in the Appalachian range and northern Midwest. Thus began a race that fundamentally shifted the industry.

When breeders use selection to improve a plant or an animal, they prioritize which traits to accentuate over others. Sometimes through luck, like finding a summer-flowering berry plant on a ski slope, but more often through the painstaking method of growing out thousands of trial samples, plant geneticists have altered all the fruits, vegetables, livestock, and poultry we eat, as well as the flowers we raise in our gardens and the pets we cherish in our homes. Not all desirable traits can be selected for in a single breeding strain. For example, in selecting cows to produce a high volume of milk, butterfat content and nutritional value declined. You can't have everything. There's always a trade-off.

Commercial growers tend to want qualities that guarantee income or at least preserve income. Yield (how much food can be grown per acre), shelf life (how long can food be held), size of the item (how can the harvest be maximized and labor minimized), as well as a few other qualities that may not be apparent to consumers like disease resistance, winter hardiness, or firmness (how much mistreatment in shipping and handling the food can withstand), are qualities breeders select for. Flavor is somewhere on the list but rarely high.

California growers were committed to developing a national market for their day-neutral berries and cared foremost about qualities having to do with size and longevity. It's no surprise then that Bringhurst, working at UC Davis and receiving funding from the California Strawberry Advisory Board, focused his work on bringing day neutrality into berries that were shelf stable for seven to ten days and could consistently pass the USDA grade A size requirement that berries not be less than three-fourth inches in diameter; traits derived from the Chilean, less flavorful side of the family. Built for battle, California berries were short on taste, long on durability, hardly a sensuous eating experience. But they met the specs and goals of the growers. Bringhurst's California day-neutral was released in 1979.

Eugene Galletta, on the other hand, working in Maryland developing berries appropriate for northeastern and midwestern farms, chose to sacrifice shelf life and berry size in favor of flavor. Growing out and testing over twenty thousand plants, flavor and acidity were paramount for him; traits more easily accessible from the Virginia side of the family. He achieved great flavor, fragrance, and day neutrality but he failed to breed a berry large enough to meet USDA grade A standards. This meant his berries would never be embraced by larger commercial growers and instead were pegged as best for gardeners or small growers. Galletta's berries, the Tristar and the Tribute, were released in 1981, just about the time that Bringhurst's berries were beginning to flood New York's high-end kitchens as Driscoll's.

Working the stand for Rick I experience that, contrary to what gets sold in supermarkets, New Yorkers approach the table repeatedly asking for the small berries. Whether it's because there is a good mix of European shoppers who are familiar with small berries from back home or because Rick has trained his customers to be comfortable with the small berry, valuing flavor over size, is hard to say. Some customers even complain if the pints are filled with too many "king" berries, the first and largest of the eight to twelve shoots that come off the plant's crown.

Rick learned a lot of ag science at Cornell, but he also shrewdly analyzed the marketplace and the fundamental problems that beset farmers. Every farmer knows that the surest way to not make any money is to be long on a commodity when everyone else is long on it too. High supply coupled with flat demand means that market prices drop. It happens every tomato season—you can't give them away at a certain point in August. Rick has pursued off-season items and oddball varieties that curious cooks and chefs would be intrigued by. Over the decades, he has settled on a few to hone: fingerling potatoes, a superlative cooking tomato, a dried bean from the Po River valley in Italy that is creamier than anything I've ever tasted, and the Tristar berry, the key component in this strategy since it really kicks in when the tomato season is winding down.

New Jersey and Long Island farmers may have longer growing seasons, but they can't grow the Tristars because Galletta wasn't able to breed temperature sensitivity out of the berries. In the high heat of summer, the plants shut down and stop producing fruit. Up in the Catskills, Rick and a few others come to market with fruit that is actually enhanced by the cool mountain nights, its complex flavors deepening, the sugars slowly increasing. Growing fruit at the edge of their viable range can produce extraordinary flavors. Champagne growers know this better than most. They grow chardonnay and pinot noir at the extreme northern limits of where the vines can survive and still ripen. It's hard to argue with this approach given the prices that people pay for Krug or Cristal.

Most careful winemakers will tell you that complex flavors develop in slowly maturing fruit, the result of warm days paired with cool nights. Rick's June berries are exciting because they are the first fruits of the market season; his August berries are more than passable but when a cold snap came through the other night, bringing temperatures down to 37°F on the first of September, the sugars in the berries that Saturday skyrocketed. Normally we think of ripening and sweetness as increasing with sustained heat but increased sugars due to cold is not as counterintuitive as it might seem. It's the maple sugar process in a hyper-condensed time frame. During daytime photosynthesis, sugar is produced in the leaves and driven down into the roots for storage overnight. During a subsequent warm day, the sugars come back up the plant and into the berry. Lucky us.

Wine growers also know that great flavor is not just about gunning for high sugars and ripeness in their grapes. Proper acidity matters too, a factor not lost on most good cooks. I ask myself if the acid level is right in a dish as often as I consider if the salt levels are right. A sauce might have great depth of flavor, richness, and complexity, but if the acidity is too low, it tastes flat or even feels heavy. A dash of vinegar or a squeeze of fresh lemon juice enlivens our mouths, bringing vibrancy to the sauce and life to the dish. That's the beauty of Galletta's Tristar; there's sweetness, acid, delicacy, and allure—the magic of Wasatch Mountain wildness. In every pristine pint I experience a gift: from the grower, from the breeder, and from the climate where they grow.

California won the berry race. It's found in every hotel's complimentary breakfast, sold in every supermarket, but it is also hard, flat in flavor, white in the center and grown so large that it takes several bites to gnaw away at one, nothing you would rave about to a friend. But here in Union Square Greenmarket, Galletta's berries win hands down. Chefs pass through all morning picking up flats from the back of Rick's truck and all 208 flats that he and his crew of five picked over the last two days were sold out by 4 P.M. Pop one into your mouth, notice the fragrant, bracing candy that awakens the senses. It might take you back to your childhood, take you elsewhere to a garden where maybe you once picked berries, or take you inward savoring how sweet the fruit is and how good it is to be alive.

In the kitchen I prefer to get out of the way and let the berries speak for themselves. Sliced and spooned over freshly made goat cheese cheesecake or setting them atop a lemon panna cotta always made me happy. By far the best use we ever came up with for them was a cocktail created by Michael Cecconi at Savoy, called the Red and Black, after Stendahl's novel. It's essentially a strawberry margarita made with muddled Tristars and combined with tequila, black pepper syrup, and lime juice and finished with a salt, sugar, and black pepper rim. Make one or three and raise your glass to Gene Galletta and the trinity of excellence in agriculture: the breed, the grower, and the place. Small is indeed beautiful.

THE RED AND BLACK

MAKES 1 COCKTAIL

Named after Stendhal's novel by Savoy regular Henry Grosman, the Red and Black became the seasonal house drink. People knew to come around from June until October to enjoy this addictive cocktail. Developed by bar manager Michael Cecconi, it's a turn on a margarita that offers complex flavors and wonderfully drunken fruit at the bottom of the glass to slurp. Plan on making at least two rounds for each person. It's that good.

> 1 ounce Black Pepper Simple Syrup (recipe follows), plus more for
> dipping the rim
> Spice Rim Mix (recipe follows)
> 5 Tristar strawberries
> 2 ounces (60 ml) blanco or light reposado tequila
> 1 ounce fresh lime juice

1. Prepare the black pepper simple syrup and the spice rim mix a day ahead.
2. Dip the rim of a rocks glass in a shallow puddle of simple syrup, shake off excess syrup, and then dip the rim into the spice blend so the spice adheres over the entire rim. Set aside upright while you prepare the drink.
3. Carefully remove stems from strawberries, preserving as much of the flesh as possible. Using a spoon or a wooden muddler, roughly mash the strawberries in a cocktail shaker. It is not preferable to make a puree. Pour the tequila, lime juice, and syrup into the shaker. Add ice, shake, and pour cocktail into the spice-rimmed rocks glass.

BLACK PEPPER SIMPLE SYRUP

2 cups (480 ml) hot water
2 cups (400 g) sugar
¼ cup (25 g) freshly crushed black pepper

Combine all ingredients and stir until the sugar is dissolved. Allow to cool and then store in a Mason jar in the refrigerator for 24 hours. Strain through a fine-mesh sieve before using. Keeps for 2 weeks in the refrigerator.

SPICE RIM MIX

¾ cup (150 g) sugar
1½ tablespoons kosher salt
1 tablespoon freshly crushed black pepper

Put all the ingredients in a small bowl and toss to thoroughly combine. Keeps well unrefrigerated in a sealed container for at least 2 weeks.

FIREPLACE COOKING

What is it about fires? Why can we gaze endlessly into dying embers and speak truths or share dreams with the people we're sitting next to, with little sense of time? Fires are totally mesmerizing. Why else would Richard Nixon have lit a fire in the White House in D.C.'s sweltering August heat the night before resigning? What's roasting marshmallows on a camping trip all about if not finding a way for kids to safely engage with this fascination—initiates as both fledgling fire tenders and cooks.

I love everything about a real wood fire: gathering tinder; the one match challenge; smelling the resiny odors; hearing the cracks and snaps of burning logs; feeling the warmth from the slightest flame, an immediate antidote to the chill creeping in as the afternoon light fails. The smallest curl of smoke exiting a chimney announces that civilization is staked out here. People leap to call someone like me a pyro, as in a pyromaniac, which implies aberrant behavior, someone akin to an arsonist. On the contrary, I believe that part of our humanity is to love the magical transformation of the forest into heat and light. It's an alternate sun, an earthbound source of warmth and light. Call me a pyrophile.

Most of all, I love the taste of the fire in my food and the perfect dry roast obtained from fireplace cooking that no designer oven can ever offer. My first self-cooked meals were prepared on camping trips over an open fire. Those delicious meals—made even more delicious after hiking all day—had the added bonus of being prepared without the modern conveniences of a gas stove or a refrigerator and primed me for more culinary explorations. Beyond its immediate pleasures, being able to elicit a satisfying pot of oatmeal over a reluctant fire from damp wood, softened me up to all kinds of challenging conditions to come. It defined my outlook that I can cook anywhere, on anything, an attitude that has served me well. Fuel, pot, food, ignition: that's all I need to cook dinner. Anything else is a bonus.

Prior to taking possession of the Crosby Street space, I suspected that there might be a fireplace hidden behind the luncheonette's stainless steel wall lined with coffee urns and a flat griddle. There were fireplaces upstairs and my measurements confirmed a two-foot discrepancy between the exterior width of the building and its interior width. Upon getting the keys, I immediately suited up in the denim coveralls that would be my uniform for the next five months and pried away some of the grease-laden stainless steel on the back wall. Jackpot! There was a brick projection directly beneath the fireplace upstairs and open space in between two brick outcroppings indicating a hearth of some sort. I was ecstatic, triumphant even, although I knew hadn't accomplished much beyond a bit of demolition. But the discovery of the fireplace confirmed the worthiness of my site selection and fueled my excitement. It was a good omen to be sure.

I was convinced that it was worth having a real working fireplace in a New York City restaurant regardless of the renovation cost. Many tried to dissuade me, saying that a fireplace was an indulgence that would become more of a nuisance than a useful amenity. I knew otherwise and could not be deterred. Surely there were spots that had propane gas fireplaces with faux logs but very few that had the real thing. I knew that even a 10 percent increase in the construction budget would repay me many times over. It would be singular and go a long way towards communicating the openness, warmth, and lack of pretention we were trying to create. If the first smart thing I did was discovering this backwater location, then the second was committing to the restoration of the flue and chimney regardless of the cost. I knew intuitively that wood-burning fireplaces are not mere embellishments but anchors of civilization and comfort in a room. Ours would offer New Yorkers a marvelous reprieve from the harshness of urban life or the chilling winds barreling down Broadway.

Our restaurant did become that cherished refuge. The fireplace, along with the two that we added later when we expanded to the second floor, was a major element in establishing Savoy's reputation as New York's most romantic restaurant. During heavy snowfalls couples would trudge through the snow to sit by the fire. January, a traditionally slow month in New York City restaurants after all the December partying, would consistently be either our second or third best month of the year. People longed to take in the fireplace and the hearty winter fare we paired with it.

Our masons suggested that we lift the hearth off the floor to give us a place to store firewood and to offer customers an eye-level view of the fire from their seats. Predictably, everyone wanted to sit near the fireplace. During the winter, a day didn't go by without someone making a reservation request to sit near it. The pressure mounted around Valentine's Day when callers would try as early as November to reserve a table for February 14 and try to convince us that the entire future success of their relationship depended upon getting a fireside deuce. Our percentage of marriage proposals in house was quite high and I know of at least one baby who was conceived after a romantic dinner at Savoy, although I am quite sure there were many others.

Cooking in the fireplace came later. On a whim, during our first New Year's Eve, I stationed a cook by the fireplace to grill shiitake mushrooms over a small hibachi pushed into the hearth. Aside from the complication of coordinating service with the kitchen, it was clear that this was great theater for the diners, added great flavor to the food, and took another step towards connecting our visual aesthetics with the simplicity and directness of our cooking. If we were committed to pulling back the curtain on where our food comes from, how it is cooked and who is cooking it, then this took us three giant steps closer. I bookmarked this idea, for later use.

* * *

Mom-and-pop restaurants are rarely as finely planned as a newly built and well-capitalized restaurant: the coatroom might be a temporary rack set up in a fire exit corridor, the bar might double as the host stand with no actual greeting area at the entry door, deliveries and trash disposal might be through the front entryway, and pastry production might be staggered with savory work because there is only one oven and limited work space. A lot gets shoehorned into very small spaces and priority is always given to seats, i.e., direct revenue generation. Compromises: we all have to make them, but small restaurants in high-rent districts trying to maximize use make lots of them. I was able to get building department approval for only one bathroom because the premise was a pre-existing restaurant but for even a wine and beer license, the State Liquor Authority (SLA) requires two bathrooms. When the approved drawings came back from the building department, I whited out the representation of the toilet, drew a pencil line down the middle to create a separating wall with two toilets, made a Xerox copy for the SLA and sent it off to Albany. Approved. Those days are gone.

The most challenging condition for us was not having an area to wait for a table. Diners with reservations would gather just inside the front door, which also happened to be right on top of the phone and host stand as well as near the entry to the bathroom and a few feet away from the kitchen door. Hooks for coats lined the wall from the front door to the phone stand. When we were cranking, the host was on the phone trying to take a reservation, the servers were trying to clear and reset tables, customers were trying to get to the single bathroom toilet, and the holding area at the door would become increasingly restive if a waiting guest's table wasn't ready in a matter of minutes. When our largest table and only six-top would finally turn, the exiting diners had to push past the six others waiting to take their place all while retrieving their coats. I'm not one for foul language, but I think the word clusterfuck accurately describes this moment.

We were aching for more space, not just to do more business but to do better business, to offer a nicer dining and work experience for everyone involved. The opportunity came just a few years later in 1995 when we were able to expand to the second floor. It couldn't have come at a better time. Susan and I had started a family; our son, Theo, was three when the second floor opened and our daughter, Olivia, was born the following summer. I wanted flexibility to be able to be with my kids during their waking hours, to read bedtime stories and to be involved in their social and school lives. Nothing out of the ordinary, it's what most parents want and struggle to accomplish.

This desire for balance meshed nicely with the growing needs of our key managers, John Tucker, the general manager, and David Wurth, the chef de cuisine. Both had been with us for several years and needed bigger challenges and fatter paychecks. I proposed offering them each 10 percent of any company disbursements in return for a three-year commitment. Delegating responsibilities to managers who were completely committed to our success gave me the sense of security and stability I needed going into the expansion and to be with the family more frequently. I trusted that increased revenues from the expansion would pay for the profit-sharing arrangement. It was attractive to John and David too; they would receive a bonus if the restaurant thrived and we now all sat at the table when discussing operational and strategic plans for the restaurant. I drafted a simple agreement and we all signed it.

More than anything else, the restaurant needed a waiting area to transform that nightly barrage of bodies at the door into a civilized experience. In other words, we needed a bar, a lounge, a coat closet, and a second bathroom. Additional dining space, a place for a cocktail before dinner or an after-dinner nightcap were all welcome and potential revenue boosters, but that wasn't the initial goal.

Believing that we couldn't integrate the two floors and serve from one kitchen—David wanted limited involvement in the expansion project—I began to think about independent concepts, a restaurant within a restaurant, similar to Chez Panisse only in the reverse, where they serve a prix fixe menu downstairs and run an à la carte menu upstairs. The fireplace seemed like the obvious focus for the dining experience. I remembered my New Year's Eve fireplace shiitakes but also an older and more fundamental conversation that I had in 1985 with Richard Olney, the cookbook writer, during a visit to his home in southern France.

Sitting in front of his stone cooking hearth, lined with mortars and pestles in graduated sizes, various iron fish grates, a small adjustable grill, and a clockjack rotisserie, all the accoutrement necessary for superior hand-hewn food, Richard pontificated on the inherent structural failure of restaurants to deliver excellence. His critique was that from the inception of the restaurant, when public cooking transitioned from the tavern, with its preparation of a single dish served to all the guests, known as table d'hôte, to the restaurant setting where individual choice was offered, à la carte, soul had been lost in the food itself. There had been a tradeoff: the ability to compose individual plates in a sophisticated setting gained, the power and depth of flavor that comes from whole joint cookery in a communally seated tavern lost. A measure of control over the meal was also lost; the chef had ceded power over to the dining room.

Cooking à la carte means being able to accommodate groups of varying sizes at different times. This necessitates deconstructing a dish into its constituent parts so that they can be partially prepared and then assembled when the dish is actually ordered. Animal proteins get cut off the bone into individual four- or five-ounce portions and vegetables are blanched separately in water to advance their cooking and reduce the time necessary for what we call "pickup," the final preparation of the plate. Although this approach is in keeping with the comptroller's directive that portion control is key to the financial success of a restaurant, it also is a style of cooking that can never approach the quality of flavor achieved when all the elements of a dish are cooked as an ensemble and their flavors meld together. Richard counseled that this mechanistic approach was antithetical to good cooking, more akin to manufacturing and, as with all manufactured items over handcrafted ones, there is a resultant decline in quality, in this case flavor. Instead, he lobbied· for cooking whole dishes, birds roasted on the spit, fish on the bone, entire saddles and haunches of lamb roasted over embers, gratins cooked and served when done, no holding time.

Before we sat down to lunch I made a careful pen-and-ink sketch in my journal of his clockjack, or *tournebroche*, a small spring and gear wind-up rotisserie designed for fireplace cookery, the anachronistic tool in his fireplace that most intrigued me. The next several pages are recorded in wildly loopy cursive, no doubt a direct result of all the wines we drank over lunch, ending with multiple tumblers of 1900 Grand Champagne Cognac from Lucas-Carton, the famed Belle Époque Parisian restaurant. Listening to him, I began to fantasize about a restaurant concept in which large-format celebration dishes were the focus of the cooking, and the meats and fishes were cooked on the bone.

I returned home still intrigued by both the mechanical gadget and the idea of trying to cook in less mechanistic ways. It went against everything I had learned and practiced in restaurants up to this point. As the sole concept for a future restaurant it clearly wasn't going to work. That's not how restaurants are generally organized and though I was familiar with swimming against the tide, I knew that the framework needed to be recognizable.

I developed a plan for the second floor dining experience that moved us in this direction. I thought that if everyone was eating the same meal even if at staggered times, we could elevate the quality of the food and alter the way we thought about menus and menu development. We could get out of the manufacturing mindset, compose dishes that were less about an assemblage of deconstructed parts and more about home cooking at its best.

I built a small professional kitchen in the galley area where the residential kitchen had been and had a skilled Italian mason build out the fireplace to accommodate our goal of trying to do restaurant cooking in it. In designing a small kitchen and dining room independent of the main kitchen with a separate prix fixe menu, I created a laboratory for culinary experimentation. I could offer young talented cooks the opportunity to explore their cooking style without being burdened by all the complications of running an extensive menu and the staffing needed for execution. It became the breakout kitchen for some terrific cooks: Caroline Fidanza, who went on to become the first chef of Brooklyn's renowned Diner and owner of the beloved sandwich spot Saltie; Andrew Feinberg, later chef-owner with his wife, Francine Stephens, of Franny's; Jody Dufur, Westchester chef; and Todd Ahrens, the kosher chef at one time of Baron Herzog Winery. All of them used the opportunity to create carefully curated meals and deeply delicious food.

Each night we offered a set three-course menu largely composed of hearth dishes that changed on a daily basis. I was committed to giving a taste of the fireplace in every meal, year-round. We began to learn about cooking with live fire. I bought a version of Olney's *tournebroche* I'd captured in my sketchbook, using it for guinea hen, rabbit, chicken, and capon. We discovered that there are all kinds of areas close to the flames that allow for gentle cooking or give a hint of smoke to the food. We could cook lamb *à la ficelle*, French for "on a string," by tying a leg of lamb onto the chimney damper lever and then twisting the joint in one direction and allowing the string to unwind and rewind in ever-shortening alternating revolutions, much like the way a twisted playground swing alternates the direction of its revolutions until coming to a stop. The string didn't burn and the slow radiant heat was a superior cooking method, far more gentle than a grill, without any of the trapped moisture of an oven or the dehydrating effects of a convection fan: a true roast. We loaded up Mason jars with dried beans, garlic cloves, a fistful of herbs on the stem, salt, a healthy shot of olive oil, all topped off with water and set them six or eight inches away from the fire's center. Over the course of their meal, customers watched the slow-motion theater of a see-through pressure cooker next to the burning logs produce the most unctuous and flavorful cooked beans imaginable. Called *al fiasco* because traditionally Italians use a wine bottle for cooking the beans, this is a safe and simple technique that anyone with a fireplace can try. It produces some mighty stellar beans.

It wasn't long before we expanded to cooking cassoulets in the fireplace and teaching servers how to tend to the stew and then serve it tableside. William Rubel, author of *The Magic of Fire*, taught us how to bury vegetables in the embers and slow roast them there: sweet potatoes, onions, carrots, squashes, from which we made salads or side vegetables. In the summer we cooked more in the back kitchen but remained committed to one item from the fireplace in every meal. We would light a fire in the afternoon, smoke some fish for an appetizer or roast vegetables, and then dress them with a vinaigrette of sherry vinegar and pimenton, the Spanish paprika made from peppers dried over a wood fire, accentuating the fire elements of the dish.

The tool and the dish that became the signature for the dining room experience was the iron salamander, essentially a branding iron that got its name in the seventeenth century because people thought it looked like a salamander with its "head" buried in the coals, its "legs" propped up on the hearth, and its "tail" the handle. We used it to finish off crème brûlée: burning granulated sugar sprinkled atop a gently cooked custard to create a thin sheet of brittle caramel reminiscent of my best marshmallow moments. We gave every diner a taste of the fireplace at the meal's conclusion regardless of whether or not they opted for dessert: a mini crème brûlée. The dramatic puffs of burning sugar caught everyone's eye but the fragrance was marshmallows by the fire, a hundred percent.

As charming and delicious as the experience was, the fireplace prix-fixe menu was a tough sell. Maybe it works in more community-minded Berkeley or because Chez Panisse has a few decades of international fame under its belt, but New Yorkers don't like being told they don't have choice. Masters of the universe get twitchy when they lose control, especially of what they are eating; they don't take kindly to being told what to do under most circumstances. Countless parties would book and then call back saying "I'm not sure if my business associate eats fish" or "My partner doesn't eat squab so I'm going to have to cancel." In the second year we offered a choice in the entrée course: a meat or a fish. That helped. We also began to write a menu for the week instead of trying to change it every night, giving us more time to polish the dishes and for everyone to practice describing the food. In the third year we offered a choice in every course. It never ceased being an uphill battle.

It also wasn't efficient. Running two menus with two sets of mise en place created more waste and increased the number of ingredients subject to deterioration. Chef up and chef down didn't always happily play in the sandbox together and coordinate buying. Labor was also inefficient. Executing the upstairs menu wasn't a one-person job when we were busy but not really a two-person job either. I would hire swing shifters or offer culinary interns assistant shifts.

During a very slow summer, I happened to be interviewing a potential new accountant. When I told him that the two dining rooms were booked separately and that we did not allow diners to eat from the downstairs à la carte menu in the upstairs dining room—even if we were fully booked downstairs—he looked aghast, set down the dismal profit and loss reports we were reviewing and said, "You can't do that." The sickening truth was that I knew he was right. I'd had a notion of what I wanted to do, but I was turning away interested diners and with them the money needed to pay rent and salaries. Looking back across the table at this accountant whom I didn't really know, I couldn't hide from the truth or continue justifying my complicated, labor-intensive pet project. After four years of tweaks and recalibrations I finally admitted that it was unsustainable.

I anxiously approached Nicole Wester, the downstairs chef at the time, and asked what it would mean to serve the à la carte menu upstairs. Ever the optimist, she just shrugged and said, "It's OK. We can do that." Not a patsy by any means, especially in the face of all the chauvinistic pushback she got from certain male cooks uncomfortable taking direction from a woman, Nicole would say yes whenever she could. It was a huge relief; buy-in from everyone on the staff is important but from the chef it's critical.

My best chefs were ones who knew how to offer hospitality from the kitchen side, who found ways of saying yes to accommodate customers and owners while still remaining committed to their artistry and holding a high standard for the food. A server's or manager's primary responsibility is to be hospitable and accommodating whereas the kitchen staff's primary responsibility is to make delicious food. Good social skills, however, are harder to come by. Historically, a lot of ingrained negative behaviors by chefs were tolerated, creating divisions between the front and back of the house. I always worked hard to dismantle these old habits. Those with more rigid views of their role either cycled themselves out or I had to remove them from our culture by firing them. Thankfully at this critical moment this wasn't the case.

Even though the prix fixe menu concept didn't prevail, the fireplace remained the heart of the restaurant. People still came because it gave them the feeling that they were in a country inn or in someone's home outside of the city, far removed from the multitude of churn and burn spots. I had taken Richard Olney's un-restaurant vision of fine food and melded it with who I was as a chef, thinker, and restaurant operator in New York City. Echoes of his viewpoint always reminded me to protect good taste and good cooking in the restaurant. The hearth is always the center of the house.

FIREPLACE BEANS
(BEANS *AL FIASCO*)

Fireplace cooking doesn't require fancy equipment. All that's needed is a Mason jar; lacking a fireplace or a campfire, the beans can be cooked in a covered pot, but it is less dramatic. The slow, even cooking produces wonderfully flavorful beans, and the glass is a window into the cooking process. The method utilizes the heat of a mature but not roaring fire. Traditionally, this is done in a wine bottle (fiasco in Italian), but the Mason jar lets you easily spoon the beans out of the jar. Serve with grilled meat or wilted greens. I prefer Sorana beans but scarlet runners or cannellinis all make great versions. Avoid white navys. They are inferior in flavor and texture.

1 cup (about 185 g) dried beans, soaked overnight
5 cloves garlic, peeled
1 (5-inch/12 cm) sprig rosemary
1 bay leaf
½ teaspoon salt
1 teaspoon freshly cracked black pepper
⅓ cup (75 ml) good olive oil

Combine all the ingredients and 2½ cups (600 ml) water in a (1-quart/960 ml) Mason jar. Place the lid loosely on top—steam needs to be able to escape during the cooking process. Set in the hearth of the fireplace 8 to 10 inches (20 to 25 cm) from the active fire. Feel with your hands that this distance is hot but not unbearably so. Rotate the jar every 15 minutes for the first hour to ensure even cooking as the beans begin to simmer. After 2 hours check to see if all the liquid has been absorbed. Taste them to see if the beans are fully cooked. Add more water if necessary to complete the cooking. When the beans are tender and brothy, they can be served immediately. Allowing them to simmer overnight in the fireplace as the fire dies down produces a caramelization of the beans against the jar walls that is delicious and a consistency more like a rough puree.

GARLIC

I love garlic; Susan loves it even more. If I use three cloves to season a pan of broccoli, she uses six, maybe even eight. For me, garlic is a seasoning; for her, it's a vegetable. In the depth of summer when Keith Stewart, an organic farmer from Orange County, New York, has fully cured his superlative garlic and starts bringing his colossal bulbs to the greenmarket, I buy them in earnest. There is only one problem. I can't seem to accumulate a supply; as fast as I buy it, Sue uses it. Their big, moist, and easy to peel cloves are irresistible. It's only when colder weather sets in and the available bulb sizes diminish, that I begin investing in garlic futures and attempt to get ahead. I squirrel away bulbs far from Sue's sight, in an attempt to bridge us all the way to spring and the next crop. Over the course of a few market visits I take a position on at least three dozen bulbs appropriate for storage in my unheated bike room, which doubles as an urban root cellar. My goal, having calculated a minimum allotment of one bulb per week, is to make it to late April when the ramps hit the market. Not that ramps are a substitute for garlic but as another member of the *Alliums*, the onion family, their arrival signifies to me that I've made it to the other side, to spring and the promise of a new crop.

Getting to April requires careful selection. Squeezing the bulbs, feeling for firm cloves and tightly wrapped skins, are good signs; the dried outer leaves are the plant's first line of defense against dehydration, rot, and infestation. Keith's variety of garlic peels easily, both its charm and its Achilles' heel; the shelf life is shorter than some other varieties, a result of their scantier clothing. With my garlic bunker in place by December, I begin doling it out, two bulbs at a time, into the dry ingredient bowl on the kitchen worktable. It's a little game Sue and I play. If I only put out one head I fear she might suffer from GSS, garlic scarcity syndrome, and go looking for the bike room stash. I also have garlic needs and require assurance that when the time comes, there will be a healthy supply for my wintry lamb braises. But two heads seem to mollify her and they keep the house workweek dinner mainstay, Sue's pasta dish of garlic, kale, and Calabrian chiles, tasting just right. Let's face it; Sue is an "ajoholic." Like any right-minded enabler in a codependent relationship, I want to supply her with only the good stuff, although I was slow to understand what the good stuff was.

I grew up in a time and place where garlic bulbs were sold in twos, tucked inside a little cardboard box with a cellophane window so you could look in on the jailed bulbs and see how they were faring. I don't know what the cardboard box was about. Was it supposed to extend its shelf life? Was garlic perceived as "stinky" and thus might taint nearby vegetables or shoppers as they pushed their carts around the supermarket? Or was garlic seen as needing additional marketing and branding? I'm not sure, but that garlic, packaged for the mainstream American shopper, was for the most part, awful.

In the restaurants where I worked prior to Savoy, garlic was delivered loose, in five- or ten-pound bags. Dishwashers peeled it during slack moments in the evening service. Once peeled, it was someone's task to take the bucket from the dishwasher and whiz the entire batch in the food processor, drowned in oil (probably not even olive oil), and set it out on the counter beside the salt cellar for kitchen-wide use. Increasingly yellow throughout the week from oxidation, we used it casually, dolloping a spoonful into a sauté pan with some mushrooms or to quickly mix with herbs for a lamb marinade. Only later did the health department deem chopped garlic under oil to be conducive to the anaerobic development of botulism and made it illegal, although the practice persists in many commercial kitchens. This was before plastic tubs with easy to pour handles chock-full of pre-peeled garlic came rolling into kitchens with a simple phone call to our produce guy. It was also before Chinese import garlic dominated the market, neatly lined up in purple mesh bags (and incidentally, irradiated). We treated garlic as a base component in stocks or sofritos, barely varying from one day or one month to the next. It was a commodity staple, never an ingredient of distinction.

In my home kitchen, supermarket garlic is often an exercise in frustration. The heads have lots of leaf paper around them, and the large cloves are situated around the perimeter of the bulb, with a progression of ever-smaller, ever-more annoying to peel cloves the closer you get to the center. Bruising the little ones to facilitate peeling them results in garlic leaf paper sticking onto my fingers, ultimately forcing a choice in annoyance and desperation:

abandon the project, throwing the little bitties into a stock or the garbage; or soldier on with more time spent for diminishing returns, yet having the satisfaction of seeing the job through. Once I learned that the Spanish have a term for cooking with unpeeled garlic, *ajo en camisa*, garlic in their shirts, I became emboldened to opt for the former. I'd toss them into a stew optimistically hoping that the roughage would disappear into the braise.

Keith's garlic was different. At the cutting board I immediately noticed that there was less surrounding leaf paper; the cloves were generally all the same size, a single row circulating around a hard inner stem, the hardneck; and easy to peel, maybe even pleasurably so, especially after countless instances of having my fingers gummed up with garlic oil and lots of thin clove paper confetti. Roasted, the flesh was creamy and sweet; rubbed raw on some toasted bread for bruschetta it was delightfully pungent, not at all acrid; and tossed into a mushroom sauté with chopped parsley and olive oil, Italy's culinary holy trinity, it rounded out the perfect balance of earthy, herbal, and fruity flavors. This wasn't just well-seasoned food, this food sang.

The farmstand signage referred to the garlic as rocambole, a variety of hardneck garlic, one of the two subspecies of garlic, scientifically known as *Allium sativum*. *Allium* is the genus name for all of the onions, leeks, chives, and ramps. *Sativum*, regardless of whether the genus is *Cannabis*, *Croscus* (saffron), *Pisum* (peas), or *Allium*, means cultivated. Originating in central Asia, garlic has been cultivated for almost as long as humans have been practicing agriculture, not far behind wheat, rice, beans, and lentils. Ceramic facsimiles of garlic heads have been found in Egyptian tombs dating back five thousand years. Over these millennia, garlic spread out from central Asia across the entire globe, becoming a key ingredient in countless cuisines. Selection of garlic for desirable traits to humans: big cloves, early harvesting, survival in a broad range of climactic conditions, has been so intense that the plant is now genetically sterile, unable to produce flowers that can be cross-pollinated to produce fertile seeds. Garlic only reproduces clonally, meaning that the genetic makeup of the offspring plant is exactly the same as the parent. It is now dependent on aid from devoted farmers to plant individual cloves in the soil each fall for next year's crop.

Unlike corn or tomatoes whose antecedents have been identified in the wild, no pre-cultivated equivalent has been found for garlic. One could liken our desire for large-cloved garlic and its resultant sterility to our desire for copious amounts of white turkey meat, which after heavy selection by breeders has produced birds so top heavy that not only are they unable to walk but they cannot mate without human assistance. In evolutionary terms, garlic might represent a huge success story; it passed along the Silk Road and other trade routes, was introduced into the Western Hemisphere by nineteenth-century colonialist trading relationships, and successfully adapted to a wide variety of environments on a global scale.

Keith's crop is part of that success story too. His original stock of thirty bulbs was a gift from a neighboring gardener who had been gifted them from a friend after smuggling them into the United States from Calabria, Italy, many years earlier. From those thirty bulbs or approximately 200 cloves, and nearly thirty years of successive cultivation, Keith has grown his stock into an annual crop of almost 90,000 heads—a success story for both the garlic and for Keith. It is also exposes some of the dangers of over-selection by humans. The garlic gene pool has become so narrow that garlic are highly susceptible to disease and increasingly dependent on pesticides and fungicides to thrive.

The term hardneck refers to the last leaf a garlic plant produces in the spring. Instead of producing a wide planar leaf suited for photosynthesis, this leaf develops into a woody shoot that projects higher than the plant's growth up to this point. It develops a small arrow-like tip, and begins to twirl around, turning in upon itself, much like the graceful twists of a French horn or a serpent. The tip develops into a flower, or more accurately a false flower, that will mature into tiny garlic bulbs called bulbils. They can be used to grow new garlic plants but they are not true seeds, since pollination, the exchange of genetic material between two separate individuals, didn't occur. Hardnecks are classified into a subspecies named *Allium sativum ophioscorodon*, "serpent headed garlic," referring to the hardneck's curls and twists. Most garlic farmers cut the "serpent" or the "neck" soon after it has developed but before it hardens, believing that deprived of the "topset" bulbils, the plant will direct more energy into developing larger cloves in the soil. Except for the handful that don't get clipped because Keith enjoys their poetic beauty, wavering blue green in the summer breeze, it is someone's Herculean task to cut each and every one of the ninety thousand serpent heads.

The shoots are known on the West Coast as garlic whistle tops, on the East Coast as scapes. I was intrigued by their loping curls when they first started showing up in the market. They reminded me of Karl Blossfeldt's early-twentieth-century photos of magnified seeds, buds, and flowers. In trying to mimic his photographic poetry, I would often grill the scapes whole and then arrange them on top of a steak or over a piece of fish, a vegetative dance or a graceful brushstroke overlaying the entrée.

I began to take them more seriously as food. I prepared them like Szechuan-style string beans with ground pork, red peppers, soy, and ginger only sans garlic since the garlic was the bean. Recently I've taken to using the early tender scapes cut superfine along with cucumber, salt, and pepper, all folded into thick yogurt to make a rich and flavorful tzatziki dip. Tender scapes also make a terrific chimichurri; the bright raw flavors are explosive and vibrant but balanced by the new plant growth's sweetness. It has raw garlic power without the pungent hard-hitting edge of raw cloves. Scapes stiffen and become woody as they age and reach skyward in order to facilitate the wide dispersal of the bulbils. Beware of what you buy. One week can make a huge difference in the tenderness of a scape. Some trimming is almost always necessary of the tough lower sections, reserving only the pliable tender tops.

The *ophio* prefix in the subspecies, *ophioscorodon*, refers to the "serpent" scape, but what's the meaning of the *skorodon* suffix? Garlic in Greek is *skordo*, and a Greek dip of pureed potatoes, garlic, olive oil, sometimes bound with bread or almonds, is called *skordalia*, a dish we served at the restaurant. The menu read *skordalia* for many years until Jerry Winter, then a Savoy manager and later my partner in Back Forty, pointed out that shoppers and tourists reading the menu in the window seemed to be put off by all the foreign terms I used. He suggested that "Greek potato dip" might sell better. Once rebranded, it became the most popular afternoon snack to accompany a glass of wine. Using scapes as the garlic component makes a beautifully verdant and delicious rendition of the classic that I have dubbed "ophioskordalia."

Selling scapes makes me think about provenance—whether it's a Louis Vuitton bag, a Jackson Pollack painting, or vegetables at a farmers' market—provenance can be a tricky thing to nail down. Although "know your farmer" is a slogan bandied about there is another factor besides trust impacting provenance. What items are worth the effort to falsify? "Wild" salmon maybe or "local" tuna, but there is no fraudulent hardneck garlic. Given that hardneck garlics require more work, yield less per acre, and have a shorter shelf life, selling scapes is a diligent farmer's small opportunity to recoup some of the income lost by not planting the softneck varieties of garlic with their higher financial return. The very presence of the scape or the hardneck is the verification system of garlic being grown for taste, not yield. With a single harvest, we benefit in two ways: when scapes are cut, the garlic bulbs get buffed up and we get the treat of an early hint of garlic flavors to come. Keith sells the majority of his clipped scapes, and more each year as people discover their culinary value. He holds back a supply of fully formed bulbils as nature-provided crop insurance until the spring crop has established itself. Once assured that the new crop will succeed, he composts the remainder.

California, and in particular, the broad fertile valley surrounding the Gilroy area, is where most U.S. commercial garlic is grown. Almost all of it is the softneck type; there is no scape. Hardneck garlics require a winter dormancy period and are happiest in the Northeast and Midwest in winters resembling the harsh cold of their ancestral home, central Asia. They don't thrive in sunny California but the softnecks—*Allium sativum sativum*—do. Illustrating just how cultivated these alliums are, their name, *sativum sativum*, could be read as *cultivated, I mean really cultivated*. The softnecks are so intensely selected that its scientifically distinguishing feature is that it doesn't flower or send up a scape and so is entirely dependent on human cultivation for its survival. Softnecks are probably what was in the cellophane-windowed boxes of my childhood and what's in the Chinese purple net bags: prodigious but they don't deliver on flavor.

Garlic's wildness may have been bred out of it but scapes aren't part of the industrial food supply and probably never will be. They are the happy byproduct of a grower choosing gustatory values over profit motives; its provenance is pretty well assured. So buy some scapes. Stick a handful in a vase to gaze at their beauty, cook them up Szechuan style, or even better make some ophioskordalia. A few weeks later, buy some garlic from the same grower who was selling the scapes. Look for a hard center stem, the clipped hardneck. You won't be disappointed.

Questions of provenance also refer to a historical point of origin as well. Although the wild ancestor of garlic has been lost, the largest concentration of *Allium* species—over seven hundred species and all of them edible—is found in central Asia. This is its ground zero from where the global radiation of alliums originated. Connecting areas of high biological diversity with the origins of domestication is a theory originally developed by Nikolai Vavilov, a Soviet botanist and geneticist who just after the Russian Revolution traveled the world collecting specimens, cataloging species diversification and working on developing drought-resistant varieties of wheat for the newly formed USSR in the 1920s. He identified and mapped eight centers of biodiversity worldwide, where crop domestication probably began, and where the wild plants, or "landraces" as he called them, should be preserved along with their habitats. In Vavilov's view, both seeds and ecosystems needed to be preserved as a gene pool repository for future breeders given the ever narrowing of genetic material by plant breeders. He founded the world's largest seed bank, the Institute of Plant Industry, in Leningrad. .

As a Darwinian, Vavilov believed that specific traits appear randomly and can only be selected from individuals over successive generations. Stalin objected to this approach for practical and political reasons. Practically, he needed a quick fix to the famine that resulted from the disastrous forced collectivization of farms and massive crop failure in 1932 when millions of people died. Politically, Darwin's randomized and individualistic view of genetic change flew in the face of Stalin's determinist outlook. Believing that class struggle and hard work could be internalized to produce permanent broad social improvement, Stalin wanted scientists to demonstrate the existence of determinism in the scientific world as well. He wanted research to show that individual adaptations to environmental conditions could be directly inherited by future generations—or in political terms, struggle would produce permanent change. Vavilov informed Stalin that there was no quick fix. It would take ten years to develop drought-resistant wheat.

Stalin found a willing lackey in Trofim Lysenko, a scientist from a peasant background who assured Stalin that crop improvements could be passed onto future generations in one to two generations. He was made head of the Institute of Genetics and began to isolate Vavilov. Seed Bank funding was cut; Vavilov was no longer allowed to make international expeditions to collect seeds or attend scientific conferences outside of the Soviet Union where "bourgeois" science was discussed. Vavilov was arrested in 1940, imprisoned, and died in jail of starvation in 1943. His devoted colleagues at the seed bank valiantly protected the repository during the Siege of Leningrad, throughout the brutal winter of 1943–44, from both the Nazis who desperately wanted the institute's seed stock for their own politicized crop improvement programs, and from the starving residents of the city, who desperately wanted to eat the wheat and grain collection in order to survive. Many of Vavilov's protégés died protecting the repository. After Stalin's death, Lysenko and Lysenkoism were repudiated both scientifically and politically. Vavilov was posthumously rehabilitated and the Institute of Plant Industry in Saint Petersburg was renamed the Vavilov Institute in his honor.

Vavilov's idea that landraces and their environments are crucial resources is relevant to many crops: wheat, beans, apples, and garlic. This became clear to me one day when I read a sign at Keith's stand that stated, "Buy our garlic to eat, but not to plant." I inquired and was told that "white rot," a persistent fungus had infected the soil on Keith's farm as well as many areas of Pennsylvania, New York, and New England. Not wanting to participate in its spread, Keith was giving his customers a small view into the perils and challenges of growing food in our modern world without reliance on fungicides. Because garlic only reproduces clonally, it is difficult to develop disease-resistant and pest-tolerant varieties. Having wild or landrace varieties to breed back into the commercial lines is not available to garlic breeders. Recently though, searching in central Asia, at garlic's genetic epicenter, botanists have found older garlic varieties that exhibit superior disease resistance.

In July, after the scapes have all been cut and the garlic cloves mature, the leaves begin to dry up indicating that the plants are ready to pull. Once harvested, Keith cures his crop, a process of hanging the bulbs in a dry, well-ventilated area so that the outer leaves can desiccate, protecting the interior cloves from mold, rot, and dehydration. For us cooks, this is a great culinary moment; the garlic is as vibrant and moist as its ever going to be, making it a complete joy to cook with.

It is the perfect time for pounding and pasting, to make aioli—the combining of *ail* (garlic) and *oli* (oil) together—in the true Provençal tradition.

Jean-Baptiste Reboul's 1897 book *La Cuisinière Provençale* offers the note "it is worthy of always having on hand" with the following recipe: "2 cloves of garlic per person, 1 egg yolk, pinch of salt, spoon of warm water, and juice of a lemon and a half liter of good olive oil." Notice the purity here; it's garlic and oil with a little help from some friends. Note too that Reboul is not shy about doling out the garlic: two cloves per person. Sue and Reboul would have had a lot to talk about. Recipes for honey siracha, maple mustard, and horseradish sun-dried tomato aiolis are not to be found in this classic, in its twenty-seventh edition, when last I checked.

There is a kind of culinary alchemy that occurs when you pound garlic in a mortar and pestle to build an aioli. I start with a few cloves and begin by bruising them, then adding a bit of salt for friction—actual grist for the mill. Pounding releases the active flavor ingredient, allicin. When the cloves are pure paste and maximal allicin levels have been attained, begin mounting the olive oil directly into the mortar. Building the aioli in a mortar is marvelous to watch develop: adding warm water or lemon juice at critical junctures so that the emulsion doesn't seize or get too tight, sensing what the sauce needs. A food processor could do the job quickly and with less risk of breaking because of the power and speed of the motorized blade, but in a mortar you get the satisfaction of having actually built something. It takes time and a bit of muscle but there's a relationship between you and the sauce that develops as you build the sauce. At the table you'll appreciate it all the more. On some occasions we don't have time to make it in the mortar and as we say in the restaurant "just whiz it." It gets the job done quickly and invisibly but it's not the same, texturally or conceptually.

The synchronicity of garlic's and basil's maturation is probably no accident, a co-evolutionary event that did not escape the happy tongues of the Genovese and Provençals who consider making pesto or pistou—inclusive or exclusive of pine nuts depending on which side of the Ventimiglia border you're on—part of their regional heritage. The linguistic roots of the words "pesto" and "pistou" are from pestle, the manner of making is imbedded in the social fabric of the Mediterranean. One might go even further, suggesting in a bit of culinary Lysenkoism, that after a succession of generations of mortar and pestling basil and garlic, the recipe and technique are now genetically passed down to future generations. On a trip to Liguria, my taxi driver spoke in rapid-fire Italian our entire ride explaining to me how to really make the best pesto. His steering wheel–free gesticulations demonstrating the pestle process fueled my belief that building the sauce manually was clearly still the preferred production method. Put the food processor away, just once, maybe on a day when you really have nothing else to do and experience that it is a different sauce.

Regardless of the season, there is no match to the rocambole hardneck garlic when it comes to good cooking. But get it at its best, in high summer when it's fully cured and sticky with garlic oils on the knife. I have come to realize that whether it is scape chimichurri in June, a hand-built aioli in August, or *ajo en camisa* in October, Sue's right: in our kitchen, garlic is a vegetable.

OPHIOSKORDALIA

Using scapes as the garlic element in preparing skordalia—the traditional Greek spread of potatoes, almonds, garlic, and lemon—brings a green freshness to this traditional dish. It was an afternoon favorite at Back Forty West, accompanied by a glass of wine and mopped up with freshly made pita bread. I love this spread warm so consider making it just before serving, but it can easily be made ahead of time and refrigerated—allow at least an hour for the potatoes to come up to room temperature before serving.

1 pound (455 g) fingerling potatoes
1 teaspoon salt, plus more for cooking the potatoes
¾ cup (105 g) whole raw almonds (skins on)
1 cup (120 ml) olive oil, plus more for roasting the scapes and
    serving
10 garlic scapes, woody sections of stems trimmed off
Juice of ½ lemon
Salt
Freshly ground black pepper

1. Preheat the oven to 350°F (175°C).
2. Peel the potatoes and boil them in lightly salted water until tender. Drain in a colander, reserving ½ cup (120 ml) of the cooking water. The reserved water will be used to get the consistency right in the final preparation. Either mash the potatoes with a masher or pass them through a ricer or food mill. **Do not use a food processor for this.** You will get a pasty, gummy product.
3. Lightly toast the almonds on a baking sheet in the preheated oven for 10 minutes or until golden. Using the same tray, toss 4 of the scapes in a splash of olive oil and roast in the oven for 10 to 15 minutes, until the scapes have softened and picked up some lightly caramelized color. Cut the roasted scapes into 1-inch (2.5 cm) lengths and set aside while you make the skordalia.

4. Roughly chop the remaining 6 scapes; in a blender, combine with the toasted almonds and whiz to make a paste. Add the olive oil, lemon juice, and salt and whiz to create a loose green puree.

5. Fold the puree into the warm mashed potatoes. Add reserved potato cooking water as needed to create a texture that is easy to scoop up with a piece of bread. Season with black pepper and taste for salt.

6. Scoop the dip onto a plate and garnish with a drizzle of olive oil and the roasted scapes. Keeps in a sealed container in the refrigerator for 1 week but bring to room temperature before serving.

CALÇOTS

Thanksgiving is this nation's greatest food holiday, a mostly insular gathering of family to celebrate the harvest. I love the grand potluck spread our family brings to the table, but as a holiday, I've never really loved it. Maybe it's because I have worked so many of them, feeding more people in a single day than five others combined during a normal week. The work and stress usually left me more gaunt than plump. In addition to the genocidal and colonialist history surrounding the holiday, my discomfort with Thanksgiving is philosophical. It is a holiday about the past, a look back at the harvest, now in the cellar or the barn and is by implication a declaration of limits: there isn't any more until spring. Potential is now the actual. It can feel a little dour or conservative; it's a celebration, but with a lid on it. I am more drawn to the spring holidays—Passover and Easter—the ones that look forward with hope and optimism to the new season and celebrate rebirth and limitless possibility. As a restaurateur, it has been in my nature to want to feed others, many of them strangers, with the potential that they might become new friends.

I lean towards celebrations that embrace everybody, where our commonality is part of the experience. Dance floors are more familiar spaces to co-mingle with strangers than dinner tables. Personal space dissolves into the communal, everyone moving and shaking to the same rhythms. Public gatherings en masse—whether watching fireworks, attending a political protest, or a rock concert—create boundary-breaking camaraderie. What's a rock concert without turning to a nearby stoner and mutually nodding in rhythm to a great guitar riff? It's rare to experience food events of this sort.

Annual church suppers and volunteer fire fighter pancake breakfast fundraisers offer that experience, but they are less common than they used to be and ones that still exist often feel more nostalgic than vital. There are pockets around the country where singularly focused food fests still persist: crawfish boils in Louisiana; crab boils on the Eastern Shore; fish fries in

Wisconsin; and "beefsteak" feasts in New Jersey and New York, but all of these are relics in danger of disappearing.

My first experience with anything of this ilk was the Allen's Neck Friends Meeting House annual clambake in Dartmouth, Massachusetts, held the third Thursday in August. The menu comprises enough clams, mussels, tripe, sausage, sweet potatoes, corn, and onions to feed 500 paying guests and 125 volunteers. It's part construction project, part picnic, with the volunteer crew layering up a hillock of food to cook under a tarp. Starting with a base of fire-heated rocks, followed by armfuls of rockweed spread over the stones emitting littoral steam vapors for cooking layer upon layer of wooden trays filled with the clams, sausage, corn, and the other accompaniments, the creation is wrapped in canvas, a lid to this huge steaming pot, timed for a 1 P.M. unveiling. Guests bring their own utensils and napkins for easy cleanup and community-baked pies cap off the meal. Good food and good feelings abound with the shared joy of being both a participant on this day but also across time. At 130 years and counting, the menu constant, and the guest list slowly evolving, the clambake remains a focus of fun and funds for the community. It's not a raucous or lusty affair by any means; it's a Friends fundraiser after all.

***

I yearned to create this kind of feast tradition at Savoy, an event not conceived to stimulate business on slow nights or garner PR but one that built community in our urban landscape. I had done annual events, like a noncompetitive cassoulet cook-off with five or six chefs each making their version of the classic dish, a nonprofit receiving a portion of the proceeds, and customers walking around tasting and drinking. As much as these were great fun and had become annual events, they didn't embody the food tradition I sought. They lacked the common table.

My next experience with the allure of a grand communal meal was in Spain, an hour outside of Barcelona in a region known as the Valls. In 1997, along with seventy-five other American chefs, journalists, and food thinkers, I tumbled off a bus late one spring morning having barely downed my cortado and churros. In front of a stone farmhouse stood a couple of rusty box springs, where instead of mattresses, the box springs supported piles of freshly pulled leeks getting torched by blazing vine cuttings underneath. Once a batch was properly charred, the leeks were wrapped in paper and new recruits were laid on the springs to grill another round.

These chargrilled leeks, known in Spain as *calçots*, are planted in the spring, transplanted in the fall to winter over, and then harvested the following spring. The word comes from *calçetines*, the Spanish word for socks. Needing to protect the plants from the winter freeze, farmers hill up insulating soil around the leeks, which looks like socks on the legs of the protruding leeks, hence the name. In late winter, when temperatures rise and photosynthesis begins again, the well-rooted calçots begin growing and mature long before any newly seeded annual plants.

Their market appearance is proof to Spaniards that the winter is over and a new season has arrived. Residents of the Valls elevated the visibility of this winter survivor by creating a feast dedicated to its consumption—the *calçotada*. During the late winter and early spring, hiking clubs, Rotarians, family reunions, and company parties, from Barcelona to Tarragona, all schedule calçotadas in the Valls.

We were ushered inside the farmhouse where long rows of tables were set up for a feast. Once seated and red wine poured, round after round of calçots began to arrive along with bowls of earthen-colored romesco sauce, the almond and chile sauce typical to the region. Eating calçots is a hand operation; utensils are frowned upon. Awkward at first, it wasn't long before everyone was pulling back the charred layers and using the calçots to scoop up some romesco, dangling them down into their mouths, like cartoon-style spaghetti eating, and washing it all down with freely flowing red wine.

I was already in love with romesco's robust flavor. A combination of chiles, tomato, roasted almonds, garlic, olive oil, and bread, we had been making it at the restaurant for years. I was a fan of the entire family of nut-bound sauces found along the Mediterranean coastline from the Costa Brava all the way into Italy, which includes Liguria's pesto as well as other nut and herb pastes known as *picadas*. Romesco was a house condiment at Savoy whether spread on toast to garnish a bowl of soup, dolloped atop grilled beef or lamb, or thinned out as a sauce for a grilled black sea bass. We relied on it to round out a dish or provide a flavor boost. It wasn't until this day in the

Valls that I understood how romesco and calçots in unison offered people the opportunity to enjoy eating with their hands and dispense with all pretense.

Everyone was giddy, their hands a charred calçot ashen mess. When people reached their calçot quota, they would amble over to a communal marble fountain and wash up, acknowledge the moment with random diners also in need of a cleanup, before heading back into the festivities for round two. This time, platters of grilled lamb, botifarra sausage, and white beans were in abundance. Not usually prone to overconsumption, I wanted to keep eating just so I could extend the bliss. After what felt like an entire day, I stumbled out of the farmhouse, the sun now low in the sky. I looked up, full with food and joy and shouted out to the gods how glad I was to be alive, that this moment was as good as any ever needed to be. In a sort of spontaneous combustion, I began dancing in the field in front of the farmhouse to the sounds of some local musicians.

Back home, rather than tell people about the experience or show them photos, I decided to recreate the event and begin a Crosby Street tradition. First, I developed a supply of calçots with Guy Jones, an Orange County organic farmer I had done business with since before I opened Savoy. For several years, the restaurant had extended a springtime credit line to the farm. We fronted Guy several thousand dollars to buy seed and pay early labor expenses before he had much of a revenue stream. In return, Guy would issue us credit for our loan with 10 percent added on as a goodwill interest payment. When I asked him if he would plant leeks in the fall and hold on to them over the winter for early spring harvest after they had fattened up, he readily agreed. This was even better than a line of credit for both of us; it was a new early spring line of merchandise. At first, planting the calçots was an experiment, planted solely for our benefit. Before long, calçots were appearing regularly on Guy's spring product inventory list for all his wholesale customers.

The first Savoy calçotada was indoors, upstairs in front of the fireplace, with Betty Fussell, the food writer, who had been on the same trip, as guest speaker. Her enthusiasm was infectious and the meal was delicious. But there was a lid on the experience; we needed to grill outside over a big fire and gather people around it, more like a beach bonfire. The following year we pushed out onto the street and set up the calçot grill on the sidewalk. I looked into getting a city permit for a street fair and realized that the bureaucratic red tape necessary would ultimately end in denial. Instead I decided to try and stay under the radar on Crosby Street. After all, I wasn't trying to close or redirect traffic on a thoroughfare; I was just setting up a grill on the sidewalk of our quiet cobblestoned block as if it were my front yard. Passersby would query, "Do you have a permit?" by which they meant did I have a permit to light a grill on the sidewalk. I would just offer a general answer "Yes, I have a permit" and then whisper to the cook working beside me, "I've got plenty of permits: a permit to collect sales tax, a permit to operate a commercial kitchen, a permit to light candles on the table."

In eighteen years of grilling on the block we were never shut down although we had a few close calls. One year the FDNY responded to a call that there was a fire on the street. Three trucks raced up to the corner, sirens blaring. When the captain viewed four guys in chef whites working a grill, he barked into his walkie-talkie to the dispatcher "Tell the chief, it's a street barbecue." The crew clambered down off the truck and approached us. "Good evening, gentlemen." I said, "Is there anything I can help you with?" "You have an open fire here." I nodded in agreement, pointed to the fire extinguisher at my side and said, "You know, we both make our living controlling fire." This did not go over well. He stared back at me—blank—without the slightest acknowledgment of camaraderie. I realize that greasy restaurant flue fires represent a significant percentage of calls the fire department receives and that my claim to parity wasn't going to fly. The captain looked around, considered the situation, and in some acknowledgment that I also wasn't a complete joker, he warned me, "If I get another call on you, I'll be back to hose you down." Phew! We finished up the evening—and all the others—without the city providing assistance to extinguish the coals.

Tables were deliberately set without flatware, forcing people to eat the calçots with their hands, to embrace dipping and redipping the charred onions into the romesco sauce. Lacking the marble fountain, we supplied hot towels, Japanese restaurant-style, cleaned everybody up, and only then offered forks and knives for the meat course: grilled lamb, house-made botifarra sausage, white beans, and Kenny Migliorelli's wintered-over broccoli rabe. The meal finished up with *crèma catalana*, otherwise known as crème brûlée, caramelized with red-hot salamanders from the outdoor fire.

Most years, there seemed to be synchronicity between our chosen date for the feast and the first flush of warm nights when everyone sheds protective clothing and spills out into the streets in search of food, fun, and a mate. It was as if the planet had started the party even before we lit the charcoal. I'd hire flamenco troubadours to play guitar and percussion while strolling through the restaurant, providing a soundscape that further transported people away from their busy urban lives and concerns.

And then there were the *porróns*—blown-glass flasks that resemble the goatskin wine totes that sheep herders carried—and the game of trying to drink from one without touching the vessel to one's lips. I've never been a drinking game kind of guy but this one appealed to me. I not only excelled at it, able to fully extend my arm while supplying a continuous stream of wine, but I took it upon myself to teach and encourage all the calçotada guests to attempt it themselves. In a departure from tradition we poured rosé. It was part of embracing the seasonal shift from winter to summer. Before long the entire room was clapping for those brave enough to attempt the challenge. As instructor and lead cheerleader, I invariably drank too much, a rare but worthy sacrifice for the cause. Sometimes I'd dance with the musicians, twirling through the room, spinning myself right back to that afternoon in the Valls and into a stratospheric place filled with joy and optimism.

Year after year, friends brought friends; its reputation spread widely. Some years we did two nights; I learned to book rolling seatings, and when I had both Savoy and Back Forty, we even did evenings at both locations. Like the Allen's Neck clambake, calendared for the third Thursday in August, I designated the first Tuesday in May as the date for the Crosby Street calçotada. For nearly twenty years, with only one postponement when unseasonably cold weather slowed the calçot growth, the calçotada, along with daffodils and the running of the Kentucky Derby, marked the new season upon us.

The calçotada was everything I wanted in a food holiday. I'd write each year on the postcard, "It's my bacchanalian homage to spring's return." It had become a religious holiday for me, and a tradition in and for our community. As a celebration of winter's end and spring's arrival, it embodied an optimism about a future, filling everyone who participated with the hopefulness of possibility and opportunity.

ROMESCO SAUCE

MAKES 1½ TO 2 CUPS/360 TO 480 ML

(ENOUGH TO ACCOMPANY CALÇOT FOR 6)

Here is my version of the classic Spanish sauce. Consider it a condiment to use in myriad ways starting with as the sauce to accompany grilled calçots, but you can also use it to top grilled meats, as a spread on toast to complement a hearty soup, or as a sauce for grilled or baked fish (use some stock or broth to loosening the romesco to create sauce consistency). This is a simple recipe—it's mostly about gathering the ingredients and combining them in a food processor.

1 cup (140 g) whole raw almonds, skins on (½ cup/70 g almonds plus ½ cup/70 g shelled hazelnuts is also a classic and delicious combination)

2 red medium bell peppers

Olive oil

3 slices sourdough bread, cut into 1-inch-thick (2.5 cm) pieces

5 ancho chile peppers

5 cloves garlic, peeled

3 cups (540 g) chopped plum tomatoes

2 tablespoons pimentos

½ cup (120 ml) red wine vinegar

Juice of 1 lemon

Salt

1. Preheat the oven to 350°F (175°C).
2. Toast the almonds for 10 to 12 minutes, until the nuts are tan and have a toasty but not acrid flavor.
3. Char the bell peppers over a gas stovetop or a fire until the skin is blackened and the flesh is tender. Peel the charred skin, then seed and stem the peppers.
4. Liberally coat the bottom of a 10-inch (25 cm) pan with olive oil. Add the bread and fry it over medium-high heat until golden and toasty on all sides.

5. In a cast-iron pan, lightly toast and soften the ancho chiles. Remove from the pan and immerse the chiles in a small bowl of water; let soak for 20 minutes until they are moist and rehydrated. Open up the chiles and discard the seeds and stems.

6. In a food processor, grind the almonds, bread, and garlic until fine. Add the wet ingredients—red peppers, anchos, and tomatoes. Add the pimentos. Puree until all the ingredients are incorporated but still have texture. Drizzle in ½ cup (120 ml) olive oil, the vinegar, and lemon juice and blend to combine. Season with salt.

7. Keeps in a sealed container in the refrigerator for 1 week.

ALTERNATE TRANSPORT

I slept through my alarm; a 4:30 wakeup call was far from normal for me. My habit was to go to bed between 1 and 2 A.M., getting up at 8, with only a razor-thin margin of error to ingest some caffeine, make breakfast for the kids, and whisk them off to school on my market bike. On the bell curve of parental drop-off timing chefs are never on the early ascending part of the curve. Those data points belong to business-suited parents, dashing off to make 8:30 meetings in their office building digs. I was on the descending side, particularly if it was a late night that involved some drinking. On market days—Monday, Wednesday, and Friday—after drop-off, I would head to Union Square to buy what was needed for the current menu.

The 5:30 A.M. phone call following the ignored alarm was a problem. I had missed my rendezvous with a trucker in the far reaches of Brooklyn, who was dropping off a specialty breed Ossabaw pig that I had arranged by phone to buy from Eliza MacLean of Cane Creek Farm in North Carolina. The pig had hitched a ride north on a tractor trailer full of industrial hogs headed for a commodity meat distributor on Utica Avenue in Brooklyn. The driver informed me that it was too late to come to Brooklyn. But I needed that pig. It was the featured guest at a sold-out event we were hosting in a few days celebrating the publication of Peter Kaminsky's book *Pig Perfect*. Failure to snag it was not an option. People had paid up front to taste an Ossabaw, highlighted in the book, and this was the only one in all of New York.

Dragging myself out of bed and throwing on yesterday's clothes, I was annoyed with myself for missing the alarm. Clearly, I had no pull with the guy. What I thought of great significance: New York City's first dinner organized to serve a black pig with ancestry dating back to the late sixteenth century, when explorer Hernando de Soto dropped pigs on the sea islands along Florida's southeast coastline, was lost on him. The driver was making his weekly run between the Carolinas and New York, and heading home with an empty tractor trailer before traffic got too bad was foremost in his mind.

"If you meet me in Bayonne in an hour, you can pick it up there." Bayonne? I had driven through it countless times; every transit to and from Newark airport includes a traverse through Bayonne halfway between the airport and the Holland Tunnel. But stopping off there? Never. Bayonne is part of the Meadowlands, low-lying estuarial land sandwiched between the Hackensack and Hudson Rivers, only paved. Staten Island is a stone's throw across a narrow channel. Cliché or not, I thought of it as a place where guys went to get fitted for cement boots. It's where you dispose of meat, not pick it up.

I jumped into our small Mitsubishi hatchback. It was early January, the light a dull flat gray, the first snowfall predicted for later in the day. I followed directions to the address provided by the trucker and at 6:30 A.M. I pulled up to a street lined with a series of loading docks all gated shut with chain-link fencing. Snow had begun to fall, enough of a dusting to show the imprint of my lone approach down the solitary street. There was absolutely no one in sight. I was creeped out. None of the businesses showed any signs of stirring. In the middle of the street though, a truck was idling. Was this my connect? I pulled the car up behind the trailer. A man in jeans, cowboy boots, and trucker's cap stepped out of the cab and greeted me. It felt like the perfect location and timing for a drug deal. Walking around to the back of the trailer, he threw open the roll-down door, exposing a virtually empty trailer except for a single carcass lying in the middle of the floor, like a lonely victim. "Is this what you're looking for?" I felt like an accomplice to a crime. He directed me to back my car up, end to end with his. We muscled the carcass onto our shoulders and heaved it into the open hatchback. Only after sliding the passenger seat as far forward as it would go and tilting the seat towards the dashboard, did my quarry fit into the vehicle. It was 220 pounds, human-sized, more linebacker than ballerina. One foot refused to stay tucked in allowing the hatch to close and we had to give it a crack and a shove. Scenes from *Frenzy*, the Hitchcock movie, were running through my head, where the murderer breaks the rigor mortised finger of his victim to fully hide her in a sack of potatoes as the film cuts to the detective breaking a breadstick in half while dining with his wife. I was spooked but glad to now have dominion over this very special pig. I drove off, headed towards the Holland Tunnel, thinking that if things went smoothly, there might be enough time to still take the kids to school.

As I approached the tunnel, I began to panic. This was not long after 9/11 and police were permanently stationed at the tunnel entrances, randomly stopping cars and trucks to inspect their contents. I'd heard stories from farmers of being stopped during the frequent orange alerts and having to answer a litany of questions regarding their truck's contents. I dreaded having to explain the situation as reasonable as this all might seem. "Is that a body in your trunk?" "No, officer, it's a pig . . . for a dinner I'm doing at my restaurant. . . ." In attempting to avoid answering any of these questions, I took the lane furthest from the squad car and slipped through with my "corpse" undetected. I delivered it to the restaurant and later that morning we dove into breaking it down, beginning the prep for the dinner.

Eliza's pig (or at least its center section) would make one more unconventional lap before landing on people's plates: a bicycle tour through SoHo, Little Italy, and Chinatown. It is very difficult to cut beautiful chops without a band saw to split the carcass in half and to remove the chine bone, the portion of the vertebrae where the ribs attach. I surmised that I could get the job done swiftly if I rode the pig in my bike to Chinatown and found a butcher shop, where for a modest tip, someone might be willing to make two passes with a band saw. I was rebuffed at several spots but finally found a willing butcher (dangling cigarette ashes supplied free of charge). Back at the restaurant we rubbed the loins with a paste of garlic, anise seed, and pimenton, let it rest for several days, then smoked and spit-roasted them the night of the event. The servers carried three plates at a time up the rear stairs into a dining room of fifty eager diners, concluding the Ossabaw's journey from North Carolina to our second floor dining room via Bayonne and Chinatown—probably not the journey people envision when they think of farm to table.

Over many years, my education as a chef had solidified my belief that a chef's work begins well beyond the kitchen door, out in the marketplace, foraging for the best ingredients and building relationships that lead to a deeper understanding of those ingredients. Bocuse had said that starting with great ingredients was a fundamental requirement for a great cuisine—in the French sense of both the place where cooking occurs, in the *cuisine*, the kitchen, and the breadth of recipes collectively shared by a group of cooks, a *cuisine*. I knew that sourcing was key to our daily production in the kitchen and to the quality of our repertoire. Even in later years when I spent less time in my kitchens, I never relinquished hunting for and supporting the viability of more flavorful and more sustainably raised ingredients. Dogged persistence, the underlying driver that there had to be a way, has served me well.

Great producers are rarely part of the mainstream distribution system. For a long time, mainstream food—or wine—distributors didn't understand that difference sells, that some chefs and wine buyers might view difference as an asset instead of a liability. They were still wedded to the idea that their customers wanted and needed consistency, uniformity, and predictability. Today's peaches need to look (and sadly, taste) exactly the same as yesterday's. This year's vintage of cabernet only varies slightly from last year's so no re-education needs to happen. Keep buying it, keep the product stream plentiful and flowing. The goal was to impose the manufacturing model on our food supply in order to minimize change in food production and on our expectations from the food supply. Cooks, buyers, tasters, and citizens of the world began to express a preference for variation and difference in taste. People wanted to celebrate the evolution of availability over the course of the season and to taste the differences in wine from one region or vintage to the next. In getting away from the mainstream food production, chefs sought out new obscure ingredients: anise hyssop, cape gooseberries, blowfish tails, heritage pork, Barb Scully's Damariscotta River oysters, double-smoked bacon from Tennessee (the list is long). We, and by "we" I mean a whole generation of chefs across the nation, became the champions of small producers and gastro-diversity, viewing small growers as custodians and protectors of taste and quality. We upended the marketplace with this approach and the big producers are still trying to catch up and even capitalize on this value system. I've seen advertisements for Lay's trying to brand their potato chips as being locally produced and McDonald's flashing the faces of their producers as if to imply that the food is not corporately grown and industrially produced.

It is one thing to celebrate small producers, but it is a whole other thing getting small farm product consistently into the restaurant. Farmer-producers are often devoting their energies to growing and distribution, and marketing is more of an afterthought. So we often worked together to think creatively about how to improve their distribution and how to create alternate methods of transport to get ingredients from farm to kitchen. We supported various

attempts at creating distribution hubs, aggregators, and trucking companies to bring local products down to the city and helped numerous farmers
think about how to better price and market their products. We needed them
to succeed.

I was not a huge proponent of next-day air-freighting of food across the
country. Its excessive expenditure of fossil fuels flew in the face of our pro-
fessed environmentalism. But given my "all things in moderation" philosophy,
I was open to any and all modes of transportation. My personal preference
for intracity travel was the bicycle. I had been riding a bike in New York for
decades. I love swiftly cutting through traffic, the immediacy of being able
to ride directly to wherever I choose, and the lack of barriers between me
and my urban landscape. There is a pirate, almost renegade nature to it. On
the streets of New York, cars, particularly taxis at that time, ruled the road
and so as riders we had to take a commanding presence to survive. I had
no need for a health club; I got my workout by moving through the city,
running errands, exploring neighborhoods and streetscapes in a way that
a car never can.

I started shopping at the Union Square Greenmarket before opening
Savoy, having discovered it when I worked at Huberts on Twenty-Second
Street in the early eighties. In the early Savoy days, my English three-speed
bike with a front basket and rear panniers sufficed to haul my purchases
to the restaurant. Soon I was overstuffing them, hoping that a profusion of
bungee cords would forestall any purchases from ending up on the road. On
heavy haul days, I'd ride away from the market with so much weight in the
rear that the bike was on the verge of tipping backwards. Increasingly, this
was neither efficient nor safe; but philosophically, hailing a cab wasn't an
acceptable solution either. One day, walking in the East Village, I came upon
a bike locked on a signpost that seemed to be the answer to my needs and
dreams. It was a well-used European-looking rig with its front wheel hyper-
extended in front of the handlebars and a large cargo basket in between—a
front-loaded stretch limo bicycle. I needed that bike. I left a note asking the
owner to phone me. A few hours later I heard from George Bliss, the bike's
owner and operator of the Hub, an alternative bike shop filled with innovative bicycle designs, not of the high-performance type for racers but ones for
whom biking was a political act. Constantly moving from one subsidized rent

space to another, the Hub was part community education center, part bike shop. George had a vision that bikes could operate as the neural fiber of our cities and he pioneered a pedicab business with a goal of incorporating them as more than just a tourist alternative to the horse-pulled hansom cabs found along Central Park South. Based on a design from Copenhagen's Christiana district, the bike I saw that day is known as a long john. George rented it to me for $10 a month to test if it would suit my needs before purchasing one and put me in touch with Jan Vander Tuin of Eugene, Oregon, at that time the only man in the United States building long johns. One trip was all it took; the bike was up for the task and I couldn't imagine shopping in the market ever again without one. I immediately placed an order with Jan but tweaked the design, giving him custom specifications for the cargo bay so that one wooden apple crate and one plastic stacking vegetable bin could easily sit side by side. Some restaurants buy delivery vans and display their logos on the side; I bought the long john and had custom-made panels with the Savoy logo decorating my "stretch."

The change was dramatic. I could buy with impunity. I actually began challenging myself on how much I could haul. In the lead-up to Thanksgiving I relished testing whether I could load up the entire order of squashes, apples, quinces, and Brussels sprouts and bring it back to the restaurant in one run. I wanted local apple cider on draft and, lacking any distributors handling kegs of quality cider, I arranged with Eve's Cidery, from the Finger Lakes, to bring kegs to the greenmarket. I'd transport them in the bike to the restaurant and literally, re-cycle the empties back. I used the bike to transport small equipment for repair or for purchase: meat grinders, mixers, food processors, even once, a new dishwashing machine. Every May on either side of our calçotada festival, I'd borrow a six-foot iron outdoor grill from fellow chef-restaurateur Marc Meyer and ride it balanced astride the cargo bay rails, extending three feet in both directions left to right, commanding space the width of an automobile.

I affixed a small yellow decal to the bike frame that reads "The Revolution Will Not Be Motorized," a riff on Gil Scott-Heron's song, "The Revolution Will Not Be Televised," ever a reminder to me that I was engaged in alternate transport, in demonstrating the viability of doing things differently, in disrupting and not accepting the status quo. "By any means necessary," another trope of the political change movement, guided me as well. Originally spoken by Jean-Paul Sartre and popularized by Malcolm X, I applied it to the politics of sourcing and getting properly grown or raised ingredients into the restaurant. A different kind of redressing persistent wrongs, I was on a change mission, not to be deterred.

If the bike was my means of insurgency, it was also the family "car." Theo became quite practiced in providing the reprise to people's incessant queries about the bike: "A guy out in Oregon made it." While some parents pulled their cars out of the garage to do the morning school drop-off or arrived in a cab, I would take the kids to school in the bike then ride to the market to shop, deliver to the restaurant, and then go home for a quick shower or some quiet time before heading to work for the afternoon and evening.

Most days the bike was parked in front of the restaurant, but not as decor. I used the bike to backhaul wine to the house that we didn't have storage capacity for in our small restaurant wine cellar. I maxed out at eight cases of wine on the bike, maintained a zero breakage record (although a case of apples once spilled all over the intersection of Seventh Avenue South and Bleecker Street). People closely associated me with the bike, especially in the market. Even today, some people either don't recognize me if I'm not with it or alternatively ask me where the bike is, if I'm riding my English three-speed sports model. It was the tool that allowed us to forage the city for ingredients and thrive as a truly market-driven kitchen.

* * *

Biking wasn't the only alternative mode of transportation we embraced. I was keen on getting local seafood into the restaurant. Throughout the nineties, annual harvests of Peconic bay scallops were so small that there was no commercial market. Massive algal blooms, the result of poorly treated sewage from Long Island townships and the nitrogen–rich runoff from golf courses and heavily fertilized agricultural lands, meant that in 1996, the entire New York State commercial harvest was fifty-three pounds. I had grown up on these small, incredibly sweet scallops. They tasted like seafood candy and held a special place in my sense memory. Bay scallops were a product worth going to some effort to obtain, not to mention trying to revitalize for the region. In 1997, the population had revived. Restoration efforts were already underway and, when the season opened up on the first Tuesday in November, I was able to buy five pounds from Charlie Manwaring at Southold Fish who mainly reserved the take for locals.

The first delivery was made by Karen Karp, a customer and part-time resident of the North Fork. She became our scallop ferrywoman, picking up from Charlie and dropping off at Savoy when her travel schedule meshed with ours. When it didn't, we had another solution: the Hampton Jitney, the local bus company. It stopped directly across from Charlie's shop and for a $10 luggage fee, the jitney would transport our cargo into the city. The only catch was that we had to meet the bus at its last stop before it headed back out to the East End. So I'd pedal up to Third Avenue near Grand Central Terminal and collect my bag o' bays.

No one else in New York City was tapping into this great local ingredient, not to mention heralding the environmental success story that putting marine conservation regulations and good land use practices into place were now benefitting everyone. My scallop ceviche with Trinidad pepper vinegar was proof positive that regulating our behavior can be economically expansive, not restrictive. The scallop population continued to rebound and after a few years it was possible to buy them wholesale or at the greenmarket. I retired the jitney "burro" even though using it was an offbeat reminder to my employees that tenacity is an important quality in a chef.

Foraging for ingredients not only raised the quality of our ingredients but influenced my repertoire as well. I'm not just speaking about peppering dishes with the novelties and esoterica, which offer market distinction, but about access to ingredients that allowed us to prepare traditional dishes: finding good-quality salt cod meant we could perfect making brandade, the delicious southern French classic spread made from poached salt cod, garlic, and olive oil; having a source for blood allowed me to serve a true civet, a dish of hare or rabbit braised in red wine and then finished with blood to enrich and thicken the sauce. It is a regional dish I had fallen for during a bicycle tour in the southwest of France when I went to cooking school but in our hyper-sanitized steak-centric world, the meat wholesalers out of the Gansevoort Market cannot sell fresh blood. A byproduct of the slaughter, it is rarely collected, much less sold by U.S. abattoirs and requires special handling. Given that most Americans don't have a hankering for blood sausage, there was more money to be made and less effort invested by selling it to farmers as bloodmeal fertilizer or as protein in animal feed for livestock and pets. I was able to get our poultry and rabbit supplier to begin collecting it for me. He delivered it once a week in empty two-liter Dr Pepper bottles, which we stored, discreetly labeled, in the main reach-in. A quick squirt of blood from a plastic squeeze bottle into an off-the heat saucepan—to avoid curdling—produced a sauce full of umami flavor. Our blood-thickened civet wasn't a fashion statement like the blood popsicles and blood cocktails of bad boy culinary hipsterism that came later, but its depth of color and flavor transported people into a medieval tapestry depicting a grand banquet after the hunt. Our "Dr Pepper" sauce qualified as another kind of alternate transport: transport through taste.

Rejecting a dependency solely on the available foods from Hunts Point–based wholesalers, we began finding small producers all around the country who were on similar paths: searching for flavor, preserving old ways of growing or processing, and looking to make connections with other kindred spirits. Increasingly, ingredients arrived via mail and UPS. Cornmeal came in from small stone mills in the south, hominy from the Mohawk reservation in western New York, wild rice from the White Earth Land Recovery Project in Minnesota, lamb from Pennsylvania, and wild mushrooms from Oregon. We were building an alternate distribution channel, recognizing that it wasn't highly efficient but holding out hope that a better and more efficient one would evolve from these small acts. We knew it was a work in progress but never could have imagined that internet search engines with centralized fulfillment centers scattered around the country would become the next iteration of direct buying.

This new system, where seemingly every business and household shops online with packages overnighted from all over the globe, obviating the need to walk down the street to a local brick and mortar business, might resemble my direct but distant buying relationships. There are fundamental differences, though. We weren't trying to save money or time. Our direct buying was about accessing better product from producers who didn't have the volume or the inclination to attract wholesale distribution. Today's online shopping is efficient but the elements of localized wholesalers that we rejected—user passivity and provenance opacity—remain. People shopping online have little connection to the producer. We're getting our delivery tomorrow and we're no wiser for it.

Not all suppliers were the result of my own research. Sometimes people found me or came by referral. I can't remember if I learned about Mountain Dell Farm from Leslie McEachern, the owner of Angelica's Kitchen, the pioneering East Village vegan restaurant, or from Marja Samsom, the chef-owner of the Kitchen Club, a wonderfully idiosyncratic restaurant up the block from Savoy. Both women were renegade chefs forging new ground, also committed to breaking free of the food industrial complex. With Leslie's and Marja's imprimatur and a phone number, I called Mark Dunau and Lisa Wujnovich, listened to the week's offerings, liked their vibe and placed an order. Mark pulled up the following Tuesday in front of the restaurant in a vehicle that looked like it had just come off a caravan trek across the Sahara. A huge Chevy Suburban with a full-length roof rack rigged with ten blue-and-white Coleman coolers strapped on with black bungees, another fourteen stuffed in the interior, its wheel wells were bubbled and pitted from countless winters of road salt spray. It looked like it was provisioned for three weeks in the desert. In fact it was delivering vegetables to eight downtown restaurants. My bike might have been the appropriate technology for my meager two-mile intraborough round trip from the market to the restaurant but there is a place for larger vehicles. This was clearly one of them.

Dirty, holey T-shirt, black jeans, unruly hair, and smudged glasses, Mark was serious about his food and about his way of doing things. His vegetables were delicious, photos of the farm showed well-groomed fields, and stapled to every invoice was one of Lisa's poems, another kind of view from the land. Over the course of the two decades we did business with Mountain Dell, we funneled tens of thousands of dollars from the urban economy, sending it upstream into the rural town of Hancock, New York, allowing Mark and Lisa to continue farming, continue nurturing the soil on which he planted year after year, and to raise two children. The '82 Chevy Suburban was a veritable workhorse, making the weekly three-hundred-mile round trip circle, hauling over one thousand pounds of vegetables on each run. The Chevy carried on until 1998 when it received a full body transplant, a "new" 1988 frame dropped onto the old chassis. When finally put out to pasture in 2009, it had logged over five hundred thousand food miles between Hancock and New York City.

My individual tales of source sleuthing might appear unremarkable or even quaint given today's marketplace where direct sourcing is the rule, not the exception. Internet searching and air-freight fulfillment are incredibly powerful tools. I use them every day and my foraging is immeasurably easier because of it. But our commitment to alternate transport ultimately created an alternate history, one that opened the door for novel producers to thrive and for values like taste, sustainability, and climate change impact to rise to the forefront instead of profit. Searching for alternate means of transport was more than a driver of my sourcing; it was part of my OS, my operating system. Without the aid of search engine algorithms, I had become well practiced in the art of foraging: for ingredients, for inspiration, for connections, for solutions.

PORK SHOULDER WITH PIMENTON RUB

Properly raised pork makes a huge difference in taste over commodity raised meat. My favorite cut to roast is the pork butt, which is actually the shoulder. It is both tender enough to roast or grill and full of flavor because of the activity level of those muscles. This can be done in the oven or on the grill with some wet chips thrown on the coals to add a bit of smoke.

2 tablespoons fennel seed

2 sprigs rosemary, leaves stripped, stems discarded

4 dried chile peppers, such as Thai or arbol chiles

2 tablespoons pimenton

6 cloves garlic, peeled

1 tablespoon salt, plus more for serving

2 teaspoons sugar

⅓ cup (75 ml) olive oil

1 (4- to 5-pound/1.8 to 2.3 kg) pork butt

1. On a cutting board, using a sharp chef's knife, chop together the fennel, rosemary, chile peppers, pimenton, and garlic to create a paste. Transfer the spice mixture to a small bowl, season with the salt and sugar, and stir in the olive oil to loosen the paste. (Alternatively, you can use a food processor or mortar and pestle to prepare the marinade.) Spread the paste all over the pork butt and allow the meat to marinate in the refrigerator for at least 12 hours or overnight. I usually put the pork in a zip-tight bag for ease and efficient use of refrigerator space.

2. Bring the meat to room temperature, letting it sit for at least an hour before roasting it. Preheat the oven to 400°F (205°C).

3. Put the pork on a rack, if possible, so that the heated air can circulate around the meat freely. (Alternatively, roast the pork in a cast-iron

pan or Dutch oven.) Cook for 20 minutes, then turn down the heat to 375°F (190°C). Cook for another 30 minutes, then check the internal temperature—I like to pull the pork out when it registers 135°F (57°C) on a meat thermometer. Let it rest for at least 20 minutes before slicing. Sprinkle with salt before serving.

ROSEMARY

Some ingredients are our culinary friends. We rely on them to make a dish sing, to make us look good in front of our guests. Lemon zest is one of my friends. Trinidad peppers, a scallion-cilantro garnish blend, an anchovy melted into a sauce, are all reliable pals. Sprinkled on top of a dish or added in the final moments before going out into the dining room, they add brightness, life, and punch.

Rosemary was not a member of this inner circle. Without knowing exactly why or when, its fragrance had stopped appealing to me. It seemed medicinal, even aggressively acrid. When I would toss it in at the end of a sauce reduction to extract a final burst of herbal flavor, I often ended up with a sauce more assaulting than sensuous. I blamed myself, thinking somehow I lacked the finesse to control the herb; my reckless side was getting the better of me. Where were the perfumes redolent of the dry, sunny, and stony Mediterranean landscape I imagined would be so right with a piece of roasted lamb or rounding out the garlic and olive oil in a pot of simmering Tuscan beans? I was schooled in the traditional French and Italian dishes associated with the fragrance, but I only wanted to employ ingredients that would make me feel and look good. Rosemary had lost its appeal. So I steered clear. That didn't stop it from coming into the restaurant in bounteous cellophane bags from our conventional produce supplier. It was a staple, always on call in the herb bins, for infusing into our cured olives or frying with the French fries.

One late fall day when all of the tender herbs had long succumbed to frost, I bought a bunch of rosemary from an organic farmer I frequent, but rarely bought herbs from. I found his bunches puny and prices tony. I may always be in pursuit of the finest ingredients but that doesn't mean I'm not price conscious. I keep walking when I read signs for $8/lb string beans or $16/lb lamb shanks. I used some of the sprigs I'd just bought and made a garlic, salt, rosemary paste in my suribachi, a Japanese mortar and pestle with ribbing in the bowl that provides much needed friction, and rubbed it on a porgy. I charcoal grilled the fish in the backyard. Sue and I marveled at how astonishingly flavorful it was and how happy its rosemary-ness made us. I wondered whether I had finally stumbled on the ultimate application or if I had figured out the right dosage for my tastes. Maybe I did have finesse after all. I was in love again.

My remaining sprigs lay forgotten in the storage bin because of a busy social schedule. After several weeks, I noticed during a refrigerator rummage that the rosemary had begun to dry out, becoming brittle. Not quite the toasty crispness of supermarket jar kiln-dried rosemary but it was dry enough so the blades could be broken from the stem. Handling it, I could feel the resin on the leaves and branches, the oils concentrated. It was a decided contrast to the verdant and bushy rosemary I would buy from one of the market's more conventional farmers. When those herbs lay in the restaurant herb bin for the better part of a week, they would blacken and lose much of their odor. Performing triage was pointless; what green needles remained had lost their fragrant qualities. Disgusted with the herbs and with myself for squandering them, I'd pitch them in the trash, declaring it a total loss.

My spindly bunch was different. Feeling the tacky resin on my fingers, I began to wonder. Was this farmer growing a different variety than my conventional farmer? My heart sank at the notion that I might have to become an even bigger agro-dork than I already was and become an expert on rosemary cultivars and obscure heritage varieties. My obsessiveness is legendary, the butt of many family jokes especially about farmstand stops during summer vacations. I am notorious for getting into agricultural ramblings with conversation-starved farmers about ancient melon or bean varieties, putting my curiosity ahead of getting everyone to the lake for a swim. Only angry shouts from inside the hot car finally get me on my way.

Was this my imagination or was there really something here? I set up a comparative smell test for myself but also for Sue, the supremely sophisticated quality control member of our team. With wine, I am loaded with technical knowledge—appellation, soil type, property site, winemaker—informing my sensibility. Sue doesn't accumulate that information; I just pour her a glass and watch what she says. Whether I am opening the good stuff or when we are having weird wine from an unheralded province, I just pour and wait to see what she notices or remarks on. I gave Sue the blind rosemary smell test, saying nothing, just asking her to close her eyes, smell, and tell me which one she preferred. My blind tester selected the organic rosemary deeming it "more fragrant, a more intoxicating perfume."

So why is that? Thankfully for my family and our future swimming excursions, it turns out there aren't all that many varieties of rosemary to choose from. All the varieties are *Rosmarinus officinalis*, deriving from the Latin *ros marinus* meaning "dew of the sea," a reference to their native marine habitat on the Mediterranean coast. *Officinalis* refers to rosemary's medicinal or herbal uses. The *officina* was the storeroom or dispensary in a monastery where all the dried herbs were kept and dispensed, the pharmacy in other words. Other plants with the *officinalis* designation are asparagus, borage, quinine, ginger, sage, watercress, lovage, lemon balm, and dandelion—all stand-up medicinal herbs. The main differentiation I could find in seed catalogs concerned selecting for cold hardiness. Farmers need the plants to survive through whatever winter is on their farm.

If the flavor wasn't about variety, then what did account for the difference? If it's not nature, then maybe it's nurture. There are two factors to consider with conventionally grown produce: the nutrients and the nutrient delivery system. Fertilizers are categorized by their varying compositions of three important elements: nitrogen, phosphorous, and potassium—N, P, K for short. If you look on a bag of fertilizer there will be some numeric like 24–6–16 or 10–10–10 on a conventional bag or 2–4–2 on an organic one, indicating the percentage of these three elements in the bag. Not recognized or accounted for in this labeling system are the micronutrients found in complex organic matter that have a profound impact on plants. That's why organic farmers always add a diversity of materials to their soil, building complexity and health rather than treating the soil as a neutral substrate for delivering nutrients to the plants. I have often heard farmers say that they are soil farmers first and vegetable growers second. Cattle ranchers say something similar; they are grass farmers first, livestock farmers second. This is "you are what you eat" with one degree of separation. I've also heard organic farmers describe their legacy as leaving behind the gift of land with thirty years of soil improvements and enhancements on it, a qualitative wealth that will outlive the farmer. The conventional model does deliver the goods, at least in terms of quantity, but narrowly views soil as a transmitter or vehicle to get the growing done, not as a treasure itself. Some conventional farmers use turbocharged fertilizers getting their N–P–K as high as 20–20–20. The plants respond with vibrant growth and high yields but there is a price to pay for it. One is that conventional synthetic fertilizers are produced from fossil fuels. In pursuit of cheap fertilizer, we search for cheap oil and have adopted a foreign policy (and a defense department budget) to secure it, with disastrous results—the overthrow of legitimately elected governments, war, infrastructure destruction, and repression of opponents to corrupt regimes in the oil-producing nations. Accounting for these externalized costs, organic agriculture might pencil out as a far more economical choice.

The numerics on the fertilizer bag matter but the delivery system for getting those nutrients to the plant is also important. The preferred delivery system for conventional farmers is dissolving the fertilizer in water and then spraying the mixture. Frequent and heavy irrigation allows for rapid absorption of the synthetic fertilizers and the plants then grow quickly and robustly. From a water consumption standpoint this may not represent much of a problem in the Northeast but in some drought prone regions of the country like California and Arizona, it is a serious issue. Dependence on quick uptake of water also goes against the very definition of the qualities we most want from our food: intensity and concentration of flavor.

Flavor is diluted with the addition of excessive water. Beware of vegetables that show growth cracks from taking up too much water too quickly; more water means less flavor per bite. Is that why the bushy dill from Florida at Whole Foods lacks a high dill quotient? It looks great in an Instagram photo scattered on my rice and grilled fish bowl, but the flavor is merely a suggestion of dill. This may also explain why the now ubiquitous arugula topping on every restaurant salad bears little resemblance to the spicy, peppery arugula with leathery leaves I buy from various farmers at the Union Square Greenmarket.

Trying to get too much too fast from a plant or from an animal has its costs. The steer that is pushed to be ready for slaughter in fourteen months with the aid of hormones has less flavor than the steer the takes eighteen- to twenty-four months to grow out to its full weight. Some chefs have discovered that they prefer buying the meat of older dairy cows with the deeper flavor that comes with slow extended growth rather than purchasing meat of a younger Angus steer bred for meat. In the wine world people talk about old vines and hang time. Winegrowers prefer stressed vines because as the roots spread deeper into the soil stratum in search of water, they absorb diverse minerals and nutrient material, which translates into complexity in the glass and lower yields often mean greater flavor.

The same can be said for restaurants. When restaurant operators take as many customers in a certain time period as they can, we call it "pushing the book," i.e., exceeding the limits of the reservation book. The dining room may look full and thriving but inevitably mistakes get made and then written off as collateral damage. An "acceptable" level of dissatisfied customers, plates returned to the kitchen, and employees feeling stretched beyond their capabilities are examples. We can taste the "push" in the food and in the experience, all too common in New York City restaurants.

My spindly rosemary comes from Keith Stewart's farm in Orange County, New York. Throughout the winter, Keith keeps his rosemary plants in unheated high-tunnel greenhouses that shed the rain and snow, protect them from the hard cold, and allow him to provide just enough drip irrigation of water to stave off death by dehydration. Summer takes care of itself; there's less rainfall and plenty of warm days so even if it's not quite the rocky landscape of Cannes or Nice, the plants thrive.

A hot and arid environment stimulates oil production in the plant, in other words, its essential rosemary-ness. The oils are thought to help retain the water inside the plant and slow down transpiration. Ironically, the very thing we desire in quality rosemary is prevented from developing when grown under an intense water-rich, irrigation regimen.

I understood the important differences between organic and conventional farming. In trying to find a balance between financial viability and my ideals, we bought bulk items from conventional sources: onions and carrots for stock, for instance. I'd spend the premium dollars on the local, organic products that showed prominently on the final plate: the beets we cut into a salad, the fennel shavings on top of a roasted piece of fish, not the herbs that melted away in the cooking. I'd get delivered the verdant bushy stuff thinking that my dollars "went further." The difference might have been invisible to the eye but not to the tongue.

Now when I cook something with rosemary in it—my beans *al fiasco*—you can be sure they're made with the rosemary I formerly viewed as spindly and puny. I look fondly at these needles abundant in resinous oil. I swoon over a simple rosemary garlic paste rubbed on a piece of fish or melted into potatoes cooked in duck fat, their starchy sweetness woven with the magical duo of garlic and rosemary, neither with the slightest hint of acrid harshness. My organic choice isn't about health and morality and good stewardship of the planet—although all that matters—but rosemary from Keith's slow-growing, faux-Mediterranean landscape in Orange County, New York, makes my food taste better. I am getting my money's worth, and more important, rosemary is now a member of my inner circle of culinary friends.

GRILLED PORGY WITH ROSEMARY PASTE

SERVES 2 AS A MAIN COURSE

I love porgy. It is inexpensive in the United States but a member of the dorade family of fishes, which are highly prized in Europe. The flesh is sweet and it is ideal to grill whole. The recipe calls for making an herb paste to rub on the fish after making a few cuts on each side to receive some of the herb paste. I use a Japanese mortar and pestle called suribachi to make the paste because its ribbed sides create a textured surface for more efficient mashing, but a traditional mortar and pestle will work too.

1 (2-pound/910 g) porgy
3 cloves garlic
2 teaspoons salt
1 sprig rosemary, stripped (or 1 tablespoon leaves)
½ teaspoon black peppercorns
2 tablespoons olive oil, plus more for grilling and serving
Grilling vegetables such as eggplant or peppers to serve with
   the fish
1 lemon

1. Scale and gut the porgy. I do it at home in the sink and keep the fish in the plastic bag it came in. Use either a fish scaler or the back of a knife to remove the scales in the bag so that the scales don't fly around the kitchen. I do gut the fish on the cutting board and remove the gills along with the guts. Wash in the sink and pat dry. (Alternatively, you can ask your fishmonger to scale and gut the fish.) Make three 3- to 4-inch-long (7.5 to 10 cm) cuts on each side of the fish, from dorsal to ventral, partway into the flesh.

2. Make the paste in your preferred mortar and pestle, starting by mashing together the garlic and salt. (The salt is grist for the mill, helping to break down the garlic.) You should almost have garlic syrup when you are done. Add the rosemary and peppercorns, and continue to

pestle the mixture until nearly smooth. Some rosemary bits will remain. Moisten the rosemary-garlic paste with the olive oil.

3. Rub the paste in the cavity of the fish and into the cuts on each side of the fish. Refrigerate for 3 hours before grilling.

4. In a charcoal grill, build a medium fire. Grill some peppers or eggplants using the intense heat of the young fire. Brush the porgy with oil and then place it on the grill over the coals. Cook for 5 to 8 minutes, until the skin is nicely charred. Flip the fish using a spatula and repeat on the other side but for less time, 3 to 5 minutes. Remove to a plate and squeeze lemon juice over the entire fish. Drizzle with more olive oil. Enjoy the magic of *rosmarin*, an herb from the dry heat of a Mediterranean climate married with seafood from nearby waters.

DINNER SERIES

We go to some restaurants precisely because the menu never changes: the local Greek diner's all day offerings of western omelets, lamb moussaka, tuna melts, and a joyously greasy burger; a French bistro for *soupe à l'oignon gratinée*, roast chicken, steak frites, and tarte Tatin; or a steakhouse for its New York strip, creamed spinach, and wedge salad of iceberg lettuce, hothouse tomatoes, and Roquefort dressing. These restaurants are selling dependability and predictability, the ability to ever-satisfy a specific hankering and a certain sentimentality. Their promise to never take those dishes off the menu means that we can reenact important sense memories whenever we choose. Some restaurants structurally build change into their menus; the "If it's Tuesday, it must be bouillabaisse" weekly rotation found in brasseries strikes a balance between predictability and creativity. Menus printed daily or a server's recitation of nightly specials tries to communicate vibrancy, but they offer little insight as to the motivation of the chef.

There are restaurants that we go to expressly in search of something new. As diners, we offer ourselves over to the restaurant or the chef to show us their stuff whether it's inspired by seasonal availability, a traditional cuisine, or from the interior of someone's imagination. For cooks, our sources of inspiration can come via a variety of means: dining in other restaurants, reading cookbooks, following Instagram postings of other chefs, reworking classics, visiting farmers' markets, and of course traveling.

I wasn't a cook of the dreamy imaginative sort; I didn't need to invent combinations that had never been tried before. I preferred dishes based on ingredient combinations that built on traditions from another time or another place. My weekly foraging at the farmers' market provided a palette of ingredients but the prompts for my culinary creativity came from the written word: culinary histories, foodways cultural studies, agricultural-related environmental writings, and cookbooks. Books by Paula Wolfert, Jane Grigson, Marcella Hazan, Colman Andrews, and Claudia Roden got worked hard early on, as I tried to absorb all I could about foods from particular places, cuisines integral to their cultures. The publication of books like Alice Waters's *Chez Panisse Menu Cookbook*, Michel Guerard's *Cuisine Minceur*, or Diana Kennedy's *Recipes from the Regional Cooks of Mexico* were all culinary events that stimulated lively conversation in the kitchen and rounds of experimentation. Scouring those books for technique and ideas, we were hounds for fresh ideas that would keep us moving forward and on the cutting edge. I would read books and then menu doodle in notebooks, later editing and extracting the best ideas to actually attempt in the pan and on the plate. I look back at pages of unrealized ideas and see that there are still ideas worthy of execution.

My favorite part of *The Chez Panisse Menu Cookbook* was the back section called Memorable Menus, a compendium of menus from events but without recipes; they were sketches, food haiku. Merely listing the dishes served at evenings dedicated to Edouard Nignon, a chef-writer I'd never heard of, Paul Draper's Ridge winery, or a Gertrude Stein–themed dinner was all I needed to dive into the kitchen and attempt to create my version of the dishes in those entries. There was another takeaway though—the idea that dinners can be more than just thoughtfully balanced menus; they can be celebratory, communally shared events.

The dinner event series at Savoy began when Ray Sokolov spoke extemporaneously at the Passover Seder and my sister suggested that I organize dinners like what Ray was doing right then. I knew she was right and immediately began planning a series of dinners for the upcoming fall of 1994. I titled it *The Politics of Eating*, and declared it "a cultural and historical exploration through dining," wanting to distinguish it from the more traditional theme dinners that restaurants often organize like "The Food and Wine of Tuscany" or "A Beef and Bordeaux Blowout." Our dinners would have a conceptual underpinning and we would build menus that highlighted ideas.

Ray was our first guest speaker on old-world and new-world ingredients, the subject of his recently published book, *Why We Eat What We Eat*. That series also featured Michael Pollan, then senior editor at *Harper's*, Jeff Weinstein, *Village Voice* food critic, and Chris Letts, a longtime friend and then education director at the Hudson River Foundation. The series focused on biodiversity, heirloom foods, wild seafood depletion, and ecologically sound eating—topics that have never ceased to interest me and our customers, and over twenty-five years later are still relevant.

Dinners were a set price including wine (originally $65) and ran on two consecutive nights, usually Mondays and Tuesdays, our slowest. I would design a seating plan for all the attendees; seating was communal. This allowed us to maximize the available space and it offered me the opportunity to thoughtfully place people together whom I thought would enjoy each other. Many friendships and a few business partnerships were begun over the evenings but regardless of these tangible accomplishments, the seating plan added to the evening's conviviality and experience of shared purpose.

We began using postcards as our main outreach at the end of our first year in business, with a wonderfully playful cartoon depicting a roadside Savoy sign and one of Susan's pies rotating atop the billboard, proclaiming, "this ain't no greasy spoon," drawn by Alan Bruton, an architect in training by day and a server by night. We notified our customers twice a year about the fall and spring lineup of events, with a few meager lines allotted to other messaging like "Come Eat!" "Now Accepting American Express," and the denouement, in the fall of 2005, "Our website is finally here!" The last postcard was a year later, after which all events were promoted online. During those ten-plus years though, planning, producing, and writing the postcard was a project I cherished. Not unlike working within the confines of our small restaurant space, I loved the challenge of using every square inch, compressing poetic enticements to attend four dinner events into 275 words.

As we were never big on swag beyond matchbooks, business cards, and a fifth anniversary T-shirt, our postcards became our strongest promotional materials. The cards were regular and dependable signals emitting from our Lower Manhattan beacon, reminding all its recipients that life, food, and vibrancy could still be found on Prince and Crosby Streets. People cherished our semiannual posts, tacking them on bulletin boards and hanging them with refrigerator magnets, personal reminders of special evenings or memorable trips to New York or simply because they were beautiful to look at.

The images came from a variety of sources: one of our landlords and prior resident Jody Saslow's 1972 photograph of the building's exterior; a photograph by customer George Woodman; a woodcut by Flavia Bacarella, the wife of farmer Keith Stewart; and a Bruegel woodcut entitled *The Fat Kitchen* I accessed from the Met print collection archives. For our tenth anniversary in 2000, I licensed a pen and ink portrait by J.J. Sempe, artist of innumerable *New Yorker* covers, of a chef riding through the city on a bicycle loaded up with produce. I considered it a spiritual if not personal portrait and justified the expense as destiny, if a bit indulgent. That card announced dinners with environmental philosopher Wendell Berry, chef Rick Bayless, British wine expert Jancis Robinson, and Lower East Side appetizing maven Mark Russ Federman from Russ & Daughters; a stellar lineup.

Dinners began with my opening greeting and introductory remarks by the guest speaker, framing the evening's discussion. Food and talk would then alternate in a gentle volley. This kept the talks from becoming ponderous lectures. It was dinner after all. By the time we neared dessert, I would return to offer final food commentary and the speaker would take questions. I always considered it a measure of success when, after the third or sometimes even the second course, I had difficulty getting people to stop talking among themselves and turn their attention to the speaker.

During a game dinner with Corby Kummer, I had a tableside interaction that provided the springboard for my next phase of programming. The dinner's pièce de résistance was Scottish wild hare, prepared as a true civet with a blood-thickened sauce and garnished with bacon, prunes, and wild mushrooms. A very happy group, tucked into the corner table with a view into the kitchen, motioned me over and shared with great amusement several pieces of lead shot found in the hare's flesh: evidence of weaponry from the chase. The party turned out to be a poet's table: Galway Kinnell, Philip Levine, C.K. Williams, and their wives. While apologetically refilling their glasses with more deeply spiced Quintarelli Valpolicella, I used the opportunity to propose to Galway that we collaborate on a poetry dinner. Everyone thought it a fine idea and we toasted over yet more Quintarelli, to a dinner the following fall with autumn poetry as the focus.

Our previous dinner speakers had all been in the food business: growers, food writers, winemakers. This was the first time I had tapped a customer from a field outside the food world to tell a story. Coinciding with our expansion to the second floor in the fall of 1996, I now had a dining room I could use independently of the main room and expand our definition of what a restaurant could do and provide to its customers. It was a salon, an arena for discussion and exploration of ideas lubricated by good food and fine wine. I was able to merge my roles as chef, host, thinker, connecter in a single evening: my Gesamtkunstwerk taken to another level.

The dinner with Galway was magical. Rather than read his own work, he selected poems that ranged from Shakespeare and Yeats to Stanley Kunitz and Lucille Clifton. The communal tables were strewn with fall leaves that Sue and I had collected on a weekend hike and a fire burned in the fireplace. With Galway's carefully sonorous readings and our dinner of spice-rubbed guinea hen, wild mushrooms tossed in fall herbs, and roasted Seckle pear tart, the evening was a complete evocation of autumn. After plating the guinea hen course, I sat down in one of the lounge chairs in the adjoining room and let Galway's words wash over me. Deeply satisfied, I sensed that I had accomplished something precious and rare. The room was meant for this kind of collaboration. I had hit a vein, rich with possibilities.

There were subsequent poetry dinners: Mark Strand on winter, Donna Masini with poetry of New York City, and a favorite, Charles Simic, reading his own poems, which are sensual, laden with food imagery, and easily accessible. Years later, the poetry dinners morphed into a poetry cocktail slam with guest bartenders pouring cocktails inspired by a poet or a poem. Bob Holman, the designated poet in attendance, led an entourage of drinker-listeners behind him as he toured all the tables, drank every cocktail and then gave wonderfully spirited and reverential readings of each selected poem.

Stephen Jay Gould, the scientist and popular writer about evolutionary biology, lived part-time in SoHo during the months when he taught at NYU and often stopped in for lunch. Mustering my best food scientific fluffery, I approached the table and proposed a dinner topic on something very broad like "the impact of Darwinian evolutionary forces in domesticated crops" to which he grimaced and replied, "I don't know anything about that. I'm an invertebrate paleontologist, specifically, snails." I quickly transformed his rebuff into a more modest proposal. "Then, how about an all-invertebrate dinner?" to which he readily agreed.

I began contemplating fun ways we could highlight the diversity of invertebrate species. Mollusks (clams and mussels), cephalopods (squid and octopus), and crustaceans (crabs and lobster) were obvious choices. My menu riffing soon led me to consider sea urchins, insects, and the plants that populated the earth prior to the ascendance of vertebrates: algae, mushrooms, and the nonflowering plants, botanically known as gymnosperms, which includes all evergreens and the city's widely planted ginkgo trees.

In an homage to Gould's snail research, the menu opened with a periwinkle course, moved on to an abalone and seaweed salad, and a bowl of every kind of bivalve I could lay my hands on: cockles, manila clams, bay scallops in the shell, green lip mussels, little necks, razors, *palourdes*. The entrée was a cuttlefish and lobster stew in a squid ink broth thickened with pine nuts, and we ended with honey panna cotta and bee pollen cookies.

The most daring dish of the evening though was the Japanese custard, *chawan mushi*, with sea urchin, matsutake mushrooms, and ginkgo nuts steamed in the sea urchin shell. I had never worked with urchins before nor had I ever seen the shell used as a cooking vessel but the drama of serving uni custard in its own shell was irresistible.

The project entailed procuring sea urchins in the shell, figuring out how to effectively cut them with scissors to extract the uni intact while still preserving its fabulously beautiful purple-green spiny shell as a cooking vessel. With the uni extracted, I went off to forage ginkgo nuts on the streets of the city. Finding female trees (the males do not produce fruit) that were dropping fruit wasn't too difficult. Although there is a good concentration of ginkgoes along Chrystie Street and Sara Roosevelt Park on the Lower East Side, the foraging competition is stiff from women in Chinatown who gathered them before I usually wake up. Invariably I would arrive, finding only smashed ones on the pavement. The West Village offered a more dependable supply. The day before the dinner, in a chilling drizzle, I collected two night's worth of nuts, several hundred. Andy Feinberg and I cleaned them, first ridding them of their vomit-smelling flesh, then cracking and gingerly extracting each one from their shells. On the afternoon of the dinner we did a tester of the custard in the shell; it was glorious: silken, delicious, and visually striking. We then went ahead, set up sixty shells in hotel pans, loaded them with the uni, gingko nuts, and matsutakes, and then as the first course was going out we topped them off with the custard and began baking them.

When we checked them midway, it was clear that we had a serious problem; many of the urchin shells had cracked from the heat, and bain-marie water was seeping into the custards. Instead of a smooth and ethereal custard, the dish was threatening to become watery egg drop soup. We culled out the completely ruined ones and cobbled together fifty presentable custards.

Following the overprescribed Gould dinner, when some close friends of the house had cancelled two tickets just moments before the dinner started (tickets that had been sold out for over a month), our general manager John Tucker turned to me and said, "*Lion King,* Pete." I gave him a quizzical look, not comprehending. "*Lion King.* It's like tickets to *Lion King.* You pay up front and if you can't make it to the performance people don't call the Broadway theater and give them a sob story. You find someone to take the tickets." It was brilliant. This began pre-sale ticketing for all future events. John created forms and people faxed us their requests along with their credit card number. It was cumbersome but we never got burned again. As fax machines became obsolete, we moved to direct internet sales.

If the Gould dinner had been momentarily problematic, then the Michael Pollan dinner in 2001 for the publication of *The Botany of Desire* precipitated a major restaurant crisis. *The Botany of Desire* is divided into four chapters, each describing a human desire and the plant that humans had adapted through natural selection in pursuit of that desire. Two chapters—Sweetness: Apples and Power: Potatoes—had grown out of dinners Michael and I collaborated on back in 1994 and 1997. With the apple and quince dinner, Michael had begun researching Johnny "Appleseed" Chapman and developed his theory that Prohibition was a major cause of the collapse of North America's cider industry. Our heirloom variety dinner looked at new varieties and explored the issues around genetic engineering, specifically the Bt potato.

In planning the dinner, I wanted to build a menu that would reflect all four chapters. Apples and potatoes were easily integrated into the menu. Since the Beauty: Tulip chapter was about visuals not taste, we decided to place sumptuous vases of various colored and shaped tulips on the tables, reminiscent of the Dutch seventeenth-century fascination with the genetically unstable and forever morphing flowers. All that remained was the Intoxication: Marijuana chapter. Remember, this was more than a decade prior to recreational marijuana being legal anywhere in the United States.

On the postcard for the dinner, I had made a passing reference to the marijuana chapter. After naming some potential dishes we'd be eating, I footnoted with "Sorry, no hash brownies." We were fully booked for both nights. In fact, the dinner had generated so much interest that I moved it into the larger dining room. One morning, prior to the dinner, I was speaking with the pastry chef and her assistant. With a draft menu in hand we were discussing the wording for the dessert: apple cherry crepes with calvados ice cream and finalizing the petits fours to serve with coffee. Usually a fairly taciturn person, the pastry chef lightly offered that since I had mentioned hash brownies in the postcard, I could probably score some weed from the women upstairs.

She was referring to the two women, a fashion stylist and a DJ, who lived on the third floor of the building, with whom we shared a common stairway. When they smoked weed, which they did on a regular basis, the perfume would seep into the public hallway. This wasn't a problem during the day when the staircase was only trafficked by (envious) employees but at night guests would occasionally get a strong whiff. Hosts were instructed to make light of the scent if diners mentioned it ("Ah, downtown New York! Gotta love it").

We all laughed at her suggestion and I began to riff on the theme, suggesting that if she made both hash brownies and faux hash brownies we could indicate the difference with signage allowing diners to make informed choices. I left the kitchen amused by the conversation and particularly happy that, having shared this light moment with the pastry chef, our relationship seemed to have reached a new comfort level. Oh, was I ever wrong.

That was on a Friday. Things were set in motion for the dinner. I spent Saturday with my kids and planned on returning to the restaurant on Monday to execute the menu. On Sunday afternoon the sous chef called alerting me that the pastry chef had turned in her restaurant keys and walked out, saying something about not being able to work for a lawbreaker. I spent the rest of Sunday afternoon trying to reach the pastry chef by telephone, futilely leaving messages about her misunderstanding my intentions, showering her with apologies, all to no avail. The event had triggered something larger for her regarding life in NYC and my transgression was just the nail in the coffin about this crazy town. Within a week she had packed up and moved back to Texas.

Bottom line for me was that I was out a pastry chef with a hundred people coming over the next two days for a special dinner with the dessert spotlighted as one of the key elements of the evening. Scrambling ensued. I hated being in that predicament, but I also knew how to think flexibly and I began crafting several scenarios, although there wasn't much wiggle room on this one. No one in the kitchen was skilled enough to step in, even temporarily.

I turned to Susan, who, four years completely out of the restaurant, eight years since last working as a full-time pastry chef, and now a mother, was completely immersed in the worlds of two young children and their social and developmental needs. In other words, her mindset was as far away from the pastry bench as one could be and she had no interest in remembering the moves required to produce dessert for one hundred people. Her first reaction was a horrified "Don't ask me!," but when it became clear that there were no other choices, she agreed to prep the desserts. I went to my desk and sent out an all-points bulletin for a temporary or a permanent pastry chef and tried to focus on the rest of the dinner. Sue produced a delicious and professionally executed dessert and the dinner was a success, with no one the wiser.

I used the dinners as a means of pursuing my own studies. In an even exchange, I shared my intellectual journey and people got to eat. We covered a wide range of topics: Claude Lévi-Strauss's anthropological theories in *The Raw and the Cooked* with Katherine Alford; wild mushrooms; "Islamic Influences in European Cooking" with Clifford Wright; "Spirituality in

Food" with Elizabeth Luard; "Ossabaw Pigs" with Peter Kaminsky; "Terroir in American Wines" with Jancis Robinson; oysters; "Natural Wines" with Ed Behr; "Cask-Conditioned Ales" with Garrett Oliver; more oysters; "Ethnobotany of the Southwest" with Gary Nabhan; "Marcel Proust" with Richard Howard; "Joseph Mitchell" with Mark Singer; and oysters yet again. I was rarely short on ideas.

I understood the powerful ways in which a shared meal and shared ideas build community, but I hadn't experienced the power of fragrance to do the same thing until the choucroute dinner with Adam Gopnik in 2006. Smells often have more sway than visual appearances. I walk into restaurants and assess the health and happiness of the business by its odors and sometimes walk out. Is the fry oil old, is the garlic sweetly sautéed or aggressively browned? Does the place have a stale or rancid odor of neglect?

After assembling family-style platters of house-made sauerkraut redolent with juniper berry, peppercorns, and bay leaf, piled high with several types of house-made sausage, fireplace-smoked pork belly, and steaming fingerling potatoes, I walked into the dining room and was knocked over by the commanding fragrance enveloping the entire room. It wasn't as if at previous dinners we didn't plate the entire room's food at the same time; we did. But those dishes hadn't necessarily lent themselves to releasing the kinds of aromas that this grand and traditional dish did. With the choucroute platters, everyone had become participants in an edible communal aromatherapy and in the course of all the deliciousness got a history lesson as well. Adam offered insight into how the internal emigration in 1870 of Alsatians to Paris after the Germans defeated the French in the Franco-Prussian War led to the proliferation of brasseries in Paris and choucroute became the "soul food" of Paris. From our choucroute dinner and that single fragrance, a dinner miniseries arose. My other collaborative dinners with Adam on cassoulet and bouillabaisse offered similar opportunities to eat well and listen to an insightful cultural perspective on French cuisine and history.

I targeted writers on book tour, whom I contacted through their publishers, to speak at dinners. Wendell Berry, the father of the food environmental movement and a critical thinker about sustainable economies, was scheduled to be in New York in October of 2000 for the release of his

185

novel, *Jayber Crow*. We pulled out all the stops for Wendell that night with a harvest meal: Asian pear salad with a date vinaigrette and liver toast, Taylor bay scallops with charred poblanos and roasted turnips, spit-roasted capon with chestnuts and Jacob's Cattle beans, and quince apple pie. Guy Jones, our *calçot* farmer, attended and brought enough just-harvested root crops and hearty greens for every guest to go home with armfuls of excellent organic produce. In the intimate setting, Wendell read passages from his new book and took questions about his hopes for a regenerative agricultural approach to farming.

Fergus Henderson, the British hero of eating all the nasty bits, regardless of the animal, passed through New York in 2005 to promote the U.S. publication of *Nose to Tail Eating*. It was one of the few times we actually turned our kitchen over to another chef, becoming sous chefs and commis to help someone else realize their vision for a meal. Fergus's menu comprised tripe, beef heart, bone marrow, and pig's trotters capped by his Eccles cake with Lancashire cheese. Lots of nasty bits.

Over nearly twenty years and a hundred special dinners we pushed ourselves as cooks and restaurateurs to develop new skills or work with new ingredients. Customers benefitted from our growth. We incorporated particularly delicious preparations from the dinners into our repertoire: Paula Wolfert's nut *picadas* as sauce and broth thickeners, Fergus's trotter gear, and Colman Andrew's Ligurian recipe for *salsa marro*, a fresh fava bean and mint mash come to mind. Our takeaway from the brewmaster Garrett Oliver was to add a beer engine at the bar so cask-conditioned beer was always on tap and, after *The Art of Eating* publisher Ed Behr's evening on natural wines, we offered a greater variety of those wines.

Less tangible though were all the ways that the dinners built and embodied community. At the conclusion of most evenings, I'd bring out all the cooks to take a bow and experience the heartfelt appreciation of the diners, in sustained applause, far more visceral than servers coming into the kitchen and telling the cooks, "The folks on table twenty-four are really loving their meal." By participating in the menu development and execution of meals based on literature, poetry, and politics, I impressed upon the kitchen crew that while cooking is a craft, it was also an art, not in a high-brow kind of way that can lead to twee food, but an art as one of many creative expressions in our culture. Our interplay with writers, poets, and thinkers gave even greater weight to the value of our work. And by value I mean something far greater than our day-to-day restaurant transactional exchange of food for dollars.

* * *

We go to some restaurants because the menu never changes, to others because the menu always changes, and then there are the restaurants we go to because we are changed by the menu.

PIETRO'S CANESTRINOS
DI GREAT JONES STREET

The last time I grew anything out from seed I was seventeen and ended up getting arrested. In those pre-sinsemilla days of marijuana horticulture, dime bags came with buds, anywhere from peppered to chock-full of seeds needing to be removed before you could roll a tight, clean-burning joint. Curious nature boy that I was, I decided to moisten the discards on a wet paper towel just as I had done in elementary school science class with lima beans, barely a few years earlier, and seeds being seeds, they germinated. After growing out in small pots on my bureau beside the bedroom window, I transplanted them outside just beyond the lawn's railroad tie edge. Sadly, I never got to reap the benefits of the harvest. The police intervened; they dug them up, took lots of incriminating photos, and directed my parents to bring me down to the station to be fingerprinted and booked. I was living in the Berkshires that summer, painting our country home, while listening to the Watergate hearings unravel the high crimes of Richard Nixon, and hydrating myself with no less than a half-gallon of milk every day before 6 P.M. I was a growing boy (choose either word for emphasis).

My plants had grown magnificently. Or at least that's how it looked from the black-and-white photos the sergeant showed me. Even though terrified about my fate, I was still able to observe that the plants were over five feet tall, bushy, full of leaves, clearly thriving in our canopied hardwood forest and nearly ready for harvest. The police, who readily agreed with my assessment of the plants' ample productivity, determined that the quantity clearly indicated "an intent to sell," and charged me with a felony. When I appeared before a judge, I soberly cowered, having had a small but more than sufficient taste of the crushing power of the state. What I didn't share with his honor was that although I never had any intention of dealing, I still thought it was really cool that from a handful of small seeds you could produce twenty-five magnificent marijuana bushes capable of smoking up scores of people. It was a "Jack and the Beanstalk" tale for the hippie generation. I couldn't comprehend how the innocent act of collecting these little dry spheres, with the addition of water, sunlight, soil, and minimal human intervention, could transform into a threat to society.

I am not sure if that experience arrested my horticultural development, but it was forty-six years until I chose to grow anything out from seed again. Over the years, I had bought herb pots at the market, transplanted and tended ivy and coleus in the restaurant window boxes, but germinating from seed seemed like a deep dive I was never comfortable taking. For starters, our outdoor space in the city has always been shady and even growing healthy herbs requires better light than we have. I also felt that when I wasn't at the restaurant, I needed to cease with the chef mindset. If I was going to grow anything, it would be flowers for beauty and contemplation. I cultivated tree peonies and lilies, hostas, and ferns. I was satisfied with that.

What changed? Maybe it's that the guy who lived on the top floor of our building and colonized the entire roof into a vast tangle of plantings had moved out. I now had the mental space to consider the roof part of my home and by extension to consider cultivating plants on our tar beach. Or it might have been that farmer Rick Bishop, on a slow February market day when he hoped to sell enough potatoes to cover the gas back to Roscoe, said in his infectiously optimistic way, "Hey, you've got to see this little treasure that I just got. First time ever." I was intrigued of course, ever a sucker for insider info. Rick reached into the cab of his truck and returned with a seed packet. It sported a color ink-jet image of the tomatoes I buy from him every September. I put them up—both chopped raw and cooked—ever-ready and versatile for a quick pasta or to augment a wintry soup or stew. From the Hudson Valley Seed Company, it was labeled: Cesare's Canestrino di Lucca. I immediately lusted after a packet of my own.

Linguistically, this slew of names obviously points to Italian origins. Who is Cesare; what is a Canestrino; and why Lucca? What's in a name? A whole lot if you actually take the time to find out. Working backwards, Lucca is a city in Tuscany, located barely twenty miles from the Ligurian coast, a perfect place to grow tomatoes and last I checked, in a country where people have a deep love for tomatoes.

You might expect that where a plant displays great biodiversity is also where you would find a deep appreciation and utilization of that plant. Sometimes that's the case. Peppers hail from Central America and the diversity of peppers in the area's regional cooking is breathtaking. Cooks routinely come home from Oaxaca hauling a mixed bag of dried chiles or tubs of mole in varying colors they've never encountered before. Similarly, the center of origin for potatoes is in high-altitude Ecuador and markets there, even in the smallest villages, sell scores of potato varieties.

Tomatoes are different. While their genetic origins in the wild are in Peru and Ecuador, the vegetable was not widely domesticated until it was brought to Mexico where the Aztec culture developed both a taste and a cuisine for the *tomatl*, the Nahuatl word for them. It's from there, that in the early sixteenth century, Hernando Cortés encountered various *tomatl* salsas and sent seeds back to Europe. The Spanish and Italians quickly incorporated the new food into their cuisines. Southern Italians in particular quickly appreciated its culinary value possibly owing to the harsh climate down the boot and the need for a crop that could thrive in the region's low water and high heat conditions. It's hard for us to imagine what authentic Italian food looked like before the arrival of the tomato. We can barely think of Italian food divorced from the tomato. Not only do we refer to an entire category of Italian restaurants as being red sauce joints, where tomato sauce is at the heart of the menu, but Italians go to all kinds of culinary extremes to preserve and process tomatoes—sun-drying, roasting, and bottling in vast quantities—unmatched by any other vegetable available in the Mediterranean. Many Italian families, and their immigrant descendants in the United States, make passata each year, essentially passing tomatoes through a food mill, cooking it into sauce, and then bottling it for later use.

It's not just in the kitchen that the Italians demonstrate their obsession with tomatoes; they cherish them in the garden as well. Everyone seems to grow a treasured variety of their particular region. There are different tomatoes for every use: for slicing with mozzarella, for preserving as sun dried, ones that store on the stem for use later in the fall and winter, early season tomatoes, late season, and of course for making sauce. As with pasta (which most people buy and would never consider making fresh in their homes), tomato sauce is produced by large-scale commercial operations mostly located in the south of Italy: Calabria, Sicily, and Puglia. The region of Liguria and Lucca in particular are not areas of industrial tomato farming, rather populated with market farmers and home gardeners. There, they cherish a local variety for its flavor density and great sauce-making capabilities. Because of its delicacy in handling, this variety is shunned by large-scale commercial growers and passed between neighbors and families, a reserve held back each year for seed stock. It sometimes appears in small, localized seed catalogs. This Luccan variety is called the Canestrino.

I grew up thinking there were essentially three kinds of tomatoes: the rock hard flavorless ones available year-round that come on BLTs and burgers (from Florida); the torpedo-shaped sauce tomato, Romas (from California); and the farmstand slicing beefsteaks, dripping with juice that my father waxed incessantly about throughout the month of August (from Jersey). Cherry tomatoes were not on my radar. We, Americans love a great raw tomato salad. Maybe that's why tomatoes are the nation's most frequently planted garden vegetable.

Greenmarket farmers introduced me to heirloom varieties, old varieties cherished for taste even if they weren't necessarily the best performers (good food shouldn't be confused with good stock portfolio management). Heirlooms have all sorts of "flaws"; they don't ripen evenly, are misshapen, or have dark colors not typical of our expectation that tomatoes must be red. There were old American varieties—Brandywine, Radiator Charlie's Mortgage Lifter, Cherokee Purple, Aunt Ruby's German Green, and Striped German; foreign heirloom imports—Black Krim from the Crimea, Opalka from Poland, and San Marzano from Italy; and new breeds—Sweet 100, Green Zebra, Yellow Taxi, and Pink Berkeley Tie Dye. The rainbow of colors and sizes was thrilling, requiring little more than arrangement on the plate, a sprinkle of salt, some red wine vinegar, and a drizzle of olive oil to make a superlative dish.

Starting sometime in the nineties, any farm-to-table restaurant worth their salt had an heirloom tomato dish on their summer menu. There might be a direct correlation between heirloom tomatoes becoming trendy and chefs flooding the greenmarket when they realized that there were heirlooms tomatoes at Union Square that couldn't be purchased elsewhere. Tim Stark of Eckerton Hill Farm rode this wave of tomato interest hard.

His specialty was growing heirloom tomatoes, but he also figured out ways to market and package them, offering chefs easy access to his marvelous diversity. Tim put together a three-tiered system: mixed flats of large slicing tomatoes of varying colors, quart boxes of medium-sized fruits with a wide range of shapes and colors, and clustered half-pints and pints of super-special cherry varieties—Mexican wild cherries and tiny currant tomatoes. The ease he offered chefs was brilliant marketing. Most mornings, Tim's stand was mobbed with chefs clamoring to pick up flats off the back of his truck.

All of these tomatoes were picked at or near peak ripeness. They were all about juicy sweetness balanced with lively acidity. But those same fine attributes in a fresh tomato do not cross over to the stove. When cooked, the liquid releases, takes a long time to reduce, and the very freshness that was so alluring is lost. Often with very little flesh, the time required to reduce the tomato juices down into sauce takes so long that the flavor is altered—the extended cooking produces more caramelized flavors, the acidity ameliorated but the sparkling freshness is gone. What if the work of concentration and reduction was done prior, by the plant? That is what paste or sauce tomatoes like the Roma, San Marzano, Amish Paste, and the flavor king of them all, the Canestrino, offer.

Canestrino means "little basket" in Italian, descriptive of the folds and crenulations on the ovoid or sometimes more pear-shaped fruit. They are late arrivals in the market—end of August, though mostly in September—when tomatoes have been flush in the market for several weeks and are actually starting to flatten out, if not wane. That's when Rick starts harvesting his Canestrinos, around the same time that cooks begin to think about conserving and season extension. Probably originally attracted to their unique shape, I brought some home and was immediately astounded by their density and great flavor. Roughly chopped there were no juices leaking and barely any seeds to remove. Tossed into a pan of sautéed garlic and onion it reached sauce status in a matter of minutes and the flavors remained fresh and lively. I began buying flats both for the restaurant and for home, freezing both quick-cooked sauce and raw puree, to offer more culinary flexibility later. The freezer wasn't just a repository of red sauce for on-the-fly dinners; my frozen Canestrino pints became the heart of my winter braises and hearty minestrones. The more famous San Marzanos, even with their special DOP status granted by the Italian government, wished they were this good.

Canestrinos are tricky to grow and store (would Rick have it any other way?). They go from firmly ripe to mush in the wink of an eye. More than once I have kept a flat in my bike room for a few days, too busy to process them immediately, only to return and find a leaky mess underneath them and when picked up they completely collapsed. Not suitable for the industrial food complex with its need for uniformity and durability, Canestrino's delicacy dictates that the cook give themself over to the tomato. Humans are not in charge, the tomatoes are. If they are not going to be eaten today then at least process them now for later use. The industrial model does not want to acknowledge and cede power to the plant. The imposition of power, the requirement that plants conform to processing specifications, is more its style. And so taste is compromised.

The Canestrino is local to the region around Lucca and not widely known outside the region. Several Italian food mavens from other regions I checked with had never heard of the variety. This is where the Cesare part of the name comes into play. It refers to Cesare Casella, a chef who during the nineties and early aughts ran and sometimes owned several delicious and important Italian restaurants in New York City. There is an air of good-food love surrounding Cesare, much like the bouquet of rosemary he always keeps tucked in his lapel pocket regardless of whether that pocket is on a chef coat or a sports jacket. The rosemary is kind of a schtick, but kind of not. Cesare is about flavor and taste, through and through. In that pursuit, he introduced many singular ingredients to the United States by giving seeds to Rick to plant: wild arugula; nineteen different varieties of shelling beans, including the Sorana from the Po Valley—the creamiest bean I have ever cooked; and the Canestrino di Lucca. Cesare got burnt out on being a restaurant chef in NYC and now advises a farm in Orange County, New York, that works with developmentally challenged individuals, involving them in farmwork and food production. Without Cesare's transatlantic seed migrations, chefs and avid cooks in New York City wouldn't have access to this sauce making wonder. Nor would a whole lot of Guatemalans, where the Canestrino is simply and accurately known as #1. The seeds traveled to Guatemala with some of

Rick's workers after their seasonal H-2A visas came to an end. Stashed in the air filters of their cars being shipped back home, to avoid any questions at the border, the Luccan seeds are wending their way back towards the tomatl's original place of domestication.

My own packet of Cesare's Canistrino di Lucca seeds arrived by mail in early April. I downloaded information on how to grow tomatoes from seed and went about putting two seeds, each one-half-inch deep, in a dozen peat plug containers filled with soil, watered them, and proceeded to wait. I set them on top of our radiator, a warm offering of encouragement. After about a week, teeny green heads began to pop through the surface. Each morning when I came down to make coffee, I'd inspect for new lives and take a census while misting my brood. The kick I got from seeing them develop was better than my morning cup of joe. By the end of the second week, I had a 100-percent germination rate. I hung a Gro-Lux bulb very close to the starts so that they wouldn't get gangly and watched as they slowly grew a second set of leaves, their first true leaves, ones recognizable as tomato plants. Soon, they even had the odor of tomato plants. After about a month I began to "harden them off," giving them a taste of the real world by setting them outside in the garden for a few hours but bringing them inside overnight. In mid-May I moved them up to the roof and planted them in large three-foot-cube planters that previously held peach trees that hadn't survived after the top floor neighbor departed. In early July, I spied the first classic little star-shaped yellow tomato flower. I allowed that I might really succeed in producing a crop. Green fruits began to develop but I quickly noticed that some were blackening on their undersides. Frantic, I consulted with farming guru Baba Rick, showing him photos. He told me this was black rot, the result of a calcium deficiency in the soil, and to immediately go buy some garden lime, dissolve it into a slurry, and amend the soil around the plants. His prescription worked and in early August I harvested my first 'mater—an eight-ounce beauty—more canestrone (a big basket), in my opinion, than canestrino. Success!

I harvested a few more over the next week, then a big haul in mid-August when I started to see new troubles. Leaves were yellowing, plant tops were wilting and failing. Dr. Rick identified it as early blight, not fatal to the plants but compromising to their health and productivity. If too many leaves died or withered, photosynthesis would be compromised, which would translate into fewer and less flavorful tomatoes. Daily, I clipped the ailing leaves, hoping to slow the blight's spread. My haul was curtailed but still healthy for our house of two.

With ample flow from the roof down to my apartment, I decided to stew some tomatoes together with some eggplant. It's a late summer recipe that is almost rote for me—eggplant, tomatoes, onions, and garlic stewed together with the seasoning options to be determined in the moment: add capers, raisins, and vinegar and it becomes caponata; zucchini and basil steers it towards ratatouille; or add in some chile peppers and garnish with grated ricotta salata and serve over pasta, alla Norma style. I opted for the later. With this rendition I used a handful of Pietro's Canestrinos di Great Jones Street—my homegrown, Great Jones Street tomatoes. Transportation distance? Eighty feet, from roof to skillet.

It is a gift to have fruit of such quality come from the soil on my roof, from my efforts and attention alone, independent of any direct economic transaction. As with my choice not to expend fossil fuels to get food from the market to the house or restaurant by riding a bicycle, I can grow food with little monetary expenditure, only paying for seeds, maybe some fishmeal to enrich the soil, and a few stakes to keep the plants from falling all over themselves. It's not about the money saved. Growing your own is a way of not being entangled in the clutches of the corporate farming system, where tomatoes are selected for qualities I do not share: uniform size, red even color, durability for transnational shipping, and sadly with little regard to taste. If shopping from farmers all these years at the market has been a form of urban resistance and taking charge of how and with what I fuel my body then I ratcheted it up this summer by growing my own. Growing is an act of resistance.

The little seeds that cooks often squeeze out and discard so they have a smooth sauce contain all the information for making a new crop and for sustaining life. How a little speck as big as a pinhead turned into five-foot-high plants full of little yellow flowers that every couple of days would transform into green orbs that plump up, then blush pink and in time turn red, replete with the "little basket" folds on the surface that resemble the folds on Rick's tomatoes, is a marvel to me. Rick and I are little more than stewards or shepherds, cherishing these tomatoes year after year, saving and sharing the seeds from one year to the next.

Seed companies may trademark their crosses and selections, but at its core, each seed contains DNA reaching back thousands of years with a story of cohabitation in its environment; information that cannot or should not be owned. The idea of seed ownership belies an anthropocentric view of the tomato when in fact, the tomato does not belong to us, we are just beneficiaries of its wealth. Native Americans teach planting three kernels of corn in each hole: one for the crow, one for the worms, and one for humans. In this worldview, there is no arrogance, no presumption of ownership or implied hierarchy in the order of things. We are one of earth's creatures, among many.

So Cesare brought some seeds over from Italy who shared them with Rick Bishop who shared them with Zach Pickens who grew them out for seed for the Hudson Valley Seed Company where I had received a $100 credit as a thank-you gift for a fundraising dinner I had cooked for Food and Environment Reporting Network and applied some of my credit to obtain a twenty-five-seed packet and grew them out and made seven dinners for me and Sue, and put four pints in the freezer for later in the winter, and saved a few dozen seeds for next year so that I can grow them again and give them away to friends and family. This wonderful Bible-like chain of begetting tells an alternative story of how to access delicious food without any money changing hands. You could get arrested for spreading ideas like that.

PASTA ALLA NORMA

SERVES 4

What better celebration of the Canestrino tomato than to make a pasta sauce and pair it with eggplant, another star ingredient of peak summer? Basil and ricotta cheese round out this sumptuous dish. I like to buy the long Japanese eggplants, but the large Italian varieties will easily work as well.

Olive oil

2 Japanese eggplants (each about 9 inches/20 to 25 cm long), sliced into ½-inch-thick (12 mm) rings

4 cloves garlic, minced

3 dried chile peppers, such as Thai or arbol chiles, broken up

6 Canestrino tomatoes, roughly chopped (about 2 cups/360 g)

½ cup (15 g) loosely packed basil, roughly chopped

Salt, for cooking the pasta

1 (16-ounce/455 g) package dried pasta

4 ounces (115 g) ricotta salata

1. Generously coat the bottom of a 10-inch (25 cm) skillet with olive oil. Working in batches, add the eggplant slices in a single layer and sauté them over medium-high heat until nicely browned on one side. Turn the slices over to brown them on the other side, then remove to a paper towel–lined plate. Repeat with the remaining eggplant slices, adding more olive oil between batches as needed.

2. Lightly toast the garlic and chiles in more oil. Add the tomatoes and increase the heat to high. Cook off the liquid until a sauce consistency is achieved. Add most of the basil along with the eggplant. Reduce the heat to medium and stew for about 20 minutes, until the eggplant is softened and the flavors have melded.

3. Meanwhile, set up a pot of salted boiling water for the pasta. Cook the pasta to al dente and drain, reserving 1 cup (240 ml) of the cooking liquid.

4. Toss the pasta into the pan with the sauce and twirl until well combined, adding some reserved cooking liquid, a little at a time, to achieve your desired sauce consistency. Garnish with the remaining basil leaves and grate the ricotta salata on top.

FINDING COMMUNITY

In high school, I wrote an essay comparing Huck Finn to Dean Moriarty in Kerouac's *On the Road*. Appreciating the corollaries with my life, I decided at sixteen I was ready for a journey. I convinced the school principal that by doubling up on required history classes and taking English lit in summer school I could fulfill my requirements in three years. The summer program was an intensive creative writing and literature class at a private school in a neighboring town.

We were four in the class: two boys, two girls. Everyone was there for personal enrichment. My school's classes averaged twenty-four students; this felt like a college honors seminar. Absent any prior history, the other boy and I bonded, seeing a mirror and worthy foil in the other. His name was Tony; he was fast-tracking graduation as well. We were good sparring partners, teasing apart the themes of the assigned readings. The teacher must have had a dark side, given the summer selections—*Long Day's Journey into Night*, *Hamlet*, and *The Glass Menagerie*—all bleak portrayals of poisonous relationships between troubled young men or women and their mothers. The darkness didn't perturb us; we were uplifted by Shakespeare's brilliance and fascinated by O'Neill's tragic world of addiction and abuse. My compositions were like botanical drawings keenly observed from nature and carefully rendered; Tony's were gonzo surrealist dreams retrieved from inside his head in fast brush strokes, full of bawdy irreverence.

We shared an obsession with chefs and restaurants. His was Typhoid Mary, the asymptomatic patient-zero, who worked as a private chef in and around New York during the early decades of the twentieth century and infected over fifty people with typhoid, many of whom died. Tony loved the twisted underside of a cook knowingly serving up sustenance with a side of death. Mine was tame, even naive, in comparison: Alice's Restaurant, Arlo Guthrie's eighteen-minute-long talking blues rag recording on war resistance. It was the summer of '72; opposition to the Vietnam War was at a fever pitch. As much as I was in awe of Guthrie's anti-war monologue, I was equally intrigued by the notion of Alice's Restaurant, a country restaurant as communal hangout. I wanted to run away to Stockbridge, Massachusetts, find Alice and Ray, and join the family.

After class we used to go back to Tony's house, get stoned, and listen to music. The one album we played over and over again, never getting enough of it, was the psychedelic soul sound of "Time Has Come" by the Chambers Brothers. It spoke to our cores—"I don't care what others say, time has come. . . ." The beat of the cowbell bent time, gradually slowing to a halt and then reactivating the song after a stoned-out moment of emptiness. The cowbell has never been put to better use.

I'd ride my bike home after those afternoons, content knowing I'd bonded with a kindred soul also set on breaking free from our cushy milieu. Like summer romances that can't sustain into the fall when old alliances are reasserted, we went separate ways when class ended in late July. I considered our friendship a near miss, one that could have developed into something deeper if life hadn't intervened.

I didn't make it to Alice's but that summer I got as close to a commune as I think I ever will. I spent that August on a farm in northwestern Connecticut, a back-to-the-land homesteading project. We raised and slaughtered rabbits, chickens, even a heifer. I learned to use an adze and a drawknife to prepare logs for erecting a log cabin, built teepees, and refurbished a two-hundred-year-old dairy barn. Homesteading emphasized self-reliance and reclaiming the crafts our culture had turned our backs on: gardening, animal husbandry, and preserving. I was engaged and energized by working with my hands. Kitchen work was a short leap away.

After my brief Vermont kitchen experience and three years of college in California, I found my way back into commercial kitchens and returned to the East Coast to seriously pursue cooking as a career. I tried to enter the culture of New York's midtown French houses but wasn't a good fit for a classical brigade kitchen. I couldn't abide the verbal abuse and the necessary submission to unquestioned authority. I bristled at saying, "*Oui*, Chef." An exploratory visit to the Culinary Institute of America was also a nonstarter. The curriculum was old-school and it looked more like the dorm mayhem of *Animal House* than a rigorous training program.

I returned to the city determined to find a good house to work in and with kindred spirits.

I landed at two of the city's most influential restaurants during the eighties: first in 1980 at Barry and Susan Wine's Quilted Giraffe, on Second Avenue in the Fifties, where France's nouvelle cuisine met New York's nouveau riche; and then later in 1985 at Huberts, Len Allison and Karen Hubert's earnest and moderately priced Gramercy Park restaurant that broke new ground by serving nascent farm-to-table fare (known at the time as New American cuisine). Both couples were American, their skillsets more akin to film auteurs than chefs. They showed little interest in emulating or gaining acceptance from New York's classic high-end establishments. Eschewing traditional culinary résumés, they hired people for who they weren't more than for who they were. What these owners lacked in culinary chops they made up in vision, gumption, and the ability to elicit high-quality, innovative food from a band of passionate and dedicated young cooks. With zero culinary pedigree, both restaurants rose in the city's competitive marketplace, garnering three (Huberts) and four (Quilted Giraffe) stars from the *Times*. These successes were representative of the cultural break occurring in New York's upscale kitchens, away from European dominance. We were young Turks, members of a generation of American cooks nationwide defining a new aesthetic for sophisticated dining.

Without a chef elder guiding our development, we relied on each other, sharing knowledge we'd gleaned elsewhere (often at the very French houses we were dismissive of). Denied the clear map for career progression that the brigade system offered with its kitchen organization, akin to military rankings—commis, entre-metier, poissonier, sous chef, defined rungs to climb on the hierarchical ladder—we referred to that "gated" community as the French Mafia. Knowing we were locked out offered many of us the freedom to pursue free-spirited, sometimes haphazard advancement paths and European walkabouts in search of kitchens with a deeper grounding.

After six months at Quilted Giraffe, I was adrift. I didn't relate to QG's notion of nouvelle cuisine: cream of enoki mushroom soup, caviar-filled crepes tied with a chive bow and beef tenderloin with demi-glace sauce, gold-leaf dishes lifted from meals eaten at highly rated Gault&Millau (the nouvelle alt-guide to the tired and passé Michelin) spots in France.

Someone, I can't remember who, told me about a culinary teacher in Boston named Madeleine Kamman and handed me a copy of her book *The Making of a Cook*. Taken with its intelligence and rigor, I made a swift trip to Boston in search of her cooking school but came up short. She had just relocated to Annecy, France. Following the trip's only consolation, a balmy summer-night ballgame at Fenway, I tore off a letter declaring my need to study with her. "This is the perfect moment in my life and in my professional development to catapult me forward. I will do anything that needs to be done—take out the garbage, stand on the porch and watch through the window—anything." Hard to turn down, right? Wrong. The class was full, as was the spring semester. Disappointed but still determined to expand my knowledge base, I dreamed of a *stage* at Frères Troisgros, a three-star restaurant known to be more adventurous than chez Bocuse. I arranged a sublet for my SoHo apartment but had yet to buy a ticket, set an actual departure date, or give notice at work. Lacking a plan for where to go or how to start, I was going to wing it.

One Saturday night, at the end of service, the customer pay phone near the bathrooms rang. It was my girlfriend telling me I needed to call a woman named Didi in Boston right away. It had something to do with Madeleine Kamman. With a handful of quarters at the ready in case it was a long call, I listened to Didi tell me that someone had dropped out and if I could get myself to France in two weeks time I could join the class. "Oh yes, indeed. I will be there." I hung up the phone and gave my notice.

Two weeks later I nervously wandered through the old city of Annecy to Madeleine's apartment, unsure of my surroundings and of my bet on her wisdom. From the very first morning, as I excitedly scribbled away in my notebook, amazed to be learning the geology and climate of different regions of France and Italy in a cooking class, I knew I had hit gold. Madeleine drew the connection from geography and what grew in the region to how cooking what was on hand developed into a regional cuisine. After the morning lecture we would cook some of the dishes for lunch, drink wines from the area that expressed the terroir, then call it a day. Oof, that was tough. On side trips to Paris we scoured the city for regional restaurants still serving food from the Landes, Périgord, the Pays Basque, and Provence. Madeleine directed us to seek out the kitchens of female chefs, the best practitioners of older flavors, traditional dishes. In Lyon she cautioned me away from eating at chez Bocuse, instead sending me to La Voûte Chez Léa for tablier de sapeur (breaded tripe, fireman's-style) and cervelle de canut (literally translated as "brains of the silk workers," a dish of fresh cheese curd with chives and shallots), and to La Mère Brazier, the house of Bocuse's early training under France's first female three-star chef. I rode my bike through the Auvergne, Cévennes, and Larzac in search of the old dishes, what Madeleine called "*le vrai cuisine*"—real food. Casssoulet and bouillabaisse? Those were for tourists. I was on the hunt for the best versions of tripes à la mode de Caen, le grand aioli in Arles, pieds paquets (lamb's feet and tripe) in Digne; I discovered salted liver in Albi, snails with walnuts near Montpellier, kugelhof and kouign-amann in the north. Even in 1980, those traditions were rapidly disappearing.

I came home a very different cook. Madeleine had given me a viewpoint and a metric by which to design dishes, judge menus, and frame my culinary explorations. I was done with haute cuisine, the pursuit of refined tastes to the point that the soul, the guts had disappeared from the plate. Cooking what was on hand, in season, and close to the land was what I wanted regardless of whether it was the food of provincial Europe or of the American countryside.

With this new perspective I landed at Huberts and joined a team more like a circus troupe, with each player bringing to the kitchen a special set of skills they were perfecting, than a traditional kitchen strategically organized to produce a single vision and menu. It was a delicious free for all, with everyone committed to raising the visibility and the status of cooks, moving beyond its blue-collar service class stigmas. We saw ourselves on par with other creatives working with their hands and bodies—artists, athletes, and rock musicians.

It was grounding to be in a business that valued sensuality and the pleasures of the table as a necessity of life. I loved learning about the earth's edible delights by taking wine classes, tasting cheeses, visiting producers, and sharing my knowledge with others. I didn't associate any of it with succumbing to temptation or corporeal excess. Decadent and sinful weren't words I used to describe the foods I most enjoyed preparing. More wasn't necessarily better.

The quandary is that the allure of restaurants and our collective prosperity is linked with consumption and indulgence. In restaurants that really crank, managers drill into servers the importance of upselling. They even track each server's sales average per customer, using it as part of a performance review. As an owner I was torn, disapproving of transparent upselling techniques—"I just want to let you know that the chicken takes a while. Do you guys want to split a salad to start?"—but thrilled when servers earned the trust of diners and could turn them on to some of the rare gems that I had proudly procured. We are able to tempt diners into even better rewards than they planned for themselves. Sommeliers whisper that they have the latest release of a boutique Oregon winery pinot noir or scallops pulled from Peconic Bay that very morning. All the diner needs is a credit card to access these experiences.

The flip side for the restaurant industry is that the blowout evening, a pinnacle marker of success and arrival, replete with a multicourse tasting menu and prodigious consumption of top-shelf alcoholic beverages, became license for all to indulge and sometimes over consume. After hours, with easy access to open bottles and the illusory fast money from cash tips, industry employees had quick relief from the stress of a night service. Sadly, abuse is rampant in restaurants. How could it not be? The "staff drink" is free, and the community is dependent (thrives) on consumption.

I wasn't a teetotaler, but I was a nerd. I participated in plenty of postmortems to rehash the evening's service at the nearby watering hole. I needed the decompression beer and debrief like everyone else, but I didn't use the shift drink as a prequel to a night of adventures. As much as I longed to connect with my peers and feel part of a community, I viewed my line-cook shifts as if they were school, or if not school, then sports practice and I was in training to become an athlete. Sleep, diet, and fitness were all required parts of the regimen. I wasn't going to join a club, if gaining acceptance meant overindulging. Yet, I always felt a tinge of sadness, getting up from the table when others stayed behind for a round of rounds—my self-imposed exile.

Showing up for a shift, on little sleep, with a partier's special cologne of perspiration, stale tobacco, and metabolized alcohol, had professional consequences: a dulled palate, diminished mental acuity, and a slowed response time. It could be tasted in the over-reduced braises or scorched pans of vegetables forgotten in the oven. In much the same way that the lifestyles of rock musicians and abstract expressionist painters were glorified in spite of their self-destructive habits, chefs' lifestyles were similarly glorified. I was convinced that in addition to the pain of the accompanying hangover, there would be a career price to pay for the excesses, that bad actors would not prevail. Clearly, I was wrong about that (at least for a while). Keeping myself apart from the carousing cook culture meant I also sacrificed acceptance by and visibility with many of my colleagues. The New York chefs gaining notoriety were the living-large partiers, relishing their misfit status. I was torn: I wanted nothing to do with their activities and I was envious of the attention they were getting.

Feeling particularly isolated during my chef but pre-Savoy years, I decided to organize chef potluck picnics. Quilted Giraffe and Huberts alumni were at the core but it had a broader guest list: Alfred Portale, newly installed at Gotham; his girlfriend, later wife, Helen Chardack; Traci Des Jardins, then at Montrachet; Michael Rose, Felipe Rojas-Lombardi's chef from the Ballroom; and Anne Rosenzeig of Arcadia all participated. Here were the seeds of an alt-chef community, but after three annual events, we opened Savoy and my focus shifted.

In the summer of 1994, I found myself on a bus heading from San Francisco to Fetzer Vineyards for a gathering of a group called Chefs Collaborative 2000. Earlier in the year, I had reluctantly attended their New York "charter signing," a ceremony with local chefs proclaiming a commitment to source sustainably. I viewed it as a publicity stunt, absent of a substantive action plan. I had scorn for the chefs who showed up for the photo op but hadn't shown much commitment to good sourcing. The gathering at Fetzer turned out to be different. Set in the middle of a magnificent Mendocino County organic garden and vineyard, many of the nation's most exciting new generation of chefs had convened to share their life paths and their commitment to weave their personal values into their culinary endeavors. An ethical outlook underpinned the good food and good times.

The retreat was low-tech and high-octane. Many of us camped in tents at the vineyard including Sue, me, and Theo, our then one-year-old son. With a portable crib in tow, Theo took his afternoon naps under the shade of an olive grove while I listened to panel discussions about seed sovereignty and the dangers of seed patenting, joined open mic sessions on the successes and challenges of buying directly from farmers, and enjoyed comparative farmstead cheese tastings. I'm not sure what made me happier: drinking in the analyses of the food system with all its new vocabulary or finding so many other chefs similarly thirsty for the same information. This was a club I wanted to be a member of, one that believed that the "best" needed to be grown and produced in ways that sustained life, the planet, and the people making it. I had found my people, my kin, even if dispersed across the nation.

* * *

Tony came back into my life shortly after this, in late 1995. He had similarly dropped out of college, found the food world a welcome place for his curiosity, worked in a tourist town restaurant, and decided to become a chef. In New York, he took over the kitchen of one of those doomed-before-it-even-opens restaurants, the ones where somebody's rich backer or lover lets them play out the fantasy of owning a restaurant. Opening in a large space, undercapitalized and without a liquor license, they quickly ran out of money, were unable to complete the dining room renovation, and then in trying to save the sinking ship, fired the chef (my friend and former employee) when he objected to eliminating the sous chef position, dumbing down the menu, and outsourcing all bread and dessert production. Tony happily complied; it meant less work and fewer people to manage. He promptly dragged a desk into the middle of the kitchen, replete with a dirty ashtray to collect the cigarrette butts he smoked during service, and a perpetually half-full rocks glass containing some high-proof, brown liquor. Tony was hoping this would be a cushy gig where he could spend most of his time writing his next kitchen murder mystery. My partner from the summer of our liberation had stooped so low: taking owners for a ride, sending his dishwasher out during shifts to cop drugs, and worst of all, not making good food. Instead, what he was making was a big "fuck you" statement to the owners and their diners (which they soon came to understand).

By this time in my career I was deeply invested in personalizing every aspect of our work—putting a face on the food by knowing my producers, making their work visible to others, knowing my customers, and empowering my employees to have a voice and a role in the creative process. Not only did I want to reform the way food was raised, I wanted to transform the exploitive nature of the workplace and emphasize the artistry and craft in our career—work that had become increasingly devalued. Cooks had been seen as disposable and interchangeable, as were the ingredients; everything and everyone was tailored to maximize profit in the industrialized food supply.

Tony was satisfied to buy whatever protein was cheap, sear it in a hot pan, baste it with a lot of butter, and then serve it up, presuming that the customers didn't care and would never know the difference. He was smugly dismissive: everything and everybody was expendable. I was right there with him and angrily dismissed him for accepting it. This wasn't a near miss, this was a story of roads diverged. My anger was further fueled by what I found to be his pretentious demeanor. One expression of that was he no longer went by Tony. He was now only Anthony—Anthony Bourdain.

* * *

The Chefs Collaborative Fetzer retreat was a tectonic shift in my relationship to the chef community. The organization, only a year old, was an offshoot of Oldways Preservation Trust, a group dedicated to exploring and celebrating the cultural importance of traditional cuisines, especially the Mediterranean olive oil reliant ones (funding came from the OPEC of the olive oil world, the International Olive Oil Council). They organized press junkets of the highest order.

I attended an Oldways trip to Morocco the following year. Jammed together on buses with other food influencers from around the globe, we ate *mechoui* (whole spit-roasted lamb) with our hands, I got hopelessly lost searching for ras el hanout in the Fez souk, and helped prepare a Marrakesh luncheon of little fish with charmoula, the bold and bright sauce that would soon become a Savoy classic. My brief immersion into a place and its tastes made clear that cuisine was an expression of history, ethnography, geography, and natural history—my subjects of interest in and out of college. I knew with my belly and my heart that I had chosen the right career and was hanging with the right group of people. The grand, weeklong mash-up of culinary professionals spawned countless friendships and collaborations that still endure decades later.

As an Oldways spinoff, Chefs Collaborative aimed to look at the full range of food sustainability concerns, specifically for chefs. The early years of the organization were electric with our urgency to unravel the truths about the food system and to figure out how we could improve our sourcing and kitchen practices. We did this as a community: teaching each other, tapping experts to school us, and then reframing our newfound knowledge for hands-on kitchen use, offered freely in our growing community. Everyone I met at Collaborative gatherings had a different life story to tell. There were disgruntled academics, frustrated painters, rebellious theater majors, all fascinating nontraditional journeys peppered with work stops at non–New York restaurants largely unfamiliar to me.

We were trying to create a language and a framework to sift through the complexity of food and agriculture issues. Realizing that food choices are political and that food is a lens through which to examine our culture, the Collaborative wrestled with a range of topics and published broadsheets that illustrated the complexity of choices rather than prescribe to chefs a single position: organic versus local agriculture; wild versus farm shrimp; grass versus grain fed beef; fair trade labeling of tropical ingredients; and genetically modified organisms (GMOs).

Kitchen technique mattered as well. We toured the nation with comparative salmon tastings: frozen at sea Alaskan; fresh, wild Pacific King; the less popular sockeye; and Atlantic farm-raised, highlighting where the intersection of taste and information could help chefs decide for themselves which they preferred. The Collaborative ran demonstrations on whole animal butchery: how to cut the animals, how to utilize all the parts, and how to do it profitably.

The Collaborative set a large agenda and went far beyond trying to be an organization providing feel-good gatherings for its members and doling out "best chef" awards. Wanting to change the way people eat and how food is produced in this country is radical. A lot of people and a lot of money are invested in maintaining the status quo. Chefs from Julia Child on down to Thomas Keller have repeatedly said in the press that taste is all that matters, criticizing examinations of how or where food is raised as incidental. Predictably, we came under attack for being part of a nanny culture, prescribing or legislating how people should eat. We were pegged as high-minded, anti-business, pious eco-chefs. Even Tony took pot shots at our approach because it threatened his renegade, live-large credo of eating, drinking, and doing whatever felt good.

In 2000, I received a call from CNN asking if I would comment on the newly published tell-all restaurant book *Kitchen Confidential*. Even though I had read an excerpt in the *New Yorker*, I speed-read the book, looking to enumerate all the ways that Tony's kitchens were not my kitchens. Fish could be fresh on Monday just as easily as you could be served old fish on Friday; my cooks would happily select a great steak and cook it medium-well, not save grizzly end cuts for the medium-well diners; and I'd never had sex in the walk-in (although its privacy did come in handy for conferences when nowhere else was unavailable). My oppositional screed probably boosted sales. People are hungry for the raw truths and lascivious behind the scenes tales even when truths are exaggerated for literary effect.

I can be earnest—sometimes overly so—to the point that local chefs have been embarrassed to share their sources with me, thinking I would judge their sustainability correctness. I was on a crusade, hoping to shift the culture of indulgence and ignorance that resulted in degradation, societal and environmental. Tony was romanticizing restaurants as havens for the misfits—where anything goes, any abuse is not only acceptable, but glorified. Whether it was the powders snorted or the asses grabbed, it was all part of the pirate's life. Tony was the fox in *Pinocchio* singing "Hi-Diddle-Dee-Dee" as he packed all the boys off to Pleasure Island. This was not the life for me. His words unleashed not only more male privilege and exploitation, but they held disdain for efforts to change the unjust world we were part of.

Regardless of the critiques from Bourdain and his chef buds, I pressed on with my involvement with Collaborative. What I found compelling was the information sharing that happened, often over postmortems drinks following a culinary event or board meeting. We exchanged information and sources: where to buy true wild rice, compared notes on favorite dry beans, why small-batch Austrian vinegars were terrific. And we exchanged favorite authors with more gusto than restaurant recommendations, novelists who tapped into the spirit of our longings: Annie Proulx, Louise Erdrich, Wallace Stegner, John Berger; and must-read nonfiction writers who set the broader stage of our concerns: Wendell Berry, Jared Diamond, Wes Jackson, Carl Safina, Mark Reisner.

I finally had the community that had eluded me in the New York scene. I would come home from meetings juiced up from the connections I was forming with like-minded chefs. Greg Higgins from Portland, Oregon, introduced me to making house charcuterie; Odessa Piper to seeing landscapes as foodsheds, akin to watersheds; Chris Douglass from Boston pioneered casual but sustainably sourced cooking with Ashmont Grill, a model for the future Back Forty; and Rick Bayless from Chicago was meticulously shining his sustainability light into as many dark corners of his operation as he could. Susan encouraged my Collaborative outings, even when they added pressure to our intense home life with two small children, because I always came home reinvigorated, with new ideas that pushed me and the restaurant forward.

Residing in separate cities had its advantages. With fewer opportunities to feel competitive and protective of information because of the constant need to maintain an edge in the ever-tightening and fickle local marketplace, we shared the daunting and discouraging parts of our careers: the challenges of making money, keeping it profitable, and the constant hiring and labor headaches. We also compared notes on not participating in the dominant culinary culture of bad boy chefs cooking loud, showy food.

Our cooking—what came to be called farm-to-table—was having its fashionable moment in the food media. My outsider pursuits were finally on the inside. Maybe I wasn't asked to pose naked in a blender ad but I was being recognized by the peers I held in high regard and as the organization's chair from 2000 to 2006, I became a national voice in this good food conversation. The Collaborative's mission and work was reflective of my core values—living in moderation and acting in ways that protected the earth and our future.

***

Tony and I began to intersect again around 2004. We were both enamored with Fergus Henderson, the British chef with his nose-to-tail ethic. Whole animal use appealed to me because it further "personalized" the meat we were sourcing, honoring the single animal's life that was sacrificed for our eating pleasure and committing ourselves to use every part, to waste nothing—the antithesis of selfish excess. I was intrigued to delve back into traditional cultures and find recipes that utilized the odd cuts and unfamiliar organs to make delicious food from privileged people's discards. Tony liked the taboo-breaking, boundary-crossing elements of eating all the nasty bits. He loved the shock value of eating outrageous foods because it placed him outside the mainstream culture and let him wave a flag for the foods previously relegated to poor people's plates. Tony wrote the introduction to Fergus's American edition of *Nose to Tail Eating* and for its release I hosted a dinner with Fergus at Savoy. Tony did not attend. Maybe he held a grudge from the CNN clip. I don't know.

At this point Tony was shifting his focus. He began to rail against the industrial food companies—the real enemies of nature and humanity—for not paying people a living wage and for pursuing profit at the expense of taste, health, and the environment—all things the Collaborative had been actively working on since its inception. He also began applauding and celebrating the decolonized non-European cuisines of the world. Luxe French dining was no longer on a pedestal for him either. The "time has come" for eating, and living, in moderation, even if it doesn't sell magazines and television advertising or buy country houses and fast cars. I hoped that Tony and I would once again sit around the table, not talking about Hamlet or Eugene O'Neill but about our mutual belief that good food can be produced without the destruction of cultures, land, or people's spirits in the process. Sitting around that table was one of those near misses that could have happened if his death hadn't intervened.

* * *

Even if the primacy of farm-to table cooking has passed and the Collaborative has struggled with its relevance, I carry forward the knowledge that I am in a community of people who have chosen this work because they feel awe and gratitude as we feed ourselves from this miracle of life. It's a community that ranges far beyond the world of chef bros into a richly complex food web of cooks, farmers, ranchers, fishers, foragers, bakers, winemakers, brewers, and writers. We move forward committed to preserving and protecting that miracle.

TAKE BACK THE KNIFE

As a young cook, I vowed never to put a burger on the menu wherever I was the chef. Burgers were antithetical to everything I stood for. I was pursuing a career that didn't conform with my parent's expectations of becoming a white-collar professional. I thought that the best way to bring legitimacy to my career path was to associate myself with the upper class, fine dining traditions of European restaurants, with their ornate platings and hierarchy of preparations that boasted all manner of sauces, reductions, coulis, and concassés. A burger on the menu would open myself up to the critique that I had more in common with grillmen working at the local diner than with the world of artisans and craftspeople creating beauty and pleasure for sophisticated tastemakers.

I wasn't alone. Despite the burger having been elevated to gourmet status in recent years, it has often been a point of contention between chefs and owners. There's a moment in the life of many restaurants when an owner (or a vocal minority partner) who promised to be hands-off in the kitchen, giving the chef full reign to design the menu, has to face the reality that their restaurant might not be the hit they dreamed it would be, especially with rent and payroll obligations quickly approaching. From the owner's perspective, burgers are a panacea, a quick fix to broaden the restaurant's appeal. So the owner "suggests" that maybe a burger would help make the menu more approachable and boost sales. For the chef, the menu may be a personal statement of their creativity and a burger represents the owner caving in to pedestrian tastes. I was a cook in several of those restaurants and watched the burger become the object around which many chef-owner relationships unraveled. And then I became that owner, too, though when I finally did put a burger on the menu at Savoy, I had come to consider it a triumphant expression of my food philosophy. What had changed?

During the first few years of the restaurant, we were developing relationships with farmers and producers beyond just those who sold at Union

Square Greenmarket. There was a weekly delivery of ultra-rich heavy cream from a dairy in New Jersey, always arriving under dark of night as if it were interstate contraband, contained in a bladder bag with a white rubber dispensing nozzle like milk in a college cafeteria; Mark Dunau of Mountain Dell Farm would deliver his vegetables in a rusted out '82 Chevy Suburban with five hundred thousand miles clocked on the odometer; Maytag blue cheese and Frank Morton's muslin bags of pristine lettuces and herbs arrived in cardboard cartons via UPS.

Up to this point our whole animal "program" (a term I've always found overly self-conscious and smacking of corporate-speak) consisted of ducks from Kevin at KNK Poultry, who learned poultry farming from Paul Keyser—the man who coined the term "free range" and pioneered raising chickens on grass in the United States, the occasional lamb from Biancardi's Italian retail meat shop up on Arthur Avenue in the Bronx or from John Williams, a "lamb specialist" over in the Gansevoort meat market. I didn't learn about Niman Ranch pork until 1999 in *The Art of Eating*'s summer issue, and Flying Pigs Farm, the stellar pork producer in Shushan, New York, that became our main local supplier didn't start up until 2000. In 1993, our farm-to-table ethic had barely evolved beyond lettuce to salad bowl. We bought what we could, always on the hunt for new sources.

In meat, the majority of what was available to us was commodity production. As chefs and diners, we were the last stop on an industrialized meat pipeline that had been designed and refined over decades to efficiently produce large quantities of cheap meat for national distribution. Dating back to the beginning of twentieth century, most animals were shipped live to the stockyards of Chicago and Kansas City for slaughter; those carcasses were then shipped whole to urban areas for final breakdown by local butchers and meat distributors. After World War II, processors began to move their slaughtering facilities away from city centers for hygienic reasons but also to increase efficiency by processing meat closer to where the animals were raised. Mechanization of processing and advances in the cold chain meant that instead of transporting whole or half carcasses across the country, meat packers could aggregate cuts, seal them in Cryovac plastic bags to reduce dehydration and extend shelf life, and ship all the same cuts together in one refrigerated carton. This became known as boxed beef. It facilitated specialization; supermarkets and butchers could order only the cuts they needed. No longer constrained by an animal's anatomical limitations—there are only two hanger steaks on each carcass—a refrigerated case could be filled with a seemingly endless supply of a desired cut. Local butchers no longer needed to promote briskets to a steak-loving clientele. The briskets were shipped, maybe to Katz's or some other Jewish deli for pastrami, and the grill cuts went to Keens and other steakhouses. Specialization was heralded as a boon for everyone, especially the consumer. Waste was reduced, Cryovac packaging extended the meat's shelf life, and best of all, prices dropped. As prices dropped, U.S. meat consumption increased and the beef business expanded.

Streamlining the meat industry took many forms, some impacting how the animals were raised: hormone injections in young steers sped up their growth, administering sub-therapeutic antibiotics (antibiotics given without an infection present) in their feed promoted weight gain, and maturing animals confined in corrals while fed a grain diet obviated the need for ranging on vast tracts of grassland.

Standardized meat cutting and marketing was also important. *The Meat Buyers Guide*, a spiral-bound handbook first published in 1961 jointly by the USDA and the National Association of Meat Purveyors (NAMP) illustrates this drive towards standardization. Filled with photos and diagrams, ones we have all seen posted behind a meat counter or in the front of meat chapters in compendium cookbooks, the guide codified the specifications for each cut, established nomenclature, and assigned a numeral to each one. As a young chef, I studied the *Guide*, learned some of the numbers, and even placed my late-night phone orders using NAMP-speak, "For tomorrow I'll take a case of 189s (full tenderloins in Cryovac), two 179s (dry-aged strip loins), and a 109 (a rib roast)." As with any shared common language, there is clarity gained but with it there is also a loss of cultural intelligence. Beyond the narrow range of cuts I had been introduced to, I had no idea how to cook any others. Aside from a few pockets of holdout butcher shops (in New York City those shops were mostly run by old-world Italians), meat cutting had moved out of the city, to huge processing plants in the Midwest.

The drive to standardize meat fabrication also brought about a shift in tools, from the hand to the machine: the band saw replaced the boning knife.

A fast, straight-line cutting tool, the band saw is like a surveyor, imposing straight borders onto a carcass's natural contours. It's not that the band saw is a bad tool, at times it is indispensable, but its use distances the butcher from seeing meat as muscles on a body of nuanced design. Standardized NAMP cuts were determined more for the convenience of the butcher than by differentiating muscle groups by how they taste or should be cooked. So we ended up with the rib eye cap, or *spinalis dorsi*, possibly the most delicious and tender cut on the entire animal, sitting on top of the NY strip, cut in half, and often overlooked or trimmed away by uninformed chefs because it is thin in comparison to the mother lode of the center-cut loin. Only now, with the raised awareness around meat, can you find butchers lifting off the spinalis and treating it as the premium cut it is. At only four portions per animal you probably will never see it on a menu.

The shift from the knife to the band saw also heralded the triumph of the rear leg over the front, of brawn over intelligence. The shoulder, or front leg, is a far more delicious piece of meat but requires skillful knife work to separate cuts that are good for grilling—the flatirons, the *teres major*, and the skirt steaks (all popular cuts in this moment)—from the remaining muscles, which are excellent for braising. The rear leg is large, has only a few muscle groups, and little of the connective tissue that so wonderfully melts in a slow braise. Think of our own bodies. Our shoulders and arms, the deltoids, trapezius, and pectoral muscles, are far more complex anatomically with a vast range of capabilities as compared to our legs, the quadriceps, big hunks of muscle, which are more single-minded functionally, evolved for locomotion and hauling a load.

All of these changes offered gains in efficiency and thus cost savings. The narrowing in capacity of all the players along the food chain ended with chefs like myself, who ordered or cooked by the numbers and lacked the breadth of culinary knowledge to prepare all the varied parts of an animal.

* * *

No one really taught me how to butcher mammals. I figured it out by myself, probably beginning with frog and fetal pig dissections in high school biology class, progressing to chickens at my first restaurant jobs (squab qualified as advanced training at the finer spots). Doing this well required a sharp knife, focus, and plenty of practice but also the desire to understand anatomy, to look at meat as muscles on a body, with similarities to our own. Graduating from poultry to rabbits and lamb was easy. Both fit on a kitchen cutting board and could be broken down into manageable pieces with a boning knife and a small cleaver. I perfected the near surgical breakdown of rabbits, observing along the way that mammalian front limbs float freely, with no bone-to-bone attachment. Instead of sawing straight through the scapula and the thoracic ribs as traditional band saw cutting would do, it could be lifted away from the body, the muscle group intact.

With lamb, I learned how to butcher the primo cuts, the ones people pay top dollar for, the loin chops and racks or rib chops, and observed that they represent a tiny percentage of the whole animal. These desirable grilling cuts have equivalents in beef—the New York strip for the loin chop and rib eye steaks for the rib chops. Known as the middle meats, these cuts represent often only 20 percent of an entire animal. From the vantage point of maximizing use of the entire animal, the premium we place on steakhouse meals dominated by thick grilled chops creates a huge quantity of discounted meat that gets sold off as grind.

When I was working as a line cook, sometimes on a day off, I would wander over to Florence Prime Meat Market in the West Village and settle into a corner where I wouldn't get in anyone's way and watch the butchers cut while they kibitzed with customers. I learned tricks for cutting veal scallops and how to seam out a beef shoulder clod. I was trying to expand the breadth of my knowledge, but it was still a limited enrichment course.

I knew far more about the vast array of fruits and vegetables than I did about meat. My entry into understanding meat production came about via a dignified and rather tweedy gentleman farmer who wandered into the restaurant one day offering us herbs and specialty potatoes from Lithgow Cottage Farm, his upstate farm amid the horsey estates of Dutchess County. I was skeptical. Was this a rich man's ploy to avoid paying property taxes on a palatial estate? And did I really need a weekly delivery of specialty potatoes? I had barely awakened to a potato world beyond the binary one I grew up with—Burbank Russet or Red Bliss. He left us with a sack of potatoes to experiment with and we were immediately hooked. I never learned whether it was a tax write-off, but this was my introduction to Stephen Kaye and to the deep flavor of the European fingerling varieties. We enthusiastically bought whatever he grew and even jostled for position with other restaurants in order to corner a controlling interest in his small asparagus harvest. After a couple of years, Stephen announced that potatoes were too much work for not enough money and that he was moving into raising cattle. We were disappointed and intrigued. As city slickers, it was hard for us to imagine that cattle might really be less work than potatoes, although we certainly understood that there was more profit in a grilled steak than in the spuds that went with it.

In the summer of 1994, Stephen rang me up, asking me if I would be interested in buying one of his Dexters when he slaughtered them the fall. Dexter? What's that? The only breed names I knew were Black Angus for meat and (remembering back to third-grade social studies) Jersey, Guernsey, and Holstein for dairy. Having already instructed me in the virtues of La Ratte, German Butterball, and Carola potatoes, I was ready for Stephen to act as my Virgil on a journey among Dexters, Red Devons, and Scottish Highlanders.

Stephen gave me a crash course in the cultural history of cattle and beef genetics in the British Isles and North America. Black Angus, the predominant beef breed in North America, were never highly regarded for flavor but are large, big-boned animals, well suited to the wide-open rangeland prevalent in the western United States. The logic is that as long as one animal has to be kept alive and healthy it might as well be a big one. In the British Isles though, where grazing pastures are more limited in size, smaller animals are preferred and taste is a distinguishing factor. "British beef is far superior to anything produced in the Americas. Everyone knows that," Stephen counseled. He was raising Dexters, a dual-purpose breed, prized for both dairy and meat, selected for their excellent eating quality and adaptability to enclosed pastures.

The first year, Stephen offered us a single loin, a prime cut with the tenderloin and the strip loin attached in one piece. I decided to cut it into porterhouses and sell them by weight, as is done in Tuscany—*bistecca alla Fiorentina*. The beauty of these Dexter porterhouses was that the portion sizes made sense for a single diner while still leaving room for dessert. I loved telling the servers that we would bill based on the varying weights; customers could select steaks for $29, $37, or $45. The meat was unlike anything I had ever tasted before. I could taste the land, the grass, and the earth's minerals in the meat. It was deeply satisfying. I wanted more; I envisioned a steady, year-round supply. Only there wasn't one. Stephen had killed what he had raised that year, but he promised to expand the herd.

The following year, 1995, I doubled down and went in on half a Dexter and decided to highlight it with a special fall dinner. Delivery day was set seven days after the kill date at the Pine Plains slaughterhouse, which had to be booked months in advance, not unlike scheduling a CT scan. The Sunday before the kill, Sue and I decided to go have a look at our steer before its life was sacrificed for our customer's dining pleasures. Our son, Theo, two at the time, accompanied us, saddled up on a horse for the first time, and we all leaned over Stephen's paddock fence, gazing at the reddish-brown specimen that in two weeks' time would grace the plates in our dining room. I can't say I understood in any emotional way what was about to happen to the steer, but I did try and look him in the eye and emote my gratitude for the life about to be sacrificed.

The meal was my first foray into celebrating whole animal cookery. I went overboard and served too large a menu: grilled heart, braised tongue, steak tartar, oxtail-stuffed cabbage in beef consommé, sauerbraten with spaghetti squash pancakes and grilled T-bones with Stephen's German butterballs and his French shallots. I vowed this was the beginning of how we were going to deal with beef going forward but the reality of a steady and reliable supply was still a long way off.

Trying to make the logistics work, Stephen used an array of slaughterhouses, all of which presented challenges: long trucking distances, uncooperative operators, or sloppy workmanship. Committed on his end to making local beef viable, Stephen formed a cooperative of local meat producers to increase supply and even bankrolled a Hudson Valley butcher to launch a wholesale distribution business, but the operators were not entirely scrupulous.

At Savoy, producers would cold call, having read about our commitment to buying farm-raised meat; some were not local, but they were raising animals thoughtfully with regard to both the animal and the environment. Desperate to gain traction, we tried them all. For a while we purchased from Conservation Beef, a joint venture between the Nature Conservancy and Montana ranchers formed in an effort to promote land preservation through selling beef at a premium over commodity pricing. The idea was to make it profitable for ranchers to continue ranching instead of being lured into subdividing the land and selling it off in twenty-acre "ranchettes." The project was slow to catch on and the grant monies supporting it dried up. Everybody was casting about, looking for ways to make beef profitable and economical for both the rancher and the end user in the face of a system that was structurally designed to be a race to the bottom: driving prices down, squeezing everyone along the line, and raising meat in environmentally, ethically, and hygienically dubious conditions.

I wanted to be the most agile cook I could be, as familiar with a vast diversity of cuts and meats as I was with the diversity of fruits and vegetables available in New York City. I wanted to become schooled in all these cuts and expand our culinary repertoire, confidently preparing them, with delicious outcomes for our customers. We would reject the boxed beef, the Cryovac bags of slimy months-old meat, and make a show of force by reclaiming the lost intelligence and flexibility of butchers and cooks. We would disengage with the industrialized food system and eat all the nasty bits. We would take back the knife!

Local producers needed to sell their meat in bulk, more akin to the old style of shipping carcasses. The meat was delivered as primals, three or four massive pieces from each side. Stephen might have taught me about breeds, pasturing, and cattle feed but he didn't school us in butchery. We were going to have to teach ourselves how to make the whole project cost-effective by fabricating the cuts that were good for grilling or braising and reserving the remainder as trim for grinding.

When I think of the word "trim" I envision a quick haircut or some fabric snipped off pants to shorten them up, or even in the kitchen, the sinewy bits removed but not discarded when we bone out a joint, and then brown them off for a sauce with a stock made from the bones and some vegetables. Trim is diminutive in relation to the whole. On a steer, though, trim often represents a majority of the animal's weight. As exciting as it was to cook dishes like grilled heart agrodolce or braised tongue with salsa verde and share them with our diners, we weren't going to pay for the half steer with an offal organ recital and there is only so much one can charge for a steak. We were going to need to find a good use for all the trim, the bulk being on the hind leg.

To be honest, I'm not a leg man. Bogart might have appreciated Bacall's gams but as a chef I can't join him in appreciating their appeal. Gams or *jambes* in French, rear legs, are a problem. Even on a pig, the rear leg is the least desirable fresh cut. It's too tough for grilling or roasting and for braising it lacks enough connective tissue to dissolve into wonderfully soft collagen. The Europeans turn gams into *jambon*, *jamon*, or ham, depending on your tongue. The Italians and the Spaniards figured out that the best treatment for a pig leg is to cure it on salt for at least a year and then slice it thinly, hence *prosciutto* or *jamon*. Pork legs, however, are still in scale with humans. A home cook can prepare a ham for a holiday party and then after a week of ham sandwiches, it's gone. But on a steer, the scale is outsized; a hind leg can weigh seventy-five pounds or one third of the carcass's half-weight. That's not a volume of meat to ignore or throw into the scrap pile; it needs to be used, money made back against the original cost. So what's to be done with all that trim? Obviously one solution is to grind it up and make a burger.

Rather than feel defeat that I had given into the market forces, descending to the lowest common denominator of American fast food, I decided to embrace the burger with gusto. With our DIY approach to so much of our cuisine, we added a professional meat grinder to our equipment arsenal, experimented with blends to get the lean to fat content correct, and decided to make the entire burger plate an expression of our food philosophy: we made our own pickles and ketchup. Never one to shill for corporate America (we chose to commission hand-tooled leather check presenters for our guests rather than use the American Express embossed ones found in most establishments, and served China Cola, an herbal carbonated drink instead of buying Coke), I certainly wasn't going to allow a bottle of Heinz to sit on tables in my dining room.

The meat in our burger was delicious: freshly ground by us, from a single grass-fed animal, locally sourced, and usually from someone we knew—unlike some supermarket patties that can comprise meat from over two hundred animals that stood knee-deep in manure with nary a blade of grass in sight. A renowned food writer and burger aficionado claimed it "deserves a place in New York's pantheon of burgers." Depending on how you view it we had either extracted ourselves from the toxic industrial food system or we had successfully created a profitable model for change in the way meat gets raised, processed, and eaten in this country. Either way, the tide had turned.

STONE FRUIT

Before we settled on Savoy as the name for our restaurant, I wanted to call it Pie. There were other early contenders: Fresh; Hand to Mouth; Mosaic; Saturnalia; Fernandel. When we floated these prospective names by friends, each choice elicited varying degrees of derision. I get it; Hand to Mouth conjured up a livestock disease or the most meager of food offerings, neither of which promised to be enticing to potential diners; and very few New Yorkers had any associations with Fernandel, the French actor from Marcel Pagnol's films. But I was serious about Pie. I went so far as to design a metal cutout sign to hang from the building cornice of a slice of pie with a crimped edge and a few vent holes. I longed to join the tribe of crafts people in the guild tradition who historically hung images of their trade outside their shops: a pair of scissors indicated a tailor; a boot silhouette, a shoemaker; or the giant eyeglass frames that still hang on Delancey Street outside Moscot, the optician. You know what's on offer before walking in. English need not be spoken. All ye who enter will find pie.

I wanted to do this because first of all Sue makes the best pie I have ever eaten, and it seemed foolish not to lead with our best card. It also embodied everything we stood for about cooking and deliciousness. Pie isn't pretentious. The best crusts are the product of skilled hands demonstrating the craft and less a mechanical construct made with precision tools (hence part of my impetus for the name Hand to Mouth). It's a dessert of the home more than it is a dessert of the pastry shop. Pie is everything we want as eaters: crispy, flaky, buttery texture on the outside offset by an oozy, rich inside. That's what fried chicken is, after all, and many a fortune has been made on that dish. It's all I desire for dessert, and if no one is looking, for breakfast the morning after.

We didn't name the restaurant Pie because in the end it was too limiting; both for Sue from the production and menu side but also because naming a restaurant after a dessert would shift the focus away from so much of the meal. And what if our diners didn't like Sue's pie as much as I do? Fresh was probably ahead of its time; Saturnalia was probably a better name for a debauched swingers club. In the end, Savoy, a name that referenced Europe without being European, rich with good associations—Stompin' at the Savoy, the Savoy cabbage, and the Savoy Hotel—served us quite well.

If my cooking is about the journey then Sue's is about the destination. I traffic in stews and sauces, amalgams that do not divide into clear and controllable parts. Sue prefers to inhabit the world of pie where there are only two elements (or maybe three, if you count à la mode, which she pretty much always insists on). There is the crust and the filling, the inside and the outside, both of which have to be exceptional. Why then do most pies fail so miserably? Let me count the ways—crusts are tough and overworked, soggy, too thin, under baked, flavorless, and boring from using insipid fats; fillings are gloppy with too much cornstarch and not enough real fruit, overly sweet, over spiced (note: cinnamon is not a coloring agent for apples).

Another of my arguments for naming our seasonal farm-to-table restaurant Pie was that pie isn't a static dish and some rendition is always in season: strawberry rhubarb, blueberry, blueberry gooseberry, sour cherry, peach, pear cranberry, apple, apple raspberry, pecan, lemon meringue, coconut cream, and chocolate hazelnut. My favorite time of the year for pie is when the berries and the stone fruits overlap. It's two moments actually: there is the rising crescendo when blueberries and peaches (or in good years, apricots) overlap in July; and then the glorious ride down off the summer's peak heat waves when raspberries reappear in September for a second crop and the peaches are still rolling in. In both cases, Sue introduces the two fruits to each other inside the dough, melding them to become one—acid and sweet, perfume and spice, a marriage made in oven.

I didn't know the term "stone fruit" until I looked at a jar of English-made fruit conserves in Dean & DeLuca that contained a mix of them all: plums, cherries, apricots, and peaches—a winemaker's field blend, only for jam. But stones? We called them pits. The English always seem to have a proper term for everything. It's not just civilized as much as it is scientific and properly descriptive. The stone comes by its name honestly; its single seed is encased in a hard coating of lignin as in the Italian word *legno*, for wood. Bird beaks and human mandibles are generally not up to the task of cracking them. Access is severely limited to the precious kernel of life locked inside the stone.

The majority of the fruits we eat have countless seeds within each fruit-ing body, offering multiple opportunities to reproduce. Strawberries, melons, bananas, oranges, pears, figs, pomegranates, apples, grapes, cranberries, all spread the risk or, if you're a genetic optimist, spread the opportunity for continuing their line by diversification. Disseminating many seeds widely and quickly is like the male model of sperm production: low energy input, high numbers, and thus a greater possibility that one sperm will hit the jackpot and score an offspring.

Stone fruits follow a more female reproductive model, producing a limited number of eggs, devoting more resources and energy into ensuring the success of each single offspring: one seed per fruit. With only one shot, one opportunity, the lignified seed coat acts as a vault protecting the future offspring: higher risk requires a higher level of security. The flesh surround-ing the seed is also at an elevated level of sweetness and nutrient density, whether to provide enticement to an animal traveler to ingest and carry the seed elsewhere or by becoming terrific compost augmenting soil fertility when the seed finally germinates.

Other fruits not categorized as stone fruits but still single-seeded take a similar Fort Knox approach to seed protection paired with ultra-high nutrient density: dates, mangoes, olives, coconuts, and avocados come to mind. Stones resist rot and crushing blows from a jaw or a beak, and can even withstand the acid barrage of traveling through an intestinal system only to emerge in a new location ready to grow. Stone fruit trees invest a lot of time developing the fruit, sequestering solar energy throughout the hot and long sunlit days in July and August. There is no rush to maturity, no quick June strawberry after a May flowering with hundreds of seeds on each berry. Lucky us—in their very nature, these fruit trees have evolved to choose producing qual-ity over quantity and we reap the benefit of that choice—slowly developed depth of flavor and an abundance of sugar surrounding each encased seed.

Sue's culinary mindset is similar to that of the stone fruit's reproduc-tive strategy. She prefers perfecting one thing at a time rather than trying to juggle multiple projects or attempting to develop simultaneous mastery in a broad set of skills. Experimentation and taking chances are not her thing—practice, with extreme attention to detail, is. Too much information and too many variables, like the constant influx of tickets being called during a dinner service, can overload her. But give Sue a prep list, a quiet kitchen in the morning with few other employees around, and she can produce an enormous volume of quality work. Reducing variables and then controlling them is integral to her quest for excellence. It's a worldview, applicable to friendships, child-rearing, or her current creative outlet, ceramics.

Making pie dough is something of a double bind: if you need a recipe you can't make it, but if you know how to make it, you don't need a recipe. A painstakingly written recipe will only get you so far, just as reading instructions on how to ride a bike won't get you up, balanced, and ready to circle Central Park. There's too much feel and balance involved, too many decisions that are unconscious and instinctual. I'm not saying measurements don't matter; they do, but strict obeisance to the measurements will not necessarily produce a good result. The missing ingredients, not divisible into parts, are focus and practice.

Every recipe you'll ever read for pie dough begins by calling for cutting chilled butter into flour. For Sue, if you followed those instructions, already all is lost. Butter is third on her list of items to chill, beginning with putting the steel mixing bowl in the freezer; then the flour; and finally the butter, cut into the requisite little cubes—all enjoying a sub-zero hiatus together for several hours. Only then does she hook up the bowl to the mixer and mechanically paddle the butter bits into the flour. Once crumbly and pebbly, she adds water (iced, of course) but as they say in the all the cookbooks "until it just comes together," a phrase maddeningly lacking in precision. During those few hydrating moments, all Sue's attention is focused on the bowl's contents, watching it come together. (Heaven forbid, if I ask a question at that moment!) She is trying to discern the moment when the least amount of water necessary has been added to create cohesion. That is key! Water + flour + mechanical action = gluten-strand development, a quality we might like in bread dough but if overdeveloped in pie dough, you need a knife and fork to break through the crust. The goal is to bring everything together with a gentle squeeze of the hand while still having unincorporated bits of butter visibly distinct in the dough. This helps make the dough flaky. When baking off in the oven, the butter melts away, creating space between the dough layers, and simultaneously fries the dough. Done right, the flakiness resembles the more complex laminated doughs of puff pastry and croissant doughs.

I have never doubted that Sue knows what she is doing and will make a pie that can bring all mouths at the table to complete silence. The difference is in her sensitivity to how the dough is coming together and how long to work it. So often in the creative process there is self-doubt, a lingering voice suggesting that we are impostors, wolves in chef's clothing. Maybe we need that bit of the fear to keep us on edge and striving. Sue has been using the same dough recipe for decades—she learned it in 1988, from Brendan Walsh, the chef at Arizona 206, a bustling Upper East Side spot serving southwestern cuisine. Invariably, she will look up at me as we both are lost in the dreaminess of the fork-tender, flaky, buttery, warm fruit heaven of her pie and she'll say, "I think I figured it out." "Oh yeah, you figured it out all right," I say. "About thirty years ago." But practice, we must. Today is a new day and we are only as good as today's creation. Sue's pies are always good, often excellent.

I am a more restless cook, desirous of change. Savory cooking has more variables at play than pastry and invites a looser approach. Thankfully the ratios between ingredients in soups or braises are more forgiving than they are in baking. I repeat flavor combos that speak to me, but I rarely attempt a replay of yesterday's game. It's not like I'm trying to make food that hasn't been made before; my dishes are recognizable, riffs on riffs, expositions on themes previously tasted or previously cooked. I don't have a signature dish; instead I have a signature approach.

There is a tension in the artistic process between repetition and innovation. Dolphy and Coltrane couldn't have produced free, unbound sounds if they hadn't practiced their scales. And then practiced them some more. We need both. I love the place where repetition liberates me from the need to think so I can direct my attention elsewhere. From repetition I have learned some hard-earned lessons—how hot a pan needs to be so that the fish skin won't stick; what a pork chop cooked to pink really feels like to the touch; how to look up from cutting onions and observe what's going on around me.

It's extreme to characterize Sue as rigid, unwilling to explore, and me as a fearless, wild improviser at the stove. During our whole-pig buying period she did experiment with incorporating lard into her dough, gradually replacing some of the butter until arriving at her optimal blend. Lately, she's been playing with pie spicing, adding Sarawak black pepper into her apple tart spice mix in addition to the traditional clove, cinnamon, and allspice. For me, having a set of ingredients to cook with but no direction known can be scary; all my self-doubt has license to emerge. Two things help subdue the imposter voices: remembering that prior successful improvisations were grounded in technique and watching Sue's methodical and careful work. There is an element of fear each time I wander down an unfamiliar culinary road in shaping a dish even though most of the time I arrive at a delicious plate of food. Remembering that Sue's meticulousness is a key ingredient in a great wedge of pie, I double down on my own commitment to strive for excellence in each step.

* * *

My favorite stone fruit is probably the apricot, aptly called by sixteenth-century naturalist Thomas Muffet (of "sitting on a tuffet" fame) a "plum concealed beneath a peach's coat." I search out the ones with red-freckled cheeks, those that submitted to some serious sunbathing before being picked. Fully ripe they are great to eat out of hand but cooked their concentrated juices, whether as a compote to slather on bread and butter or slow-baked halves to accompany a roasted duck breast, are incomparable in balance—high-pitched in acidity matched by a luscious sweetness. All grouped under the genus *Prunus*, the range of stone fruit diversity is enormous—sour cherries (the only cherry worth using in a clafoutis or pie), peaches (including the intoxicatingly perfumed white peaches), and nectarines along with beach plums, sloe fruit (for making sloe gin), and almonds (the sole genus member whose flesh we generally discard, only valuing the kernel). Also included are all the plums—the spherical Asian plums, often brightly colored—the yellow shiro and crimson Elephant Hearts—and the more elliptical European purple plums, sometimes almost blue with a foggy bloom obscuring their true hue. They arrive in the market at that wonderful June-July moment—after the evanescent strawberries but in advance of the apples and pears with their durability and long storage capacities—full-on summer, in other words.

I have three favorite stone fruit growers: Red Jacket Orchards, for their red-freckled apricots; Samascott Orchards, for their diaphanous green gage plums (so easily bruised, I can barely get them home, but oh, so sweet and silken in texture); and Locust Grove, the multigenerational farm of the Kent family on the Hudson who grow damsons, a small almost wild plum that refers back to the place of origin for all the plums, to Persia. The original term was *damascene* as in "from Damascus" but in a global game of telephone the name transformed into damson.

I seek out foods that might retain more of their pre-cultivated pre-modern taste—Tim Stark's wild Mexican cherry tomatoes, Franca Tantillo's Andean *papa amarilla*, or Chip Kent's damsons. I fantasize that in sharing the same sensual experience as ancient peoples I am connected to those people across time. With one foot in the twenty-first century in NYC's Union Square and another in an open marketplace in ancient Syria, I feel the continuity of human desire and thus of our humanity every time I cook with Kent's damsons. They're not pleasant to eat out of hand but cooked down, the tannic skins give true heft to the sweetness they do have. We would put a spoonful of damson compote on our cheese boards, and at home I like to spread it on toast with ricotta or farmer's cheese for breakfast.

Along with the damson, the Kents grow numerous varieties of European plums. On a peach, the skins are an annoyance; cooks often remove the itchy peach fuzz by blanching them quickly in boiling water and peeling them. Plum skins, though, have an astringency that is integral to their great flavor and balances the sweetness of the flesh—acid and sugar all in a single bite. The Kents grow a small number of plum trees that they labeled as German plums; smaller than the Italian varieties but densely flavored. They have only a few trees and throughout the fall I have a history of pestering the stand manager every week for them. When they finally arrive, without a prompt Lucas will say, "Pete, they're here." I would often buy a case of them, knowing that by the following week they would probably all be gone, and then hold them in the wine room for a special dinner or slowly dispense them to the pastry department for tarts.

Sue doesn't have the market cornered on stone fruits in our household; they are terrific in savory cooking. The way I successfully introduced Olivia, our daughter, to tomatoes was by serving her my turn on the summer classic panzanella, the traditional stale bread and tomato salad, where mine uses an even mixture of tomatoes and stone fruits, their blended juices hydrating the stale bread. Finished with a mix of herbs, red wine vinegar, and olive oil, it's a great picnic accompaniment (improving en route) to grilled chicken, roasted pork, or as a stand-alone. My favorite foray into things peachy, though, is tapping into the bitter almond flavors found in the leaves and the stones of all the *Prunus* genus members. The similarity in flavors made sense after I learned that almonds and peaches occupy the same *Prunus* subgenus. It's no wonder that *crème d'amande* as a base filling for a baked peach tart is so sublime; they are kissing cousins sharing the same bed of a tart.

A few of my old European cookbooks suggest adding a few peach leaves when steeping milk to deepen its flavor (not unlike flavoring potato or bean water with a bay leaf) and one even suggests adding them to tomato sauce for depth. But it's the kernel, the treasure hidden deep within the stone, the one the tree has restricted access to by constructing the stone that offers astonishing flavor. Every time I taste a *crème anglaise* (custard used as sauce or ice cream base) steeped with kernels (the French call it *noyau*), I marvel at the flavor. As if I'm a co-conspirator with the tree, I am protective of the value of the treasure while also delighting in sharing the culinary-botany lesson with select cooks lest they sweep all the pits into the trash. With a hammer for smashing the stones and a towel covering them to reduce kitchen shrapnel, I collect what the tree doesn't want me to have. The labor-intensive process of smashing kernels repays the laborer fivefold in flavor. Tasting the infusion, I finally understood what bakers were striving for with marzipan or almond extract doused biscotti. It's not quite the Old Testament taboo against cooking a kid in its mother's milk but there is nothing like a peach or apricot tart surrounded by a pool of *noyau crème anglaise*—the fruit accompanied and amplified by its nascent offspring.

Sue's clarity of distinction between piecrust and filling versus my fluidity of process and ingredients when making a braise or a soup crosses over into how we approach personal relationships. I don't mean to suggest that Sue views things as more black and white than I do; she appreciates the subtleties and contradictions in human interactions. But when lines are crossed, when deferring to someone else is no longer self-protective but self-destructive, she has clarity that I sometimes lack, willing to call people out when they have gone too far. I'm more forgiving, more comfortable in the stew. As a friend and an employer I've expended a lot of energy listening and trying to understand someone's position, working to appreciate the validity of their viewpoint, rather than call them out for being wrong. A gradualist, wanting to inspire change in people, I often had difficulty firing people.

Both of our approaches have validity but mine has gotten me into trouble when people cross boundaries, sometimes even violating my space. For all my diplomatic skills and social grace, I can lack the ability to draw the line, to know that the pie dough stays on the outside and filling on the inside. Without Sue and her clarity to throw me a line, I can end up drowning in someone else's psychic soup—one more place where my pastry chef partner brings definition and rigor to my life.

When I shared my pie dough of life observations with Sue, she whimpered, mostly in jest, "But I only have a few friends," and I said, "Yeah, but you make great pie." We both laughed.

SUSAN'S PEACH-RASPBERRY PIE

MAKES ONE 12-INCH (30.5 CM) DOUBLE-CRUST PIE

Here you go: Sue's extreme directions for making pie, in her words. The fine points are all included, but you'll only really master the technique by finding your way yourself—and then by repeating the unpleasant task of making and eating pie until it's excellent. These notes are a great starter kit. Sue has found that it is best to make the pie dough a day ahead, when there is the luxury of time to do so. The dough can be multiplied, portioned, shaped, and tightly double-wrapped in plastic wrap then stored in the freezer for about 6 months. The rule of thumb when making pie dough is that all ingredients should be cold.

For the crust:

¾ cup (1½ sticks/170 g) unsalted butter, cut into ½-inch (12 mm) cubes

3 ounces (85g) lard (can be substituted with butter), cut into ½-inch (12 mm) cubes

1¼ cups (155 g) all-purpose flour

1¼ cups (170 g) bread flour

Pinch salt

1 teaspoon sugar

Ice water mixed with ¼ teaspoon white vinegar or lemon juice (Note: I usually make a cup of this mixture knowing that I will only use a small amount of it. The amount required will vary with ambient humidity levels. I always mix it in a measuring cup with a spout so I can drizzle it into the flour/butter mixture with control.)

For the filling:

7 or 8 peaches

¼ cup (55 g) packed brown sugar

¼ cup (50 g) granulated sugar

2 tablespoons cornstarch

Cinnamon, to taste

Nutmeg, to taste

Allspice, to taste

Cloves, to taste

Black pepper, to taste

1 cup (125 g) raspberries

For assembling the pie:

Egg wash (1 egg, gently beaten with a bit of milk or cream)

Coarse sugar, for sprinkling

1. **MAKE THE CRUST:** Chill a 12-inch (30.5 cm) pie pan in the freezer.
2. In a mixing bowl, toss the butter and lard with both flours, the salt, and sugar. Place in the freezer for about 30 minutes, or until the butter is really cold. (Note: Oily butter leads to tough dough.) Using a stand mixer with a paddle attachment (or do it by hand if one isn't available; a food processor is not recommended), break down the butter into smaller pebbly, sandy pieces while incorporating it with the flour mixture. With the mixer running, drizzle ice water down the side of the mixing bowl in a thin, steady stream, adding just enough water so that a handful of the dough mixture holds together when squeezed. (I remove the paddle attachment two times during the mixing process, and with a rubber spatula, rotate the drier flour up from the bottom of the bowl to ensure even water distribution. This step really helps!)
3. Remove to a work surface. With the heel of your hand, smear the dough away from you bit by bit. This is known as *fraisage*. Repeat once; this step will make for a flakier crust. Gather the dough together, divide in half, and knead quickly into neat flattened circles. Let rest in the refrigerator until cold, for the better part of an hour. (Little trick: Sometimes I put dough in the freezer for about 20 minutes to speed the chilling process, then transfer to the refrigerator for the remaining time.)

4. The dough should remain cold for the entire rolling process, so working as quickly as possible, roll out one circle of dough to about ⅛ inch (3 mm) thick. Using a pizza cutter, trim off any ragged edges, then place the dough in the chilled pie pan. Press the dough gently into the bottom edge, trimming if necessary so that the edge of the dough lines up with the edge of the pie pan. With a fork, prick the dough all over. Place in the refrigerator. Roll out the other circle of dough to the same thickness. Let it chill in the refrigerator.

5. **MEANWHILE, MAKE THE FILLING**: Cut the peaches into eighths by cutting quarters, then cutting the quarters in half perpendicularly, making chunks rather than thinner slices. Discard the pits.

6. In a medium bowl, combine the peaches, both sugars, the cornstarch, and spices. Mix very well until the fruit melds with the sugars and cornstarch and the mixture is moistened. Add the raspberries last and mix them in gingerly so they stay intact.

7. **ASSEMBLE THE PIE**: Preheat the oven to 400°F (205°C).

8. Pile the filling into the bottom crust so that it forms a mound, then pat it so that no peach slice points are sticking up. Using a pastry brush, paint a thin layer of egg wash around the rim of the bottom crust. Place the remaining rolled out dough over the filling and trim the edge so that the round is a bit wider than the bottom crust. Fold the edge of the top crust under the edge of the bottom crust, squeezing them together. Crimp the edge with fingers, a fork, or the handle end of a butter knife.

9. Brush egg wash over the entire pie in a thin layer (avoid pooling in the crimped crevices). Sprinkle coarse sugar evenly over the egg wash, going lighter at the edge. With a paring knife, make slits in the top crust, as decoratively as you like so long as there are enough of them to allow steam to escape. (Note: This may be done while the dough is still flat but after it has been chilled. Placing it on its own baking sheet lined with parchment works well for this alternative method.)

10. Place the pie on a sheet pan in the lower part of the oven. When the edge of the pie takes on some color, after 10 to 15 minutes, turn down the oven to 375°F (190°C) and bake until the fruit bubbles out of the

vents, approximately another 45 minutes, or until the top of the pie is deep golden brown. (Note: I move the pie to the middle part of the oven for the last 10 to 15 minutes of baking to avoid the bottom getting too dark.) Let the pie set at least 30 minutes before serving. It's excellent for breakfast too!

PETE'S "THIS SAUCE IS THE PITS"

This is a simple crème anglaise that is infused with the crushed stones from any stone fruit. I collect cherry pits as well as apricot and plum stones in a bag in the freezer until I am ready to make this sauce. (Peach pits are tough to smash with a hammer so I usually avoid them.) I infuse the milk with the crushed stones and then strain it all out before moving on to make the anglaise in the traditional method. Serve with stone fruit pie or tart.

15 apricot or plum stones
1 cup (240 ml) milk
¼ cup (50 g) sugar
Pinch salt
4 egg yolks

1. Lay the pits out on a cutting board. Cover them with a towel and smash the pits with a hammer. The towel keeps the bits from flying around the kitchen. Once they are all broken open, put the shells and pits in a small saucepan with the milk. Gently steep for 30 minutes to infuse the flavors into the milk. Taste to determine if the infused milk tastes like almonds. If so, strain and discard the pits.

2. Return the milk to the pot. Add the sugar, salt, and egg yolks and whisk together well. Switching to a wooden spoon, warm the sauce over low heat while stirring. As the yolks begin to cook, the custard will thicken. Remove from the heat when a candy thermometer registers 165°F (74°C), or test the thickness of the sauce by drawing a line across the sauce-covered wooden spoon with a finger. If the sauce on the wooden spoon holds the line, then it can be taken off the heat. Cool while still stirring, until you can put a finger in the sauce without it feeling unpleasantly hot. Refrigerate until ready to use. Keeps in a sealed container in the refrigerator for up to 1 week.

THE ICEMAN COMETH

Without a doubt, the most important outside professional relationship a restaurant maintains is not with its lawyer, accountant, or even its IT guy; it's with its refrigeration repairman. You can put off phoning your attorney for their legal perspective and you can place the company tax return on extension—revisiting it three months later—but fifty pounds of freshly ground beef getting warm in the walk-in box needs immediate attention. In this grand city where every third truck parked in a commercial zone seems to be making an HVAC service call, finding and keeping an excellent repairman is harder than you might imagine.

Excellence is defined by a combination of attributes: swift response time, proper diagnoses, quality work, and honesty. Swift is always at the top of the list. Why else would one of my repairmen early on have named his company Justin Time? (His name wasn't Justin; it was Tracy.) Lots of companies reference their chilling abilities: AC Coolman, Igloo HVAC, Deep Freeze Repair, but what's paramount when a box is down, especially if it's the walk-in, is promptness. The response can't be "We'll get someone there late tomorrow morning." It needs to be "I will swing by on my way home," and invariably showing up sweaty, dirty, and cranky but ready to go another lap.

The latter response was what I always heard from my main man for over two decades: Wing of Wingstar Mechanical, a Chinese-American man born in Hong Kong, living in Queens, who works with a small team of men, some of whom are equally fastidious. Trained as an electrical engineer before taking on the impossible task of trying to maintain consistently cold temperatures in New York's hot and cramped spaces, Wing never failed to take my call. His first words were always, "Hullo, Peter? What's going on?" As if to say, "I know you wouldn't be calling unless something was wrong so cut to the chase. What's up?"

In return, Wing's invoices got paid before all others, except our small farmers. There could be no delays in cutting Wing checks, not if we wanted him to always take our call or remain at the top of some imaginary preferred client list. Our dependency was real. Having a box go down is serious business. Product is at risk, expensive proteins are losing shelf life, health and hygiene concerns quickly come into play, and depending on the failed item, customers don't stick around if the beer is warm or the dining room is stuffy.

Wing entered my world when he found a solution to a problem other contractors had been unable or unwilling to solve: providing sufficient and well-balanced air-conditioning in the restaurant dining room. AC in restaurants is always tricky. Particularly in small operations lacking a centralized system and with kitchen exhausts that are forever pulling the surrounding air up into the flue, someone is always dissatisfied with the temperature. At Savoy there were two large window units at one end of the dining room with the entry and the kitchen located at the other, and I desperately wanted to find a way to install a third unit at that end. Every potential contractor I walked through with either ended with an outright "Can't be done" or they failed to follow up with a job quote. I couldn't get a bid too high to reject. Enter Wing. Intrigued by the challenge, he walked through the space several times and proposed a Byzantine but plausible solution. It required running piping on a circuitous journey through two brick walls, across the kitchen ceiling, up a floor and a half to a back roof that was only accessible via an eighteen-inch-square roof hatch. He didn't think it was particularly difficult (read expensive) although it would involve hammer drilling through brick in four different locations. Right then I knew that he was my guy for this job and probably for many more to come.

**

Utilities are the largest fixed expense of a restaurant, after rent and insurance. Cooking gas represents less than a third of that bill, the two-thirds-plus being electricity, of which the majority goes to running "boxes": walk-in boxes for bulk storage, lowboys on the cooking line, stand-up reach-in boxes for backup materials, bar fridges, wine coolers, beer boxes, ice makers, and freezers. At Savoy, we had fifteen individual refrigeration units, not counting dining room air conditioners, which during the summer months would spike an already high bill. Our electrical demand was year-round, huge, and we paid handsomely for it.

With gas and stoves, cooks transform the raw into the cooked; it is action grounded in the present. The steak or chicken you order and I transform by grilling or roasting in the oven is an activity happening in the now. With electricity and refrigeration, I'm not transforming anything. I am anti-transformative, resisting change, attempting to extend the lifespan of our perishable-filled holding tanks. It is action grounded in the future or in my forecasts of the future. My stove is what I can do for you today; my walk-in box is what I hope to do for you tomorrow. Placing orders with suppliers on Thursday night for the inventory needed for two Friday services, a rocking Saturday night, and a jamming Sunday brunch is an optimist's bet on the future. And it's always a bet.

Every time a box would go down, the odds on that bet quickly headed south and my anxiety levels would rise. How long would it be out, would I lose product, would the health department come at this inopportune moment, and how much would the repair cost? The very sight of Wing's satchel, the red and yellow rubber hoses with attached brass gauges lying on top of the bag like a stethoscope, was a salve. The doctor was in the house even if I hadn't seen the man himself. Major repairs might involve the unit being down for several days, which in our tightly allocated space, ranged from a major irritation to complete havoc. I can't count the number of times we worked through lunch service with a prostrate repairman under our feet, fixing the very refrigerator we were using. Wing's presence in the kitchen was not only tolerated but welcomed by all the cooks. Everyone knew he was there for us.

Gas stoves and ovens are fairly simple mechanisms, not fundamentally different from cooking over a wood fire. They offer more precise control with regulating valves to open or restrict the flow of gas. Ovens get turned on when the first cook walks in to open the kitchen and remain on until the dinner service is over. There isn't much to break, door hinges being the most common mishap, the result of cooks yanking and slamming the doors in unending repetition all night long. When I did have a breakdown, heaven forbid if I called my tatted-up stove repair guy, Repairmaster Dave, at 11 A.M. on a Friday because he was usually already headed upstate for a weekend of motorcycle racing and kicking back. "I've got a super busy weekend," I'd plead. "Just crossed the bridge," he'd reply. I'd beg. "I'll hook you up with a fat steak and a beer." "Nope, sorry, Pete. I'll be there first thing Monday morning." Click. Annoying, but generally not a disaster. With an oven, the workarounds are fairly easy; menus get adapted and simplified, baking shifts to other ovens. Over time and through necessity, I learned to do many of the oven repairs myself, keeping a kit of thermocouples, hinges, hooks, and springs around to save money and keep the operation flowing smoothly.

A refrigerator is wholly different: neither a modernized version of older equipment nor mechanically simple enough for my rudimentary tinkering. Invented in the early twentieth century, it represented a complete technological shift—just as the light bulb was fundamentally different from burning candles and kerosene. Prior to refrigerators there were ice boxes (that's what we called our refrigerator when I was a kid because my parents grew up with them in their kitchens), nothing more than its name, a well-insulated box with an area for holding a large block of ice that chilled the surrounding area and whatever might be put inside. No electricity required, no running parts, no constant hum in the night. The only service required was a weekly delivery of ice.

In temperate zones, this worked pretty well; there was a localized industry harvesting cut ice from lakes and rivers in the winter and then storing it in heavily insulated warehouses for later use. Hauling ice to hotter places was expensive, a losing proposition—between melt and energy expended. Cities like Las Vegas or Miami could never have developed without the invention of more efficient methods of supplying cold.

Modern refrigeration systems cool an enclosed area by physically moving heat from one area—inside a box—and transferring that heat elsewhere—outside the box. The box could be a dining room with a central air conditioner or a small dorm fridge chilling milk on a servers' station for coffee service. Regardless, the process and mechanism are the same: piping filled with coolant runs into the box, absorbing the warmth of the enclosed area—thus lowering the temperature—and then out of the box, dumping the warmth into the surrounding air. Today, refrigeration units are ubiquitous; most apartments in New York City run with a minimum of two: one in a window for air-conditioning and one in the kitchen for perishable foods.

Fifty years ago, most people only owned one. A hundred years ago most people had none.

* * *

Consider an icy glass of lemonade left unattended on a hot day. Some might observe that the ice is melting in the lemonade and that after a while it will be warm. And that would be true. But in the relational "it goes both ways" approach to life, there is a more dynamic, transactional description of what is occurring. If something (the lemonade) is getting warmer, then something else (the surrounding air) is getting colder, even if the surrounding air is immeasurable or infinitesimally small, given the air's huge volume in comparison to the volume of the chilled glass of lemonade. This heat exchange process continues until the two bodies have equalized in temperature. Since the cold lemonade is a far smaller mass than the surrounding air, the lemonade will rise towards the air's temperature.

Using the lemonade example we could theoretically cool down the city on a hot day with a massive block of ice. Taking a less grandiose approach, by defining smaller volumes of space, say, inside a Coleman cooler, and increasing the quantity of ice from a couple of cubes to a ten-pound block, we might be able to keep beer and some watermelon cold to slake our thirst on an outing to the beach.

To mechanize this action, we'd have to replace the static block of ice with a system of pipes carrying a slurry of chilled liquid running continuously inside and outside of the insulated box. As the super chilled slurry comes into the box, temperature equalization begins: the slurry warms and the air temperature inside decreases, moving closer to the slurry's temperature. Traveling outside the box, the warmed slurry would need to be relieved of its heat, chilled again to continue the process. Finding a more efficient cooling material than H_2O and developing a method of continuous cooling were the technological hurdles that engineers needed to surmount to develop the modern refrigerator. The method is known as the vapor compression system. Vapor refers to the coolant inside the piping because sometimes it's a vapor—gaseous—and at others a liquid. Compression refers to the action necessary to liquefy the vapor, to begin the process again.

I time stamp my awareness of how the principles of the vapor compression system play out in our daily lives to a watershed moment in my relationship with Susan. On an early ski trip to Colorado, unmarried and still novice travel companions, we unpacked our toiletries in a high-altitude Aspen hotel bathroom and Sue wondered why her shampoo bottle had swollen as if someone had pumped air into it. My smug and curt response was "PV = NRT." She stared back at me like I was speaking in tongues. I guess I was. I was using the scientific shorthand to describe Boyle's gas law, named after Robert Boyle, who in 1660, observed that changes in the pressure, volume, and temperature of gases inversely affect each other. Every intro level chemistry student commits this theory—distilled into the formula PV = NRT, where P = pressure, V = volume, T = temperature, and N and R are constants—to memory.

Being at high altitude means that there is lower air pressure. That is why we flatlanders get so tuckered out when we first go to the mountains; there are fewer molecules of oxygen in every breath than we are accustomed to at sea level. For Sue's shampoo bottle, the decrease in pressure and without a change in temperature, the volume of the shampoo bottle had to increase, making it expand. From then on Sue and I began pointing out examples of Boyle's law to each other, particularly in our culinary world. After stretching plastic film across a bowl of hot charred peppers, why did the film become concave as it cooled? Why did my glass Mason jar filled with fermenting cabbage explode? Why did the CO_2 tank nozzle of the beer system have frost on it after a bartender had improperly attached the beer lines to it and all the gas escaped? Now an inside joke, one of us would just point and say to the other "PV = NRT."

The vapor compression system controls pressure and volume in order to create changes in temperature. The best way to modulate those changes is to use a compound whose boiling point—its change from a liquid into a gas—is at a much lower temperature than water. The first vapor compression systems used ammonia as the coolant. It was very effective at cooling but when the gas accidentally leaked, it was highly toxic to humans. If refrigerators were to become standard in every home, they needed to stop killing the users. As young physicists, Albert Einstein and Leo Szilard designed and patented a refrigerator in 1926 that lacked moving parts, so it was less prone to developing leaks. It used a method different from vapor compression known as gas absorption.

Most other engineers stuck with the vapor compression model but searched for compounds as effective as ammonia but without the risk to human health. The alternative came in 1928 with the development of chlorofluorocarbons (CFCs) marketed under the DuPont brand name Freon. They were a dream family of compounds: they had low boiling points, were nontoxic to humans, and didn't corrode the piping systems they circulated in. The dream only lasted about fifty years when it was discovered that although nontoxic to humans, CFCs were destructive to the ozone layer and everything on the planet. With the 1987 Montreal Protocol, all signing nations agreed to phase out CFCs and replace them with more expensive but effective coolants called hydrofluorocarbons (HFCs). These are the coolants used today.

A description of the vapor compression cycle illustrates its genius and also reveals its fragility. Since cycles are continuous, this description could begin anywhere but I'll begin as the coolant leaves the refrigerator. It is warm, having absorbed the heat inside of the box and is also gaseous because it is under low pressure. The piping travels outside the refrigerator to a compressor, a piston-driven motor, which pumps the gas into a smaller volume, increasing its pressure. The pumping and pounding of the compressor create a lot of vibration around the compressor and the surrounding piping. This is the sound we hear when we hear a refrigerator "working." Compressed but hot, the coolant moves to a condenser, a set of metal baffles like a radiator in reverse, where the heat is thrown off into the surrounding air. As the temperature of the gas falls below its boiling point it becomes a liquid again. Now, both cool and under pressure, the coolant travels towards the box and here is the magic moment of cooling. The liquid passes through a tiny nozzle, called an expansion valve, and is released. No longer under pressure, the liquid coolant turns to gas, its volume dramatically increases, and (as Boyle predicted) its temperature drops. The cold gas rapidly moves inside the refrigerator and spreads across an array of fine metal fins that—like alveoli in our lungs exchanging oxygen in our bloodstream—exchange the heat between the ambient refrigerator air and the coolant inside the fins. A fan circulates the air in the box, the air temperature drops, and the coolant, now warm and gaseous, returns to the compressor to begin the cycle anew.

* * *

A warm refrigerator required a call to Wing. The most common cause of temperature loss is due to leaks in the closed system. Subjected to the relentless pounding of the compressor piston and its rippling vibrations, it's no surprise that welds and connections eventually develop minuscule fissures, leaks invisible to the eye. Big ones that cause a grand whoosh of refrigerant into the atmosphere—rendering the refrigerator useless—are easily identified but slow leaks can be annoyingly difficult to locate. This is where Wing's careful diagnosis and quality work came to the fore. An excellent repairman is part detective and has to want to find the leak. They can't be thinking about going home because it is a hot Friday afternoon in July or get distracted by cooks constantly coming into the walk-in grabbing things they need for dinner service. Focus and will are required. Most of the time Wing's guys were persistent enough to find the leak but occasionally they would not find it, pressurize the system with new gas, and cross their fingers, hoping they weren't the one sent back on the next repair call if the pressure fell over a week or a month. With particularly vexing leaks, Wing would assign himself the task and ruthlessly pursue the breach. Dressed in a simple mechanic's uniform, a blue short-sleeved shirt, the Wingstar Mechanical name embroidered in gold above the shirt pocket, he would always come find me to give me his report before leaving the jobsite—never writing an invoice for several weeks until the refrigerator was proven to be successfully maintaining pressure.

What happens to the heat that is thrown off at the condenser after absorbing the heat from inside the refrigerator? Some refrigerators are self-contained with the mechanicals directly attached either on top or in back—as in most home refrigerators. With this setup, the heat is dumped right into an already hot kitchen. This adds further heat to the room and increases the need for additional cooling, a bad cycle that only ends when the demand is reduced at the end of service or the outdoor temperature drops.

If the mechanicals are not located with the box, then it is known as a remote unit and the heat gets tossed wherever the condenser is placed: outdoors on a roof, in a backyard, or in a low-use area like a basement. Central AC units are also designed this way. The cumulative cooling of all the bedrooms, dining rooms, and refrigerators around the city increasingly heats up the ambient air and the surrounding stone and concrete, only increasing the need for more urban cooling. The more we stake out cool areas for our internal, private lives, the more we create heat in the commons.

It's not hard to imagine what the global implications are for the sake of my sleeping comfort, my need for a cold beer at the end of a hot service, or my desire to seat as many customers in the pleasant dining room with a seven days a week restaurant operation. The heat has got to go somewhere. It doesn't disappear. In the scientific world this is known as the first law of thermodynamics. Others call it karma and what goes around comes around.

If there isn't a gas leak, a common—and expensive—repair is that the compressor burns out from the constant activity of pumping and needs replacement. On these occasions Wing would come into my office, almost apologetically looking down at the ground, shuffling his feet with the pawing motion of a tentative horse and gingerly deliver a physician's prognosis on our patient. Sometimes the compressor would be under warranty and switched out; other times, Wing would put a good spin on bad news, telling me that after fifteen years we'd beaten the actuarial tables for compressor lifespans and that I'd enjoyed the money not spent during the additional years.

The vapor compression cycle is the keystone of our entire international system of food transportation and the delocalized food system that we all participate in and depend on. Without it, the vast, nationally distributed farms of California or Florida couldn't have developed, salmon from Norway couldn't pass in Los Angeles as fresh, and I couldn't sit in a restaurant in Chicago happily eating yellowtail sushi from Japan. Developing a coolant that would make ice obsolete was an important step, but compressors required a power source. A massive amount of electrical power and a highly developed grid to distribute it is the other leg critical to the food system. With an electrical socket and a power grid behind it, cold can be manufactured anywhere.

Our collective demand seems to continue unchecked and sometimes the grid fails to meet the demand. During an August heat wave in 2003, energy companies across the Northeast and Midwest made a set of errors and, in a matter of minutes, 55 million people lost power for nearly two days. Having experienced localized outages before and with a lot of product in the walk-in, I immediately sensed trouble was brewing. I jumped on my bike and rode up to the West Fifties where Manhattan's only remaining wholesale icehouse was located. When I arrived, there was already a line down the block. I spied one of the Ottomanelli "boys," the multigenerational family of butchers on Bleecker Street, a few people ahead of me. He looked at me with newfound respect. Instead of seeing me as a chump chef who only showed up when I was in a bind, needing a last-minute leg of lamb because of poor planning and willing to pay retail, I was now the forward-thinking chef whose food was going to stay cool over the next few days as we rode out the heat wave and waited for power to be restored. I bought the last two fifty-pound blocks of dry ice, put them on my bike, and rode back to the restaurant down Ninth Avenue through the biggest snarl of traffic I have ever experienced. With every traffic light out, it was true mayhem, even with pedestrians voluntarily directing traffic.

Caused by a guy at an Ohio power plant who threw the wrong lever when demand surged, no one wanted to take responsibility for the blackout or pay out insurance claims on the losses. My losses? Two days of business revenues including part of a weekend. Covered by insurance? Nope. Because post-9/11, the premiums had gone through the roof so I could only afford a seventy-two-hour waiting period before my insurance coverage kicked in. At least I didn't lose product. The hundred pounds of dry ice in the walk-in kept everything cool, and interestingly, I noticed that the food was in even better condition after two days of being cooled by dry ice. Everything was perky, still fresh from the market, with no signs of dehydration.

Why was everything so perky? Consider again the glass of lemonade sitting on a picnic table on a humid day in Montauk and not, let's say in the dry heat of Phoenix. There would probably be condensation beading up on the outside of the glass, dripping down onto the table. That's what coasters are for, my mom would remind me. The water collecting on the coaster is the moisture being removed from the surrounding air. Although it might be minuscule, the icy lemonade will have lowered the humidity of the surrounding air on that summer afternoon. If this were happening inside a walk-in box or in your home refrigerator, the humidity in the air would also be condensing on the fins (that's why refrigerators drip more in the summer) and the air would become drier along with everything in the box as well.

By design, then, walk-ins are dehydrators and dehumidifiers; they are tough on vegetables and brutal on delicate fruit. They are not places a chef concerned about quality should leave product for very long. They remove water from everything and everyone who enters, which sometimes is just what we wanted. At the end of a hot summer night, beers in hand, we'd fill out the prep sheet in the walk-in, enjoying the transpiration from our chefs coats. As if the breeze were coming off the lake or at the shore, I would get super-chilled.

I realized that part of our job as good cooks is to protect our ingredients from the very walk-in they are in. Like learning to regulate the flame at the stove, chefs also need to actively gain control of our refrigeration as it impacts our ingredients. Using the best quality zip-tight plastic bags makes a huge difference. Misting as grocers do in their open cases helps keep greens hydrated, and my precious day-neutral strawberries were either immediately transferred into plastic lidded containers or stored in more passive cool rooms, like the wine room. Critical too is minimizing inventory to promote faster turnover. It shortens the time between harvest and consumption, an improvement that is only possible with short supply chains, such as buying several times a week at the Union Square Greenmarket, and a watchful eye.

***

I never quibbled with the price on an invoice from Wing and after we began working together, I never shopped around to see if I could find better pricing. No doubt I could have, but a corollary to "what goes around, comes around" is "you get what you pay for." With Wing honesty was paramount. I learned this in a moment of cultural misperception. As careful and respectful as Wing and his guys always were, they never cleaned up after themselves. Broken timers and expansion valves were left around in the basement for us to throw away. I mused that this was akin to the habits of the Chinatown butchers that cut pork for me with cigarettes in their mouths, a different sense of hygiene and propriety. With some trepidation, I confronted Wing about it one day, asking his men to be more respectful of our work area. After all, I was pay-ing his guys for their work, the least they could do was leave our basement as clean as they had found it. With no offense taken, Wing responded that this was his clear directive to all his employees. He never wanted there to be a question as to whether or not the part was actually broken, leaving open the possibility that the part might get taken away and installed elsewhere and of course inversely that I might be receiving someone else's used parts. Equipment, whether old or new, was our property and he had no claim on it. It was ours to dispose.

On so many occasions we wanted to show our appreciation for getting us back up and running by offering the gift of our skills, a meal, but his men always declined. This was another Wingstar rule: no one was allowed to accept food or drink from clients beyond water. Wing didn't allow any cozi-ness or blurriness in the relationships. Occasionally, under extreme pressure from the chef or at the end of a very long day, Wing would let us cook him a burger and give us the pleasure of giving back to him.

***

That completes the laundry list required for refrigeration repair excellence: prompt response, proper diagnostics, quality work and honesty. But with Wing there was one additional item: gratitude, not something I expect in business. At the end of the day it is transactional. I need service; he provides it; I pay for the services; everybody is happy. Even in the dining room it's transactional; customers need food or a glass of wine; we provide it, they pay for it. Hopefully everybody is satisfied. But in fact, we long for something more meaningful, for interactions that aren't transactional. We have favorite restaurants because we are seen and with that recognition comes a story or a tableside visit or maybe an extra taste from the kitchen or the bar. Having those opportunities is what kept the restaurant business vibrant for me. In the world of repairs and maintenance, though I don't expect to have that kind of interaction. It's get the job done and go home.

Wing came to me one day and said, "This is my twentieth anniversary of being in business, and since you are one of my first customers, you can choose not to pay any single invoice you want to this year. No changing your mind, no waiting until the season is over, but you can pick any bill and cross it out." Such an Eastern philosophical outlook I thought, making an offering but leaving some of it to chance. It was like throwing the I Ching on behalf of my refrigerators. Regardless of which invoice I selected, twenty years in, I knew we were both winners.

Before the summer heat had hit hard and stressed out any of my aging AC units, my walk-in evaporator went down, corroded and irreparable after twenty-five years of hard use, clearly a serious four-digit repair. His men were on the job making the repair when Wing stopped by to check in on their progress and chuckled to me, "Maybe you are going to pick this one." It was early enough in the season that worse could be coming down the pike, but I said, "Yup. No doubt." There was no resentment; the gift was given, the offer made and now it was mine to use. Even if a bigger job came along later in the summer, there was no second-guessing my gratitude for having a man with such integrity on my side.

THE HIVE

It's going to be a busy Saturday night. Although I stopped cooking on a daily basis many years ago, I'm still happiest when I'm immersed in the flow of the operation. Running plates to tables, jumping behind the line to make a few salads, or polishing glassware during a busy service is part of my natural elevated state of rest. Sometimes I am tempted to do it in other people's restaurants when I see they are struggling to keep up. It's part of why I drift behind Rick's farm table and bag up potatoes or make change.

I arrive on these kinds of nights late in the afternoon, after whatever lunch mayhem there may have been is over, ready to hear the tales, attend to some small tasks, and then participate in a busy service, in a supporting role, where many others are the night's stars and everyone is playing their well-practiced part.

Cooking for one is about sustenance, getting the needed calories to survive. Cooking for two is about sharing. The French word for friend, *copain* (hence "companion" in English), means to share or break bread together, *co-pain*. From that one word, food and friendship conjoin and community around the table is built. As much as I loved cooking for Sue and myself during our many months of COVID-19 quarantine, my professional life was to cook for lots of people, an undertaking that required building a large community. Writers and painters might thrive in solitary sanctuaries, but I need the thrum of the restaurant hive—a complex, interdependent food community.

The restaurant functioned on two floors. There was a front staircase guests used to go to the second-floor dining room. Food was never run up those stairs. We shared it with the third-floor neighbor and needed to keep it free of the internal stress inherent in busy moments; there was a back stair for that, running from the kitchen up to a second floor kitchen that functioned as a pastry kitchen by day and a server station by night. I'd make big bi-level laps through the house all night long, always beginning at the front entry door.

The door host, an ebullient Harvard grad has been working the book, moving reservations around like puzzle pieces to liberate a few more deuce time slots without slamming the house. Simultaneously she's fielding late calls and confirmations with a perkiness I envy. The book and the door are in the best hands I could imagine. No aggressive diner insisting on being seated immediately is going to knock her off balance. Her bright spirit never fails to soften the angry edge of anyone walking in the door. The floor manager swings by to take note of tonight's VIPs and get a sense of the evening's flow. Tall, with proud posture, he is an inspiration to watch on the floor. When pouring a tableside taste of a wine by the glass, he takes a half-step back, giving the taster the space to consider and evaluate. As polished and diplo-matic as I have become, I can still get into it with a customer. I don't easily roll over when someone returns the penultimate bottle of Barbaresco from a great winemaker in a stellar vintage because "it's bad" and wants me to open the final bottle. Besides modeling what great service looks like, he provides useful contrasting evaluations of employees to my own and regularly gives me book titles to read.

It's time for staff meal, to get everyone fueled for the evening's work and to go over the game plan for the night. The cook puts up family meal and before anyone has tasted it he explains why it isn't his best effort. A server rejects the apology and passes along wisdom she received in her acting class, "No qualifying allowed." It's wisdom I internalize and hope to inspire in others. She's one of the servers who developed and mastered the perfect crab boil spiels, "What to Expect When You're Expecting Crabs," a description of how the evening works and the quick tutorial, "How to Crack a Crab and Eat Every Morsel." I grab a plate, sit and listen as people share stories of their "weekends," talk about politics or the latest films. Then the manager, ever dressed with downtown casual elegance, espouses a few fine points of good service. He uses last night's wrinkles as learning opportunities for tonight without a hint of disappointment or discouragement. I'm glad he's running the meeting; I've given these director's notes more times than I care to remember and by now there's probably a perceptible hint of ennui in my delivery. After the chef has described tonight's specials, the manager calls "break" and everyone gets up, busses their dishes, and makes their final preparations for the evening.

Even though the wine fridge gets restocked at the end of each night, replenishing what was purchased, invariably wines get improperly stocked. In expectation of a busy night, the French server, the only foreigner I successfully sponsored for green card status, goes down the wine list, organizing two of each bottle for easy access. Some servers can identify wines by bottle shape and lead capsule color, the labels only serving to verify their pick. It's a level of detail articulated by someone not just doing the job, but by someone committed to doing a great job. Meticulous and at times domineering, she demands excellence from co-workers if she is going to comfortably pool the tips. She isn't shy about letting me know when she feels I've dropped my standards and aren't demanding enough of other employees. Wine cooler set, she goes upstairs to the section of the dining room where she is working.

The food runner takes coffee orders from all the cooks, getting the line pumped up for a busy service; mostly, it's double espressos. The chef is calm; his cooks have all completed their prep. He is the one who perfected the burger blend, combining meat from the shoulder, the rear leg, and a bit of aged fat for taste. The cooks pick thyme, snip chives, and tell kitchen yarns about former kitchens or departed cooks, the more salacious the better. I offer up an entry into the "you can't make this shit up" category. A pastry chef from years back came to work even though he was very ill and made a special-order dessert for a wedding rehearsal dinner party, inoculating the entire party with his gastrointestinal ailment. Many attendees spent wedding day with their head in a bucket. Our insurance company refused to offer any compensation unless the client officially sued us, an ordeal I refused to put them through given the ruined wedding. I opted to return all the money along with gift certificates for all the guests to eat a "flora-free" Savoy meal.

I can howl with laughter recounting the story, but in the moment I was mortified that I was responsible for causing pain for so many people. I'm on a roll and offer up another one: the time a line cook, flying high on a cocktail of substances, kicked in the glass front door at 1 A.M. because the manager refused to return his sexual advances. As a topper, I share the time I was physically threatened by a manager's husband after I fired her, necessitating backup from the NYPD. As much as these tales are fun to regale people with, highlighting the inanity of running a restaurant, they are like fishing stories, mythic and anomalous. The day after day story of the ongoing work is the story of people working together, collaborating to cook good food and to create dining experiences where people feel at ease.

The first ticket comes into the kitchen: two heirloom tomato salads, a striped bass, and a duck—the salt-crust baked duck being our signature dish. The technique came from Romy Dorotan, back when Sue was his pastry chef, and was refined by David Wurth, our first chef, in his daily morning process of roasting a tray of ducks for the evening crew. I sliced thousands of them in dinner service and developed many of the sauces and garnish sets for the duck breast entrée, but I rarely participated in the daytime part of the procedure; the intricate secrets of salt crusting were known to others, passed from one daytime cook to the next.

The tomatoes are sliced to show off variety of color and shape and just barely dressed with vinegar, salt, and olive oil. They are at peak ripeness, juicy and flavorful. Knowing that deep refrigeration kills the aromas of tomatoes and shuts down the ripening process of stone fruit, one chef commandeered space in a wine room I had built in the basement a few years back. The beverage manager and the chef now jockey for space every summer within the wine room's tiny forty-square-foot plan but there is mutual respect, knowing that each is devoted to serving superlative products. I may have provided the capital to pay for the infrastructural improvement but others implemented practices that forever raised the bar on our food.

Excellence can come from any person regardless of their job description: a meticulously organized reservation book, a stack of grease-free sheet trays, a tidy walk-in at the end of a hectic day, vinaigrettes that taste right every time, salads that are never overdressed, burger temps hit nearly every time. Doing a job well requires a dedication in each moment, making a personal decision over and over again on the part of each employee.

The tomato plates come up in the pass and are ready to take to the table. Tonight's runner is the guy who defined what the runner's job really is: the pace at which plates need to be carried up the back stairs, the necessity of a watchful eye, looking to bus empty plates on the cruise back through the dining room when returning to the kitchen, and maintaining total command of the tickets as they come up. No longer hanging in order of when they were spit out of the printer, he's discerned what the new order should be by attentively listening to the cooks' conversations. Off to massage therapy school soon, his legacy is imbedded in the house, methods that will be taught to all future runners.

A few more tickets have been called: sardines, a green salad, two grilled shrimp, and a chicken liver pâté. The duck breasts are roasting in the oven, the apricot sauce reducing in the pan when a server walks into the kitchen with a special request. "Can we grill the striped bass for a guy who wants it plain, no sauce, no oil?" She's the Bosnian powerhouse who not only called out a (soon to be former) manager for putting his hands on her body, addressing her as "Beautiful" instead of using her name, and directed her not to offer desserts to customers because he wanted to go home, but caught him comping an expensive bottle of wine for a friend. She then directly reported it all to me. That's what you call a keeper, not just in the usual sense of someone worth keeping around but someone who protects what the place is and stands for. Having these kinds of people on staff meant that I didn't have to be there all the time because they embodied what the place was trying to be and the standards of the house. From dishwashers and prep cooks to baristas, door hosts, and operations managers there were many keepers. All of them deserve to be named.

It's not like we ever achieved total Dream Team status. There are always people who are just warm bodies, just passing through or not cut out for this level of focused work. They cycle out; whether they chose to move on or I had to move them along is unimportant. Skills aside, some people don't mesh with our culture: abusive language and treatment of co-workers, non-collaborative work habits, setting their own rules or culinary standards, not getting the manner of service and the style of food, or undermining my authority with other employees. Staffing is a constant process of honing, matching personalities and skill sets with one's vision.

The bargain that we strike on the job—work offered in return for money—is, at the end of the day, transactional. Plenty of employees do just that—they do the work—which is sufficient. Owners can't demand more, even if we might hope for more. When employees go further and join in with the culture of the enterprise, offering a piece of themselves, of their heart, to the project, the workplace flourishes. I view these as gifts, not rights. I remain grateful to have been both a witness and a beneficiary of myriad gifts that allowed the restaurant (and me) to thrive.

Before leaving the kitchen, the Bosnian artist grabs a rack of glassware from the elder dishwasher, who once owned his own restaurant uptown and, in his words, is now taking it easier, washing dishes six evenings a week, free of ownership worries. He moves slow but he moves smart. He tips the full garbage bin over on its side before pulling the bag out so as not to lift the weight directly upward, an energy-saving trick I still employ at home. Everyone dreads his annual six-week vacation each January to go home to Mexico because the young placeholders can never keep pace on a busy Saturday night.

I follow the server up the backstairs; we chat while I help her polish a few glasses. I survey the room and say hello to a couple, who have been longtime fans. Every server knows them, and they them. The restaurant is an extension of their home, a dining room with better food, a service staff, and tables for gathering with groups of friends larger than their apartment can accommodate.

I step into the office off the second-floor dining room that's tucked behind the restroom and hidden by a mirrored door. The general manager, who has made organizational projects her raison d'être, is hard at work assembling a survival kit for when a two-hundred-amp fuse blows, as it invariably does in the depths of August's heat. Her floor service shift is long over—lunch service wrapped up hours ago—and now she is taking this quiet office time to move some projects forward. Contained in a plastic box are simple schematics of the electrical service, spare fuses, a tool to replace them without electrocuting oneself, and precise procedural instructions, nothing she ever thought she would learn about. The box sat in its perch not far from the summer tomato stash in the wine room long after she moved to New Orleans. It's but one reminder of her contributions among many computer folders organized, wires untangled, and time invested over many years.

We chat for a few minutes about another keeper, now running her own business, an assistant pastry person who had once called me into the kitchen to show me the paltry nature of the industrial eggs we were buying from our dry goods supplier. "Surely we can do better than this," she said, showing me thin-shelled eggs with pale-yellow yolks and watery whites. She was right. It was time to raise the bar, to be more of what we represented ourselves as. I found a greenmarket source and added a case of eggs to my weekly run. It was another advancement contributed by someone hard at work in the hive.

I drop down the front stairs to the bar and restaurant entrance. I've gone full circle. The bar is full, people waiting for tables and plenty there for a casual hangout, to grab some bites and a few rounds of high-grade cocktails. Tonight's bartender happens to be our drink creator and bar manager. On certain mornings, he preps out jalapeño mezcal infusions and batches of cucumber juice for all the bartenders to use throughout the week, but tonight he's performing behind the parabolic bar with an audience. A cocktail shaker in each hand, he makes the rhythmic music of banging ice hard against the cups, before ending his percussion solo with the rippling splash of the contents pouring into a couple of waiting rocks glasses. Everyone seems happy.

The door host grabs a stack of menus and a wine list and gathers up the two couples who've just reunited, tells the bartender where she's about to seat them so he can transfer their check, and takes them to a table. She quickly returns to her home base and fields a phone call from someone looking for a last-minute table. "Sure, swing by. We'll make something work." I dread the day she will give notice but I know hosts do cycle through the house fairly rapidly.

Sometimes I am thrilled when people give notice, not because I am going to be freed of dead weight, but because a cherished employee's departure represents a personal success or triumph in their lives. This is particularly true with front of the house employees whose primary talents often lie outside restaurants. The stereotype that New York servers are all actors has a grain of truth to it. Our servers may not have all been actors, but most are here to pursue an art: visual, dance, music, film production, in addition to theater. The arts don't usually pay a living wage for quite a while, and for some, never will. It's the day job—the restaurant gig—that pays the rent and food bills. Diners may not realize this but every time you dine out, you are a patron of the arts. Filling out the tip line on your credit card slip is a direct subsidy to New York's artists and its art scene. When servers gave their notice because they secured a job in their field, I felt a personal pride that my restaurant had been their safe harbor as they worked to establish themselves. I loved toasting those departures over staff meal—"To one more artist quitting their day job."

The kitchen is peaking. There are lots of tickets hanging and without an extra set of hands, a slackened pace will drag the entire house down. The chef slips behind the line and plates a handful of desserts because the cold station cook is overwhelmed with all the appetizers on order. I run desserts out to the two regulars and as a way of saying thanks, I add in a small bowl of the pastry chef's newest sorbet—made with black currants supplied by customers with a house in Vermont. She's the keeper who a few years back, when finances were tight during a particularly slow summer, agreed to do pastry in the morning and then work the salad station through lunch even though she was six months pregnant and had to swing her ever-widening belly aside in order to open the refrigerator door.

Under this roof countless *copains* were formed, lifelong friendships including several marriages (with offspring now in tow). We broke bread, undertook a common task, and together everyone brought their best to my passion project. It's 10:30; all the reservations are in, there haven't been any major hiccups, and I can head home. But not before heading back to the kitchen.

Mohammed, the overnight porter, has arrived. He helps push out all the additional work that hits the dish pit when cooks start closing up their stations, changing containers, switching out fish trays, along with all the pans that have been used in the late-dinner rush. Only after helping with all of that does he take on the unpleasant but necessary overnight, deep-cleaning projects. He always greets me with "I am so glad to see you" and a beaming face. It's unfathomable to me that he can be so positive about life—living alone in the Bronx, away from his wife in Guinea, here without documentation and little hope of that changing. Using highly caustic degreasers to strip fry oil away from all the surfaces where it has accumulated, cleaning the kitchen mats littered with the food droppings from a busy service, he works solo through the night, listening to the Quran read aloud from his phone as his sole companion. Every night upon arrival, when Mohammed hugs me and says "I am so happy to see you" I think to myself, "What troubles do I have worthy of pulling me down?" He stays through the night until dawn, when he proudly turns over a sparkling kitchen and buffed dining room to the morning cook. The house is ready for another day, another dance in the hive.

GRENADA PEPPERS

I am used to competing with chefs for ingredients; that goes way back. Prior to opening Savoy, I remember once approaching Alvina Frey's farmstand, grower of the best string beans this market has ever seen, when a fellow chef saw where I was heading. In a move reminiscent of a junior high school student blocking their test paper with their arm lest anyone see the answers, they gathered up all the beans, plopped the more than ample bag on the scale and then turned to greet me. There is no question that they were the rightful owner, just as the test taker was entitled to their privacy, but my annoyance was similar, and upon completing their purchase any sense of camaraderie between us evaporated, forever.

Contemplating a role reversal, I vowed never to completely wipe out a stand's supply, to always leave a bit behind, particularly for the shopper right behind me, even if it was a token amount. Whether it's for mushrooms and berries in the forest or okra and tomatoes in the market, this is good foraging etiquette and not a bad approach for living on the planet and for treating resources and people. It's a non-extractive utilization of the market. Leaving some behind recognizes that there are others who matter, others who keep the market healthy, diverse, and vibrant. The vibrancy from the diversity is part of what makes the market such a wonderful place to shop. It raises the deeper notion of whether or not we are living and acting from a mindset of scarcity or abundance. Is there enough for everyone to go around? As a chef, does my ability to excel or distinguish myself in the crowded field of restaurants derive from controlling access to ingredients or from my ability to cook delicious food?

I know all about the early bird catching the worm, but with school drop-off when the kids were little, I couldn't get to market before 9 A.M.; I was not the first (but by no means the last) chef to pass through. Scale was also an issue. Some restaurants are of a size that dwarfed my purchases, gaining buying leverage based on volume. Fortunately, this disparity also

259

worked to my advantage because my needs were more moderate, more easily accommodated. For a time, Gramercy Tavern was my most formidable competition for coveted items in limited supply. Their purchaser, Modesto, a towering Dominican man, consistently arrived earlier than me, piling his cart high, stack upon stack of tomato and berry flats and bulging blue plastic bags filled with black Tuscan kale or frying peppers. After Modesto had repeatedly cleaned a farmer out of some shell beans prior to my arrival, I approached him one morning, and braced myself for another disappointment. "Modesto, did you already take all of the cranberry beans again?" His immediate response was "Peter, tell me, Peter, what do you need?" and immediately offered me part of his cache. Big hearted and sympathetic, he crafted a strategy for lean times that looked out for both restaurants. Instead of ten flats of berries going to Gramercy, they might end up with nine, with one going to Savoy and the Gramercy chef (Tom Colicchio or Mike Anthony, depending on the year) was none the wiser.

Not all chefs or their buyers are as community-minded in their approach. Some chefs use the market as just one more place from which to extract resources, albeit a better one than the Hunts Point wholesale distribution hub. Some angle to gain exclusive control of a farmer's supply, trying to buy up the entire crop, thinking that this will give them a leg up in the competitive marketplace of New York City restaurants. This approach is an extension of their philosophy that cachet is dependent on offering and selling exclusivity. Whether it is about getting a coveted reservation or offering ingredients that no one else has access to, these chefs and restaurants are selling the allure of scarcity.

The market, though, never felt like a place where it was right for farmers to collude with a chef's need for exclusivity. Not a complete angel either, I wouldn't share information and sourcing with the chefs who cultivated their air of superiority. If knowledge equaled power then I liked holding my insider knowledge, doling it out only to those I deemed deserving. When John Schmidt of Muddy River Farm (a stand often overlooked by chefs) started bringing in New York State–grown artichokes, I kept that information under my hat, not wanting to advertise my discovery right into oblivion. Ultimately though, I prefer building camaraderie and exchanging gastro-knowledge with my community and shared the info.

But there was one ingredient that didn't bring out my best self, that for years tapped into my feelings of resource scarcity. It was a pepper. Supply was indeed short, and it wasn't the chef community with whom I was in competition. Come Labor Day, when kids are back in school and the Montauk post office has rehung the "They're gone" sign, the corn and tomatoes that raced hard in August to produce fruit are now in decline. Not so for peppers; they're just finding their pace on the backstretch of summer, actually thriving in September's sustained heat and scarce rainfall.

Pepper nomenclature is confusing and Christopher Columbus, responsible for so much cross-cultural misunderstanding and misappropriation, is to blame for this too. In pursuit of a westward oceanic route to the east, Columbus's sights were set on India, its spices, and in particular, the highly prized black peppercorn. Thinking he had made it to Asia, Columbus called the Caribbean islands the West Indies. Peppercorns, the berries of *Piper nigrum*, a climbing vine limited to hot regions near the equator, were called pimiento in Spanish. When Columbus was introduced to chile peppers in the Americas, he conflated them with peppercorns and called them pimiento as well, even though they are botanically unrelated. These peppers, part of the nightshade family of tomatoes and eggplants, are known as the *Capsicums*. Most of the peppers we are familiar with are of the species *Capsicum annum*: jalapeños, bell peppers in all colors, poblanos, Hungarian wax peppers, shishito, and Padróns. Tim Stark of Eckerton Farm was for decades the sole Union Square farmer growing an array of another species: *Capsicum chinense*, the more exotic, flavorful, and incendiary peppers and specifically, my object of desire, the Grenada seasoning pepper.

My competition for the Grenadas was a host of Caribbean women who would show up in the market at sunup cajoling, pestering, and begging Tim to sell them his entire day's haul before he had a chance to set up his stand. I never had the opportunity to invoke my "never wipe out the table" practice because they were an invisible force, arriving before I was even out of bed. I considered myself lucky to get a half pound, and I got that only by begging Tim to set some aside and hide them in the truck. For me, Grenadas are a unique flavor and special ingredient that I delighted in sharing with my cooks and customers. For the persistent island ladies though, these seasoning peppers were part of their cultural heritage, a culinary lifeline to a distant home, a far more powerful motivator than my desire to cook with novel ingredients. That seemed to me a more worthy reason to lose out.

The Grenada seasoning pepper is named after its namesake island in the Windward Islands of the Lesser Antilles, close to the South American mainland. The *chinense* peppers developed in the Amazon basin and radiated from there into the southern islands of the Caribbean. It is bright yellow with the occasional orange blush, thin-skinned, and rarely bigger than a walnut. Its sensual folds and ripples characterize all of the *chinense* peppers, prompting Caribbean people to name one of its hotter kin, the Scotch bonnet, after the highlander wool hat known for its multiple pleats and pom-pom tuft. Crack one open and the fragrance is intriguing: full of floral and citrusy flavors accompanied by a nasal tease, a tingle suggestive of an underlying arsenal of heat. Grenadas have all the fragrance of habaneros or Scotch bonnets and only a fraction of their heat. Another island variety of *chinense* is known as 7-Pot pepper because it packs so much heat and flavor that it is only discarded after offering its powers to multiple stews.

I'm not sure that Columbus declared that he discovered America or if others assigned that honor to him, but I relate to the thrill of making a discovery. Just as lots of people liked to consider that they "discovered" Savoy, I used to act like I had discovered the Grenada pepper. This was complete folly given that Tim Stark had gotten the seeds from a Windward Islander and had been growing the peppers for several years, displaying them each week for all to buy. I staked a claim as being the first (or only) white mainstream chef to "discover" the Grenada because come September, when Tim's cash crop, tomatoes, are mostly in decline, most chefs have moved on from his stand and so the Grenadas stayed off their radar. The arrogance of this Eurocentric worldview and my own participation in a kind of eco-colonialism does not escape me. I longed to taste the island women's stews cooked with their five-pound 7 A.M. purchases of Tim's Grenadas. I was certain they were a bold celebration of flavor.

***

The *Capsicums* are a miraculous group of plants. Once the Columbian Exchange (the less pejorative term for the botanical and zoological sharing that commenced after Columbus "discovered" the Western Hemisphere) began, Portuguese and Spanish explorers transported peppers all across the globe, where they easily adapted to many diverse climates and were embraced by the peoples of Asia, Africa, and most of Europe. The botanical success of the *Capsicums* is a result of a combination of factors: they grow prodigiously; can be easily selected and bred to express different traits; and probably paramount is their taste—attractive, powerful flavors that come in small packages.

Other new-world "discoveries," beans, potatoes, and corn, are more nutritionally significant, which might explain why they became the caloric staples for millions of people worldwide. The tomato, another star ingredient of the Americas, took several centuries to become the overwhelmingly dominant vegetable in worldwide production. But no other ingredient spread as rapidly and became foundational to as many cuisines as the *Capsicum* peppers. Their appeal is not nutritional but rather their abundance of flavor. Pinch for pinch, no other plant group comes close to *Capsicum's* seasoning power, which explains why they were so quickly embraced in Asia and Africa, and play a central role in Spanish, German, and Middle Eastern cuisines. And of course, in the traditional pepper-rich cuisines of Mexico, the Caribbean, and the Amazon basin, peppers were appreciated long before colonial forces began spreading their genetics around the world, an ecological form of imperialism. It's kind of incredible to imagine what Hungarian, Szechuan, Hunan, or Indian food tasted like before the sixteenth century, without access to this crucial ingredient in their cuisines.

If every painting is in some ways a self-portrait of the painter then every pepper selected to reflect the climate and taste preferences of a culture is a self-portrait of the people breeding it as well. Adapting to so many different palates and desires, there is a vast trove of shapes, colors, flavors, thicknesses, and heat levels. Grenadines breed them for their seasoning, Middle Easterners for their stuffing capacities, and Hungarians for their qualities dried and ground into powder.

Peppers are a culinary antidote to scarcity and people's experience of poverty. Carbohydrates, the major caloric fuel in many diets, tend to be neutral in flavor (some might even call them bland) and animal proteins are dear, whether they are hard to come by or expensive to purchase. Peppers dry extremely well, offering a year-round, unrefrigerated dose of big flavor, and bring life and interest to meals that might otherwise become boring. The financial analyst side of Tim readily agrees with this analysis. His juice-laden tomatoes, which sell for $5 a pound, make the month of August his Black Friday. Tomatoes may be Tim's cash crop, but the soul of his operation lies with his peppers. His tiny mix-and-match half-pint boxes of pequeño pimentos only bring in $3, and most people only buy a half pint compared to the average tomato sale of three pounds at $5 a pound. Pepper power goes a long way.

The top row of my spice rack represents my classic French training: vials of bay leaf, black peppercorns, coriander, and fennel seed, mainstay flavors in so many European stews and braises. The bottom row, though is overrun by *Capsicums*: Aleppo, pimenton, smoked chipotles, and gochugaru, with a nearby spillover collection of Hungarian paprika, raisiny anchos, and dried green Hatch chiles. Widely varied in their flavor profiles, my chile choices often steer the direction of the dish I'm cooking.

What is it that we humans love so much about peppers? What explains our fascination and, for some, obsession? Much of it is about the heat. Black peppercorns are pungent and aromatic, but they aren't actually hot in the way that *Capsicums* create the sensation of heat on our tongues (and other sensitive mucous membranes in our bodies). Stimulation from a pepper "tells" our brain that we are touching something hot. The nervous system sensation of burning is real, no different than if we ate a spoonful of extremely hot soup. It's a wake-up call that something is happening, a prodding that reminds us to be in the present. We are awake, alive. People the world over love that stimulation, that provocation if you will, of eating hot sauce or jalapeño poppers and experiencing the edginess, the border between the humdrum and the vibrant. It's no different than the jolt I get from jumping into the frigid pool at the Russian & Turkish Baths when I go for a schvitz or charging into a lake on a cool summer morning. When daily routines can become desultory, we use peppers to tingle our skin, our body's edge, in order to re-experience the joy of living.

Social scientists call this pursuit of exhilaration benign masochism or constrained risk, when we ignore the message of the physical sensation and enjoy the experience because, in this case, we know we aren't actually getting burned. I don't agree with the masochism theory. The endorphin rush that comes along with a sweaty forehead and a runny nose is an experience of heightened awareness. Deeming it thrill-seeking belittles the feeling of euphoric indestructibility we get, the way that meeting the challenge of a flaming tongue can serve as a metaphor for acting boldly in the world. Mao Tse-Tung said "the food of the revolutionary is the red pepper. Those who cannot endure red peppers are also unable to fight." May his culinary insight have longer resonance than his political beliefs.

I like raw sliced serranos added into a bowl of pho with basil and sprouts or to posole with shredded cabbage and lime garnishes, and I love three strong shakes of fermented hot sauce on a taco. But I am not a chile head. Heat is measured in Scoville Heat Units (SHU), a vaguely defined and subjective measure of the amount of sugar or alcohol needed to add to a pepper tincture to ameliorate its heat effect. I like eating hot peppers but not scorchers: ones with ratings that range from poblanos (2,000), and espelettes (2,500), to jalapeños (8,000) and serranos (8,000–20,000), and even the occasional Thai bird pepper (75,000–100,000) or the Brazilian Cumari pepper (100,000) in a vinegar dipping sauce or sprinkled raw over some braised meat. But the bro culture reverence for the Bhut Jolokia (ghost) chile (1.5 million) or the Carolina Reaper (at over 2 million) has no appeal to me. On that, the Caribbean women and I are in agreement: we are in search of seasoning (Grenadas are about 1,000). At 2 million Scoville units it's no longer about flavor; it's about endurance. As much as I can enjoy pushing my limits, this isn't one of the areas I choose to test them. Sue, on the other hand, who developed the habit of popping pickled cherry peppers as a child to delight her dad, has been known to liberally squirt "Cardiac Arrest" hot sauce on her barbecue, regretting it moments later but still proud to have gone to the other side and survived.

The fluidity of pepper characteristics and breeding is a result of their very biology. Bees, other flying insects, and the wind readily cross-pollinate between pepper plants. In order to ensure that a variety grows true each year, growers geographically isolate their pepper varieties. Tim used to grow Trinidad peppers, kin to the Grenada, but over time after too many accidental crosses with other *chinense* peppers of far greater heat, there was genetic drift and Tim's Trinidads went from being a seasoning pepper to ferociously hot. I once unwittingly served a whole pickled pepper to a customer and set their mouth aflame. Easy cross-pollination is also a blessing. Tim developed a cross of a cherry pepper with a serrano and now sells basketfuls of his Eckerton pepper. I love it sliced raw on top of a simple lentil or bean stew.

As scarce as the Grenadas were for many years, their abundance of flavor is what prevailed. In time, Tim grew more, some under hoop houses to extend the season, and other farmers (including the Campo Rosso folks who interned with him) are now growing *C. chinense* peppers as well. The Columbian Exchange instigated the abundance of pepper diversity across the globe and that diversity resides in NYC, in its markets and in the kitchens of its shoppers.

GRENADA PEPPER PUREE

Break open a Grenada with your hands; notice how it almost snaps when you crack it. Inhale the heavenly perfume. This vinaigrette is fabulous to drizzle over raw fish—maybe some blowfish that come through the mid-Atlantic in September. Or present it over vegetables—cabbage that has been roasted on the grill, or onions roasted in the oven. If you can't find Grenadas, substitute with a mild member of the C. chinense species: aji dulce, lemon drop, Habanada, or Trinidad seasoning peppers.

1 small onion, sliced

3 cloves garlic, sliced

6 tablespoons (90 ml) olive oil

8 Grenada peppers, seeded, stemmed, and roughly chopped
(reserve trimmings for the vinegar; recipe follows)

1 bay leaf

4 whole allspice berries

3 sprigs thyme

½ cup (120 ml) champagne vinegar (or other white vinegar)

1 teaspoon salt

Good olive oil, for finishing

In a 10-inch (25 cm) pan over medium heat, sauté the onion and garlic in 2 tablespoons olive oil. When the onion is soft, add the Grenadas (if you want to make a larger batch, you'll need twice the volume of onion), along with the bay leaf, allspice berries, and thyme. Sweat until the peppers soften, about 5 minutes. Add the vinegar and simmer for a few more minutes. Remove the allspice and thyme, then puree the pepper mixture with a hand blender or in a standing blender. Blend in the remaining 4 tablespoons (60 ml) olive oil. Season with salt. Either lay the puree down on a cold plate and top with sliced fish crudo or dress roasted cabbage with the puree and drizzle with good olive oil on top.

GRENADA PEPPER–INFUSED VINEGAR

This recipe involves sweeping up the pepper trimmings and putting them in a bottle of vinegar instead of dumping them in the trash. Take the reserved seeds, stems, and ribs and just push them into a bottle of apple cider or champagne vinegar. For extra credit, add a few cloves of garlic or some allspice berries and thyme sprigs if you like, but most years I just stuff the trimmings in the bottle. Replace the lid. Let sit for 1 month in a dark place before beginning to use. Use for vinaigrettes, to season a soup or sauce or add acid to brighten just before serving, or as the vinegar in a slaw. You will find myriad uses after you experience its intriguing flavors. Keeps indefinitely in the vinegar section of your pantry.

ONE STEP FORWARD, ONE STEP BACK

As cramped as we were for space at Savoy, desperately needing it if we were going to continue with whole animal butchery and hamstrung from taking on any other culinary projects, I came around to the idea of opening a second place with great reluctance. It was seventeen years before I opened a second set of doors.

When we first opened Savoy, the business completely depended upon me to operate. Quite happily, I was cook, menu creator, bill payer, human resource director, sommelier, maintenance chief, with probably a few more functions that I am forgetting thrown in as well. I loved having all those responsibilities, not because I am a control freak but because I thrived on the diversity of the skills required, on my ability to straddle being artist, businessman, and plumber. I was empowered by the self-sufficiency.

I had employees of course but my mindset was that they were there to support what tasks I couldn't do on my own or get done in time. I viewed everyone as adjunct to me. Is that what the organizational charts of mom-and-pop businesses look like? Regardless, it is the organizational model we opened with in 1990. All of the important restaurants I had worked in or modeled ourselves on, both French and American, had been built on this model: La Colombe d'Or, the Quilted Giraffe, Huberts, Chanterelle. This shifted later as I began hiring people to take charge of departments and my primary function became to support them. A manager who was deeply interested in wines took over the list. I hired a chef who had prior experience both managing a team of cooks and developing and implementing a menu. I was there to help provide focus, to articulate standards, to help people with what got difficult for them, and to keep articulating our style and approach for everybody. I was coach more than chef creator.

I wasn't clear about how to grow or if I even wanted to grow if growth meant expansion. I didn't embrace the concept of the concept restaurant and didn't dream of having multiples or creating a restaurant group. I also didn't want to be in my shop every night watching every plate go out. I wanted to go home and read to my kids before bedtime. I was also acutely aware of how tenuous and fleeting success in the restaurant business can be. Taking on another location or having a vision of multiples seemed to ignore the fundamental fact that running a restaurant had become extremely challenging.

Prior to opening, a renowned Italian restaurateur, sitting in his large fashion magnate–financed restaurant, bestowed me with some key advice. "You see this place? Even this is a nickel-and-dime business. That's the only way you are going to make money." He detailed a long list of areas where the nickels had to be scrimped—from the cost of cheese and janitorial supplies to insurance and obviously, labor. On a napkin, he drew a diagram of how to play an accounting shell game with credit card tips to create some off-the-books tax-free cash to augment the meager pay of cooks and dishwashers. I won't say I was haughty, thinking that the "nickel and dime" approach didn't apply to me, but I do remember rejecting the notion that I was getting into a business where I'd be focused on micro-managing costs. I wasn't going to be a mere shopkeeper shaving expenses on inventory and labor to make a profit. The balance of my attention was going to be focused on creating profit through delicious food. (As for the tip check scheme, I did tuck away that one for later use.) Fundamentally I believed—and it was true for many years—that if I purchased intelligently, didn't waste product, and worked hard there would be more cash coming in than going out. It was a simplistic if naive equation for what was supposed to be a straightforward business—cooking good food for hungry people.

Another successful restaurateur I sought advice from prior to opening preached that expansion was the only way to ensure stability and success because of the growth opportunities it could offer key employees. I was never convinced; that approach always felt like a Ponzi scheme predicated on an ever-expanding universe of restaurants and diners. I didn't believe in the theory from either the supply side or the demand side. I spent most of my career seemingly wrong about that. As the number of restaurants in New York City expanded almost every year, dining became a new form of entertainment and, with a strong economy, New Yorkers seemed to eat out more than they cooked at home. Many operators have embraced that approach and built empires. I didn't want to build an empire. I just wanted to have an atelier in which to do our work and do it at a scale where the cooking remained a craft, not a manufacturing enterprise.

Jerry Winter, a Savoy manager for several years, had left New York and upon returning, proposed doing a project together but suggested that rather than open another fine dining establishment—a formula for more headaches—we try and exceed customer expectations by lowering the bar with a tavern or a roadhouse with professional, friendly service and really good food. I saw the wisdom in his perspective and the burger fit nicely with this approach. The place would be casual, fun, and an outlet for all that trim.

Jerry found an interesting property in the East Village with outdoor dining space and ample prep space to fabricate meat; it could act as a commissary for both restaurants. The basement, even with its low ceiling height (prep and pastry cooks over five foot eight need not apply) gave us the opportunity to comfortably butcher and properly age the animals we were buying. In time I had a stainless steel rack custom-built for aging meat on one side of the beer walk-in, where, absent moist vegetables, the humidity was perfect for dry-aging our premium cuts.

We named it Back Forty after the colloquial term for the least developed and least accessible part of a farm, referring to back when 160-acre homestead grants from the federal government were divided into four equal quadrants. Lacking road frontage, the "back forty" was a place to get lost, to be closer to nature and to breathe. Many people in the Midwest still refer to their second homes as their "back forty," regardless of how many acres they have—a trailer parked on a woodlot or a lakefront cabin both qualify. It's people's happy place. Ours was 2,500 square feet in two adjoining storefronts and the adjacent yard, located on Avenue B, a residential back eddy of the East Village, far removed from the intense street life of St. Marks Place or Second Avenue. It was a neighborhood needing a casual, American-style restaurant with good food. We opened in 2007 with a grass-fed burger central to our menu.

Back Forty was a huge hit; people appeared to be burger starved. On a typical Saturday night service, if we did 140 covers, 75 might be burgers. The grill cook could barely keep up with the orders much less handle another menu item like a grilled piece of fish. I quickly realized that our volume demanded more grill space than the twenty-four-inch-wide grill we had installed. I redesigned the cooking line to accommodate a larger grill just before an avalanche of burger-eating clubs reviewed us, all of them raving about the grass-fed burger. People wanted meat from sources they could trust. We had built a reputation on the ethics and effort we put into our purchasing. It gave people the comfort to eat what they deeply desired—but mistrusted in more traditional venues—namely meat, and specifically burgers. A common refrain from customers was, "This is the only place I'll eat a burger."

Grass-fed meat may have acquired cachet as a term but what it really means, what it really tastes like, and how you cook it properly were questions that in pursuit of the answers set all of us—cooks and customers—on a steep learning curve. Stephen Kaye had taught me that good meat begins with good grass, something that grows easily in New England and is increasingly difficult to sustain in the West with overgrazing and frequent droughts. The conventional feedlot model of bringing the food to the animals instead of forcing them to range for their feed is brilliant on first flush. It upturned the beef industry and provided a vital component to further consolidate and industrialize the meat industry: animals could reach slaughter weight in fifteen to eighteen months instead of twenty-four to thirty-six months, thereby reducing the amount of time, acreage, feed, and labor needed to grow out cattle. Cowboys be gone.

But there were unforeseen consequences as well. Grain-fed animals have a less-acidic stomach pH, allowing E. coli to thrive. When combined with the unsanitary feedlots where the steers are literally standing in their own manure, the animals become massive vectors for bacteria. The number of meat contamination incidents has increased dramatically, some resulting in deaths and large recalls. The surrounding lands don't fare too well either. Huge lagoons of waste are accumulating where the majority of feedlots are—in western Colorado, Kansas, Nebraska, and the Central Valley of California—sometimes leaching into surrounding groundwater and impacting human as well as environmental health.

What about the taste of the meat? The rich, nutty flavor and silky mouthfeel from grain-fed meat became the dominant flavor we came to expect from U.S. beef. The industry uses intramuscular fattiness, known as marbling, as the standard for grading meat—prime having the most fat, well integrated into the musculature. We became accustomed to the taste of corn in our meat rather than the taste of the grass and the land. South American countries and much of Europe still finish their meat on grass and that meat tastes different. In addition to more fat, another byproduct of raising meat in a confined feedlot is that since the animals move less, their muscles are less active and produce less flavorful meat. For many Americans, the cut of choice at weddings and other catered events is the tenderloin, a cut sadly lacking in both flavor and texture; but it is tender. We seem to prefer easy eating beef with little flavor over a cut that is more flavorful but toothsome and requires some chewing.

Our challenges as cooks and for servers as communicator-ambassadors were to prepare it well and to educate people about what they were eating. With less fat marbling, we needed to find fat on different parts of the animal to include in our burger blend. Aged fat from the strip loins helped deepen the flavor. We learned to cook it less because the meat dried out more easily. When cooked medium-well to well-done, the more mineral, almost livery flavors became prominent, so servers discouraged customers from getting their meat so well cooked. Weaning people off the umami bomb of unctuous grain-derived fattiness mixed into their large protein dose took time. Even critics reviewing the restaurant were slow to understand and appreciate the superior flavor of grass-fed beef. They were wowed by another trend occurring simultaneously, the U.S. production of Wagyu beef, the breed of Japanese cattle whose genetics, when combined with a super-grain-fed diet, produces the highest percentage of USDA-graded prime meat in the nation.

With Wagyu beef being an extreme example of that fatty grain-fed profile, lots of chefs jumped on this bandwagon and perpetuated a false association between fat and flavor. Large marketing budgets by big producers and historical taste preferences help maintain grain-fed meat as the dominant product in the marketplace regardless of both its impact on our personal and environmental health and the shift in taste preferences by many farm-to-table chefs. Taste preferences have been slow to shift. The recent explosion of "plant-based" burgers may begin to shift that narrative. Sadly in trying to persuade people about the evils of meat its proponents often fail to make a distinction between the deleterious impact feedlot grain-fed meat has on the environment and the lighter ecological footprint of grass-fed beef, which contributes to soil health and fertility.

Back Forty opened in the fall of 2007; business growth was a slow, steady build. We offered good value to people, especially in light of the 2008 financial crisis. The place had a nice vibe, friendly service staff, and we strived to be more than just a burger joint. We made terrific cocktails without the pretentiousness of the twee mixology scene. Shanna Pacifico, the opening chef, had her finger on the culinary zeitgeist and developed many dishes that resonated with the customers, most notably pork jowl nuggets, the transformation of a weird cut into a must-buy dish to start off every gathering of friends for dinner.

We became known for our weekly crab boils in the summer, my re-creation of the spicy crab picnics traditional to Maryland's Eastern Shore. Building on the feasting tradition of the *calçotada*, Back Forty's outdoor space and more casual style was the perfect spot where crab boils could happen.

Buckets of steamed crabs are dumped directly on tables wrapped in newspapers, an arsenal of wooden mallets for claw cracking are at the ready, and pitchers of cold beer are always nearby, the perfect accompaniment to wash down spicy crab flavors. Fire isn't involved, but fun, abandon, and the lack of any pretense is. In place of romesco sauce as the flavor driver, a house-made spice mix is liberally doused on the crabs before they are steamed and as with the calçotada, everyone throughout the restaurant was doing exactly the same thing at the same time. The menu: corn on the cob, steamed potatoes, string beans, corn bread, and of course plenty of hard blue-claw crabs.

I had experienced one or two crab boils many decades earlier and knew they were roll-up-your sleeves, get-your-hands-dirty affairs much loved by people in the Virginia, Maryland, D.C. area. I had tapped into a deep need in people that I didn't know existed. People's memories are a powerful force; this was a need way beyond just dinner. Walking around to tables, visiting the scores of happy crab-picking diners, people would glance up at me and say, "You must be from the D.C. area" or exclaim, "I feel like I'm home. Are you from down there too?" "No, I just love what this tradition is and wanted to re-create the spirit here." Crab boils occurred at the nexus of summer's ease, when the goodness of life seems as if it could go on forever. Each Tuesday, whenever someone prised a sweet nugget of crabmeat from a back fin and chased it down with a slug of crisp Narragansett lager it was a celebration of the rich abundance the ocean offers us. It was also a conduit to fondly remembered gatherings past or the basis for future memories spent in the garden of Back Forty.

On Saturday nights, it was three-deep at the bar while waiting for a table and, in good weather, the backyard would fill up soon after we opened the doors and stay filled all evening. The place was jumping without being a scene. It was attracting upbeat diners looking for a good food without the trappings of a serious dining experience.

It was thrilling to be running a place again that was humming on its own, generating its own energy and new ideas instead of Savoy, which constantly needed an energy infusion and a staff rejiggering every time a manager or chef departed. Back Forty's vibrancy extended throughout the house. A group of young servers were looking to take on management responsibilities and Michael Cecconi developed the Back Forty cocktail, a maple bourbon sour—that people ordered as Back 80s and Back 120s. If the staff were less knowledgeable about wines and food, they had spunk to make up for it, and their personalities had room for expression in ways that fine dining places demanding more reserve can quash. For me, there was also a freedom in being less emotionally attached to each decision and physical appointment in the place. I could let go, knowing that Back Forty was an idea or a business venture, rather than the extension of me that Savoy always felt like.

I would bounce between the two restaurants over the course of the week, checking in, holding management meetings at each location, helping people think about how to do their jobs better and then go home to my family. Not unlike the shift many parents experience in their parenting styles between the first and second child, I was committed to Back Forty's success but I also enjoyed not feeling forever belted in, forever responsible. Cash flow was positive. Investors were getting quarterly checks. Jerry and I were being paid a management fee for overseeing operations. Back Forty looked like it could be a model with potential for other locations. We had the supply, the culinary knowledge, and now, the customer base.

Over on Prince Street, our two decade-old restaurant was showing signs of age—in aesthetics, in our customer demographic, and the lease end was closing in. Our first lease, signed in 1990, was for ten years with a starting rent of $3,000. Five years in, we had the opportunity to expand to the second floor and after negotiating with my ground floor landlords I extended that lease an additional ten years. That gave me a fifteen-year lease expiring at the end of 2010. The expansion had been a great growth step. We applied for a full liquor license, which meant we could offer cocktails and spirits and had a place for people to wait for their tables instead of blocking the bathroom door. Booking private parties on the second floor while still being open for regular à la carte business downstairs gave us a steady revenue stream, which allowed me to hire and support more expe-rienced chefs and managers. People were entrusted to make decisions, ones I reviewed but was not burdened with making on a daily basis. I willingly delegated responsibility and supported people's decision-making power. Chefs hired cooks I'd never met, sommeliers selected wines I hadn't tasted. I was fine with that; it allowed me to go home and read Harry Potter and Amelia Bedelia books to my kids.

Twenty years in, business revenues were healthy, but we could also see the flattening out of the profit curve. It was increasingly difficult to reward employees who were dedicating themselves to the project, given the ever-rising fixed and operational costs of the business. It was hard to keep talented people stimulated and well paid. I had expanded the universe by going seven days, but the pressures were unrelenting. The nickels and dimes weren't accumulating fast enough to continue rewarding staff and cover all the costs.

Facing a new lease at nearly double what I had been paying, I was at a crossroad; should I stay or should I go? Four years earlier, I had opened the more casual restaurant in the East Village, partly to hedge my bets in anticipation of the Savoy lease endpoint, but I was also dipping my toe into the "all boats rise when you take on more businesses" expansion philosophy. It was working. Running a simpler, more efficient, less management-heavy business was in fact all those things, and more profitable. If I stayed, I had the advantage of the infrastructure I already owned that in a new location would have to be built out again at great expense. If I moved on, I had the opportunity to procure a new space that fit who we had become as cooks and operators—or wanted to become—with the opportunity to design a new kitchen and create a workspace that allowed for more projects. It might be in a new neighborhood that would rent at fewer dollars per square foot and be populated by people who resonated more with what we were doing. SoHo was no longer the neighborhood it had been when we opened in 1990 or even the neighborhood it had become ten or fifteen years after that. The art galleries had largely moved to West Chelsea, forced out by an earlier wave of rising rents, and were now replaced by retail—mostly clothing boutiques. More and more we were feeding visitors to the neighborhood, particularly foreigners who were there to shop.

I had become much more risk averse than when I opened the business. I had a family to support and, after 9/11, I felt extremely vulnerable. We were closed for a week because we were within the civil authority zone. For months afterward I could smell the smoldering World Trade Center site, an unseen but visceral reminder of our vulnerability. Everything seemed at risk. I had been so proud of my fearlessness, seeing it as my very fuel for moving through the multitude of challenges, but now it was oxygen deprived, choked closed, and I saw my fearlessness as youthful arrogance. Maybe they are two sides of the same coin. Either way I wasn't feeling like taking on more risk. I knew the landscape, both interior and exterior. I knew the neighborhood, the building, the landlords. And I had become attached to the corner and all the people that frequented it. It was home. I wasn't in favor of scrapping twenty years of knowns. I thought the richer, albeit less bold, approach was to stay put.

At the new (double) rent though, I couldn't operate with the same model as I had operated Savoy. Revenues needed to increase, which I could either reach by raising prices and raising the level of dining experience or by lowering prices, increasing turnover, and offering a more simplified one. I was temperamentally and politically opposed to operating a more elite dining experience. Temples of gastronomy, where the server's explanations of the food demand everyone's attention at the table and overshadowed conversation with old friends, with prices comparable to buying an airplane ticket to

Europe, was not a direction I wanted to head in. It demands more training, more management, and more catering to entitled people of privilege than I was interested in.

The success of Back Forty in the East Village had proven that we could serve sustainably raised ingredients, buy whole locally raised animals, and do it at a price point that worked for a broad spectrum of diners. Good healthy food wasn't only for the wealthy. Looking at the success of Back Forty, I thought the better bet was to go with doing more covers and to extend the Back Forty brand to SoHo. Shocker: I was embracing the idea of multiples under a single brand. I signed the new lease, ran Savoy for the busy winter months while planning a renovation for later that summer, and announced to the staff and public that we would be closing Savoy in June 2011.

* * *

Closing a beloved restaurant from a place of pride and strength might be rare but it is a wonderful opportunity for customers, employees, and owners. Too often places shutter in moments of crisis or shame, slinking away with a posted sign "on vacation" or "under renovation." I had the luxury of being able to plan it out, choreograph the close, and leave room for mourning and celebration, two nights of calçotadas—one of which was essentially a staff reunion—a week of set fixed-price menus expressing the height of summer's best and plenty of evenings filled with informal gatherings at tables and at the bar. None of the staff quit prior to closing even though they knew that within six or eight weeks they would be unemployed; their investment in the place was powerful enough that they wanted to see it through, to be part of whatever the closing would bring.

I was in house every night, greeting, basking, consoling, thanking, hugging all the friends of the house who came in for one last go. So many people owned a piece of Savoy—even ones who had moved away and came less often—and wanted to reminisce or have another night in the room or another taste of our romesco or a Red and Black. It felt like taking a victory lap, even though I wasn't done running the race and was about to dive into a renovation and a relaunch. Following the last dinner, we began selling off items that weren't going to be part of the Back Forty decor. It was clear from the outpouring and rapid sales that people wanted to actually own a piece of the restaurant that they already felt like they had discovered and now inhabited. Even plates or glassware that are available in restaurant supply stores that line the Bowery were imbued with the special meaning of having been used at Savoy, a physical evocation of all the good times people had in the dining room over the last twenty-one years. It was an enormous outpouring of goodwill; it gave me hope for what our next incarnation on Crosby Street would be.

APPLES AND PEARS

I drag my feet when apples first show up in the market in August; I just can't bring myself to buy them. Don't get me wrong, I'm obsessed with them. My kids will vouch for that, having been subjected to countless comparative tastings of heirloom varieties. I hear there are some decent summer varieties: Paula Red, Lodi, Vista Bella, and Yellow Transparent, but I wouldn't know, never having actually eaten any of them. Because when I take that first chomp into fall's essence, the world cleaves in two: on one side falls the soft ease of summer's long days when I wear as few clothes as possible, relaxing into the world's warmth, and on the other, the brisk, curtailed days of autumn and winter that demand warm clothing and a protective shell of resolve to ward against the elements. I opt to stay on summer's side of the divide as long as I possibly can and so I shy away from taking that bite.

In a rebuke to September's shortening days, I spend most of the month still in shorts and flip-flops, chasing summer's tailings of peaches and plums. Peaches are the transubstantiation of the summer sun's long rays and steady heat. They are delicate, impermanent, and best consumed fresh and in the moment: sliced over sheep's yogurt and drizzled with honey or baked in pie mixed with some high acid raspberries, or best of all, eaten out of hand while bent way over at the waist, with an elbow tipped awkwardly upward, directing the juices away from clothing and towards the ground. Peaches dried, preserved, and canned are rarely satisfactory, certainly never hitting the highs of dried figs or preserved apricots. I'm with the peach though; I prefer summer, when the line between inside and outside, self and not self is blurred. Those slow, languid days that stretch ever so slowly into evening lure me into feeling that I, too, could go on forever. Gradually, the waves of peach crates flowing into the market recede as the month progresses and soon apple bins will be all that arrives on the incoming tide of each market day.

I spend most of October deep into pears, though I find them infuriating. I remember when I first went to France, leaning over into a crate of pears at a

Paris street market. In the northern low light and damp fall air, I inhaled an atmosphere of pear vapors and knew I had truly voyaged to another world. Later, in a brasserie, sniffing a glass of Poire William eau de vie drew me in even deeper. I wanted to inhabit the planet whose delicate elegance was captured within the glass. I prefer poire eau de vie, which is directly about the fruit and called by its name; unlike the apple and grape distillates that go by calvados or cognac. In poire, a clear distillate, the fruit remains the object, direct and pure. Calvados and cognac are more expressive of process; the distillation and barrel aging become the object and the fruit fades.

Pears are elusive, you might even say fickle. Getting them right can be maddening for the grower as well as the chef. Hitting the perfect moment of soft, melty juiciness is always a challenge because pears mature from the center out. Testing for a softening surface or an increase in perfume as with peaches or apricots never gives a hint to a pear's internal readiness. Even when I hide a few in the fridge, trying to slow down their maturation process, a knife cut can invariably reveal a frustratingly thin mantle of firm flesh covering an underworld of mush and decay. How many times did I run my favorite pear, the miniature Seckels, on the menu as a spiced compote with our salt-crusted duck only to have their ripeness swing wildly between granular rock-hard wedges on some days to smooth creamy flesh with ethereal vinous flavors on others? Half our customers got the correct experience, hardly an acceptable batting average. Pears remain largely untamed, unknowable, their perfection outside of my cheffy control.

I rarely pick up a pear and eat it out of hand—the way I prefer apples. Chomping into an apple doesn't just divide the seasons, it's a small savage act, shearing flesh into chunks and then chewing them into submission. It's my private Iron John moment. The French aren't big on this kind of savagery. They view it as uncouth, just as they look askance at eating corn on the cob. Pears though, are more subtle, straddling that autumn cleave—one foot in summer, one in winter. They perfectly express the French notion of civilization imposed upon nature: carved and presented on a decorated plate, skin on, and splayed to reveal their buttery, weeping flesh or poached in red wine syrup with quatre épices (the four spices—clove, cinnamon, allspice, and nutmeg), sitting up straight, easily carved into with a spoon, the dark syrup mixed with swirling cream. Carefully selected over centuries within the stone walled *clos* of French gardens, there are far fewer varieties of pears grown in Europe and the United States than the unruly vigor that apples naturally produce in the North American woods.

An apple's structure is part of its survival mechanism and part of why we so value them. They don't yield their juice as easily as pears; their cellular structure is designed to resist release and deterioration, hence they have the best storage qualities of all fruits. Along with the refined and delicate succulence of pears also comes vulnerability; like peaches, they aren't very good keepers.

By mid-November only the crisp Bosc pears remain but I steer away from them. As pears, they disappoint me and I consider them to be nearly apples, just sporting a different set of fragrance notes. Susan loves them for their crispiness and prefers them for poaching because they hold their shape and don't deteriorate in the cooking process, but I'll pass. Soon apples will be my main squeeze fruit all the way from mid-November until the strawberries of early June, or mid-May if you count rhubarb. It is easy to understand why there is so much anticipation and lore around the spring arrival of rhubarb. In a pre-refrigeration world with minimal global trade, seven months is a long time to be eating the same fruit. True, I can always cross the street to Whole Foods for mangoes and pineapples from the tropics or berries from Florida and the West Coast, which I occasionally do, but in my pursuit of living by the seasons I keep those purchases to a minimum.

* * *

Sometime in late October or early November the winds have shifted around to the north bringing in cool and dry days. There is an appealing edginess to the bracing chill. The line between self and not self is quite clear; I need a sweater. I can finally acknowledge the apple. It's time to go out in search of the right one to crack into.

There are so many to choose from. Newtown Pippins, my over-the-long-haul seasonal favorites, are on the table but I pass on them for two reasons. First, because early in the season the acids in Newtowns are distractingly high; come January and February with some storage time under their belt, the acids soften and they explode with incomparable round and complex flavors. Like a new vintage of red wine that needs some cellaring, some apples do improve with storage. And second, there are more fleeting varieties in the market that if I don't partake in now, will soon be gone until next year. I rummage through the bins looking for the oddballs. I consider the russeted ones: Roxbury Russet, Golden Russet, Britain's favorite Cox's Orange Pippin, all strikingly beautiful with their roughened skin and alternative (non-red) color schemes; the Winesap, with its tiny golden starbursts against a red night sky; and the seventeenth-century Calville Blanc d'Hiver, its voluptuous hips, quite the ample Reuben's lady of an apple.

I finally settle on an Ashmead's Kernel, an English member of the russeted clan. Its faint fragrances of dusty rose and sweet anise are made easily accessible by its russeted skin, which is more gas permeable than both the glossy skin types and the lightly waxed apples coming through the industrial pipeline. Waxing an apple is a common and harmless practice used to reduce dehydration, extend shelf life; the loss of fragrance is tolerated as collateral damage. For all their extraordinary flavors, Ashmead's have a short shelf life because of their beautiful tan skin; they wrinkle and soften in a matter of weeks. But during those few weeks, oh my! When I sink my teeth into one an entire hemisphere shears with a simple torque of my wrist. It is electric, bursting with bright acids and round sugars, vibrant with citrus and spice. *Zing Quash Shwong!* It's symphonic.

* * *

You might be able to plant a radish and get a radish, as the song says, but that's not the case with apples—both part of their magic and part of what makes breeding them a time-consuming and costly undertaking, even in today's biotech world. A McIntosh tree will dutifully produce branchfuls of Macs year after year but planting any of its seeds will not produce a McIntosh apple tree. Apples are not self-pollinating and in order to produce fruit require a different apple type or cultivar to pollinate them. A lonely Honeycrisp tree, standing out in a field far enough away from any other apple tree so that a bee, with its three-mile flying radius, cannot transport pollen to it, will not produce fruit. Even on a biological level, apples, like humans, are scripted to need community and diversity. Each seed or offspring is a mix of the genetic material from both of its parents. Since the traits we deem desirable in an apple are widely dispersed along its genetic sequence there is no guarantee that the offspring will even express half of what we think of as a McIntosh, much less taste like a McIntosh. That is why biotech and genetic engineering has not been useful to the fruit tree industry. The only way to have predictable fruit of a particular variety, year in and year out, is by taking cuttings from one tree and grafting them onto the branches or rootstock of another, thus producing a clone of the original apple. So when you eat a Roxbury Russet, America's first named apple, discovered in Roxbury, outside of Boston, in the 1630s, you are eating the fruit from an individual tree genome in continuous production for almost four hundred years. That's a pretty good run. I love that aspect of eating heirloom apples, knowing that some Boston cabinet-maker and his wife might have loved eating this apple too. Our pleasures, our humanity, spans horizontally but also reaches back through time.

Left to its own devices, an average modern McIntosh tree on dwarf rootstock will produce eighty apples in a single season. When multiplied out by the ten seeds found in each core, there are 800 unique offspring crosses possible in a single growing season from a single tree! And that's only from one tree. If grown out, 799 of them might produce bunk, but one might produce a superstar. If you are a breeder trying to commandeer specific traits of chosen parents this might entail growing out thousands of seedlings, waiting three to five years to see if the seedlings express the desired traits, and then another ten years to build enough inventory of budwood grafted onto nursery stock so that orchardists could actually begin selling the fruit. This represents a huge investment of time and money.

But if you were a homesteader prior to the twentieth century working the land, the discovery of a chance seedling that had great tasting character or long storage capacity was one of life's happy accidents; it was something to name, graft, share with neighbors, and distribute around the region. Apple growing was done on a small scale, mostly for personal fruit and cider (alcoholic) consumption. It wasn't immediately a moneymaking proposition.

Here was Darwin's concept of natural selection playing out on count-less farms across the United States. A chance seedling was excellent right from the start, complex, delicious, and hardy; the selection work had already been done. All that was needed was someone skilled in the ancient and unsurpassed art of grafting from one tree to another and then others could partake in the discovery. That's how it is still done today. Three of the top five apples in U.S. production were chance seedlings: Red Delicious, Golden Delicious, and Granny Smith, while two were the result of family planning: Fuji and Gala.

Not native to North America, or even Europe for that matter, the ancestral home of apples is Kazakhstan. They began emigrating out from there around 7,500 years ago across Central Asia and the Middle East and finally to Europe. The climate of northern North America resembles that of Kazakhstan more than the milder Mediterranean climate of Europe did, and so, after apples were brought from Europe as seed or saplings, they easily adapted to our climate. Beginning in the colonial period and on through the nation's expansionist phase, the number of unique apple varieties in the United States exploded.

Apples and our young republic were on parallel paths, a kind of biological and cultural convergence when the wildness of the continent's less cultivated landscapes allowed or even promoted a pluralism of newly created trees and self-made lives. Apple growing was egalitarian; it was democracy in action and an expression of how American rugged individualism could fuel both our bellies and one of our zeitgeist myths. Finding a chance seedling worthy of propagation meant that anyone could have their fifteen minutes of pomological fame. They popped up everywhere, especially as settlers pushed westward and people carried seed with them to establish homestead orchards. Some, like John Chapman aka Johnny Appleseed, who grew out thousands of apples for early settlers in the Ohio Valley, believed that grafting was forbidden in the Bible and so only planted from seeds gleaned from the discards of cider pressings.

Apples were prized not only for their good eating qualities but also for their contribution to making good cider, and to be clear I mean cider, the alcoholic beverage, not the brown fresh apple juice that gets poured at birthday parties and Halloween fairs for kids. Because most of North America lacked Europe's suitable climate for viticulture and thus wine production, fermented apples filled the human need for getting a buzz at this young nation's table. A tankard (or two) of cider went a long way to soften the edges of a tough rural life.

Cider makers ran the gamut from on the farm home brewers to regional producers. A wide array of apples was cherished for their cider-making characteristics. In fact, the best ciders are generally made from a blend, mixing those that have bitter tannins for body and longevity with ones that are acidic, offering liveliness in the mouth, and of course with some that are sweet to round out the flavors. Cider making was localized and, when grown from seed, quality could vary widely but as a blended product these apples still had value. Only through a combination of luck and persistence could an outstanding cultivar become both named and widely known.

* * *

I grew up on the workhorse varieties of the Northeast: Macs and Macouns, Cortlands, Romes, the occasional Winesap. The Red Delicious was always lingering nearby on the cafeteria lunch counter but never showed up in my home. All of these apples had grown tired for me and for the eating public by the 1980s. Granny Smiths had hit our shores. Firm, crunchy, and with great acidity, they were a welcome and bright green alternative to the ubiquitous big Red D—the Red Delicious. As a young cook in the restaurant industry, we liked their year-round dependability. In the heat of July, Granny didn't look a day over October. This, we thought, was progress.

In the fall of 1981, when I was working at Huberts on Park Avenue and Twenty-Second Street, I discovered the Union Square Greenmarket and at it, Chip Kent's Locust Grove stand, lined with handwritten bin labels of apples I had never heard of, much less eaten. Among the Cortlands and Macs were signs for Northern Spy, Golden Russet, Opalescent, York Imperial, and Quince (my god, what was that fuzzy and fragrant thing?). Many were odd-shaped or off-color and I realized that I was far less knowledgeable about food than I thought. Here was a library with a strong history section and I happily began to work my way through the stacks.

Early apple names celebrate the discoverer or its place of origin. My season-splitting Ashmead's Kernel is named after the physician and gentleman farmer who discovered it in Gloucester, England, in the 1700s (kernel means a seed, just as pips and pippins refers to chance seedlings). My homey, the Newtown Pippin, is a variety originally discovered growing near Newtown

Creek, which divides Brooklyn from Queens. Standing on that land today would probably put you on asphalt somewhere between the National Grid electricity depot and the city's Newtown Creek Water Treatment Plant, a far cry from the pastoral setting for a tree so exemplary that Thomas Jefferson had them shipped to France while he was ambassador. I love imagining Queens in that former time. Same place, very different look.

Place-name apples proclaim their site of inception to be their most important defining feature. It conveys a sense of continuity with the land and the people living there as well as suggesting something about the micro-climate in which they thrived: Harrison, Detroit Red, Fishkill, Champlain, Shiawassee, York Imperial, Wolf River, and Esopus Spitzenburg (a rare instance of place and discoverer). I have only tasted a few: the Spitzenburg is a wonderfully tart and richly sweet fruit and I never need to eat the Wolf River again. Some remind me of its place if I've been there: Fishkill just up the Hudson and Champlain, as in the lake that borders Vermont and New York, with many lovely orchards along its shores still to this day. Others are places as yet unvisited: Detroit Red and Shiawassee. I ponder how their former landscape shaped these apples. Shiawassee in Michigan is no doubt well adapted to cold winters and a shorter season. The Harrison of Harrison, New Jersey—across the Passaic River from Newark, and hardly an agricultural region today—was a highly coveted cider apple and lost for nearly a century. Recently rediscovered, it is currently being brought back into production. My favorite place name, the Westfield Seek-No-Further, imbeds a swagger-ing braggadocio long gone from this down-on-its-heels Massachusetts mill town sandwiched between the Berkshires and the Pioneer Valley. It makes a great single varietal cider, but I've never tasted it out of hand. I've read, though, that if you time it right, there are some to be had in the Sturbridge Village Museum orchard.

Maybe sensing that you can take the Harrison out of New Jersey but you can't take Jersey out of the Harrison, names referencing physical character-istics were more poetic and evocative and offered better marketing oppor-tunities: Red Delicious (a rebranding of the Hawkeye), Black Twig, Golden Russet, Ozark Gold, Rome Beauty, Sops of Wine, Sheepnose (well, maybe not), as well as ones that spoke to the orchardist, not the eater: Limbertwig, Blue Pearmain (a derivation of the French verb *parmaindre*, to remain, thus

a good keeper), Orleans Reinettes (from *renatus* or rebirth, a chance muta-
tion, that grew out from a branch not unlike Eve from Adam's rib), and the
Keepsake (a good keeper and parent of the Honeycrisp).

* * *

In the twentieth century plummeting biodiversity and large-scale indus-
trialization of agriculture were not kind to the apple genome. Prohibition
played a role in bringing about the abandonment (at best) or the destruction
(at worst) of orchards all across the country and with it the elimination of
apples with great cider-making characteristics in favor of the more limited
sweet eating types.

After Washington attained statehood in 1899, Congress allocated funding
for massive irrigation projects that brought water to previously barely arable
land on the eastern side of the Cascades. When combined with its easier
growing conditions of abundant sunlight, low humidity, and cool nights,
the region used this competitive edge over the Northeast and Midwest to
claim the dominant share of U.S. apple production throughout most of the
twentieth century and well into the twenty-first. In 2017, 64 percent of U.S.
apple sales came from Washington State. Railroads, also federally funded,
created an efficient distribution system that penetrated the entire country
and supplied apples to a growing network of chain supermarkets. If broad
diversity characterized the apple plantings in the Hudson Valley and much
of New York State, then a narrow, limited range of types is what got planted
in Washington's eastern range.

Land-grant universities also contributed to varietal narrowing. Established and funded by the USDA, their ag departments developed improved
breeds for growers and offered advice on how to maximize production and
profit. New York State's land-grant college, Cornell, one of the nation's most
important agricultural breeding stations for apples, developed over sixty-three
successful cultivars including the Cortland, Empire, Jonagold, Macoun,
Spigold, and the patriotically named disease-resistant types, Freedom and
Liberty. New breeds were considered intellectual property and since they had
been developed with tax money, the new varieties were commonly owned
and freely available to the public. The tart and tingling juiciness of an early

fall Macoun was edible proof that federal spending was bettering the lives of farmers and diners alike.

Efficiency over diversity was the key mantra for botanists and technical advisors as they helped apply the industrial manufacturing model to the world of agriculture. For Washington State, that meant concentrating production to a whittled down list, namely the Red and Golden Delicious varieties. Washington growers worked them hard, both in the field and in the focused national advertising and marketing campaigns by the Washington State Apple Commission. With ten times the marketing budget of the New York State apple board, Washington was able to create a huge worldwide market, even in New York City, for its deeply red but not terribly delicious apples.

The first time I ever rode a subway car where all the advertising space had been taken over by a single advertiser was in 1997, when the Washington State Apple Commission ran a series of airbrushed autumnal orchard photos plastered on every surface of the subway car. Previously, ad space in subway cars was cheap, relegated to cosmetology and secretarial schools; Dr. Zizmor, the dermatologist; and the MTA's Miss Subways ad campaign. I was amazed that some savvy Madison Avenue ad firm had thought to take all the available space in a car to create a huge visual impact and disappointed that the MTA would take money from the Washington State growers at the expense of our local growers, their main competitor.

Predictably, monopolies don't tend to promote innovation, preferring to rest on their laurels; Washington State growers were no exception. In the 1980s they were caught flat-footed by the influx of new foreign apple imports from New Zealand, Australia, and Japan. Similar to how the stagnant U.S. auto industry was caught off guard by the superior Japanese cars, Gala, Fuji, Granny Smith, and Mutsu all took a commanding slice of the apple market away from domestic growers. When warned by the state's leading pomologist about the need to innovate, growers booed him off their convention stage.

Replanting is expensive and time consuming, so growers tend to be risk averse and stick with the older varieties until there is no other alternative. One variety they pinned a lot of hope on was the Cameo, a Red Delicious × Golden Delicious. Like a Hollywood blockbuster that had a lot of hype but disappointed at the box office, the Cameo failed to reinvigorate the apple industry as promised. Washington growers fell behind and suffered such huge losses ($760 million in 1997 alone) that the federal government had to bail them out in 2000 with relief funds, a prequel to the "too big to fail" Wall Street bailout of 2008.

The first successful response to the foreign apple invasion came from the University of Minnesota, another important land-grant university apple-breeding program, with the Honeycrisp. Sweet and firm, as its name suggests, the Honeycrisp was developed between 1974 and 1988, a period of deep funding cuts to public education and scientific research. To offset the cuts, the university took the novel step of trademarking the Honeycrisp, charged licensing fees to growers, and then used the collected fees to fund other breeding projects. Passing the increased cost of growing this cutting-edge apple along to consumers, the high-priced designer apple was born. With the trademark expiring in 2008, the University of Minnesota took a page out of the pharmaceutical companies' playbook and developed a new generation of branded and trademarked apples: the SweeTango and the Zestar! (the capitalizations and exclamation point are included in their registrations). These names were developed with the help of focus groups and seek to connect personal lifestyle experiences with eating the new varieties. Perfect for our untethered times, the name is not about the discoverer or about a place; it's about what the apple does to us, the eater. It's not unlike people's phone numbers, which once spoke volumes about where someone lived.

In addition to creating apples at premium prices, the university took their desire for branding and quality control one step further and created club apples, also known as managed varieties. These apples are sold in limited quantities and marketed collectively in order to maintain brand consistency and a perpetual revenue stream for the university. Limiting access also promotes their allure. The owner of the trademark maintains control of the apple beyond its nursery release by setting standards for growing, harvesting, storage, and shipping. The days of getting free advice and a stack of pamphlets from a university extension agent are long gone. Now you have to follow their specifications or have your rights to sell apples by that name revoked.

Cornell joined in and produced the Rubyfrost and Snapdragon apples, the Midwest Apple Improvement Association developed the Evercrisp, and, now Washington State, not to be outdone, launched the Cosmic Crisp in 2019. Developed by the very pomologist whom growers booed off their convention stage thirty years earlier, the Cosmic Crisps released with 12 million trees in the club program and is grown solely by Washington State orchards. Launching with a $10 million marketing campaign, growers are betting heavily that the Cosmic Crisp will counteract the steady and unabated slide in sales from continuing to grow the big Red D.

Two hundred and fifty years ago, Dr. Ashmead discovered his singularly excellent tree, crowed about it by naming it after himself, and freely distributed grafted saplings to friends and neighbors. With Cosmic Crisp, another quality apple has been discovered but it has also been patented, licensed, and marketed with specific taste and appearance parameters in order to fully monetize this miracle of nature. I can only imagine what Dr. Ashmead would think.

* * *

I come up out of the Eighty-Sixth Street Q station, the jewel in the crown of New York City's four-decade-long Second Avenue subway project. It's grand, grander than it needs to be. Maybe it was planned for the grandeur of an age yet to arrive, when the station will be a hub for a bustle that has so far eluded the neighborhood. It's been a backwater all these years due to its distance from the Lexington Avenue subway, regardless of its Upper East Side ZIP Code. Along the station's expansive walkway of white subway tile, there are huge mosaic portraits by the artist Chuck Close interspersed every hundred feet or so. They represent Close's New York arts community: his standbys, composer Phillip Glass, musician Lou Reed, artist Alex Katz, as well as less familiar subjects: the artists Kara Walker, Siena Shields, and Zhang Huan. Each portrait is done in a different mosaic technique, reflective of Close's own evolving grid imagery. The work defines New York City in this early twenty-first century moment: a mosaic of mosaics, with musicians, photographers, and artists who together comprise our diverse, vital urban landscape.

I quickly exit out of the station's southern end because I'm on a mission: to visit a greenmarket I've never been to and, specifically, to visit Ron

Samascott, a farmer I know, but rarely see. Ron, together with his brother Gary, seven other family members, twelve full-time year-round employees, twenty-five seasonal workers here on H2-A visas from Mexico, and six mostly Nepalese people running the markets in the city, produces the most diverse and best cared for apples I know of, on a one-thousand-acre fourth-generation farm called Samascott Orchard in Kinderhook, New York.

This market began tucked into a vest pocket park adjoining Saint Stephen of Hungary, a Catholic school on Eighty-Second Street, but now spills onto the sidewalk. The neighborhood is a whisper of the one that flourished here fifty years ago. In those days you could hear Hungarian spoken on the street, see old ladies with kerchiefs tied around their heads and colorful flowers embroidered on their dresses, and eat chicken paprikash at countless spots up and down the avenue. My father would take us to Mrs. Herbst's for strudel, then stop by Paprika Weiss to pick up some spices and peppers before heading back to the homogeneity of suburban New Jersey. Little of that remains, but the church still stands and not far away is the Budapest Café, where you can still get a solid bowl of goulash and a passable cherry strudel.

Although I know the street and avenue coordinates of this market, I could use vegetable echolocation to determine its location; the number of people toting bags with farm-fresh merch markedly increases in density as I approach until soon the white and green farmstand tents reveal the market's epicenter. I've often mused that in early spring I can zero in on Union Square Greenmarket by reverse plotting the radiating patterns of people carrying huge bundles of lilac branches under their arms, a stark contrast with the stolid brick and metal buildings in this constructed cityscape.

Today is no different. Divining the contents in the exodus of loaded shopping bags, the hauls are topped off with fronds of curly kale and below, bulging spheres suggest a jumble of winter squashes, potatoes, and apples. There is a nice smattering of farmers tucked into the park: a Vermont cheese producer, an organic vegetable grower from Kingston, a bread baker, a honey guy. It's quaint, decidedly in keeping with the sleepiness of the neighborhood. Yet out on the street and sidewalk, there is astonishingly swift action: two long columns of tables, covered with wooden apple crates, corral a line of customers who extend beyond the columns, heading off towards York Avenue. There's no room to browse.

I realize too late that it's best to get on line, and begin filling my bag as I move along until reaching the scale, then settle up and get out. When I excitedly step off midway through the ten-minute line to search for some arcane variety I remember wanting to share with my friend, the woman behind me is tolerant of my newbie status and offers to hold our place. My endearing passion outweighs my chump move.

On this brilliant Saturday morning in December, Samascott has thirty-five different varieties on offer, not counting the pears, potatoes, sweet potatoes, hard squashes, baked goods, and a cooler filled with frozen cuts of grass-fed beef from their hundred head of cattle. I've never counted before, I just knew they lay out a nice spread. But thirty-five? Who needs thirty-five different kinds of anything? We certainly don't need thirty-five kinds of breakfast cereal even if the center aisles of supermarkets are filled with them. But this feels different. Instead of being overwhelming or redundant, it's invigorating. There are individual personalities here. Among the russeted types there some with green underwashes, others almost orange. Some sport a final brushstroke of red, a splash of deep maroon. I snag a few Newtown Pippins with pink freckles; they must have enjoyed a few chilly nights combined with good daytime sun just prior to being picked. Plenty of red varieties have scabs of russeting on their shoulders, stretch marks of beauty, battle scars from an early cold snap. Varying girths and shapes read as delightful nonconformity, not as ragtag discards that under other circumstances would fail to make the cut for USDA commercial grade A.

Most varietal shapes don't conform to the prim upright profiles of the Red Delicious used in promotional materials from the apple marketing boards. There are flattened ovoids, as if squashed at the center, and ones almost wobbly, tilted off axis. My pastry chef was always pleased when I would come back with a half crate of gargantuan Melroses, some probably weighing in at nearly a pound each. They made peeling and coring a breeze, but she also came to appreciate the smaller Golden Russets that comprised the other half crate because of their engaging acidity.

Given that Samascott raises over seventy-five different varieties there's always a chance of catching a new release, something that wasn't available on my previous visit. Dolma, the Nepalese woman who has run the Union Square stand for the last twenty years, steers me towards my favorites. "Ashmeads are all gone but there are 460s today over there," she proclaims. NY460 is a cross, Spy × Empire (which itself is a cross—Mac × Jonathan) that the Samascott's grew as a trial for Cornell. The university never chose to name or release the apple because it wasn't a heavy enough producer but Samascott continues to grow them, even expanding their plantings by grafting new trees. I like the 460 and given my obsession with names, I'm intrigued that its namelessness has becomes its name, devoid of focus-grouped suggestive associations. It's a good apple and has many fans, being both crisp and fine-grained, with lots of Mac fragrances. The obvious commercial success stories are here as well: Gala, Fuji, Honeycrisp, displayed in double-wide crates. Closest to the scales are the premium-priced club varieties: the Rubyfrost, Snapdragon, and Evercrisp.

Call me a snob. On a certain level that's what chefs are. We are always on a quest for the best in ingredients and execution. Our work begins long before we get into the kitchen and many of us continually expose ourselves to new ingredients and look for ways to refine our techniques. Sometimes this pursuit gets intertwined with fashion and the need to distinguish ourselves in a crowded marketplace. What's new and trendy is reinforced by a public ever in pursuit of new sparkly objects and can result in an ever-revolving door of momentary hot spots. Even if some trends are doctrinaire, gratuitous, or seem misguided, the irrepressible curiosity of chefs remains at the root of all these pursuits. Curiosity fuels our work.

Being a snob isn't necessarily elitist or classist, even if some of the people we cook for are. Having an interest in the offbeat and the less pedestrian means that we can give voice to the unsung and elevate the underutilized or underappreciated ingredients, often neglected because of their localized or working-class roots. We are connoisseurs in the best sense of the word, as in the French verb *connaître*, to know, to be informed. And being informed requires not only a commitment to educating oneself but also to taking the time to discern, to notice difference and become sensitive to nuance. Some might call that the path of an artist. I'd rather extend it to all of us and say that's what it means to be alive.

* * *

A few days after I shopped at Ron's stand, I went to my local Whole Foods store and found about a dozen apple varieties available, which numerically might seem like a wide selection. They were almost entirely from Washington State, each mountainous pile nearly perfect in its consistent coloration—this one canary gold, that one dappled in red orange, the next a perky green taken right off a Beatles record label. The voluminous displays all promise a steady pipeline of supply. There's more where these came from, not just in the back, but on their way here: tomorrow, next week, next month. Like theater lights with variable color cellophane gels, the hues change but little else does, with only slight modulations in sugar or acidity. I'm not sure I can even identify any of the varieties without reading their little stickers that indicate name, place of origin, and a PLU for electronic scanning. Sizing is consistently uniform and orderly; the fruit can be laid up in cardboard boxes for maximal space use, each apple nestled in its own egg carton-like depression, isolated from its neighbors. No one apple can spoil the entire bunch.

Washington State growers are able to deliver consistency and predictability because the high desert of the Eastern Cascades offers cool nights, steady sunlight, and a federally engineered irrigation system, which together are about as close to corporate control of weather variability as a farmer will ever get. Huge tracts of land, fifty acres at a pop, are planted in single varieties to maximize management efforts and mechanization. Apples that aren't "tippy" (i.e., typical) get culled out and sold off at reduced prices for processing or get sent to foreign markets, removed from the view of U.S. mainstream consumers.

Opting to narrow selection is understandable if the goal is higher efficiency, market penetration, and increased profit margins through sheer volume. With a nationalized apple pipeline, the same apples are available in Los Angeles, Indianapolis, and Portland, Maine; availability is year-round and quality is sound but dull. There are no explosions of bright flavor, no quashes and zings of explosive vitality as with my short seasoned Ashmead's, but nothing horrid either. Corporations need tippy, people don't.

Tippy doesn't have a home at Samascott. There are no bin ends selling off items at reduced prices and they don't own a PLU sticker machine so supermarket sales aren't even a possibility. The half crate of Macs that sat out in Union Square on a hot eighty-degree September afternoon don't see another market day; they get pressed into cider. Apples get utilized in all stages of their evolution: for cider, applesauce, animal feed, and finally as compost to reinvigorate the orchard's soil. Nimble efficiency is a benefit of a short supply chain and gets overlooked when economists are evaluating market efficiency. A mealy, aging bushel of apples sitting in the receiving area of a New York City Whole Foods will never get shipped back to the Yakima Valley and folded back into the soil. It will end up in a landfill in the metropolitan area, the loss will be written off by the accounting team, and the growers will purchase fertilizer for the orchard externally.

Samascott's personal and localized selection of apples also prompts the question of what varieties are missing, what might be found elsewhere, beyond the Hudson Valley. Black Oxford, Harelson, Doc Matthews, Swiss Limbertwig, and the Slack Ma Girdle are prized regional apples of the northern Midwest, Vermont, and Maine and of Pennsylvania and North Carolina. I've heard people rhapsodize about them but I've yet to taste these treasures. Only by doing the work, by traveling to other regions can we experience the vitality and magic of an unhomogenized world.

It's time for a revised version of "The Revolution Will Not Be Motorized," featured on a sticker on my market bike. The new one should read "The Revolution Will Not Be Homogenized." How as a culture do we resist the corporate preference for tippy and how do we do it without being branded as elitist? Many years ago, on lower Mulberry Street where Little Italy bled into Chinatown, a sheet of plywood covering a closed-up storefront was painted with the image of a Clorox bleach bottle and the words "MONOCULTURES DYE OUT." I'd pass it on my way back to the restaurant from Chinatown and it reminded me to keep sharing complexity, to keep cooking the unknown and the unexplored, and to stand for the unhomogenized, in food and in culture, on the land and in the city.

I frequently hear shoppers ask the Samascott workers which apple is best for making pie. Piemaster in residence Susan always insists that I bring her back a mix of apples. She wants Macs because they easily melt into sauce and act as mortar for others, the structural Winesaps and Honeycrisps, a few Newtown Pippins for acidity, and Golden Russets for complexity and color contrast. No one apple can hit the highs we want in a pie, in a bottle of cider, or in a world. It's always about the blend.

The urban blend is alchemy: part science and part magic. It allows a world of creativity, dissent, variety, and surprise to thrive. Like Close's mosaics of sparkling and flat tesserae, the patterns indistinguishable close up, but standing back, the images come into focus, faces gazing out, scrutable and grounded in this city. I am a Winesap and you are a Northern Spy, and she is a Seek-No-Further and that guy over there is a Blue Pearmain. I need to live near all these varieties with a few Jonathans and Opalescents too, in order to be happy. That's why I'm still here in the city, climbing the subway stairs, curious to discover what surprises might abound on its tiled walls, in the city's sleepy neighborhoods, and in wooden crates piled high with Samascott apples.

FALL SALAD WITH SECKEL PEARS, FENNEL, AND PECORINO

SERVES 2 AS A FIRST COURSE

Buy the Seckel pears a week in advance if they are firm, or maybe even a bit green in hue, and set them out to ripen. If they are golden brown with red blush, then maybe they are ready to eat. Try one and see. I love their winey flavor, and their petite size looks great on the plate. Fall fennel, especially from organic growers who aren't irrigating, can produce a tender and sweet licorice slaw that, when combined with the juicy pears and offset with salty Pecorino cheese, make for a wonderfully robust salad for a fall lunch. The dressing isn't really a vinaigrette but rather tossing the fennel and pears in oil and a lively mixture of lemon and cider vinegar.

1 bulb fennel

4 Seckel pears

½ cup (120 ml) olive oil

¼ cup (60 ml) cider vinegar

Juice of ½ lemon

2 ounces (55 g) aged Pecorino, for shaving

1 teaspoon salt

Cut off the outer sections of the fennel, then finely slice the bulb with a knife or a mandoline. **Do not soak in water**. This leeches out all the delicate flavors. Quarter the pears lengthwise, cut out the core, then cut lengthwise again into eighths. In a mixing bowl, combine the pears with the fennel and dress with the olive oil, cider vinegar, lemon juice, Pecorino, and salt. The acid on the pears should enliven their sweetness but not overpower it. Taste the fennel too. Together the oil and the vinegar should make the raw slaw feel luxurious in the mouth but still raw and crisp. Plate or put the salad in a serving bowl. Using a vegetable peeler, shave cheese over the salad and serve.

THE BURGER KILLED MY RESTAURANT

Turning Savoy into Back Forty West wasn't just a rebrand with new logos, updated lighting, and a paint job. What had been my professional residence for two decades had undergone an inversion. Savoy, a restaurant serving a diverse menu that included a burger, had transformed into Back Forty West, a burger joint that offered other interesting dishes. It was one thing to have the East Village burger location as a complement to my fine-dining restaurant establishment in SoHo; it was a whole other thing for casual burger joints to be the sum of what I did.

Like not noticing how your parents' or your partner's hair has grayed, I had difficulty seeing that SoHo was no longer an arts district and had transformed into a shopping mall. I was well aware that in Christmas week, diners lugged in enormous quantities of packages requiring a dedicated coat check person to handle all the bags. I knew that every Saturday and Sunday afternoon, tourists—many of them non-English speaking—would pour into the place, their blood sugars plummeting after shopping on a breakfast of only coffee and a pastry, and that the only letters they could decipher on the menu were b-u-r-g-e-r. Come dinnertime, after the tide of humanity receded and happy hour had passed, our evenings would be dull, lacking verve. In yet another inversion of how Savoy had functioned, dinner had been the busier and more profitable service.

Many old Savoy customers mourned our closing and had moved on to other haunts. The neighborhood had also changed. The art galleries, once the driver of a sophisticated clientele to the area, had moved to Chelsea and the trendy new generation of dining spots were located in lower rent zones closer to the Bowery and the northern edges of Chinatown. The neighborhood we had pioneered when we opened in 1990, that had broken new ground for a generation of New Yorkers, had become mainstream. The cutting edge had moved east, south, and off the island.

After decades of celebrating and promoting culinary and cultural diversity on the menus, I was discouraged that the majority of customers wanted a burger—the epitome of mainstream America. It might have been a better version than the burger they grew up eating at a local diner but at the end of the day it was still a burger. That it was grass-fed was not a point of distinction. Putting the burger on the menu had allowed me to buy whole animals direct from the producers and supported my radical vision that restaurants could run independently of the industrialized food system. Now I had to buy additional meat to grind because the trim from our weekly steer wasn't enough to keep up with the burger demand and selling the odd cuts was more challenging. I looked around at my beautiful restaurant and asked myself, "How did I get here?"

I wasn't alone in that frustration. Plenty of other restaurants experience intense burger pressure from their customers. Some respond by only offering it at lunch or making it available solely in their barroom. Gramercy Tavern, one of the city's most acclaimed farm-to-table restaurants, has struggled to manage people's burger fixation and, as proud as they are of the burger they serve, the chef began actively developing other dishes to rebalance the sales mix. Others have embraced the obsession and built their reputations on it. Minetta Tavern, the Greenwich Village tavern revived by Keith McNally of Balthazar fame, sells an aged prime meat "black label burger" for a staggering $36. Arctic char and duck à l'orange are on the menu but people swarm the place for the famed burger; that single item alone represents over a third of the restaurant's total sales. And of course, there's Shake Shack, started by Gramercy Tavern's owner Danny Meyer. Now an international fast food chain serving burgers and shakes in 275 locations, Shake Shack had an IPO in 2015 and is now valued at over $2 billion.

At Back Forty West, the burger-centric menu also posed challenges to hiring qualified cooks and chefs. Aspiring cooks wanting to gain exposure to interesting ingredients and quality culinary techniques don't want to flip burgers and make kale Caesar salads all day long. As much as I sang the virtues of our farm-to-table commitment and our fine dining service, more than a few chefs were scared off by the afternoon crush of diners looking for an umami bomb and a Coke. I desperately tried to say, "We're still a cutting edge farm-to-table restaurant," but the daily printout of the sales mix told a different story—burgers were not only our bass line but had become the melody as well.

With Savoy gone, I no longer had the fine dining "carrot" to hold out as advancement. Recruitment, a problem before, was now even more challenging and I added an internal piece of defeat to the equation: that there was no point in trying to improve server wine knowledge or a cook's knife technique when any new hire would probably leave before long, forcing me to begin the process all over again. As proud as I was of how many people I taught culinary and life lessons to, I wasn't intentionally running a school. The trade-off in not building an empire or even a small multiunit company was that we lacked bench depth. When a key employee departed, we often lacked junior or assistant candidates ready to step in and step up. Operating felt more and more like a house of cards, stable in one moment, but teetering on vertiginous collapse in the next.

Maybe if the sales numbers had looked better, I wouldn't have found the phenomenon so discouraging, but we weren't hitting the numbers we needed to remain profitable over the long term. A burger and a beer, even a premium burger and a craft brewery pint, cost well under $30, compared with Savoy's more than double cover averages—dollars spent per person. I was hoping to "make it up in volume," only the place wasn't really physically or operationally designed for that. I extended hours, added breakfast and served continuously throughout the afternoon. Savoy had been open for eight hours of service, lunch and dinner combined, and now Back Forty West was operating for fourteen in the same space with only the meat cutting and the pastries produced offsite. Continuous service put extreme pressure on the back of the house. Trying to prep food and cook orders in the same space and using the same equipment was challenging. It also demanded significantly trimming the menu, a way to speed up the production process.

I had chosen the route of increased turnover and lower prices, but I was resistant to embracing this new business model. I wanted to serve casual food, but I clung to remnants of fine dining. I still wanted to crumb people's tables between courses and refused to bus glasses by inserting a finger into each one to collect them. "Get a tray," I'd grumble at servers. I was reluctant to drop a check before people asked for it. Brisk service read as brusque to me. I wanted customers to linger, to dine and to experience our creativity. "Tonight's special is grilled goat heart skewers with a salsa verde made from pounded green coriander seeds," wasn't going over well with the hungry tourists.

"Make it up in volume." What the place needed was to increase the line speed, the term used in meatpacking houses and slaughterhouses to describe the rate at which animals are moved along the slaughter assembly line through to cutting and packaging. Increasing line speed at Back Forty West meant that I needed to transform the restaurant into the fast casual model where the food is paid for before sitting down, with a healthy takeout or delivery business to offset the limitations of the small (previously called intimate) dining room. In fine dining the most important metric is always the cover average, the dollars spent per person. In the fast casual business, cover averages are fairly flat; there are no high rollers purchasing top-end wines or even extravagant appetizers to splurge on. The key metric is line speed, the number of customers that can be moved through the place during the key meal periods. Adding staff to work shoulder-to-shoulder and push people through while keeping the cafeteria-style trays of food fully stocked is money well spent. Once the rush is over, line workers can be cut and sent home.

There is an old saw in the construction business regarding selecting a contractor. Every client wants their job done quickly, at a high quality level, and inexpensively. With a contractor you only get to pick two of the three qualities: speed, quality, and cost. Want it high quality and cheap? Then speed suffers. Fast and high quality? Then be prepared to pay. In the U.S. food system, we consistently end up choosing fast and cheap and so we lose out on quality, which is ultimately about taste. The last thing I ever wanted to be part of was the fast and cheap model of production. In fact, all my work had been about developing skills and habits that were contrary to that approach. It was abundantly clear that line speed was required in order to make Prince Street work. Our decades-long commitment to celebrating culinary diversity had been reduced down to a ground beef patty barely distinguishable from the two low-end burger places that had recently opened on Prince Street, one immediately next door and the other directly across Lafayette, and both decidedly cheaper than our grass-fed, fine food, high-minded option. I preferred to operate like Chicago blues musician Howlin' Wolf does with his lovers: "I'm built for comfort, I ain't built for speed."

The cracks in the façade, the stresses in the structure were systemic as much as they were personal. The equation was no longer working and I couldn't see how to improve it. Wages were stagnant, which meant they were declining, turnover was high because I was asking too much of the space and therefore too much of people. Running a business based on low wages, high turnover, high burnout rates for employees, a race to the bottom for ingredient pricing, with a customer base that seemed uninterested or unaware of these issues was doomed. And the rent predictably and relentlessly kept escalating.

I would begin each morning by reading the restaurant log in Dropbox from the previous night; tales reviewing what mishap had occurred with a customer, which employee had acted inappropriately, along with how much business we did or didn't do. I had trained myself away from reading it at the end of the night, as I'd only end up clenching my jaw through the night. I had become a clencher, biting down as I tried to hold on and hang on to the present. Only there was no doing that. I no longer had a vision, was no longer creating or expressing a personal culinary statement. I had stalled out and was just barely holding on.

Newton's laws of motion say no work is being done when pushing up against a huge boulder even though it may require great effort. This law does not apply to the New York City restaurant business; maintaining the status quo is in fact work. Staying even, much less moving things forward, demands focus and energy. I had gone from an awe-filled, optimistic chef with passion and limitless energy for solving all the problems that arise every day to become a risk-averse and fearful man trudging down a narrow, joyless path like a burro retracing yesterday's dusty well-trodden route.

I toyed with any number of growth ideas along the way, ones that weren't just developing more restaurants, but concepts that were extensions of our beliefs and might have kept me stimulated—a butcher shop, a line of charcuterie, a farm associated with the restaurants, maybe even an inn in the countryside. With flattening profits, no fresh generation of managers to take on expansion projects, and me running out of juice, I was handicapped. I hadn't paid back either Back Forty investors the entirety of their original investments and wasn't sure when, if ever, I would achieve that goal. Earning a return on my money and my investors' money wasn't enough impetus to keep me pushing against the immovable rock. I had barely paid for my life the past few years. With one kid in college and the other in private school, a significant home mortgage (part of which represented money borrowed to finance my share of Back Forty), and an SBA loan still on the books from renovating Savoy post-9/11, I was pretty well debt-maxed. I had been dancing and dancing hard for many years; I was afraid, deathly afraid, the music was about to stop.

Sue had the clarity to encourage me to get out, pull the plug and move towards finding new challenges. "You don't have to do this," she reminded me. Sue had discovered a new creative outlet after retiring from pastry, finding her way back to making art, but this time with clay, sitting at the potter's wheel. She wasn't the wife enjoining her husband to err on the conservative side, protecting the family finances and job stability. Rather she was encouraging me to keep reaching for personal and professional fulfillment, confident that in doing so we would meet our financial obligations. As discouraged as I was and with prospects dim, I clearly saw that Sue was right.

Throwing in the towel is not something I do easily, neither in situations nor in relationships. Call me tenacious or call me blindly hopeful but moving on from people just isn't my way. More girlfriends broke up with me than I with them and even when I was distraught over my relationship with my business partner, I proposed counseling sessions months before I finally uttered the decisive words, "I think we should separate." Whether it's a pragmatic "bird in the hand" philosophy, knowing how hard it is to find good people and being appreciative of people's good qualities, or my reticence to act as ultimate judge, I do not cut ties easily. Shortly before my sixtieth birthday, I made the firm decision to get out. Once made, all that remained was figuring out how to implement my exit.

KALE AND RADICCHIO

Every change in the growing season is gradual, except for one. The market procession of ingredients feels like an ongoing revelation: from the first arrival of the wild ramps and overwintered spinach, followed by the gentle unfolding of the new radish and fava plantings, hakurei turnips and baby beets not far behind, to when the berries, corn, and tomatoes arrive en masse. Even as certain items pass out of season, gradualism is still at play. I can watch the wave of availability crest at the tables of South Jersey farms moving northward into the Hudson Valley, up into Vermont and the Finger Lakes until there is a dwindling and then it's gone. Asparagus are like that, cherries too.

But frost kills. In a single night there can be an abrupt closing of the door to the growing season, for cultivated and uncultivated plants alike. There is no predicting when a hard frost, a killing frost, as farmers call it, is going to hit. Sometimes there are the signs of its approach, a light frost one week that burns leaf tips; basil is sensitive and always the first to go. The shocked plants may later recover having only lost their outer leaves before a harder hit arrives the following week. Some years though, the executioner arrives without warning and brings the cycle up short with a decisive end. Overnight the landscape transforms. Many crops are already tired at the end of their season, having produced and pushed out fruit, their branches and structure now weakened or withering, or showing signs of disease and blight that were debilitating but not fatal. The frost then is the final blow, a decisive end to a slow decline.

Farmers are always checking the forecast for predictions of hard frost. Forewarned, they can lay down row cover, a synthetic protective fabric called Reemay, the equivalent of throwing a sweater on the crops for the night. Crews might work into the night, harvesting what's still out in the field, bringing everything they can into the barn. Even then, plenty of good food gets left behind. The only time I have ever been able to eat all the raspberries that I could possibly want was when we were visiting a farm the day a heavy frost was predicted for that very night. Unable to harvest and get them to market later in the week, the farmer said, "Have at it." He was resigned to the fact that no amount of planning could change that scenario. I couldn't help doing the calculation as I stuffed my mouth—the number of clamshells of raspberries I was eating multiplied by their $3.99 price tag at the store.

As a chef, I can prepare too. Knowing that a frost was predicted and having failed to get my fill of shakshuka breakfasts this year, I scrambled to collect the peppers and tomatoes for one last go. I also grabbed three times the amount of tomatillos I really needed; they hold well in the fridge and will push out my salsa-making capacity by almost a month. And as for the tomatoes, I'm not sure if I am just a procrastinator with one foot back in the summer or a climate change denier of an apolitical sort, but I never put up tomatoes until I get the doomsday message from Rick Bishop, my Union Square Greenmarket soothsayer, that the end is near. Only then do I grab two cases of his Canestrinos and spend an afternoon turning half of them into tomato sauce and the other half into unseasoned rough chop, both headed into the freezer for later use. Sometimes the abrupt shift came at inopportune moments at the restaurant's cycle. We weren't always ready to change up the menu, too many events going on, no chef in place, but it forced itself on us. Sometimes we kicked the can down the road by buying those items from outside the regions or worse, outside the country—haricot beans from Guatemala always look fresh as a garnish to a piece of chicken or steak.

I especially enjoy cooking with the lasts of the season. It brings a heightened awareness to my cooking. I can reflect on dishes made earlier in the season or thoughtfully ponder this final preparation. If this is my last shot at cooking eggplant what do I want to do with it? Char it on the grill, then dress it with Thai basil, lime, and fish sauce, or stay deep in the Mediterranean and simmer it with olives, capers, and tomatoes? I remember that all of these vegetables are a gift. It's my way of saying grace, of saying thank you and honoring it by cooking and consuming it.

It's easy in this global food economy to be lulled into presuming ubiquity, into taking all of this for granted. If we become blasé about the food we cook then we can extend that attitude to even the basic elements that make life enjoyable or in fact, possible, on the planet. Water and air come to mind. When we freely fill our lungs with fresh air or drink a refreshing glass of water from the tap, it's hard to comprehend that these fundamental necessities for life are not givens in all places or for all people, much less realize that by our actions (or inaction) that we are contributing to their degradation.

I'd never make it to the dinner table if I really contemplated all of this while preparing my shakshuka, but feeling gratitude is an important part of the season winding down for me. I guess that's what Thanksgiving is meant to be; only in the restaurant business, the day is anything but a wind down. Our gross revenues on that single day equaled an entire week's during a slower season. The day required a carefully executed battle plan for the week leading up to it and a full brigade the day of to pull it off. The gratitude I felt was for all the people who had been on their A-game all week that allowed the day to go off without a hitch.

I like it when I don't have advance notice that the end is coming. I might buy some of the small, late fall string beans that almost resemble haricots verts because of their slow growth rate. With that extended hang time on the vine, they are packed with minerals and flavor. Pro tip: the best vegetables aren't necessarily the ones that have burst forth in the exuberance of full sun and long hot summer days. Sometimes the best ones are those that develop slowly and under challenging conditions, like wine grapes that have ripened slowly in cooler temperatures. Sugars may develop in a flash of heat but depth of flavor develops over time on the vine.

I know these tiny string beans are an endangered October species but the farmer assures me that there will still be some next week. And then life intervenes. It could be anything: my schedule changes, an unannounced storm comes through and washes out the field, or the farmer's truck breaks down on the highway and they don't make it to market. And then poof, the beans are gone. I go back to the table and ask for the beans and the farmer shakes her head and says, "Nope. They're done." I like being denied, being reminded that we aren't in control, that life is unpredictable and unknowable. Instead of scheming about how I would have prepared them, I'm left with the memory of last week's quickly steamed beans that I tossed in olive oil, sprinkled with sea salt, and set atop a warm, herby potato salad. With the farewell also comes the promise of the return engagement. There will be another go on the string beans, on the eggplant, and all the rest. Our wealth comes, not only from what we have, but from what we don't have.

Regardless of when or how it arrives, the hard frost demarcates the beginning of a new season, at the market and in my cooking. Succumbing to temperatures that turned the water in their stems and leaves into ice and ruptured all their cells, countless crops have collapsed in their cells and in the field. Last week's shopping list is now moot—tomatoes, peppers, lettuce, string beans, the soft squashes, melons, and the soft herbs are done.

I turn my attention towards the hardy, woodier herbs: thyme, rosemary, sage, savory, and to plants that made long-range storage plans: winter squashes, dried beans, and the root vegetables. As they rise to prominence in my menus, cooking times lengthen. I lower the flame to ease from them the flavors they are retaining in their bulwark of storage cells. Hello to braises and broths, to reduced sauces, and to long-cooked meats that fall away from the bone.

* * *

From November through to May, I am always scanning the winter market for aboveground plants, not just storage crops, of which there are plenty. Deep in the winter sometimes leeks appear. They are hardy and able to withstand snow and cold, whether they are still in the field or previously pulled and stacked outside a barn like cordwood. More important, there are the brassicas, the plant group that spans from broccoli and kale to cauliflower and Brussels sprouts, all with frost hardy leaves that can withstand freezing temperatures, up to a point. In the cold weather they grow more slowly, tighten up into heads. If a heat wave in July, a time of plant perceived prosperity, causes the brassicas to bolt, sending a seed spike high up to disperse seeds as widely as possible, then in a leaner, colder time the plants hunker down and grow one protective leaf after another, tight and close to their heart, preferring to grow vegetatively and defer the risky behavior of sexual reproduction.

Over dinner Sue and I noticed that some black kale I had cooked was incredibly sweet. We had never tasted kale like this before. I'd heard farmers say that the brassicas improve after the first frost. What is that about? In order to explain what's occurring physiologically in the plant, a bit of physical

308

chemistry helps. From that, the magic and the deliciousness of kale's adaptation to cold will be clear.

In advance of a storm, doormen all over the city throw salt or pellets on the sidewalk because it melts ice or keeps it from forming. This is because the dissolved salt particles in the water lower its freezing temperature. Dissolved particles, whether they're salt, sugar, or alcohol, get in between individual water molecules and interfere with the process of freezing, the slowing down of molecular movement. The water molecules are aligning themselves with one another, like with like, thus becoming a solid. Physical motion can interrupt that alignment. That is why a forest stream can continue to run even in sub-zero temperatures. It's why orange growers mount large fans in the orchard to churn the air when a freeze sets in. Similarly, a water solution with dissolved particles in it can remain liquid even though its temperature drops below 32°F if the particles interrupt the alignment, the settling down. The greater the percentage of solutes in the water, the lower the freezing temperature will be.

Imagine then, if a plant could do the same thing as those doormen do to the sidewalk, if they could increase the dissolved molecules in their cells as a survival mechanism in cold climates. Instead of using salt, the brassicas use sugar, sugars they have been storing throughout the summer in their roots. Breaking down its root starches into sugars, the plant sends the sugars up into its veins and lower its freezing temperature. Californians don't have anything on us when it comes to great-tasting brassicas. Though blessed with a longer growing season, never-frost zones like their Central Valley can't attain the pinnacles of flavor found in post-frost kale grown in the black dirt of New York and Pennsylvania. Sugar is kale's antifreeze! Lucky us.

* * *

Come November, I drift by many stands, quickly surveying their diminishing returns and keep moving along. I'm on a mission, headed for the one stand that still has striking vitality along with a devoted following of local chefs and shoppers: Campo Rosso Farm from Gilbertsville, Pennsylvania. Owners Chris Field and Jessi Okamoto spend much of August and early September planting for October, November, and hopefully even December harvests. Contrarian farmers, their goal is to have abundance when other stands are looking meager. They specialize in Italian chicories, the beautiful red-leaved radicchios.

Chris and Jessi are also contrarian in that they are new farmers, both went into the field at age twenty-five after Chris worked in NYC as a cook/chef in high-end Italian places and Jessi worked in retail sales. For decades, the U.S. demographic flow has been off of farms and towards urban centers but Chris and Jessi went the other way, leaving Brooklyn in 2012 to intern with two greenmarket farmers, Tim Stark and Rick Bishop, for a year each before starting their own operation in 2014. Bucking the tide is always hard, their learning curve has been high in a short period, but the reception from chefs and home cooks has been overwhelming. Even so, the 2018 season was so wet in the late summer and early fall that thousands of their plants could not be transplanted for the fall crop and their radicchio inventories were severely rationed. Pre-ordering as if I were a restaurant account or getting to the market before 9 A.M. were the only ways to guarantee having some of their greens (or reds to be more accurate).

Chicories grow wild throughout the world. I grew up seeing their delicate, pale blue daisy-like flowers growing along country roads in the summer all over the Northeast. They are an important component of *horta*, the wild greens mix that women forage for in the Eastern Mediterranean. In Puglia, *fave et cicorie* is a classic dish of sustenance where the chicory is long cooked, served over dried fava bean puree, and heavily drizzled with olive oil. It is also gathered for its root, which, roasted and made into a beverage, has been used as a coffee substitute or coffee extender in lean times. A remnant from the Civil War blockade of Port New Orleans, a cup or two of chicory coffee blend in the French Quarter alongside a plate of sugar-dusted beignets is still enjoyable.

Chicories and daisies are both members of the aster plant family, which as a botanical group are all late bloomers. Asters are known in the British Isles as Michaelmas daisies, named for a Christian holiday that falls after the autumn equinox, an indication that their proclivity for cold hardiness has long been recognized. Linnaeus also acknowledged their late-season contrarian growth cycle by naming the chicories *Chicorium intybus*, intybus after the Greek word "*tybus*," the Egyptian month of January, a time of cold temps and low light when these plants thrive. It's no surprise then that the chicories and endives all grow in and are a cherished part of the cuisines of northern European countries: Belgium, France, and in northern Italy, particularly in the Veneto.

The late season growing asters are a boon to farmers and diners alike, but they tend to be bitter, especially when grown in full sun. Just as leeks have a thick cellular structure that allows them to withstand cold, the thick and fleshy leaves of chicories allow them to stand up to the cold. In taste, they range from mildly astringent to so ferociously bitter that even Italian cookbooks can recommend boiling them in several changes of water.

Italians aren't afraid of bitter. In fact they have elevated the taste to high gourmet status and even created the class of alcoholic beverages called *amari*, Italian for bitter. The proliferation of home infusions and medicinal elixirs to cure whatever ails you produced a vast selection of artisanal amari that can be found all over Italy, although they are elevated to near religious status in the north. The best known of these is Campari, from Piemonte, a key ingredient in a classic Negroni.

An openness to bitter flavors notwithstanding, Italian gardeners still strive to reduce the bitterness in their leafy vegetables. One often-used technique is known as blanching. Not culinary blanching, which means parcooking vegetables or meats in boiling water; horticultural blanching involves denying plants access to sunlight so that chlorophyll isn't produced. This both reduces bitterness in many plants and allows other color and flavor compounds to emerge or develop. Blanching is done with many vegetables: white asparagus is produced by keeping the spears buried in soil or under black plastic, celery is often wrapped in newspaper to reduce its nasty bitter tendencies, rhubarb in England is grown in the dark to promote its redness, and my favorite spring festival allium, *calçots*, are hilled up with soil all along the length of their bodies to act as protective insulation from the winter winds. The soil protects the plants from freezing but also has the unintended result of elongating the white section, which is tender and delicious grilled.

There are many radicchios, with village after village in the Veneto claiming and naming a particular variety as their own, but all are strikingly red and white leaved: Chioggia have small tight spherical heads (the ones we see most often), Verona are more ovoid, Treviso look like long slender torpedoes similar to Belgian endive, and Castelfranco are frilly and variegated like a parrot tulip. The red color, anthocyanin, is a pigment compound produced in plants under cold conditions particularly in autumn, as perennial plants are actively storing sugars in their root systems. In a tradeoff between producing chlorophyll or anthocyanin, the red pigment may allow the plant to absorb more heat from the sun, which helps keep their metabolism higher during a period of declining photosynthetic activity. The outer older leaves of the radicchios are green and extremely bitter but in colder weather, the plants begin to head up and self blanch. Their inner leaves, unexposed to sunlight, take on an interplay of white, pink, red, and even purple. Without the heat and chlorophyll production of summer, the plant's bitterness is reduced to palatability.

When I first set my eyes on radicchio di Castelfranco at Chris and Jessi's stand I was knocked out by the beauty of the plant. They were more like bouquets of flowers to me than lettuces and, even after I tossed them with some oil and vinegar, they still took my breath away. Whether it's in a salad or in an aperitif, the Italians have figured out that powerful flavors are best met head-on with different but equally powerful flavors. Their most common treatment for radicchio and puntarelle, the cultivated more dandelion-like variety of chicory, is to dress the raw leaves with a pungent dressing composed of anchovy, raw garlic, vinegar, and lemon. I needed a power faceoff like this to finally appreciate both the intense salty rottyness of anchovy and the extreme astringency of bitter greens. Tasted singly we'd never tolerate them but in tandem the dish achieves a pinnacle of balance that is wonderfully bold and invigorating.

Matching bitter with sweetness is common too. Think again of the Negroni (and I do love a well-made Negroni). What makes this cocktail so alluring and enduring is that it strikes the perfect balance between those two elements, with sweet vermouth going head to head with Campari, and citrus rind and gin aromatics there to brighten it. Sweetness works well with chicories too. Another classic Italian salad plays blood oranges and sweet fennel, even some pomegranate seeds, against the bitter red leaves. The sweetnesses all around balance the bitter greens and the easy acids from the blood oranges in the dressing are a great foil to the bitter leaves.

Fats and bitter do something for each other too. *Pissenlit*, the classic French salad with bitter dandelion leaves (also a chicory), is garnished with warm bacon lardons and a poached egg and dressed in a vinaigrette using bacon fat for the oil. Fat gives body to an otherwise light pile of leaves and the fatty meat cuts through their bitterness. The fattiness of nuts can offer necessary heft as well. Try tossing in crushed toasted hazelnuts or pounding walnuts into a dressing. The house favorite foil for the chicories was Savoy's fig anchoïade, a coarsely mortared combination of herbs, anchovies, dried figs, orange rind. and toasted walnuts. Sometimes we spread it on a toast as a side garnish to a salad and at others we eased the paste into a dressing of red wine vinegar, a mixture of orange and lemon juice, and some good olive oil, which bathed the leaves in deliciousness. In both cases, people clamored for more bitter leaves.

Cheese is yet another introduction of fat as a balancing element into a bitter salad. There is probably no better example than the classic Belgian endive salad with pears and blue cheese. In proper proportions, it is still a marvelous salad, a brilliant layering of powerful flavors. It's everything we want in a salad: crisp, bitter, wet, sweet, salty, creamy.

Another strategy gardeners have used to both produce sweetness and balance in the chicories and to extend the season is to fool a plant into "thinking" that the winter is over, time to begin growing again. This is called forcing. Many plants are forced, not just edible ones. My mom would force forsythia. On a warm sunny day in the late winter, when the tree sap was running but the full thaw was still weeks away, she would go out into the yard and clip some barren-looking sticks. Within a few days of indoor warmth and a good drink of vase water, the cuttings would swell and burst with yellow blossoms, a promise that spring was not as far off as the snows around the house might suggest.

Chris and Jessi force the Treviso radicchio variety that the Italians call *tardivo*, which means late, like tardy, in English. It's an incredibly labor-intensive process but Treviso produces spider chrysanthemum-like spears that are sweet and refreshingly crisp and sell at a premium. The plants are seeded in late August and then dug up entirely, roots and all, after the plants have experienced several frosts, usually in late October or early November. Chris looks for the anthocyanins to develop before he digs them up, a sure sign that the plants have gotten a good chill. Brought indoors, the plants are stored in the farmhouse's root cellar at about 58°F to begin a new sprouting cycle.

Many plants require a sustained period of dormancy in order to produce new spring growth. Known as vernalization, this process ensures that plants flower in the spring instead of flowering again in the fall. It is a survival mechanism for temperate-zone plants that discourages growth at the wrong time of the year to mitigate the risk of getting frozen later in winter, nipped in the bud, if you will. It sets an annual clock for the plants and promotes the accelerated growth of flowers over vegetative growth, once the plants do start growing again in the spring. Apples need dormancy to blossom properly; artichokes too.

Endive and other chicories need a period of vernalization although the tardivo varieties of radicchio do not. They begin sprouting when they bask in conditions that resemble the warm rains of spring—high humidity and cellar temperatures that are warmer than the outside air temperature. All this is done in the dark so that no chlorophyll develops. After about ten to twenty-one days, shoots called *chicons* sprout from the taproot. Exceptionally crisp because of the abundant water, filled with sugars from the root's warehouse of stored sugars, and only slightly bitter because they lacked exposure to sun, they are the perfect constituents of a winter salad. I know that many people cook tardivo but I can barely get them into the salad bowl, constantly eating spears out of hand as I'm filling the bowl. Vegetable candy: they are summer's energy, stored for next year's growth, suddenly accessed in the dead of winter for our dining pleasure. Worth every penny.

Italians have been doing this since the 1860s but it was the Belgians who developed this treatment in the 1830s with endive. They refer to it in Flemish as *witloof,* or white leaf. The discovery was accidental, but they seized on the technique with gusto and developed it into a thriving basement industry, consuming and exporting vast quantities of endive each year. The French and the Belgians, though, cook their endive adding cheese, cream, ham, and other rich ingredients; they are more intent on releasing the sugars in the chicons than on enjoying their succulence raw in salads. It was a Belgian horticulturist, Francesco Van Den Borre, hired to develop gardens at wealthy palazzi around Vincenza, who successfully applied the endive technique to endive's radicchio cousins in the late 1860s. It was immediately embraced by Italian growers and, by 1889, there was enough excitement about radicchio varieties and the forcing technique that a radicchio fair was begun in Treviso with nearly sixty growers exhibiting and competing for ribbons of distinction. The annual event continues to this day.

* * *

Seasonality in the temperate zone has been a challenge for humans and plants for millennia. Plants have adapted by developing cold hardiness: the antifreeze of sugar in kale, the reds and bitter flavors in the chicories. Human adaptation in the garden has been to learn how to use passive technologies to extend the season and to trick plants into changing their flavor balance or growing contrary to their internal clocks. But we've also shifted our kitchen practice and learned how to make forceful dressings that delight diners and make us crave eating more radicchios.

The glory of it all then is that in response to frost, the radicchios develop bright red heads and the speckled tulip petal-like leaves that excite our eyes during the darkest days of the year. We match their bitter flavors with equally invigorating ingredients and make salads that sing with life at this nadir of the sun's rotation. Chris and Jessi are contrarians tending to plants that pinnacle when most other vegetables have died back or fallen away weeks ago. Pushing their production as far into the fall as they can without the aid of fossil fuel–burning, heated greenhouses, Chris and Jessi are their own radicchio, colorfully thriving in a colder, slower time of growth.

RADICCHIO SALAD WITH FIG ANCHOÏADE

SERVES 4

This is a great fall salad. Any of the chicories can be used: radicchio, Castelfranco, Treviso, escarole, tardivo, even endive. A mix of them makes for a gorgeous display of fall colors on the plate. The dressing utilizes three key elements that cut the bitterness of the chicories—anchovies, lemon, and sweetness in the form of dried figs.

For the salad:
1 pound (455 g) mixed chicories
Small handful parsley leaves
1 fennel bulb, finely shaved (optional)
2 teaspoons fennel seeds
¼ cup (35 g) pumpkin seeds
Olive oil

For the anchoïade dressing:
½ cup (50 g) walnuts
3 cloves garlic
8 anchovy fillets in oil
¼ teaspoon dried red pepper flakes
4 dried figs, stems clipped, roughly chopped
½ cup (120 ml) olive oil
Juice and zest of ½ lemon, plus more juice as needed
Juice and zest of 1 orange
½ cup (25 g) loosely packed flat-leaf parsley

Salt

1. Preheat the oven to 350°F (175°C).
2. **MAKE THE SALAD:** Wash and spin-dry the chicory leaves and parsley. You could include some finely shaved fennel too if you like.

3. Toast the fennel seeds in the preheated oven or in a small pan over medium heat on the stovetop. When the seeds begin to release their aroma (after about 2 minutes), remove from the heat and set aside.

4. Toss the pumpkin seeds in olive oil to coat lightly and toast in the preheated oven for 8 to 10 minutes. Set aside.

5. **MAKE THE ANCHOÏADE DRESSING**: Toast the walnuts for 10 minutes.

6. In a food processor, blend the garlic, anchovies with their oil, and red pepper flakes into a paste. Add the toasted walnuts and the dried figs. Add the olive oil and the lemon and orange juices to loosen up the mixture. Add the parsley and lemon and orange zests and process. Loosen with water or more lemon juice if the texture is too tight.

7. Dress the leaves with the vinaigrette. Taste to check salt and acid levels, then sprinkle the fennel seeds and pumpkin seeds over the leaves. Serve.

TYING THE ROAST

Understaffed. Yet again. This time it was of my own creation. Knowing that this year would be the last *calçotada*, I scheduled the feast for two nights instead of the usual one and opened up on Sunday night, a night we were traditionally closed. My plan had been to publicly announce that I was closing the restaurant prior to the calçotada and turn them into blowout goodbye feasts. But negotiations with the buyer moved too slowly and I couldn't announce prior. I could only infer in some late publicity notices: "Book now! Nothing lasts forever." In any case, we were short staffed, having added the service. Additionally, in wanting to leverage the moment and bring greater attention to the calçotada, I had agreed to teach a De Gustibus cooking class two days after the calçotada, requiring yet another set of hands in a short-staffed week. More compression, stretching cooks thinner on a staff without much of a bench. The chef was off, having worked both event days, his normal days off, most of the crew were working a six-day week, and prep for the class needed to happen without additional hands. And so it fell to me.

Under normal circumstances, I would have had a designated assistant to prep for the class, gather ingredients, and support me during the event, but my designated assistant was on the line. Lunch was unexpectedly busy, so busy that an expediter, someone to call the orders and organize the plates going out, was needed. With the chef off, that burden would have fallen on a sous chef, but staff development had stalled out given that I knew I was trying to sell the restaurant and wasn't investing in the future. Eyes looked to me. I declined, prompting the prep cook to jump in and push out the tickets. With some guilt, I hung back in the corner, remaining focused on the work at hand, not getting drawn into the temporary mayhem. We were all stretched too thin. That was its own burden on me too, not my ideal image of good management or how I wanted people to view me and my management skills. Regardless, I still needed to pull all the loose ends together for the class, get my head organized for teaching, ready to demonstrate our recipes and also provide continuous entertainment for three hours.

The menu involved roasting a couple of lamb shoulders, remainders from the two whole lambs we bought for the calçotada. They were going to be roasted while teaching the class, sliced and served with grilled leeks and romesco sauce, a prefect distillation of the calçotada meal. I was nervous about the whole thing. It was just performance anxiety but I found proof to validate my anxiety wherever I looked. I allowed the patched together nature of the day in the kitchen to bring entirely into question my professionalism and any mastery I might pretend to have. I couldn't remember when I last boned and tied a lamb shoulder. It wasn't last week or last month, that's for sure. And I hadn't taught a cooking class for at least a year. Had I only received a terms sheet for the sale of the restaurant two weeks earlier as planned we would be in the final stages of the negotiation and sale by now. If it was going to take too long, I would begin to bleed money during the slow summer and I might be forced into making drastic decisions.

Staring up at me were two lamb shoulders that had been marinating in a quick herb paste of thyme, parsley, olive oil, salt, and jalapeños for a few days. Thankfully Mike, the chef, had left them butterflied for me. Somebody had my back. I grabbed the first one, slapped it onto the cutting board, and gave it a loose prelim roll to see that I had the shape right. I slid a length of string under the meat and tied an easy slipknot around the meat at one end and pulled on it, setting the right tension for my roast. I do not cut the string. Instead I create a loop with a half twist, pass it around the meat again, having now made a second ring securing my package. I do the third pass and see that it is really quite uniform, coming into shape with all the knots lined up and of equal tension, no obdurate bulges. This is going to be OK. Breathe. I do know how to do this, well in fact. I am practiced and the knowledge is in my hands not just in my head. The technique isn't one you will find in Jacques Pepin's *La Technique* or in Hugh Fearnley-Wittingstall's *The River Cottage Meat Book* nor taught at the CIA for that matter. The only YouTube video of it may be the one I record and post along with the publication of this book.

How do chefs, especially unschooled chefs, learn technique? I learned how to preserve the "oyster" on the chicken thigh from Kikuchi, the Japanese chef who got tossed out of Huberts after only about a month but not before advancing my regular poultry practice. I learned the procedure of removing the wishbone from poultry prior to roasting from Jim Pender who learned it from Guy Reuge, Sally Darr's first chef at La Tulipe, who learned it from someone in France who taught him. Cooking is a craft and in the guild tradition we learn technique orally or by demonstration, passed down by elders to apprentices who watch, express interest, and strive to get better through practice. This tying technique though is not culinary. It is actually used to sew stiches after dental surgery. I learned it from a dentist, from another sort of elder, my dad.

That my dad could be very annoying is an understatement. Infuriating is more like it. He wasn't a great listener but he sure loved being the authority, even on topics other people knew more about than he did. He once tried to give my sister's boyfriend swimming pointers until the boyfriend announced that he was Connecticut's freestyle state champion. That silenced him, but only momentarily. I would bristle at the mere inkling that he might offer advice, keenly aware when those inklings appeared, a tickle in your nose before a full-on sneeze. Over time my sisters and I trained him not to just blithely offer direction without checking in first to determine if there was interest or willingness to listen.

You can imagine that it might be tough to find one's own path amid all his noisy assuredness. College was pretty much a requirement. As for occupations, I think my dad placed the greatest value on professional careers that were like his, ones that used the word "practice" after the skill—medical practice, architectural practice, even legal practice. Insurance broker, banker, real estate developer, securities trader weren't high on his list of admired professions. Still no one was kvelling when I choose cooking as a career. Julia Child and James Beard were prominent chefs but neither of them worked in restaurants and the arc of where the career might lead wasn't clear to them or to me for that matter. Cooking was the realm where I began to develop skill and prowess. I needed my early signs of mastery to be acknowledged, particularly by my dad. This was challenging for him. It was far easier to comment on my braised cabbage with fennel seed and lemon rind by asking me if I had ever tried preparing it with red wine and cloves (aka, his version) than to taste, acknowledge, and experience something new and different.

Long ago, I decided to prepare a feast for my mom on her August birthday—unlike any I had ever done before—executing the spread solo from start to finish. I worked from Roy Andries de Groot's *Feast for All Seasons*, a grand tome that explores the seasons with both intricate and simple menus. Up in the Berkshires at my folk's summer place, I chose to prepare his veal roast stuffed with cherries and cardamom. This was before I had sniffed out all the local food sources in the Berkshires or learned about the perils of veal production. Finding veal loin was epic enough, but I located a butcher forty-five minutes away. The whole dish is something people rarely cook today. Poking a hole into the center of a loin and stuffing it is such a violation of the integrity and sanctity of the flesh even if it looks great when sliced. It's a parlor trick more than embodying good culinary precepts. Today we would serve the meat beautifully roasted on the bone with the cherry compote served alongside and a bit of jus gathered from the roasting pan.

There I was at the table trying to tie up the roast as I had seen in a butcher case or sketched in *Joy of Cooking*. The loin flopped about, not behaving; there was bulging flesh next to overly constricted sections and cherries spilled out as I handled the meat. My dad watched me struggling to get the tension right and tie the twine. I could feel the tickle coming on, the "Can I make a suggestion?" Only this time instead of saying no or girding myself, I listened. Maybe because I really wanted to make a superlative meal for my mom or maybe I had an inkling that a morsel of wisdom instead of a shovelful of ego was about to be offered and I knew I needed the help. "Let me show you how we do it when we tie sutures in people's mouths," he offered.

With clear command he demonstrated the creation of a loop with a double twist on it so that there was enough friction to hold the tension before moving on to the next loop. With a sleight of hand, magic performed by a dental wizard, he patiently repeated the motion, the break of the wrist, the rotation of the hand, slowly, repetitively, until I could see the process. One continuous string with a final hard knot and a single clip of the line. The roast was tied. Gorgeous. Ready for the oven, ready for Mom.

* * *

Back in the kitchen at Savoy. The romesco sauce was barely made, the leeks thank goodness were already cleaned by way of the calçotada, but the asparagus for the appetizer wasn't prepped. We were supposed to leave in an hour. Johnny, my assistant for the class, was still deep in lunch service and there were still two more shoulders to rock out. I found the rhythm of the loop making and setting the knots as the roast slowly puffed itself up, and came together. The movements are still known and comfortable. I admired my work, thought about my teacher, eight years gone now, and knew that he would appreciate the beauty of the craft exhibited here. Maybe it was all going to be OK.

I've been practicing this technique for over thirty years, transferring his dental wisdom into culinary brilliance for every generation of cooks that have worked alongside me as we straightjacketed countless pork loins, boned out rabbits and lamb legs so that they sat up proud and ready to fulfill their glory as a fine roast. So we practice. It's a business that abounds in practice. Book learning cannot teach how much water to add to pie dough so that it stays flaky yet still holds together, how soon to pull a piece of fish out of the oven, knowing that it will continue cooking as it moves onto the plate, or how long to work potato gnocchi with flour so that it holds together but isn't tough. These are wisdoms internalized into the very musculature of our hands, bypassing our heads. Sometimes practice can feel like drudgery, mechanical. That's when it is repetitive but without awareness. But sometimes there is a freedom that comes out of the repetitions, when internalizing the action allows it to become rote and easeful. From the ease comes a freedom to think about something else or to strive for even greater precision.

I am tying the last shoulder, I look up, think about what needs to be pulled from the basement, direct Johnny, who now has a bit of a lull in lunch orders, to pull together the romesco sauce, and collect the ingredients for the class. I calculate what time we need to call the car so we can arrive at the class with ample time to settle in. There it is, the brain space liberated by rote practice.

My dad asked a lot of himself every day he worked. He was disciplined without being regimented, even if I couldn't discern the distinction as a kid.

It wasn't rules for rules' sake or to show who was in control; his orderliness allowed him to be efficient at his work and produce the finest dental work possible, whether it was a simple cleaning or the re-creation of a tooth that resembled all the others in the mouth and felt to the tongue just like the rest of the dental family. Patients mattered but it was the practice he came back to, single-mindedly focused on improving his performance, searching for efficiencies in movement to reduce wasted motion. From practice, improvement, profit, and recognition would flow.

I brown the meat in a cast-iron skillet in front of the class, place it in the oven behind me, and set a timer so I can concentrate on demonstrating romesco sauce. Delegating responsibility to the timer is also a great brain-space liberator. Although not familiar with their ovens, I sense when it must be time to check in on my lamb rolls. I give them a two-fingered gentle squeeze. It's a Goldilocks moment. What is too soft, too rare? What is too firm, too well done? What does "just right" feel like, that when well rested will be rosy pink all the way through? My fingers know that moment. I pull the smaller shoulder from the pan, done, and put the larger one on a five-minute timer, coming back around then to pronounce it too, "Just right." After an extended rest, I clip the meat of all its loops and yank the string off in one piece, another elegant aspect of Dad's technique. It is ready to slice and serve with grilled leeks and the intoxicatingly addictive romesco sauce that I have never tired of eating since I first discovered it twenty-two years ago. Whether it's slathered on grilled bread or turned into a vinaigrette to drizzle over a platter of high summer tomatoes or whisked into a pot of clams thickening its briny broth, I never tire of romesco.

I feel pressure from Arlene, the school's founder, and my class monitor to keep things moving along. The fourth course needs to be served so that the class has time for dessert, questions, chatter, and more wine. I feel her anxiety with the prodding preference for the meat to be sliced in the back by my assistant and then plated by the De Gustibus support team. But there is no way I am giving up that performance moment, that moment of truth and pride. With each draw of my slicer towards my body, the knife in extension not compression, a piece peels off the roast, uniformly pink with only the barest bit of tan at the edges, a few crawling veins of green from the marinade like mineral ore. The meat is gorgeous. I guess I do know what

I am doing. Practice buoyed me through a hard spot. I take a modest but earned bow and exhale.

Cooking remains an analog skill in a digital world. No app can ever adjust for different-size lamb legs or know the right tension to bind the roast or know that the bit of lemon juice will make the sauce sing. I didn't become the professional that my dad had once imagined but I did dedicate myself to a craft and he knew the value of craft. In striving for excellence and precision, we get to the delicious.

EXIT STRATEGY

Most of the time, the way to get out of the restaurant business with any money is to sell the lease, the only asset with any real value. No matter how hard someone will try to convince you that the stainless steel kitchen is priceless, fixtures are worthless. An unencumbered lease represents time in the space in which to make money. That has value. Better still, if the rent is below market people are willing to pay a premium for that opportunity. And if there is a liquor license on the premise in an area where licenses are hard to come by then it's worth even more. I had all those things on Prince Street, with a caveat.

There were five years left on the Prince Street lease, negligible to any restaurant buyer. A shoe store or clothing retailer wasn't going to offer much money for the intense infrastructure build-out and they had no use for a liquor license. Without adding additional time onto the lease, I was sunk. I knew, from experience.

Things had gone badly when I sold Back Forty on Avenue B two years earlier. The landlord, the buyer, and the real estate agent were all trying to squeeze me because we were trying to sell a shuttered restaurant. I had signed a personal guarantee as part of the original lease so I was on the hook for the outstanding rent, which climbed upwards of $90,000 as the negotiations dragged on. Could it have been any worse? For a smart guy, I had really gotten myself into a jam and my partner had gone AWOL. In the end I closed the deal without taking any money out of my pocket but I had worked for over a year and a half without compensation. Given how weak my position was, getting out clean was a win, but it had bruised me and irreparably damaged my relationship with my partner.

I vowed not to repeat that situation. I'd line up the lease extension before the sale, find a new attorney, identify the buyer myself independent of real estate agents, get loose of my partner, and make the sale while the business was operating. Only I didn't expect the next "opportunity" to come as soon as it did. The Avenue B deal finally closed in July of 2015, seven months after shuttering in December 2014. Four short months after that I came to the conclusion that I had to find a way out of the Prince Street operation.

I began with the lease and securing an extension. Approaching my landlords, not your typical New York real estate owners—a jazz musician and a filmmaker—was delicate. I had always had a conflicted relationship with the two of them, having taken numerous actions during my tenancy that bring to mind the aphorism "better to beg forgiveness than to seek permission." I had understandably annoyed them and eroded trust between us by placing air-conditioning units on a back roof and diverting hot water from the boiler to feed my dishwasher instead of installing an electric booster. I was also the de facto manager and super of the building for over twenty-five years.

The jazz musician played the role of bad cop, the filmmaker the good cop. I approached the filmmaker first about the lease extension saying that I wanted to bring in a chef partner. He said, "Don't worry. We like you. We will give them a new lease when the time comes." No chef was ever going to come in with only five years remaining and a promise. This wasn't going to work for any potential partner, especially an outside buyer. So I went to the jazz musician, the more volatile one, who, during his rants would regularly remind me of my past abuses. This time he asked, "Is it personal or about business?" I didn't know how to answer, terrified what to reveal. Of course it was personal and absolutely it was about business. I felt like I was locked in a fairy tale castle not knowing which door to open. I decided that given my sometime past duplicity, truthfulness was most important and that I was prepared to accept whatever his response might be. I replied that it was personal; I needed it to extract myself from the situation and get out whole. His response was "If this is for you, then I'll do it. You paid the rent for twenty-six years, we've never ended up in court." Rapping his knuckles on the nearest wood surface, he continued, "This has let me live my life and do my music the way I wanted to and so I'm grateful. You moved my life forward. I'm cool doing the same for you." I was floored. Was it really going to be that easy? True, under the terms of the lease, the landlords would get an immediate 15 percent rent hike, but they could just as easily have taken the long view and chosen to wait and see what the market would bring in five years. That would have been a totally acceptable position for a landlord to take. Instead, he said, "You get it written up and we'll sign it."

I went to my partner and told him I wanted to sell the business. He nodded. I told him the landlords were open to a lease extension. He nodded; asked no questions, clearly lacking interest in developing a strategy or contemplating next steps. He was one foot out the door, had had his fill and was moving on. I was on my own, which was actually a relief.

My next task was to find a buyer, which I opted to do myself. My analysis of the neighborhood and the property was that the highest-paying customer would be someone who wanted to do what I hadn't wanted to—create a fast casual business—churning out lunch food for the young folks working in the surrounding buildings. After querying a former chef who now worked for a small but aggressive healthy fast casual concept, I had an initial meeting and sensed that there was potential for a deal. But there was to be no further conversation until I had bought out my partner. Even though he had expressed no interest in participating in the sale, I needed to ensure that he couldn't come back afterward and claim that I had concealed that a sale was in the works and thus deceived him as to the value of his shares.

It took me weeks to summon the courage to confront him and say in the clearest language possible that I wanted to separate, to buy him out. My desk was littered with multiple drafts of carefully scripted declarations so I could memorize my lines and practice my delivery. Finally, after spending a weekend retreat in Maine with a buddy going over the ramifications of *not* having the conversation, I committed myself to step through all the fears that might arise. I said in the plainest language I knew, "I don't think we are working well together anymore. It's not good for the business or either of us, and I think we should separate." No blame placed, just a dispassionate statement of facts and without even an implied outcome. It was meant to be the beginning of a discussion.

Thus began five months of jockeying to reach a mutually acceptable buyout number and all the while I had to maintain radio silence with the potential buyer. When the separation papers were finally signed, it wasn't a celebratory day for me, more mournful with the stark recognition of a failed relationship. After we signed all the documents, with my lawyer in attendance guiding us through the pages that required initials and signatures, I took a moment to enumerate some of the things I appreciated about his work after more than a decade of working together. Barely mumbling thanks and without any reciprocity shared, he departed. It was over, anticlimactic, one more task completed and crossed off the list.

Drafting the lease extension in preparation of the sale was fairly easy. As promised, the landlords had stuck by their word. Getting a sales agreement written with the fast casual group was laborious. Thankfully I now had a shark for a lawyer instead of a guppy. Given the demeanor of the real estate manager for the group I needed one. Combative and haughty, this guy made the process of getting to a signable document unpleasant and expensive. What should have taken two months with three or four drafts exchanged between lawyers instead took five months with endless redlined versions of documents and page after page of riders with new conditions inserted. Goodwill was quickly dissipating. I wondered if we were really going to make it to signing.

Back Forty West was still open but summer was fast approaching, a notoriously slow time for restaurants in the city. Before long I'd start bleeding money and I needed to share with employees what was going on. Why wasn't I buying new floor mats and a new juicer? Why wasn't I hiring a sous chef? I tried to get it done before the May *calçotada* and have a blowout, but the attorneys flew past that date. Once the papers were close to final and I went public with the news, it was July. We ran a week of blowout crab boils and closed on July 15 with the goal to sell all the contents in two weeks and then sign over the lease on August first.

Sue wrote a great note on the window explaining to people why we were closing and she came back to sell off all the contents; we reunited as co-proprietors. Everything was for sale: jars of Spanish peppers, chairs, waffle irons, sugar caddies, sheet trays, plates, ancho chiles, plastic wrap, metro shelving, wall art, table bases, spices, plastic containers, more plates, glassware, cookbooks, espresso spoons, vinegar, even more plates, Sue's pottery, sconces, coffee beans, pepper mills, and random bottles of booze we were never going to drink. It gave us the opportunity to look at objects together, remembering different periods in the life of the restaurant, and visit with an endless stream of customers and neighbors who came by to purchase a piece of the place and say farewell.

It harkened to when we first opened Savoy and we'd close up the restaurant together on Saturday nights, one doing the checkout and server tallies, the other placing phone orders or reorganizing the reservation book and watering plants. Servers and cooks would drift off and we were left to wrap up at our own pace, decompressing from the week's intensity. The twenty-four hour joints, Florent and Odeon, were regular refueling stops before we fell into bed, spending most of Sunday in recovery. These sale days had a similar tidal rhythm, the falling away of customers, our hired helpers departing once the "store" was closed, and once left alone we'd putter and rearrange items for the next day. Dirty and sweaty, we ate sushi and drank cold beer. My mind was dull as I struggled with the approaching vacancy and its absolute finality. We'd barely get enough rest before waking up to give it another go the following day. The last night I set a huge stack of hotel pans on the street that no one wanted to buy, gave the place a sweep, and locked up for the last time, my big key ring already feeling lighter in my pocket. I was ready to head downtown in the morning to the closing with the buyer.

With checks in hand, Sue and I took our landlords out for lunch in the neighborhood. Strolling up Lafayette afterward, we floated in a sea of European shoppers, glancing in their guidebooks, referencing phones for locations, with no idea of where they really were. No one, us included, belonged to the neighborhood. When I had found this little gem on the corner, no one knew of Crosby Street. As we departed, the office building across the street had forsaken their Broadway address and adopted 100 Crosby Street as a tonier location for marketing its commercial space. The structures were the same but none of us recognized its inhabitants; the factory workers from our landlord's day or the art mavens from ours were gone. Swept along with the tide of shoppers, I felt the relief in every cell. I had navigated some rough waters and swum to the other side.

THE VILLAGE GREEN

The Union Square Greenmarket is a grand plaza—a zocalo—regardless of the weather or time of the year. I run into chefs, old Savoy customers, chat with farmers, and talk with other shoppers I've bonded with over our devotion to particular growers or ingredients. Our conversations range from national news, who has the best peaches, and restaurant gossip to kids, cooking tips, current art shows, and finding a physician. There is a generosity to the exchanges, they are relaxed and freely offered.

On a market day in late August 2019, I am awed by this moment in the season, the crossover of summer's best—peaches, tomatoes, eggplant, and basil overlap with autumn's finest—squashes, shell beans, and pears. All the plants are in high production, pumping out offspring before the inevitable end of the season. These past few weeks I've needed the market in ways I never could have imagined. My mom is near the end of her life and is struggling to have clarity about how to die with dignity. I am cooking for her to make sure she is getting what she needs nutritionally and to bring her the best in market ingredients, ones that scream of the joys of life, offering no choice but to want to take another bite. I want to give her the market's megavitamin dose of life and convince her via the dinner table that life is still worth living.

I'm here to gather ingredients for physical sustenance but I'm also here for the community of people, the intersection of lives being lived fully and thoughtfully shared. Cross-pollination might be deleterious to Tim Stark's pepper operation but the generous exchanges of ideas and empathy that occur on our village green of a market are life affirming. I run into some old friends and tell them about my mom. I'm in a quandary of how to counsel her: "call it good," a life well lived, or encourage her at age ninety-six to keep on pushing. Her decline comes as no surprise but letting go is still painful. Sharing stories with others who have been here before is helpful. Just as I can't imagine what Indian food must have tasted like prior to the arrival of peppers and I can't imagine what the culinary and cultural life of New York

City looked like prior to the arrival of the Union Square Greenmarket, I can't imagine what life will look like without my mom.

We talk about losing parents—one has recently lost her mother after years of debilitating dementia—when we are briefly joined by a former customer, whose father's obituary was in the *New York Times* that morning. I offer condolences, share with everyone what a great spirit he'd been as a customer, and express gratitude—reflecting on how everyone in NYC benefitted from his work as a public servant. We all chat for a few moments, remarking on our commonality, the finality of life cycles, and what we are going to prepare with the spectacular ingredients from today's market haul.

My knapsack is beyond brimming; flat Romano beans, Japanese eggplant, baby artichokes, cranberry beans, Thai basil, and a constellation of peppers—Jimmy Nardello's, espelettes, and a handful of Grenadas fill the bag. The zipper can't fully close; corn tassels protrude up through the open section and fennel fronds trail behind me as I weave my way through the cars, riding my bike down Broadway. I'm also traveling home with a full heart, overflowing with renewed optimism and love for this community, this city that I get to live in. The morning's interchange and this brilliant palette of ingredients to cook with will buoy me through the day—all of it, reminding me of what's good.

ACKNOWLEDGMENTS

I have had many cheerleaders throughout the process of bringing this book into existence. Most important, my readers reflected back to me whenever I hit the right chord or made them chuckle or muse on a thought, but they also told it to me straight when my words were hollow, not entirely truthful, or struck an off note. Together they helped me find my groove and kept me moving forward.

Susan, my partner in most of the events recounted, was always at the ready to verify my memory and stimulate new recollections, and never failed to see the beauty I was striving for. Even when armed with her oversize red marker, she always offered deeply thoughtful responses to the work. Adam Gopnik's refrain, reminding me to reach for the larger story, to write about the subject as well as the object, helped direct my journey as a writer. With him as friend and mentor I could envision greater potential for the book. Katherine Alford, my colleague of nearly four decades and my culinary inside track reader—her comments on race, class, and exploitation in the workplace were invaluable. My writing group—Pam Newton, Joelle Hahn, Liz Fodaski, and Liz Logan—I needed the structure of our monthly meeting to complete my task. Reading their well-crafted pages gave me something to strive for and their feedback helped keep my stories compelling and from drifting towards insider baseball. Broader perspective, deep engagement and thoughtful feedback were also provided by Patrick Littlefield, Tevere MacFadyen, Jim Weiss, Paul Heck, Charlie Komanoff, and Roslyn Schloss. Getting the science right and in plain language came from, first and foremost, my nature pal David Daub but also professors James J. Hancock at Michigan State University, Michael Lange at Champlain College, Damian Cirelli at University of Alberta, Eric Block at SUNY Albany, and farmers Keith Stewart, Rick Bishop, Tim Stark, and Chris Field. Early and/or persistent believers who said "I want to read that book" were David Bowler, Lorrie Bodger, Andrew Tarlow, Judy Hoffman, Susie Hoffman, Hilary Reyl, Olivia Hoffman, Theo Hoffman, Jon Czeck, Robert Lavalva, Gabrielle Langholtz, Paul Greenberg, Gerry Marzorati, Michael Hurwitz, Peter Carey, Patti Ratchford, Genny Kapuler, and Noel Comess. Savoy and Back Forty memory stimulators and suppliers of forgotten bits were Jody Dufur, Mike Laarhoven, Shanna Pacifico, Matt Weingarten, Caroline Fidanza, Michael Cecconi, David Wurth, John Tucker, Charlie Kiely, Sharon Pachter, and Gil Avital, as well as Rick Bayless, Bruce Sherman, and Amy Bodiker for Chefs Collaborative recollections. Thanks to David McCormick for seeking me out after reading my Bocuse piece in the *Washington Post* and believing in the project; to Jamison Stoltz for crucial words of encouragement when completing the project felt daunting and for crucial editorial wisdom along the way.

To my dad, who taught me how to work and hold a high standard.

To my mom, ever my cheerleader from the very start, who at ninety-five, after I had been writing in earnest for two years, said, "Hurry up. I want to read the book." I'm sorry you never got to hold a copy in your hands.

And to everyone at Union Square Greenmarket—growers, stand keepers, market managers, and fellow shoppers—all whom still fuel my enthusiasm, put up with my endless queries, and share with me their own appreciation of the edible treasures at hand. As Dolma wisely observed, "We are a part of you." I feel it.